T.

Q L D

A.

① BRISBANE

WASH

① ARMIDALE

N. S. W.

② SYDNEY

A.C.T. ② CANBERRA

ADELAIDE ①

V I C.

① MELBOURNE

T A S.

① HOBART

THE HUMANITIES IN AUSTRALIA

Winthrop Hall, University of Western Australia.

THE HUMANITIES
IN AUSTRALIA

A Survey

with special reference to the Universities

Editor

A. GRENFELL PRICE

Sub-Editors

J.J. Auchmuty   A.R. Chisholm   E.L. French   H.A.K. Hunt
A.G. Mitchell   G.H. Russell   A.D. Trendall

assisted by

R.M. Crawford   R.B. Farrell   R.StC. Johnson
J.A. Passmore

Published for the Australian Humanities Research Council

by

ANGUS AND ROBERTSON

First published in 1959 by

ANGUS & ROBERTSON LTD

89 Castlereagh Street, Sydney
105 Great Russell Street, London
66 Elizabeth Street, Melbourne
164 Willis Street, Wellington

Contents

Illustrations

Foreword

By The Rt Hon. R.G. Menzies, C.H., Q.C., LL.M. LL.D.,
Prime Minister of Australia

We live dangerously in the world of ideas just as we do in the world of international conflict.

Today the popular accent is on the physical sciences, the fullest development of which is essential to the improvement of the world's material standards; of public and private health; of increased production; of transport and communications. This is good. Indeed, it must go on more and more rapidly if the expanding populations of the world are to be fed and clothed and housed, set free from poverty and pestilence and misery, and so permitted to enjoy access to the higher world of intellectual creation and reflection.

But there is a danger in concentrating our facilities too much into one channel. The troubled history of the twentieth century affords sad proof of the fact that humanity can be overthrown by mechanical skill and the worship of the purely material.

Only recently we have had dreadful examples of murder and violence used as a political instrument; publicly admitted; made an occasion for well advertised boasting.

If we are to escape from this modern barbarism, humane studies must come back into their own; not as the enemies of science, but as its guides and philosophic friends.

Perhaps the most significant sentence in Francis Bacon's immortal essay on Studies is in Latin: *Abeunt studia in mores*. For, beyond question, what a man reads, and how he thinks, will serve to fashion his personality.

Specialization will add enormously to a man's knowledge in his own field. But his service to mankind will be the greater if his interests are broad, so broad that there is no aspect of human life which lacks interest for him.

Homo sum; humani nil a me alienum puto. Physics and metaphysics are, so regarded, aspects of the same universal problem. Today the physical sciences are receiving a great deal of public attention, even though the private attention to them may be comparatively restricted. They are, so we say, practical. And so they are, practical and vastly important. The trouble is that, with our quaint instinct for dichotomy, we tend to divide studies into the practical and the useless. Chemistry is practical; the classics, and history, and literature are "useless" in the sense that they are ornaments but (so it is said) have no structural significance.

This kind of reasoning is not only fallacious, but dangerous. On one level it is leading to the substitution of jargon for good speech and writing. On another it is encouraging the idea that history, which tends to produce a sense of proportion; and languages, which tend to produce a precise understanding of words and meanings; and philosophy, which tends to explain the sources and nature of ideas and emotions are irrelevant to practical life.

If we are to advance in civilization we must bring all these things into perspective. For if the challenge to civilization, the greatest challenge of our time, is to be met, it is necessary to see that the main source of that challenge is not external but internal. Wisdom, a sense of proportion, sanity of judgment, a faith in the capacity of man to rise to higher mental and spiritual levels; these are the ends to be served by the Humanities Council, whose Survey I am honoured to introduce.

R.G. MENZIES

1st October 1959

Introduction

BY A.D. TRENDALL

THE AUSTRALIAN HUMANITIES RESEARCH COUNCIL came into being a little later than its two sister bodies, the Social Science Research Council and the Australian Academy of Science. The need for a body to speak for and look after the interests of the humanities had long been recognized, and the impetus necessary to launch it came in 1953 when Dr Brian Elliott of the University of Adelaide returned to Australia after a visit to Canada under the auspices of the Carnegie Corporation of New York, greatly impressed by the important work being carried out by the Canadian Humanities Research Council. His enthusiasm inspired Professor A.N. Jeffares, who at the time held the Jury Chair of English in the University of Adelaide, to take steps to form a similar Council in this country. It is largely thanks to his initial efforts, which met with a most encouraging response throughout the universities, that the Australian Humanities Research Council came into existence. Delegates nominated by the several faculties of Arts met in Melbourne in November 1954. They formed an interim Council, of twenty members, drew up a draft constitution and appointed an interim executive.

The aims of the proposed Council were set down in the constitution as being:

1. To promote and disseminate knowledge of the humanities, and to declare their value to the community.
2. To foster scholarship and the publication of studies in the humanities.
3. To establish and maintain relations with international bodies concerned with the humanities.
4. To correlate and assist in correlating the efforts of other bodies in the humanities.
5. To arrange or join in arranging meetings of humanists in Australia, to arrange for visits of humanists from other countries to Australia, to assist Australian humanists to study and carry out research abroad, and to assist in exchange of scholars.
6. To administer or help in administering funds for purposes of research in the humanities.
7. To assist in improving the general conditions and scope of libraries in Australia in the field of the humanities.

8. To act as consultant and advisory body in matters concerning the humanities.

With these ends in view it seemed clear that one of the first objectives of the Council should be the publication of a Survey of the present state of the humanities in Australia, with special reference to the universities, in order to provide the factual foundation upon which any necessary recommendations or actions could be based.

In July 1955 a small deputation, consisting of Professors Jeffares, Mitchell and Trendall, waited upon the Prime Minister (the Rt Hon. R.G. Menzies) to explain the aims and purposes of the proposed Council and to enlist the financial support of the Commonwealth Government in carrying them out. The deputation received a most sympathetic hearing and it was later announced that the Prime Minister had agreed to make the Council an annual grant of £4000, thus placing it on a similar basis to the Social Science Research Council and the newly-formed Academy of Science. We are deeply indebted to Parliament for the support that it has given to the Council and hope that the publication of this Survey will give some idea of the tasks that still lie before us.

Meantime an approach had also been made to the Rockefeller Foundation in New York to see whether it might be willing to provide the necessary funds for the expenses involved in the preparation of the Survey. Once again our appeal met with a most generous response and a grant of £7000 ensured that it could be conducted on a proper scale. The Council most gratefully acknowledges its debt to the Rockefeller Foundation for its contribution, which made this Survey possible.

With the funds for the proposed Survey and for the development of the Council thus assured, it was felt that the time had to come for a permanent body to replace the interim organization. Each Australian university had been asked to nominate to the Council one scholar of high distinction in the humanities. These scholars, together with the members of the interim Council, made up the twenty-six members who formed the original Council, which met for the first time in Canberra in November 1956 to confirm the constitution, elect officers and appoint standing committees, and to discuss plans for the future, with special reference to the conduct of the Survey. Sub-editors for each of the main sections were appointed, and an editorial committee was set up under the chairmanship of Dr Grenfell Price, who was to act as general editor of the volume. Under his energetic guidance work proceeded apace; preliminary drafts of certain chapters were circulated among the committee during 1957, and the arrangements were fully discussed by the whole Council at its second annual meeting in November of that year. It was decided to restrict the Survey substantially to the universities, as being of most direct concern to the Council; this is in no wise to underestimate the importance of the humanities in secondary education, which it was felt would most appropriately make the subject of a further Survey which the Council hopes to undertake after the publication of the present volume.

The individual chapters were put into their final form during 1958; each was circulated among all the members of the editorial committee, who in turn consulted their colleagues, from whom they received most valuable criticisms, as a result of which many modifications of the original plan were made to the great benefit of the Survey as a whole. It is with real pleasure that I express, on behalf of the Council, our gratitude to all those members of the staffs, both administrative and academic, of the universities of Australia, whose sympathetic co-operation has made possible the presentation of this Survey.

At the end of 1957 appeared a document of the greatest importance to the universities of Australia. This was the Murray Report: a careful analysis of the needs, material, financial and spiritual, of the universities, based on the thorough investigations carried out by a committee specially appointed by the Government under the chairmanship of Sir Keith Murray, chairman of the University Grants Committee of the United Kingdom. The results of our own Survey support the conclusions of the Murray Report, and of other authoritative reports such as those on the Australian libraries, that we have fallen behind in our cultural as compared with our material development. We do not wish to overemphasize this lag or to imply that no efforts are being made to overcome it. Indeed, it might be disastrous if our fellow humanists in other countries were led to think that the Australian governments and people were heedless of the situation or unwilling to redress past errors. The fact that the political leaders of the major parties in the federal and state parliaments accepted the recommendations in the Murray Report and that they are in course of implementation has already had a most beneficial effect upon the universities, in which, and not least in the Arts faculties, the numbers of the teaching staff had failed to keep pace with the huge increase in the student population, just as the scale of salaries had not risen in proportion to rising costs in a period of inflation, in both cases with very serious consequences.

A number of facts explain, if they do not excuse, the lag in Australian culture. First, the Commonwealth is a very young nation. It is younger even than Canada, and in the development of humanistic studies, such as literature, music and art, it is still suffering from immaturity and the slow development of its own traditions, although there are signs that in certain fields national individuality is beginning to develop.

Secondly, Australia is an isolated country. Unlike Canada, it has no vast, progressive and English-speaking nation on its frontier, and even though scholars can now fly to Europe in a couple of days, the expense is considerable, and the time-difference in the academic terms between the two hemispheres works against the easy exchange of university teachers.

Thirdly, very large parts of the more closely settled areas of Australia possess attractive climates. The long dreary winters of northern Europe or America are unknown, and for much of the year Australians tend to lead an outdoor life, with particular emphasis on local travel and sport. This may not affect the people who have reached high academic standards, but it does affect the sources of supply. It must be admitted that Australia ranks considerably lower in the world of culture than in the world of sport. Not without justification did an American publisher recently advertise an Australian publication on the grounds that it was "as Australian as a Wimbledon men's tennis final".

Fourthly, although the driving forces behind progress have been those traditional in democracies—private initiative and private philanthropy, combined, particularly in recent years, with assistance and even some leadership from the central and local governments—the relative weight of these various factors has differed considerably from that in Britain and the United States. In Australia, personal initiative and ability in the cultural sphere were evident even in the days of transportation, for example in the architectural achievements of Francis Greenway. Similarly, the vigour of private initiative was shown when the South Australian pioneers formed a literary society even before they left London in 1836. Far more important, however, was the transplanting to Australia of the British Mechanics' Institutes which, with the assistance of some local governing bodies, often evolved into municipal art galleries, libraries and museums. These, in the great cities, have divided up into those separate institutions which today are mainstays of the humanities in Australia.

Nevertheless, even when the young nation had developed great wealth, Australia saw no evolution such as the establishment of the Rockefeller, Carnegie, Guggenheim or Ford foundations in the United States. We can be deeply grateful to a number of generous patrons of the arts, such as those whose names will appear in the chapters which follow, but it is noteworthy that no Australian philanthropist has yet founded any substantial benefaction either to enable his countrymen to carry out research overseas, or, and this is not less important, to bring the humanists of other nations to this country. Yet Australia has been well represented in the ranks of those who have enjoyed the benefits of American and British generosity. It is due in no small measure to the Rhodes Trust, the Nuffield Foundation, the Rockefeller Foundation and the Carnegie Corporation that the staffs of Australian universities and libraries are, in general, of a high standard, and that Australian scholars have been able to gain some reputation abroad.

Surely the time has come when we must devote more attention to considering ways and means of making some return for the benefits we have received and how we may bring to this country a steady stream of distinguished scholars—especially from Europe and Asia—to both their and our advantage. This is a matter in which the Council hopes to be able to take active steps in the near future.

There are many other ways in which the Council hopes to overcome the "culture lag". One of the more pressing needs of the humanities in Australia is the publication of a journal of international standing which would carry articles of scholarly importance written by Australian humanists. The difficulties of publication in this country are great. In the meantime, since it will be some years before it is in a position to launch its own journal, the Council is doing what it can to assist in the important task of aiding publication by subsidizing existing learned journals in its field like *Historical Studies*, *AUMLA* (journal of the Australasian Universities' Language and Literature Association), and the *Australasian Journal of Philosophy*, and by sponsoring a series of monographs of which two have already been published and three others accepted for publication in 1959. It hopes also to assist scholars by granting subsidies or giving guarantees to publishers of books already accepted for publication. Elsewhere mention is made of the position of university presses in this country; the present would seem to be a propitious moment for a thorough investigation of the whole question of scholarly publication, and the possible establishment of a combined press with the support of all the universities and learned institutions of Australia.

The Bibliography at the end of the book shows that Australia's contribution to humane studies is an important and a growing one; the list of conclusions which sums up the Survey is evidence that we are aware of our weaknesses and that we have positive suggestions to put forward to remedy them. The Council, therefore, looks to the future progress of the humanities in Australia with confidence. Their nature and importance are so well set out by Professors Mitchell and Passmore in Chapter I that nothing more need be said here, except to stress the growing recognition of the need for these studies that is being felt in the scientific and professional faculties of our universities, which are becoming increasingly conscious of the fact that they are hardly worthy of the name if they allow their undergraduates to remain unaware that the values impressed upon them by a purely scientific training are not universally valid and that there are other values—moral, spiritual, aesthetic—which such a discipline may not impart.

One of the most interesting phenomena in the contemporary university scene is the attempt to inject some measure of humanism into scientific curricula. This can be done by means of survey or general courses, by

B

occasional lectures on different aspects of world civilization, and by many other methods, none of which seem to have achieved any great measure of success in Australia. My own preference would be for the introduction of a full three-year course on the history and philosophy of science, from the beginning of time to the present day, seen as an element in human achievement and studied in relation to and against the background of the other elements. In this way students in their first year could be introduced to the great contributions—scientific, philosophic, political and artistic—of the ancient civilizations; in their second to those of the Orient, of Byzantium, the Middle Ages and the Renaissance, and in their third year to those of more recent times. Such courses could well be integrated with their scientific studies and would serve to give a coherent picture of man's progress through the different phases of civilization. With a slight variation of emphasis they could also give the Arts student some conception of the main lines upon which scientific thought has developed, and it is surely no less important for him to have some knowledge of the attitude and approach of the scientist, than it is for the latter to appreciate the aims of the humanist. The widening gulf between Arts and Science springs from this lack of mutual understanding, and so many of our present problems arise from the lack of sympathy between the two disciplines that it must clearly be one of our major tasks to try to bridge the gap before it has widened to such an extent as to make co-operation almost impossible. It is a rather sad commentary on education today that it is extremely difficult to find people qualified to give courses of the kind referred to above, for they need that combination of humanist and scientist which our present system so signally fails to produce.

The chapters which follow the discussion of the nature of the humanities include a brief historical outline of the evolution of Australian universities and an analysis of the different types of Arts courses that may be taken in the several faculties. Then come sections primarily concerned with research and the conditions under which it may be carried out, with particular reference to library resources and other aids to scholarship. There is a study of university finances and reference is made to the far-reaching effects of the recent Murray Report. A brief survey of secondary education in its relations to the universities underlines the need for that fuller inquiry which has already been mentioned as one of the forthcoming tasks before the Council. Some attention is given to various bodies or institutions which give support to the humanities, such as learned societies, museums and galleries, as well as to other contributing factors like radio or television. In conclusion the Council puts forward a number of recommendations based upon the facts brought to light by the Survey, feeling that it is a matter of great importance that the Commonwealth governments, the universities, the public, and humanists themselves should appreciate the weaknesses that have been revealed, and realize the urgent necessity of the actions which should result. A similar survey made in Canada in 1947, also with the help of the Rockefeller Foundation, disclosed a situation which led to the Massey Royal Commission on the state of humanities, the setting up of adequate machinery and the spending of very large sums of money "to rank Canada as a civilized nation and not merely as an enormously wealthy and heavily industrialized Siberian hinterland to the world".

CHAPTER I

The Nature of the Humanities

By A.G. Mitchell and J.A. Passmore

THE HISTORY OF THE WORD "HUMANITIES" WOULD BE A STUDY IN itself, and one which could throw considerable light upon changing patterns in educational practice and in the beliefs which sustain that practice. The word has been used to distinguish the study of man, and what pertains to man, from divinity; it has served to describe the philosophical belief that, as the sophist Protagoras expressed the matter, "man is the measure of all things"; at the time of the Renaissance a "humanist" meant, substantially, a classical scholar—and, indeed, the Professor of Latin at some Scottish universities still bears the title "Professor of Humanity".

At the same time, there is an unchanging nucleus to the meaning of the word. The humanist, whatever else might be said of him, has always been a man who has sought intellectual development—and, more generally, enrichment of mind—through a study of what humanity has created.

If a humanist is thus generally defined, it will at once be obvious that there is no absolute distinction between the humanities, the natural sciences, and the social sciences. They grew up together; they form part of the Greek heritage to the Western world; together they constitute the world of learning. They demand the same qualities of mind: imagination, intellectual courage, honesty, persistence. The laboratory drudge no doubt lacks these qualities, but so does the pedant; the laboratory drudge is no more a typical scientist than the pedant is a typical humanist. The creative scientist and the creative scholar are natural allies in the struggle against Philistinism, a spirit of mediocrity, a narrow utilitarianism. The sooner they realize this, the better will be the state of our civilization.

At the same time, although humanists may lament the fragmentation of modern culture, and although they may try to do what they can to keep communications open, the situation which has arisen in Australia, where there are three distinct academic bodies—the Academy of Science, the Social Science Research Council and the Humanities Research Council— is in some degree inevitable. Even were those three organizations to join forces in a single academy, the present divisions would have to be formally recognized, for they express a real difference in approach and point of view.

Yet this difference is by no means easy to define. What, for example, of the historian? Most historians, probably, would wish to be considered humanists; and yet they might still insist, and with justice, that they ought to be strongly represented on a Social Science Council, for they certainly study society in a scientific spirit. Some philosophers, again, would be most at home in the Academy of Science, some with the social scientists, some on the Humanities Council—and a few, even in our own times, could claim membership of all three bodies. Even the linguist, now that language is conceived more and more as a social institution, may well be hesitant about his proper habitat.

Yet if there are uncertainties at the boundaries—uncertainties which usefully draw our attention to the unity of human knowledge—there can still be no doubt that a chemist is a physical scientist, that a demographer is a social scientist, that a classical scholar is a humanist. The distinction between humanist and scientist—natural or social—is not, that is, wholly arbitrary.

In the first place, and most conspicuously, there is a difference in techniques. The natural scientist works with, or in, a laboratory; the social scientist engages in field-work, or examines statistical records, or ransacks archives; the humanist's laboratory is his library. The practical interests of the three groups are in consequence very different—a fact which partly explains why they feel the need for distinct organizations. Considered purely as groups of professional workers, the Academy of Science will naturally press for the setting up of additional laboratories or research stations; the Social Science Council will look for funds with which to encourage individuals, or teams of individuals, to undertake extensive field-work; the Humanities Council will be mainly concerned with the improvement of library facilities and provision of opportunities for publication.

At the same time, there is something unsatisfactory and superficial about this method of discrimination, however convenient it may be for practical purposes. A distinction in terms of subject-matter might bring us closer to the root of the matter. Let us put the matter thus: the natural scientist describes and explains the structure of organic and inorganic processes; the social scientist describes and explains the structure of society and of the human being, considered as a social unit; the humanist makes a persistent attempt to come to a fuller understanding of the major achievements of the creative human spirit through a study of the masterpieces it has created.

No doubt this mode of discrimination still has its difficulties. Consider the case of the modern linguistic scholar. Language is clearly the concern of the humanist, in so far as it is a fundamental mode of expression of the human spirit. Yet it may be so studied—in its dependence on locality, education, social standing—as to form part of the subject-matter of social science. The logician, the psychologist, the physicist, the psychiatrist may all of them be profoundly concerned with the nature of language, and their investigations may prove to be of the first importance to the humanist.

Thus linguistics is not a subject that can be exclusively assigned to the humanities, or to natural science, or to social science. It fans out; the full study of a single utterance in language could involve the use of knowledge derived from physiology, psychology, neurology, philosophy, the mathematics of communication theory, inquiries into social milieu and historical background, the physics of sound, the practice and achievements of the literary artist. To worry unduly about whether one is a humanist can be an obstacle to inquiry—an inquirer must be free to follow his problem where it leads him. Yet, with whatever hesitation in a particular case, we still find it possible, in general terms, to distinguish the man whose central concern in the study of language is humanistic from the man who regards it primarily as a social phenomenon or as a psychological device or as a physical mechanism. For the humanistically-minded linguist will be trying to help us more fully to appreciate the character of masterpieces.

Other ways of defining the humanities readily suggest themselves, but do not turn out to be satisfactory. One such definition is that the humanist is a person devoted to the cultivation of a certain style. The scientist, often enough, thinks of himself as the person with something to say, but no skill in saying it, and of the humanist as having nothing to say, but saying it beautifully. Now it is no doubt true that the humanist cares more than the ordinary scientist about the mode in which he expresses his conclusions; he tries to write, as well as to study, works which are lucid, graceful, ordered. But if a concern for qualities of style is not always to be found amongst scientists, it sometimes is, and ought always to be. There is no excuse what-soever for the inept and clumsy writing, the laboured polysyllabic style, which disfigures so much contemporary scientific writing—and is by no means unknown even within the humanities. If the humanist feels a special responsibility as a writer, and if the character of his own studies should keep him alert to the subtleties of his language, the fact remains that he does not wish to claim any monopoly over the proper use of the English tongue. On the other side, too, he does claim to have something to say, and some-thing of the first importance.

The humanist cannot claim, either, that he alone takes the beautiful as his subject-matter. The crystallographer, the botanist, the aerodynamicist both reveal and delight in beauties of shape and line. Nor is it true to say that the humanist has a monopoly over intuition and imagination, for these qualities every creative scientific thinker must certainly possess. On the other side, the humanist, quite as much as the scientist, seeks precision, tests his ideas against the evidence, attempts to be as accurate and impartial as his subject-matter permits.

One common way of making the distinction between science and the humanities demands a somewhat more prolonged consideration. The scientist, it is said, concerns himself with "facts", the humanist with "values". On the face of it, this way of approaching the matter has been completely ruled out by the rise of the social sciences; for valuing is one of the main themes of anthropology and sociology and it is the central concern in many economic and psychological studies. The humanist is sometimes suspicious of the social scientist. Quite often, he may feel, the social scientist is achieving "scientific exactitude" only by concentrating upon superficial aspects of the phenomena he is supposed to be considering. Attempting to investigate the traditional subject-matter of the humanities by the methods of physical science, he sometimes reveals an ineptitude as a scientist only matched by his lack of humane sensibilities. Yet however critical the humanist may be of certain types of social-science investigation—and can he, examining his own conscience, wholly deny the counter-accusation that the humanist is sometimes a mere pedant, sometimes an empty rhetorician?—he can scarcely deny that the psychologist, the sociologist, the anthropologist have considerably illuminated the processes of valuation which go on in society.

The difference is that whereas the social scientist is content to *describe* processes of valuation, the humanist is trying to change, or sometimes to conserve, the valuations he finds around him. For if the humanist studies masterpieces, he must also determine which are the masterpieces, he must distinguish the shoddy and the meretricious from what is of sterling quality. His task is not merely "appreciation" but also criticism, not a blind reverence before the fashionable and the accepted but a serious attempt to estimate greatness critically, to help us to decide in what it consists, to aid us in developing that sort of appreciation which rests on a deep critical understanding. The humanist does not preach or exhort; it is not his task to bully us into admiring, but rather to reveal the admirable to us, whether in literature, in art, or in intellectual achievement.

How is this to be done? Only, in the first place, by the exercise of scholarship. To appreciate masterpieces we have first to see them as they are, and that implies, for the most part, some measure of scholarly penetration. Most obviously, we cannot understand the achievements of the Greeks unless we have a grasp not merely of the language they used but of the local characteristics—the conventions, the now obscure allusions—which conceal the work from us. The same is true of the Elizabethan and Jacobean dramatists; for if the language they use is English, it is not the English of our own time. It is easy to laugh at scholarly apparatus, and no doubt it can be carried to such a point of elaborateness and pedantry as to conceal rather than reveal the work with which it concerns itself. But without the scholar, all the same, masterpieces would often be wholly inaccessible to us; only through the scholar's persistence, his imagination, does the past exist for us as a living ingredient in our culture.

Scientists are sometimes impatient with the humanist's interest in the past. But this preoccupation is quite natural. The history of science and technology is a history of gradual gains and improvements and the stages by which science developed may be of little direct relevance to science as it operates in the present. But in the humanities the remote past is often much richer than the recent past. The humanities do not show us the gradually ascending line of achievement of the sciences. The great peaks of achievement are in the past. There are no greater dramas or epics than those produced by the Greeks at the beginning of our humanistic tradition. The theatre-goer in the last three hundred and fifty years has been less privileged than the common man of Shakespeare's London. The local and the contemporary have no title to special consideration just because they are local and contemporary. However signal may be the victories of discovery won by modern science, man is no more deeply concerned about the ultimate questions than he was in ancient Greece or in the Middle Ages, nor are his sensibilities and creative imagination more highly developed than they were when Western civilization first came to fruition.

This does not mean that the humanist is restricted to the past. He is bound to be, and quite properly, a *laudator temporis acti*, but not in a sense which implies any withdrawal from the present. For as he ranges over the contemporary world the humanist has still the same responsibility: to bring the world to a critical understanding of what is valuable. It is the humanists who draw to our attention what matters in the present as well as what matters in the past. To detect what is merely fashionable, to distinguish between the genius and the charlatan, is a task of the greatest difficulty— but one the humanist cannot shirk, for he alone can undertake it with any chance of success. Perhaps the most striking feature of the humanist, one can indeed suggest, is that for him the past is at once of very special significance and of no significance at all: of special significance because he must learn to see things historically if he is not profoundly to misunderstand them, of no importance in the sense that for him the crucial question is always: "Is that good?" not "Is that up-to-date?" That is one reason why the historical approach is so characteristic of a humanist. Even if we believe that scientists would be all the better for making a closer study of the history of their subject, the historical approach, as we suggested above, has still not the same importance for the scientist as it has for the humanist; indeed the history of science is rather a means through which the scientist begins to think humanistically about science than a part of science itself.

For, as becomes perfectly clear in the writings, say, of Sir Charles Sherrington, science itself can form part of the subject-matter of the humanities, can be seen as a human achievement and in its relation to the history of human achievements. But this sort of historical and philosophical reflection upon science is not to be identified with science itself; it requires, for its success, the temperament and the training of a humanist combined with the knowledge of a scientist. The scientist is all the better as a man for being a historian, but not necessarily the better as a scientist. In contrast, the humanist is bound to develop a historical point of view, merely as a consequence of the kind of work in which he is engaged. And this, it is fair to say, is one of the great virtues of the study of the humanities: that it encourages the development of a sense of perspective, the taking of long views rather than the quest for short-term gains. Of course every virtue has its corresponding defect. Respect for the past may degenerate into a crusty and obstinate Toryism, just as too great a concern for the immediate present can encourage tyranny in the name of "urgent reforms".

One can put the matter another way by saying that the humanities help to free us from provincialism, whether of place or of time. From provincialism of place, indeed, any form of inquiry liberates us. The scientist is inevitably conscious of the international character of science; he can scarcely believe that any one nation has a monopoly of wisdom. But just because scientific knowledge develops at so rapid a pace, just because he is compelled by the nature of his work to be up-to-date, the scientist may well fall into a provincialism of time. Young scientists sometimes speak as if the Dark Ages ended, at most, five years ago.

If the humanist is inevitably a historian, he is also unlikely to succeed in his task unless he thinks philosophically—reflects critically, at least, on his criteria of judgment. Should he fail to do this, if he is content merely to pick up and use uncritically the criteria which float at large in his cultural environment, he is very liable, as soon as he is not constrained by the rigorous discipline of scholarship, to lapse into a painful woolliness. Whereas the temptation of the social scientist is a spurious accuracy which records readily-measurable trivia at the cost of ignoring the less tractable fundamentals, the temptation of the more "literary" sort of humanist is to fall into a style which achieves an appearance of sublimity at the cost of an actual inanity.

Hard-headed humanists sometimes react against this empty loftiness by devoting themselves to antiquarian detail, no less trivial than the banalities of social science or the mere collecting spirit which is sometimes exhibited in the natural sciences. (Physical science, it is important to realize, can be at least as trivial as any other form of inquiry: but this is less obvious to the outsider, because the triviality is concealed in the decent obscurity of a learned language.) Or, alternatively, humanists may be led to embark upon what are really social science inquiries into, say, the kinds of people who find satisfaction in popular fiction, because they despair of establishing any sort of precision in the direct study of masterpieces.

Yet surely the proper way of overcoming humane woolliness is to cultivate that sort of exactitude which the humanities permit. This is not the quantitative exactitude of science but rather philosophical exactitude; the critic must attempt to employ his general categories with sufficient exactness to enable him to cast light on the masterpieces he is discussing, to make more apparent the precise quality of their achievement.

The humanities at their best, one must conclude, are a systematic attempt, first, to bring us to a fuller understanding of masterpieces by removing those historical and linguistic obstacles which stand in the way of our understanding, and secondly, to help us in distinguishing, with as much clarity as the matter permits, between the genuine masterpiece and the pretentious oddity. The first objective implies, of course, an arduous study of language; but a man is not a humanist if he is only, in the ordinary sense of that phrase, "good at languages"—he must use his linguistic gifts in the criticism of masterpieces before he deserves to be entitled a humanist. Similarly, a philosopher as such need not be a humanist: his main interests may be in, say, the foundations of mathematics rather than in the categories of criticism or the history of thought. Nor is every historian a humanist; if he restricts himself to the investigation of socio-political or economic structures, his natural affiliations are with the social scientists rather than with the humanists. But just as a humanist is handicapped—fatally, one may say—unless he is fluent in languages other than his own, so too the humanist must be something of a historian and something of a philosopher —as was long ago recognized by the founders of the Oxford Greats course.

One question arises: are the humanities parasitic? If they are defined as an attempt to come to terms with masterpieces, does not this imply that they are secondary growths, at best of negligible fruitfulness, at worst a drain on creative strength? Creative artists, creative scientists, creative philosophers sometimes think of humane inquiries in this way: the critic, the commentator, is a battener, a blood-sucker, a desiccated pedant. W. B. Yeats's attitude in his "The Scholars" is typical:

> Bald heads, forgetful of their sins,
> Old, learned, respectable bald heads
> Edit and annotate the lines
> That young men, tossing on their beds,

Rhymed out in love's despair
To flatter beauty's ignorant ear.

They'll cough in the ink to the world's end;
Wear out the carpet with their shoes
Earning respect; have no strange friend;
If they have sinned nobody knows.
Lord, what would they say
Should their Catullus walk that way?

Stung, perhaps, by the epicene malice of some failed-novelist critic, the creative writer responds with savage scorn. Yet, as we have already suggested, this much at least must be said for the humanist: that if it were not for the work of critics and scholars Catullus would no longer exist for us, except as a crumbling piece of paper. It is the critic who picked him out as a poet worth preserving; it is the scholars who make his work intelligible to us. But we can go further than this: the great critic, the great scholar, is eminent in his own right, apart altogether from his usefulness to the artist, whether as irritant or as preservative. Normally, no doubt, the critic could not himself have written the work he criticizes, sometimes severely, but that is beside the point; for it is equally true that many artists are incapable of writing effective criticism or accurate works of scholarship. A critic may lack that sort of human sympathy which enables a dramatist to bring men and women alive before us through the medium of dialogue; yet he may have a wider range of understanding of the dramatic art than the creative dramatist—committed to a particular technique and line of approach—can hope to possess. If there were no drama there could be no dramatic critics—that is obvious; but no more relevant than the fact that if there were no human conflicts there would be no drama. If the critic is parasitic upon works of art, this is only in the harmless sense in which the novelist and dramatist are parasitic upon human beings. No doubt men often fall back upon criticism when they fail as creative artists, or on the history and philosophy of science when they fail as scientists, but they are likely to be as incompetent in their new capacity as in their old one —unless chance has led them by devious means to their true field of usefulness.

The fact, however, that the humanist has works of genius as his subject-matter gives to the humanistic subjects a peculiar advantage as an educational instrument. In the early days of his training, the scientist is never directly confronted by a masterpiece; he is being trained as an apprentice, accustoming himself to the use of formulae and techniques. At a time when his humanist contemporaries are reading Catullus or Shakespeare or Plato, he is still struggling with elementary text-books. Now, no doubt masterpieces can be so badly introduced to school children—or even to undergraduates—that their greatness is obscured rather than made evident. But still the greatness is there, and even the worst-taught child has a chance of seeing it for himself.

Furthermore, through his study of literature he is brought into contact with subtle and sophisticated human beings and with societies no less diverse and complex. The infinite possibilities of the human being for good and for evil are brought sharply before his attention, whether through the medium of literature or of history. The study of science, even at its best, brings humanity before the student only in the ideal form of intellectual creation whereas the humanities introduce him to the entire range of human feeling and human aspiration. And in that process they deepen the student's own emotional responses, sharpen his sensibilities. In that sense the humanities engage, and seek to cultivate, "the whole man". That is why a humanistic education has traditionally emphasized literature rather than pictorial art or music, because of its richness in this respect. In many cases, no doubt, the confrontation is ineffective—the humanistic impression, if ever made, is erased by the commonplaces of everyday life, the platitudinous simplifications of his companions. But there is at least a chance that the student of the humanities may catch a spirit which will remain with him through the rest of his life.

One might hope that, in the same way, he would catch the scientific spirit through the teaching of science. This, though, is more difficult, partly on account of the way in which science has to be, or at any rate commonly is, taught in the schools, partly because unless the student actually becomes a scientist he will have no opportunity to continue his scientific education—in the sense that he can continue his education in the humanities merely by reading books, looking at plays or films, in a manner somewhat different from that of the unhumanized man.

Thus, however sympathetic the humanist may be to the claims of of science to form part of a liberal education, to the view, indeed, that science is one of the most remarkable achievements of the human spirit, he is yet bound to insist that if we were to sacrifice a humane to a technological, or even a purely scientific, education we should seriously impoverish not only our schools and our universities but the whole life of the community. No doubt when the humanist criticizes schemes for the reconstruction of education in an anti-humanist direction he sometimes does so in a manner which reveals that he is either quite unsympathetic to science, or determined to insist upon prior rights of possession, or grossly unrealistic about the actual practice and effects of humanistic work in the schools and universities. But if his arguments are sometimes unsound, the humanist's conclusion still stands: that an education which produces its effects through the serious study of masterpieces must take the central place in any society which has as its ideal a rich and varied life rather than the grey uniformity of a merely technological society.

If a training in the humanities is recognized (as it now seems to be) as an essential constituent of every education, various questions immediately arise about educational methods and organization. Into most of these we do not propose to enter here; but one matter of immediate practical importance cannot be passed by, especially as it is particularly relevant to our central theme. When, as in some institutions of higher learning, humanities are made a compulsory part of the courses of technologists, humanists are sometimes inclined to say that such courses can confer no more than a smear of culture, that the discipline must be shallow and scrappy, that no more than lip-service to the humanistic ideal is here intended. But if there are dangers of superficiality in such arrangements, it is for the humanist to remove them. He must accept the challenge of presenting his subject in a way that will make the best use of his limited opportunities, avoiding superficiality, narrowness, thinness and over-simplification. The humane scholar who can, or will, think of no methods of teaching his subject other than those appropriate to students to whom it is their main interest, is missing the opportunities offered by the increasing tendency to include humane studies in technological and scientific education.

There is, all the same, a certain danger in some present attitudes toward the problem of selecting humane studies for scientists and technologists. Scientists—Sir Eric Ashby for one—sometimes say that only those humanities which are "relevant" to technological education are suitable for this purpose. Such a line of approach may exclude the most characteristic and, for a scientist, most valuable parts of the humanities, those which will help to diversify his imaginative and emotional life and provide him with opportunities for taking the long and comprehensive view. Thus whereas "history of an anthropological kind" and "history of science and technology" have been recommended as courses for technologists, the emphasis, surely, should rather be on the sort of history which attempts to understand those aspects of human thought and action which a technologist is liable to ignore. The "instrumental" or "servicing" conception of the humanities has considerable dangers in it.

It would be particularly unfortunate if the idea were to gain wide acceptance that humanities courses should be developed only in so far as they are of instrumental value in a scientific or technical education, or if it should come to be supposed that such courses can be a substitute for a faculty of Arts. Any university worthy of the name must have a fully-developed Arts faculty in which humane studies are pursued with the same concentration, thoroughness and rigour as is characteristic of scientific faculties—an Arts faculty which will add to knowledge, not merely a miscellaneous collection of humanities teachers.

The scientist sometimes refuses to admit that research, as he understands it, can proceed in an Arts subject; and he assumes that no other sort of research is worthy of attention. Only sometimes, as in archaeology, does humane research take the form of discovering previously unknown facts. More typically, it is a re-interpretation or re-assessment of a masterpiece; it may be re-thinking, criticism, speculation. To see a masterpiece in a new light is no doubt to make a discovery about it, but this is not, one can freely admit, a discovery in quite the sense in which, say, a neuro-physiologist might discover a new fact about the chemistry of synaptical transmission. The fact remains that it is no less important as a contribution to knowledge, and rests upon a training no less rigorous.

If in their desire—which humanists welcome—to provide a worth-while humane element in the education of scientists and technologists, scientists extract what, in their eyes, is "really important" from what a faculty of Arts offers, and beyond that have no interest in the development of a faculty of Arts, they will find, even at the lowest level, that the humane studies will have little to offer them. Humane studies must be developed as fully in the university as other studies; otherwise they are bound to collapse into superficiality. (Just as "general science" does, if it is entrusted to men who are not engaged in fundamental scientific inquiry.) One of the most dangerous fallacies of our time is the belief that humane studies are dispensable luxuries that can be neglected with no great loss. A society which neglects its masterpieces is a society on the path to destruction.

We are often asked whether we can afford to ignore the competition for industrial power, and how there can be room for more scholars in a country threatened with enslavement as a result of falling behind in the nuclear powers race. To put the matter thus is to discuss the place of the humanities in education at the lowest possible level of controversy. On this same level of argument the humanist might ask the scientist and technologist to reflect that, as recent history clearly reveals, a high degree of development in science and technology can go along with a decline in political freedom and individual dignity, with a tyranny over the mind that makes life not worth living. One can readily imagine a technological civilization with its efficiency and its security developed to the full, yet no more fit to live in—for a man endowed with powers of thought and criticism, creative curiosity and imagination—than an ant-heap.

We need and are bound to have more science and technology—not only on practical grounds, but because science and technology are amongst the most notable achievements of our civilization. But we dare not sacrifice the humanities in that cause. If the present conflict of educational claims and counter-claims, criticisms and defences, issues in a recognition of the mutual dependence of the sciences and the humanities then we may be grateful for it; we sometimes fear that it may rather lead to a decline in creative achievement both in science and in the humanities.

In a recent article Sir Eric Ashby has carried the controversy between humanists and scientists into the field of management and government.[1] The traditional technical education in England, he says, has produced a highly trained technologist, who, because the humanities and the social sciences played no part in his education, is not fitted to manage human beings or to shape general policy. He remains the technical expert. He tenders advice and supervises operations but he does not sit on the board of his organization or take his place among those who shape its general policy. Sir Eric would like to see the position of the technologist improved, with the help of an education which would fit him to take a part in management and in the formulation of general policy.

The most significant part of Sir Eric Ashby's address is his acknowledgment that this state of affairs can be achieved only if the humanities and the social sciences are included in the education of the technologist. But a related point made by Sir Eric Ashby is of great import. With the present highly technological organization of industry, he argues, the men who manage and formulate general policy must be able to think in the manner of a scientist and a technologist. Looking at the matter from the point of view of the technologist, the happy solution, according to Sir Eric Ashby, would be to train the technologist, by seeing to it that his education includes those humane studies which will fit him to manage people and to cope with problems of general policy.

One might rather suggest that the solution is so to train the humanist that he can think in terms of technological processes and problems. The argument that since scientists and technologists are transforming the world they should also run it, that since their discoveries are creating social and human problems they should determine the solution of these problems, is a merely sentimental one. Only a thorough training in the humanities and social sciences can fit a man to take a broad view of those policies, problems and plans that involve human purposes, human satisfactions, human strengths and weaknesses, human conflicts and co-operation. Whether a man is a humanist who has acquired some understanding of science and technology or whether he is a technologist who has acquired some understanding of humane subjects might be regarded as a matter of degree. The fact remains that his point of view as an executive must be humanistic, not technological; he must treat human beings as potentially creative, not as mere cogs in an organization". Otherwise our society will collapse into some

---

[1] "Technological Humanism", *Journal of the Institute of Metals*, lxxxvi, 1957, p. 461.

form of totalitarianism, however benevolent. The humanities are more important than ever in a technological civilization; unless, to repeat a main theme of this chapter, science, technology and the humanities can learn profitably to co-operate, the outlook for our civilization is indeed a bleak one.

CHAPTER II

Australian Universities: The Historical Background

BY J.J. AUCHMUTY IN COLLABORATION WITH A.N. JEFFARES

WHEREVER THE BRITISH PEOPLES HAVE ESTABLISHED THEMSELVES AS colonists beyond the seas, there have always been present those who desired urgently to create educational institutions on the model of those in the mother countries. Nevertheless in the true British tradition there has been no uniform development and the growth of university and higher education in the North American colonies and in their Australasian counterparts has followed strikingly different patterns. It was a prime characteristic of the early colleges of what are now Canada and the United States that they were in general religious foundations and only secondarily dependent upon state support; moreover they came into being proportionately earlier in colonial development than did the colleges in the Australian states. The Australian universities, with the possible exception of Melbourne, are the result of long discussion and argument and are all, without exception, firmly organized on a purely secular and non-sectarian basis. Harvard College was established as a Congregationalist foundation in 1636, less than thirty years after permanent British colonization in the North American continent had commenced, and before the population of New England had achieved a total of 30,000. Its purpose was clearly set down in the oft-quoted words of *New England's First Fruits*, a pamphlet published in London in 1643:[1]

> After God had carried us safe to New England, and we had builded our houses, provided necessaries for our livelihood, reared convenient places for God's worship, and settled the Civil Government: one of the next things we longed for, and looked after was to advance *Learning*, and perpetuate it to Posterity; dreading to leave an illiterate Ministry to the Churches, when our present Ministers shall lie in the Dust.

In this climate of opinion, prior to the War of Independence, no fewer than nine degree-granting colleges, all save one denominational, were established on American soil. The continuing American loyalists in Canada

[1] F. Eby and C.F. Arrowood, *The Development of Modern Education*, N.Y., 1942, p. 554.

inherited the same tradition and one of their first activities after separation was the establishment of King's College, Nova Scotia, the oldest English-speaking institution of higher learning in the overseas empire,[2] deliberately fashioned to preserve the Anglican heritage which had been grievously under attack prior to and during the War of Independence.

In Australia the University of Sydney did not come into being until 1852, more than sixty years after the arrival of the first fleet and the consequent first permanent British settlement on Australian soil; in contrast to the mere 30,000 of Harvard's colonial New England the population of New South Wales in the 1850s was passing the 200,000 mark and it would certainly have been more than difficult to find among those 200,000 the equivalent of the 100 resident graduates of Oxford and Cambridge who had supported the call for the establishment of John Harvard's college. Sydney's university was emphatically non-sectarian; the Bill introduced by W.C. Wentworth into the Legislative Council of New South Wales on 2nd October 1849 would even have excluded ministers of religion from all share in the government of the university but in due course wiser counsels prevailed and the first senate did in fact include several clerical members though no religious test of any kind has ever existed in any Australian university.

In the fullness of time each of the Australian states set up its own university institution. Sydney, where the first lectures were given in 1852, was quickly followed by Melbourne, legally constituted in 1853 less than eighteen months after the state of Victoria had severed itself from New South Wales, and where the first lectures were given in 1855. The University of Adelaide was created in 1874 and fifty-eight students attended the first year's lectures in 1876. Tasmania came into being in 1890; Queensland in 1910; and after a series of Royal Commissions and other inquiries Western Australia completed the pattern in 1911. All these universities were state universities, increasingly dependent on state funds, some, such as Sydney and Melbourne, recipients of considerable aid from private donors and all, within the limits of their budgets, very similar in the composition of their faculties and the design of their courses. This symmetrical pattern was altered in 1929 when the Commonwealth Government established a small university college at Canberra which was allied by a succession of temporary agreements with the University of Melbourne and which, in its early days, made slow development as it provided for the part-time education of local members of the public service. The second world war turned Commonwealth attention to the inadequacy of research and technological facilities throughout Australia and brought to a head proposals dating back many years to meet these evident deficiencies. The Commonwealth founded the Australian National University at Canberra for

[2]W. Kirkconnell and A.S.P. Woodhouse, *The Humanities in Canada*, Ottawa, 1947, p. 20.

post-graduate instruction and research in 1946 and the New South Wales University of Technology was established by that State in 1949 with a special mandate to increase the number of technologists and applied scientists in Australia and to provide them with the means of advanced training and research. In the terms of its Act the University of Technology was empowered to establish divisions and colleges in other centres besides Sydney but so far the only university college to be established is that at Newcastle which was set up in 1951. The Newcastle University College makes a further break in any uniform picture of the Australian academic scene by reason of the link established between its Department of Arts and the University of New England. The University of New England is the first Australian example of academic decentralization. The New England University College of the University of Sydney was opened at Armidale, New South Wales in 1938 and was given independent university status in 1954 when it agreed to examine and confer degrees on those students of the University of Technology at Newcastle University College who wished to graduate in Arts. So far the University of Technology, by reason of its very special place in the academic community, has not seen fit to confer degrees in Arts but since it controls the only university college in the industrial city of Newcastle which has a population approaching 200,000, some provision for Arts degrees was obviously necessary and these have been provided by this co-operation between the universities of Technology and New England.

This temporary expedient seems already to have served its purpose as the recent Report of the Murray Committee on Australian universities firmly recommended that the University of Technology should assume more of the features of the traditional university. To that end the Committee recommended the establishment of faculties of Arts and Medicine and the dropping of the word Technology from the title. This advice has been accepted in general by the State Government and the necessary legislation has transformed the University of Technology into the University of New South Wales.

The Victorian Government has recently recognized the need for a second university in Melbourne and has set up an interim council to establish it. It is to be called the Monash University after Sir John Monash, equally celebrated as an engineer and as the leader of the Australian Expeditionary Force in the first world war. In the first instance the new university will have faculties of Medicine, Engineering and Science, to be followed by Arts.

If the academic scene in Australia had until recently a certain monotony so also the general problems have had an equal air of uniformity. When the mother universities of Sydney and Melbourne were established there were only four universities in England—Oxford, Cambridge, Durham and London; and but two in Ireland, the historic Anglican university of Dublin and the recently established examining body called the Queen's University of Ireland. Despite the existence of the four ancient universities of Scotland it was from the English and Irish colleges that staff and inspiration were derived, though in the long run it was the Scottish spirit and practice which were in many ways to prevail.

Although the prime aim of the founding fathers of Australian universities —Wentworth and Douglass in New South Wales, Childers and Redmond Barry in Victoria[3]—was in no way concerned with the provision of a literate ministry for the church overseas, nevertheless their views of the academic content of the courses in the new colleges were distinctly con-servative, conditioned by the traditional background of the great historic universities of Oxford, Cambridge and Dublin in which the vast majority of university graduates resident in Australia had been educated. The twenty-four students admitted as matriculants to the University of Sydney at the opening ceremony on 11th October 1852 were all compelled to pursue courses of study in Greek, Latin and Mathematics, in which subjects they had passed the entrance examination, as well as in Chemistry and Experi-mental Physics. Until 1874 this group of subjects was always compulsory in the degree courses though the same professors who taught them also lectured on occasion in Logic, Ancient History, Modern History and Natural Philosophy, and intermittently there were courses in French and German. At Melbourne, where only sixteen students matriculated in 1855, to be followed by seven in 1856 and 1857 and only two in 1858, the under-graduates were also compelled to take Greek and Latin (for two years), the elements of Natural Philosophy and Astronomy for one year and nine other subjects including Logic, Mathematics, History and Political Economy, as well as Geology, Botany, Zoology, Mineralogy and Chemistry. Students at Sydney today can graduate in Arts without studying any single subject compulsory for graduation prior to 1874, but they are still sheltered by the peculiar clause introduced into the Act of 1884: "Provided that no student of the university shall be compelled to attend lectures upon or to pass ex-aminations in any of the following subjects, namely:— Ethics, Metaphysics and Modern History." Wentworth and his friends of 1850, influenced by the University of London Act, were ardently secularist in outlook; by 1884 the various religious denominations of New South Wales had come to accept the university but were fearful of proselytism, hence the introduction

[3] The careers of Wentworth, Childers and Redmond Barry can be followed in the *Dictionary of National Biography*. Dr H.G. Douglass was an Irish physician who came to New South Wales in 1821, after practising for some time in France. See H.E. Barff, *A Short Historical Account of the University of Sydney*, Sydney, 1902, p. 68 and K.W. Street in *The University of Sydney Centenary Celebrations*, Sydney, 1952, p. 64.

of the additional safeguard. It is only in recent years that further legislation has permitted the introduction of degrees in Divinity.

It is a sign of the growing fragmentation of knowledge that the first three professors in Sydney and the first four in Melbourne covered in those early years the entire range of subjects taught in the two universities. The letter addressed by the Provost, Vice-Provost and Colonial Secretary from Sydney to the original committee of selection in England included a passage from the writings of Arnold of Rugby which summarizes the attitude of the early founders of the universities both in Melbourne and in Sydney: "We require for our purpose, gentlemen, scholars, men of ability and vigour of character, to become the parents of the education of a country rapidly rising into greatness, qualified to assist in laying the foundations of all good and noble principles, and to induce our youth to submit to the discipline of education for the sake of its ultimate fruits." [4] The English committee which made the appointments was itself of outstanding academic quality and looked for equally outstanding qualifications in the men it recommended. In the second half of 1852 the new professors arrived in Sydney. To the Chair of Classics, which was combined with the office of Principal of the College, had been appointed the Reverend John Woolley, M.A., D.C.L., formerly Fellow of University College, Oxford; to the Chair of Mathematics, Morris Birkbeck Pell, B.A., Fellow of St John's College, Cambridge and Senior Wrangler of 1849; and to the Chair of Chemistry and Experimental Philosophy, John Smith, M.A., Marischal College, Aberdeen, Lecturer in Chemistry in that university.[5] These were men of proved capacity and distinction and under Dr Woolley's enthusiastic leadership the university and its staff began immediately to play an important part in the cultural life of the community. Nevertheless no one of them contributed as significantly either to the world of scholarship or to the life of the evolving nation as did the first and perhaps the greatest of Melbourne's professors, W.E. Hearn, a notable Dublin graduate, formerly Professor of Greek in Queen's College, Galway, who proved a stormy petrel as well as a great constructive force in Victorian education and politics from 1854 till his death in 1888. Hearn was a polymath who based his teaching in Modern History and Literature, Political Economy and Logic upon a spirit of inquiry. His *Plutology* was an original and advanced piece of economic theory; his *Government of England* influenced later writers; his *Aryan Household: its Structure and its Development* was a work of learning, and he wrote a text-book for law students when he became Dean of the

---

[4] Quoted in H.E. Barff, *A Short Historical Account of the University of Sydney*, Sydney, 1902, p. 16.

[5] The English selection committee consisted of Sir John Herschel and Sir George Airy, the great astronomers; Henry Malden, Professor of Greek at University College, London and Henry Denison, Fellow of All Souls.

Faculty of Law, having for a short period carried out the duties of the classical professor. In order to circumvent legislation forbidding university professors to stand for election to the Victorian Legislative Council he resigned his chair and had himself appointed a dean at the same salary. Hearn was a suitable mentor, not only to his students at Melbourne as professor, but briefly to the governing body of the university as chancellor and from 1878 to the Legislative Council of which he became the "unofficial leader", and in which he devoted himself to legal codification; his enthusiasm and energy were matched by his gentleness and civilized behaviour. His colleagues were W.P. Wilson (Mathematics), M. Irving (Classics) and F. McCoy who became an F.R.S. Three of these professors came from posts at the new Queen's University of Ireland and one was a Fellow of Trinity College, Cambridge.

On his way back from leave in England, Principal Woolley of Sydney was drowned when the *London* foundered in the Bay of Biscay in January 1866. He was succeeded in the Chair of Classics by the second scholar of international repute to make his home and pursue his career in Australia. The Rev. Charles Badham, something of a character and strangely irascible in his private life, had been a favourite pupil of Pestalozzi prior to a brilliant career at Eton and Wadham College, Oxford. A prodigious linguist, the friend of Thackeray and Tischendorf, he came to Australia with recommendations from Huxley, Grote and Newman and of him A.E. Housman has written: "Badham, the one English scholar of the mid-century whose reputation crossed the Channel, received from abroad the praises of Duebner and Nauck and Cobet, but at home was excluded from academical preferment, set to teach boys at Birmingham and finally transported to the Antipodes."[6] Badham was a notable orator and an enthusiast for the most widespread facilities for educational opportunity.

On the work of these early professors the whole structure of Australian faculties of Arts and Science has been built. This university structure has slowly risen to include within its framework faculties of Law, Medicine, Engineering and Economics, though it should be emphasized that for the first thirty years or so the only fully operative faculty was that of Arts. True, Sydney had a medical dean from the beginning but it had no teaching department until 1883. It has been the practice in the Australian universities, at least in their early stages, to admit to *ad eundem* status not merely distinguished citizens and visitors but also local residents with degrees from elsewhere who may desire a local qualification and the practice may be enlarged, as currently in Western Australia and Tasmania, to include status in non-existent faculties so that the governing bodies of the respective

[6] Quoted by Professor Milgate in *One Hundred Years of the Faculty of Arts*, Sydney, 1952, p. 44.

universities may be representative of as wide a range of university disciplines as possible.[7]

The governing bodies in these new universities have developed along similar lines though with differing nomenclatures. It will have been noted earlier that it was the Provost and Vice-Provost of Sydney University College who in conjunction with the Colonial Secretary corresponded with the English committee of selection. These titles were chosen in part because of a confusion between the place of the university and of the university college in the Sydney arrangements. In 1861 the Provost became the Chancellor and ever since the normal English university practice with slight variations has been uniform throughout the Australian states and Commonwealth. The only major deviation in subsequent years took place in the early stages of the New South Wales University of Technology which had originally been envisaged on the American model as an institute with a president and a director as its representative officers. However, after six years of operation with leading officials bearing these titles the normally accepted nomenclature of Chancellor, Vice-Chancellor and Deputy Chancellor was introduced in 1955.

In the development of the Australian universities the non-academic chancellor or chairman of senate or council has played a far more significant role that his counterpart in the British Isles. Although Professor Woolley was termed Principal of the new university college at Sydney, he naturally gave prime attention to his Chair of Classics and in no Australian university was there a full-time vice-chancellor or other permanent officer of accepted academic as well as administrative capacity until well on into the twentieth century; accordingly, from Sir Redmond Barry at Melbourne in the 1850s to Sir John Morris at Tasmania a full century later, there have ever been university chancellors of proved competence and ability and of accepted public position who have in addition exercised a considerable day-by-day control over the internal organization of their respective universities. It was Barry's lifelong aim to produce "a strong university" and he "did more than any man to raise the university in the esteem of the community".[8] Outside his work as Chief Justice, in which he exercised a distinguished and impressive rather than a learned influence, Barry's two interests were the public library and the university. The foundation stones of both were laid upon the same day and for the next quarter of a century, save for overseas leave, Barry was the strong man at any executive committee of either

[7] Mr K. Cable, Lecturer in History at the University of New South Wales, has compiled a list of the *ad eundem* degrees conferred at Melbourne 1856-65 showing the original university at which the applicant for incorporation had obtained his qualification: Dublin 17, Cambridge 15, Edinburgh 12, Glasgow 8, St Andrews 7, Oxford 7, Aberdeen 4, London 3, Queen's University of Ireland 1.

[8] N.H. Olver and G. Blainey, *The University of Melbourne: A Centenary Portrait*, Melbourne, 1956, p. 17.

institution. When books arrived late for the library opening the Chief Justice himself worked long and midnight hours unpacking and cataloguing; when quorums failed to present themselves on university executive committees the Chief Justice would exercise an independent jurisdiction and legalize everything with his signature in due course. However essential this dictatorship or managerial technique may have been, it has resulted in a grave weakness of academic responsibility at the centre and has constituted a dangerous and ever-present threat to academic freedom at all levels. This is the more forcibly threatened by the at all times great and at present overwhelming dependence of all Australian universities on government support and by the tendency in these modern times for so much of the scientific and technological research, which is an integral part of the university's responsibility to the community, to be financed from government sources and to be conducted under conditions of relative secrecy.

On the other hand, the appointment of full-time vice-chancellors as the twentieth century progressed has ensured that university problems are more forcibly brought to the attention of the general public. The first of these permanent vice-chancellors, like Sir Mungo MacCallum at Sydney or Professor H.E. Whitfeld in Western Australia, tended to be outstanding professors from the previous regime. Sir Mungo was for fifty-six years a member of the Professorial Board or of the Senate at Sydney and for thirty-three years occupied the Chair of Modern Literature; Whitfeld was one of the foundation professors in Western Australia. Since 1924 all Australian universities have come to possess vice-chancellors normally with distinguished academic records, though, as we mention elsewhere, the post is still an honorary one at the University of Queensland. In the case of every new university foundation, provision for a full-time vice-chancellor is to be found in the statutes.

Sir Mungo MacCallum's career at Sydney was paralleled by that of Sir William Mitchell at Adelaide. Sir William came out from Edinburgh University as Professor of Philosophy and English at Adelaide in 1894; he established his reputation as a scholar with *The Structure and Growth of the Mind* in 1907 and as an administrator as vice-chancellor from 1915-42 and thereafter till 1947 as chancellor. MacCallum and Mitchell are not the only professors to have become chancellors of their universities after retirement from professorial chairs. We have already mentioned the case of W.E. Hearn at Melbourne but a more recent one is that of Professor Walter Murdoch at Western Australia.

The dominance of chancellors and senates, the influence of governments, the comparative weakness of academic bodies like the professorial boards, have resulted in a certain diminution of the true value of university education. The senior Australian universities are contemporary with the first three major Western universities in India. These last, influenced by the innovation of the University of London, were set up as purely examining bodies and although teaching has ever been the prime function of all Australian universities, every university in the Commonwealth, with the exceptions of Sydney and the University of New South Wales (itself a special case), has been prepared to examine and confer degrees on students who have had no opportunity to attend lectures or to mix with their peers in that fruitful discussion and competition which is the basis of successful collegiate life. Amongst the earliest decisions made by the new University of Queensland in 1911 was that which sent a Bachelor of Arts, Thomas E. Jones, overseas to study correspondence school methods in American universities and today the University of New England in Armidale is responsible for degree education by correspondence within the state of New South Wales. Without such willingness on the part of the universities of Adelaide and Melbourne to control classes and forward study outlines, higher education would have been of even slower development in Western Australia and Queensland. Correspondence courses and part-time degrees by evening study have ever played a significant role, for economic reasons, in Australian development. This is not however to say that they approach the ideal. It is significant that in England the London innovation was not copied; that the Indian experiment has not been popular; that many have denied to the Royal University of Ireland the very title of university. What has been peculiar in Australian conditions is that certain types of development have been masked or hidden by an apparently normal façade. Who stops to ask whether a degree was taken by full- or part-time study, with attendance at lectures or through correspondence lessons? This situation has affected the value of the Australian pass degree and it has increased the importance of preparation for examinations over any ideas of a general or liberal education.

The differing values associated with the varying types of study are well evidenced by the predominance of those undergraduates who have the opportunity to attend the residential colleges of the various universities, not merely in student life and activity, but also in the lists of Rhodes Scholars from the respective states. It will be recollected that all the Australian universities are secular foundations. Inevitably this situation was disapproved of chiefly by that very section of the community most likely to have enjoyed the benefits of a university education in the homeland or to appreciate the needs of its sons, and later its daughters, for such an education. This enthusiasm for the teaching function of the university even found expression in the small and sparsely populated state of Tasmania where the Education Act of 1858 created a Body Corporate with power to confer, after examination, the degree of Associate of Arts, an examination qualification also established at that period by the University of Oxford. For the two out-standing graduates at this examination in each year the Tasmanian Government provided scholarships of £200 per annum "for the purpose of enabling students to become and continue members of some university in England, Scotland or Ireland, having power by law to confer degrees in Arts, Law or Medicine". It was the expenditure of this £1600 a year overseas which in Tasmania brought to a head the long struggle which had originated with the establishment of Hobart High School in 1847 "to advance and elevate the general education of the Colony with a view to the establishment of a Tasmanian University". Were it not for these overseas students like L.K. Giblin, an economist, whose ideas profoundly influenced Australian thought and development, and R.L. Dunbabin, the professor who devoted his life to university education in his own state, the University of Tasmania which was finally chartered in 1890 and in which teaching commenced in 1893 might have been merely an examining and not a teaching body. Less than a century later, in place of the eight students per annum who were receiving a university education there is more than a hundredfold increase. The Queensland Act of 1870, by rendering it lawful for any university in Great Britain or Ireland to institute examinations in the colony, had approached the problem much less adequately.

The older universities now possess firmly established colleges. The principle of student residence is fundamental to the Australian National University and the University of New England and from the experience of the University of New South Wales it is clear that the future development of all new Australian universities must be closely associated with the setting up of residential colleges. Nevertheless the number of students who have benefited from collegiate residence has at all times been small in proportion to the total number of full-time, much less part-time, students on the rolls. Only at New England where all full-time students must live in university colleges or hostels, save for the few normally domiciled in the small town of Armidale, is the Oxford or Cambridge ideal approached; at the universities of Queensland and Western Australia alone of the others does the proportion of full-time residential students approach a quarter of the respective totals. [9]

The original colleges like St Paul's (1854) at Sydney, or Trinity (1870) at Melbourne were Anglican foundations. But other denominations, Roman Catholic, Presbyterian, Methodist and Congregational, quickly followed them, though when these were joined in the twentieth century by women's colleges the latter were largely non-sectarian. The new residential arrangements at the post-war universities differ from the old in being university rather than private foundations, controlled by the same governing body as

[9] See Table 6 of Murray Report, 1957, p. 54. The figures given refer to the academic year 1956.

that which controls the university as a whole. Until recently the public character of some of the older universities was to a large degree formed by the students and alumni of the colleges; they often provided the heads of the university societies, the editors of the university newspapers and the backbone of the football, cricket and other athletic teams; they also provided a high proportion of the honours graduates; even their pass rate was well above average, and, as we have already stressed, their numbers included an overwhelming proportion of the Rhodes Scholars who by the very principles of choice laid down by the founder enjoyed a tremendous advantage if they had the good fortune to share in a college education. However, being poor and private foundations the colleges have not been able to maintain their development and their proportionate influence with the enormous current expansion in university numbers. There is increasing recognition that additional accommodation of a similar kind must be established if the accepted benefits of the collegiate system are to be appreciated by a wider body of students.

Since the Australian universities originally grew up in an atmosphere of state rights and were themselves the creation of sovereign states, there was little attempt to rationalize specialization between the universities until after the second world war. Faculties have been created in each state to meet local demand and of the possible fifteen[10] to be found in the various Australian institutions, no less than twelve operate in Melbourne and eleven in Queensland. New England has the fewest with only four, two of which, Animal Husbandry and Agricultural Economics, are peculiar to itself. Duplication of subjects, as of faculties, has created great problems of expense and of staffing and though rationalization is frequently talked of, it has been very difficult to achieve. For instance, for many years the Medical faculties at Sydney, Melbourne and Adelaide dominated the field. But these Medical schools increasingly found it necessary to limit the intake of students from the other states; the Queensland Medical faculty came into being in 1936 and that at Perth is now in process of full development. Here was a case where additional duplication of faculties was essential but where also the vast expenses involved were an effective deterrent. All the more honour to the citizens and friends of the state and university of Western Australia, who in the past few years have raised well over half a million pounds—about a pound per head of the state's population—to ensure a fitting start to this most important development. Tasmania is still without a Medical school but there are many critics who feel that this small state is in no financial position to support additional faculties to the six already operating.

[10] Arts, Science, Engineering, Technology, Medicine, Law, Education, Economics, Music, Architecture, Dental Science, Agricultural Science, Veterinary Science, Animal Husbandry, and Agricultural Economics. There is no uniformity in faculty nomenclature. This list is only an indication of faculty fields of study.

On the other hand, in New South Wales the opinion is widespread that additional faculties for medical education are essential, and it seems clear that, as a result of the Murray Report, a new Medical faculty is well on its way.

On occasion the Commonwealth Government has given aid to ensure that in at least one Australian university some significant university discipline should be pursued. Thus a Department of Anthropology was established at Sydney in 1925-6, having for its first head Professor A.R. Radcliffe Brown, F.B.A., formerly Fellow of Trinity College, Cambridge and later Professor of Social Anthropology and Fellow of All Souls, Oxford. This has been the major anthropological department in the Australian Commonwealth and the fruit of its researches is brought to a wider audience through the periodical *Oceania* founded by Professor Radcliffe Brown in 1930 and established on a firm international footing by his successor, the present editor, Professor A.P. Elkin. The Commonwealth has also helped to support the teaching of Oriental Languages at the Canberra University College, though other Australian faculties have been and are increasingly interested in Asian studies. The federal authorities have of course been of fundamental assistance to basic and applied research in many of the Science, Engineering and other faculties, both through the Commonwealth Scientific and Industrial Research Organization and in other ways.

With the development of air services, travel times have been vastly shortened throughout the Australian Commonwealth. Only in recent years has there been any serious attempt at a Commonwealth-wide policy and Commonwealth-wide co-operation in the university sphere. The Australian Vice-Chancellors' Conference met first in 1920, the National Union of Australian University Students dates from 1937 and the Commonwealth Universities Commission was established at a crisis in Australian affairs, in the middle of the second world war in 1942. Every modern development tends to ensure closer and closer co-operation between the universities at all levels and the establishment of the Australian Academy of Science, the Social Science Research Council and the Humanities Research Council has increased the opportunities for personal meetings between representative scholars. The number of periodicals accepting contributions of a scholarly nature is also on the increase and the university world is no longer one of relative isolation whether from other university centres or from the world at large. None the less, geographic and economic circumstances still contrive to ensure less mobility and greater self-centredness than obtains in comparable institutions overseas, and increased opportunities for publication are of course not equally available in all disciplines. The natural sciences are fairly well provided for through the Australian Association for the Advancement of Science, the support of C.S.I.R.O. and the existence of a number of specialized periodicals; in the humanities and social sciences there are reasonable outlets for contributions to history, economics, philosophy and psychology, but publication in languages, particularly the classical languages, is difficult, and on the whole the Australian academic continues to feel himself somewhat cut off from the great centres of world scholarship and the outlets freely open to scholars in other and older environments. Particularly do the Australian universities feel the absence of great library resources or of any centralized national library occupying the dominating position of the British Museum or the Library of Congress.

This comparative isolation of the Australian universities has not however prevented the attraction as well as the production of great and outstanding scholars in all disciplines. We have already referred to the establishment of the mother universities of the Commonwealth, Sydney and Melbourne. Both these universities were the creation of the state legislatures and primarily dependent on state funds. The University of Adelaide, set up by an Act of the South Australian Parliament in 1874, was largely prompted by the liberality of two local citizens, Sir Walter Watson Hughes and Sir Thomas Elder, who each contributed £20,000 for the foundation of chairs—Hughes for two professorships, one in Classics and Comparative Philology and Literature and the other in English Language and Literature and Mental and Moral Philosophy, and Elder for chairs in Mathematics and Natural Science.

The founders of the University of Adelaide were sure of their aims. They wanted culture. As Sir William Mitchell in his Commemoration Address of 1942 said: "Culture was put in the care of the professors and to emphasize their function, they were given no assistants and hardly a home but salaries relatively higher than we have ever paid since. They taught what they chose and gave help to the literary and scientific societies of the town. They had plenty of time for their studies, and they were protected from having too many students by compulsory Greek. It was culture's halcyon day and the calm lasted as growth slowly came and it found itself turning from beauty and wonder to utility." Eight matriculated students and fifty-two non-graduating students, thirty-three of them women, attended lectures in 1876 and evening lectures were instituted. Today the total enrolment is about 4500.

The half-century from 1875 was the period of great private benefactions to the Australian universities; such benefactions preceded 1875 and have continued to this day but are no longer so significant a proportion of a university's income. To Hughes and Elder at Adelaide succeeded the Barr Smith family and Sir Langdon Bonython; to be matched in Sydney by the wonderful benefactions of Challis and Bosch, each of the order of a quarter of a million pounds, together with the McCaughey Bequest which also benefited the University of Queensland and by the munificent gifts of Sir Peter Nicol Russell to the Sydney Engineering Schools. At Melbourne much was forthcoming at the end of the nineteenth century for the newly established colleges: Francis Ormond not only founded the Presbyterian College which bears his name but also endowed the Chair of Music; to Melbourne came one of the latest large-scale benefactions to any Australian university—over £200,000 from Sir Frank Beaurepaire in 1954 and subsequent years for the improvement of sporting facilities. The Nuclear Research Foundation at Sydney and similar scientific and technological research projects elsewhere currently receive considerable financial support from well-known philanthropists like Adolf Basser or large industrial firms like General Motors-Holden, Imperial Chemicals and the Broken Hill Proprietary Company. Melbourne has had the good fortune in recent years to have had more chairs privately endowed than any other university including the professorships of Fine Arts and Semitic Studies which are unique in the Commonwealth. The University of Queensland is indebted to Dr Mayne and his sister for its magnificent and picturesque site of 223 acres at St Lucia where a permanently impressive series of stone buildings is in course of erection and its Fryer Memorial Library, the Mayne Law Library and the Darnell Bequest for Arts and Pacific Studies betoken a significant public interest in university development on the part of the Queensland public. Nor do great public benefactions dry up state and popular support. No university was more dependent for its foundation on the efforts and financial support of one man than the University of Western Australia, and as we have already stated, no other university has in recent years made such a successful public appeal to the people of its parent state.

The university at Perth was largely the creation of Sir John Winthrop Hackett a classical scholar from Trinity College, Dublin, who went to Western Australia as a newspaperman after a period as Deputy Warden of Trinity College, Melbourne, under another distinguished Dublin classic, the virtual creator of the college and of its reputation, Dr Alexander Leeper. Hackett became a Legislative Councillor and a dominating figure in the life of Western Australia and was closely associated both in ecclesiastical and public affairs with an equally dominating character, the Anglican Archbishop, the Most Rev. Charles Riley, D.D. In 1898 Adelaide University, then almost a quarter of a century old, established an examination centre in Perth and public agitation for an independent state university inevitably gathered strength. While Western Australia was a state of giant area and great potential, it was one of small population, isolated from the east by enormous distances; those who used cultural rather than materialistic arguments to support their case for a university were not greatly encouraged by the struggling existence of the University of Tasmania founded in Hobart in 1890.

In 1909 Hackett became chairman of the Royal Commission which resulted in the University Act of 1911, the appointment of Hackett as chancellor, and the reception of the first students in Arts, Engineering and Science in 1913. The university started with three faculties, eight chairs and 182 students; two only of these professors were in the faculty of Arts— Walter Murdoch in English and E.O.G. Shann in History and Economics. For the first time an Australian university had come into being which did not give priority to those humanistic and classical studies which enjoyed a historic pre-eminence in the mother universities of Britain. On the other hand, by a resolution of the first senate, 18th November 1912, no fees were to be charged, and Western Australia is today in some faculties the only free university in the Commonwealth. That the university did not become predominantly scientific and technological is due to the first Professor of Mining and Engineering, H.E. Whitfeld, an outstanding figure on the academic side in the early history of the university, its first vice-chancellor in the days of part-time rotation, and its first permanent vice-chancellor. Professor Whitfeld had originally been a classics graduate and throughout his life consistently maintained an attitude friendly to the humanities. Whitfeld, Murdoch and Shann gave to the university as auspicious a start academically as was given to any Australian university and when the generous Hackett Bequest totalling some £500,000 became available in 1926 the opportunity was taken to build the most beautiful and aesthetically homogeneous of Australian universities on a magnificent suburban site at Crawley; the only comparable university site in the Commonwealth is that of Queensland at St Lucia. Vast expansion at both Sydney and Melbourne has dotted with temporary buildings and anachronistic erections sites originally well designed and spacious, though nothing in Australian university building can equal the faith and achievement displayed in Sydney's Great Hall, erected in the first ten years of the university's existence when the student population was still under 100. With the establishment of its Medical faculty, the University of Western Australia now has nine faculties and the student enrolment approaches 2500.

Western Australia was the last of the state universities to come into existence; its immediate predecessor Queensland opened its doors, also in the three faculties of Arts, Science and Engineering, in 1910. The struggle for a university in Brisbane had been longer and more protracted than that in Perth. Though a first attempt had been made to establish a university by the then State Premier as early as 1873, the first Royal Commission on University Education did not sit until 1891. University bills failed to pass in 1898 and 1901 and the final achievement of a University Act in 1909 was largely due to a desire suitably to commemorate the jubilee of responsible government. On 10th December 1909 Sir William McGregor, Governor of Queensland and first chancellor, dedicated the former Government House to the uses of the University of Queensland on the fiftieth anniversary of the establishment of responsible government. A year later the first appointments were made to chairs in Classics, Chemistry, Engineering and Mathematics and Physics, the professors coming from Aberdeen, Sydney, Melbourne and Manchester. Yet despite the establishment of a Chair of Classics, the founders of Queensland's university had been compelled to put their project to the politicians and people of the state as a place of utilitarian rather than humane studies. "It was sold to the community as a kind of superior Technical College not because that was the belief of the founders but because it was the only way to get the act through."

From 1893 Sydney and Melbourne universities had severally and together promoted university extension lectures in Brisbane, and a number of Queensland external students had graduated at Melbourne. Accordingly there was a known demand for university lectures and qualifications and seventy-five students enrolled in the first year 1911 and 155 in the second. Unhappily for both Western Australia and Queensland, hardly had their respective universities begun work than the great war supervened. Today Queensland has eleven faculties and some 5700 students.

Queensland's development has been aided by the continuance of J.D. Story as chairman of the Finance Committee of the Senate throughout almost the first half-century of the university's development. Story, who joined the Queensland public service in 1885, was, together with the Governor, Lord Chelmsford, the chief support of the University Congress held in Brisbane in 1906 under the chairmanship of Chief Justice Sir Pope Cooper. He was gazetted a foundation member of the senate on 16th April 1910 and was immediately appointed to its most responsible post, the chairmanship of the Finance Committee, which he has retained ever since, associating with it the honorary vice-chancellorship which he took up in 1937 after his retirement from the public service. Such continuity of administrative experience has been of remarkable benefit to the university and the impressive buildings at St Lucia are a tribute to the significant position Story has held not merely within the university but also *vis-à-vis* the politicians of the state and state public opinion. Queensland and Western Australia are extensive yet by no means wealthy states and they are insufficiently populated; yet the measure of their achievement in university development in many fields, not least in architecture and buildings, is most impressive.

Many men of eminence have come from the British Isles to occupy Australian chairs; many Australians have achieved fame overseas, particularly in scientific fields. Perhaps the greatest of Australian scholars in the field of humanities has been Samuel Alexander, one of only three

D

Australians to receive the Order of Merit. Alexander, a posthumous child, was born in Sydney in 1859. He was early brought to Melbourne where he was educated at Wesley College and spent two years at the university before being encouraged to go to Balliol College, Oxford, where he took firsts in both mathematical and classical studies. He was elected a Fellow of Lincoln College in 1882, a year after graduation, the first Jew to be elected to such an office since the Act for their relief in 1870. From 1893-1924 Alexander held the Chair of Philosophy at Manchester, his greatest published contribution to his subject being *Space, Time and Deity*, the fruit of long years of reflection, which clearly established his status among contemporary philosophers. The outstanding original thinker to have been born in Australia, he lived to be doyen of British philosophers and was admitted to the Order of Merit in 1930 eight years before his death.

Almost as remarkable in another field is H.W. Bailey, like Alexander a Fellow of the British Academy, who occupies the Chair of Sanskrit at Cambridge. Few Australians who have read the ten massive volumes of Toynbee's *Study of History* can fail to be moved by the passages in the final volume where Toynbee refers to the extraordinary background of this remarkable man "Professor H.W. Bailey (*natus* A.D. 1899), a philologist of world-wide renown . . . had awoken to consciousness as a child on a farm in Western Australia, and it would be hard to think of a more unpromising environment than this for producing a savant in the field of Oriental Languages. . . . The books that descended from Heaven . . . were a set of seven volumes of an encyclopaedia (eagerly devoured) and four other volumes with lessons in French, Latin, German, Greek, Italian and Spanish. Later came Arabic and Persian out of which Persian took the lead (joined later to Sanskrit)."

Bailey specialized in Greek and Latin to enter self-taught the University of Western Australia. Oriental Languages, his first interest, were not then taught in Perth but he gained a scholarship to Oxford. When he went on to Cambridge it was to the Chair of Sanskrit since there was no chair in Khotanese, the language in which today he is the leading authority. Bailey may not have been able to study exactly as he desired in Western Australia but he was fortunate to have come to the age of matriculation in the years succeeding the establishment of Western Australia's university and any university in the world would be proud to have shared in his intellectual development. Every Australian university great or small can point to the academic quality of some of its distinguished graduates or to the great names which have appeared in the lists of the teaching staff.

As these pages were being written the accidental death was announced of an Australian-born scholar with a world-wide reputation in the humanities. Professor V. Gordon Childe established himself in a field as unlikely as that of Professor H.W. Bailey. Childe was a distinguished classical graduate of Sydney with a strongly developed political instinct. After a brief period in the public service he found his life's work in the study of archaeology where his brilliantly intuitive interpretations created new concepts in his chosen field. Although his chair at Edinburgh was in Prehistoric European Archaeology his many publications were equally concerned with Mediterranean and other areas and in recent times he probably did more than any other scholar to popularize and interpret our growing fund of archaeological knowledge. Childe concluded his academic career as Director of the Institute of Archaeology at the University of London. He also was honoured with election to the British Academy.

In early years opportunities for university education were open only to a limited few. The door has been speedily opened more widely with the extension of compulsory education, the increasing number of high schools, alteration of matriculation requirements and, more especially, additional scholarships provided both by the states and the Commonwealth. The student population today is essentially democratic, drawn from all classes in the community, all districts in the state. Melbourne agreed to admit women to degrees in 1879; Adelaide in 1880; Sydney in 1881. Universities subsequently founded did not discriminate between undergraduates on grounds of sex. On the other hand, no woman has yet occupied a full chair at any Australian university. This is the more surprising when we think of the early political enfranchisement of women in the Australian states and the high academic rank often held by women in older and supposedly more conservative environments. There have been Australian female lecturers, senior lecturers, even associate professors, but the day of the woman professorial head of a department has still to come.

Post-war development in the Australian universities has been feverish but it has been primarily in the scientific and technological fields. Limited expansion of Arts faculties has indeed occurred but largely to ensure additional teachers in the public schools. The influence of the study of humanities has, however, been more widely spread by the foundation of the New South Wales University of Technology (now the University of New South Wales), which demands the study of certain compulsory courses in English, History and Philosophy by all students proceeding to degrees whether they be in Science, Engineering or Architecture. This awareness of an apparent dichotomy in the modern world between the scientists and technologists on the one hand and the humanists on the other is deeply felt throughout the Australian academic community but no other university has taken equally drastic and draconian measures to meet it. The University of New South Wales, though it has no external students, is predominantly a part-time institution; the Australian National University at Canberra, also a post-war creation, is essentially a research centre. The National University has no undergraduates and its work is organized into the School of Medical Research and the three research schools of Physical Sciences, Social Sciences and Pacific Studies. Situated in the Australian Capital Territory it is, with the Canberra University College, the direct responsibility of the Commonwealth and whereas salaries, courses and conditions of employment at the University College are comparable with those in the state-supported universities, conditions at the National University are without parallel in the Australian academic scene.

It has ever been a standing reproach against Australian industrial, commercial and scientific life that it has been too dependent on overseas research and foreign discovery. None can deny the advantage to the able Australian graduate of overseas travel and study but it has become equally important, not merely for reasons of national pride, that post-graduate research of the highest quality should be achieved in Australia. Under a unitary government increased support for such post-graduate research could have been distributed over the pre-existing universities; under the Australian federal system it proved simpler to establish an entirely new university with research as its primary object.

By the very nature of its aims this new university, which has been able to enrol a most distinguished staff, has achieved success in the four established schools of the Physical, Medical and Social Sciences and Pacific Studies. So far the humanities have not appeared in the formal organization of the university, but are represented by a number of scholars distinguished in various fields.

In the second half of the twentieth century the Australian universities, despite remarkable post-war expansion, are facing a most serious crisis. They are short of buildings, equipment, and above all staff in adequate numbers to teach the increasing flood of students. In the current struggle for survival, Arts faculties have uniformly suffered an increased student-staff ratio and a continuous deterioration of library resources. The problems so created are not peculiar to specific institutions but consistent over the entire Commonwealth. In 1858 Queen Victoria accorded a Royal Charter to the University of Sydney declaring the equal validity of its degrees throughout the British Empire; in due course similar charters were issued to the successive Australian universities established during the colonial period. The equality and uniformity preserved and accepted by the Victorian charter persists to this day. In strength and in weakness the Australian universities continue to produce graduates and scholars who compete on equal terms both at home and overseas with students of different climes and newer, as well as more ancient foundations. Associated in the classrooms today with the native born are to be found hundreds of post-war European migrants and a considerable proportion of Asian students brought to Australia either through the Colombo Plan or under their own private resources.

Australian universities have come of age physically, temporally and intellectually. Their strength is accepted, some of their weaknesses known, their improvement and transformation confidently expected. The acceptance by the Commonwealth Government of a joint responsibility with the states for their development is now regarded as inevitable and the next few years should see the joint implementation of the recommendations of the Report of the Committee on Australian Universities published in 1957. This report, generally known as the Murray Report because the chairman of the committee was Sir Keith Murray, chairman of the United Kingdom University Grants Committee, was made at the request of the Federal Government and was largely concerned with the decisive problems of numbers, finance and equipment caused by post-war expansion both in population and demand. In addition to Sir Keith Murray, the committee consisted of Sir Charles Morris, Vice-Chancellor of the University of Leeds, Sir Ian Clunies-Ross, chairman of C.S.I.R.O., Dr, now Sir Alexander Reid, Chancellor of the University of Western Australia and member of the Commonwealth Grants Committee, and J.C. Richards, a former Rhodes Scholar who is assistant general manager of the Broken Hill Proprietary Company. The report underlines the need for vigorous expansion not only in the scientific faculties but also in the humanities and recommends the creation of a Federal University Commission to prevent a continuance of the present trend towards piecemeal development. If its recommendations are fully implemented then a new day has dawned in the history of the Australian universities.

CHAPTER III

The Humanities in Secondary Education

By E.L. French

THE PLACE OF THE HUMANITIES IN SECONDARY EDUCATION IN Australia, it is perhaps unnecessary to say, is not what it was a few generations ago, or even ten years ago, and is even now in process of change. The secondary school, like any other social institution, has had to make its adaptations to changing social realities. When, in a few of the private schools of the early penal settlements, secondary education was first given in Australia, humane studies were mainly classical in content and comprised the greater part of the intellectual discipline. The subjects of study, according to the schools' advertisements in the Sydney press, were Greek, Latin and Mathematics. In practice this meant a rigorous study of a Greek and a Latin "grammar", a good deal of translation from Greek and Latin authors, an introduction to prosody, and a token study of the rules used in the fundamental operations of the three basic mathematics. To these was added a study of the scriptures, history and doctrines of the Church. The early colonial schoolboy well knew, however, that the important text-books were the "grammar", the "delectus", and the book on style.

This type of secondary education, in which the classical humanities played the predominant part, was an export from the endowed grammar schools of England, which were the traditional schools of the territorial aristocracy and the bar. Its justification was that it provided the best possible means of giving a training in linguistic excellence and a discipline of the intellect, and that it was the most suitable kind of education for those who were destined to be the future leaders in Church and State. Historically, it had been the education of the class born to rule and the culture that valued reflection. As such it had come in for considerable criticism in the late eighteenth century from the rising middle classes, who were stimulating in the nonconformist academies a predominantly "modern" and utilitarian type of secondary education. But in spite of criticism it persisted in England until the middle of the nineteenth century.

Anything more different, however, than the society of England in the late eighteenth and early nineteenth centuries and that of the early penal settlements it would be hard to imagine. The society of the early penal settlements lacked any considerable social class comparable to the English aristocratic class, and it was generally inhospitable to the things of the mind. Its small official class was distinguished by a callous obsession with wealth, its community life was noted for an incapacity to rise above the level of the crude or the mundane, and its institutional life extended little further than church on Sundays and a rudimentary schooling for a fortunate few on weekdays. Just what sort of a secondary education might have commended itself to such a society can only be conjectured. Whatever appeal an education in the classical humanities may have had for the few members of the official class who had ambitions for their sons in the British army and civil service, it certainly held little for those who shared the elemental life of the quays, shops and farms. It was inevitable that sooner or later there should be a challenge to the supremacy of Classics.

The signs of such a challenge were not long in appearing. English and French, two of the so-called "modern" or useful subjects, typical of the curriculum of the English nonconformist academies, were introduced into the curriculum of the private schools as early as 1814. These were hesitant and cautious moves. The gage was not really thrown down to the classical curriculum until the year 1826, by which time the penal settlements, once thought to be ephemeral, had begun to grow into permanent communities with an oligarchic instead of an autocratic form of government, an expanding pastoral industry and export trade, a modest amount of institutional life, and a not inconsiderable middle class. In that year the Scottish clergyman, Dr. J.D. Lang, arrived in Sydney fresh from Glasgow University with a plan for a Caledonian Academy in which Classics was to be but one department among several, the others being described as "English", "Commercial", and "Natural Philosophy". Unfortunately for Lang, as for several other leading men in the colonies who tried to found corporate secondary schools in the late twenties, an economic depression arrived. Pupils were withdrawn, and the Caledonian Academy, along with other corporate schools, had to close. A second, and more successful, series of attempts to found corporate secondary schools in the colonies was made in the early thirties. Prominent among these was an attempt by Lang to found a school called the Australian College, staffed with five schoolmasters from Scotland, and organized to give an education of the kind proposed in his earlier venture. A few years later a second school directed by a Scottish schoolmaster and organized on academy lines was set up in Sydney. Other schools in which Scottish influence was paramount sprang up in Adelaide in the early forties, in Hobart in the late forties, and in Melbourne in 1851.

The secondary education given in all these schools was transplanted directly from the public academies and city high schools of Scotland which, like the private and dissenting academies of England, were distinguished by a curriculum of great breadth and diversity containing as many as sixteen "modern" or useful subjects. These were: English, French, German, History, the three basic mathematics, and two or three branches of applied mathematics like Trigonometry, Mechanics and Surveying, several branches of science, several subjects of nautical interest like Geography, Use of Globes, Astronomy and Navigation, the commercial skills of Bookkeeping and Shorthand, and the manual art of Drawing. Latin and Greek were included but rarely. It was the kind of education that was held to be well suited to the sons of middle class parents who hoped to make their way in the world of trade, industry and finance, and it was just such a class which in fact provided most of the patronage of the public academies and city high schools—the manufacturers, traders, farmers, and the better paid artisans and peasants.

This curriculum held a strong appeal for the colonial middle class parent, in whom a practical utilitarian outlook on education had been sedulously cultivated by the colonial press.

> Above all, as we have said, let us have nothing of your Eton or Winchester systems introduced into Van Diemen's Land. We object to these on account of their overgrown numbers, but more on account of the mode of education pursued in them. To keep a young mind to the age of sixteen and upwards hammering at Greek and Latin to the exclusion of other learning is in our conception, attached as we are to classical studies, the most ridiculous and preposterous of human follies.

Thus the *Hobart Town Courier* of 14th June 1833. The circumstances of life in a pioneer colony were of themselves enough to induce a practical utilitarian attitude in the colonial outlook; the rhetoric of the press intensified it. The result was that the schools controlled by the Scottish schoolmasters became the most successful in the colonies. Faced with a blunt parental utilitarianism and strong competition from the Scottish schoolmasters, the heads of the Anglican and Catholic (Benedictine) schools, who had tried to carry on with the classical curriculum, felt obliged to fall into line. In the late thirties there were signs that the classical humanities would soon cease to be the staple of colonial secondary education. By 1840 all but a few schools were teaching eight useful subjects in addition to Classics. These were: English, History, French, Geography, Arithmetic, Algebra, Geometry, and Bookkeeping. The forties saw the range of studies in some schools widened further by the inclusion of Navigation, Astronomy, Shorthand and Drawing. A decidedly middle class type of curriculum had developed in which the humanities were but one group of studies among several, and were themselves as much "modern" as classical.

The classical curriculum was not allowed to decline without an attempt being made to save it. The headmasters who had been educated in English grammar schools, men like W.T. Cape of Sydney College, a former pupil of Merchant Taylors', and J.P. Gell of the Queen's School, Hobart, a former pupil of Dr Arnold at Rugby, argued constantly for it in their school reports and public addresses. Their case was essentially that of the apologists of the eighteenth century English grammar school. The Latin and Greek classics contained "the most perfect models of composition which the human intellect ever produced" and were the finest instruments for the training of the reason—"indeed, logic, precision of expression, could scarcely exist in a satisfactory form except with such preparatory acquirement".[1] And informing the whole argument was the assumption that secondary education was ordained for the training of those who would ordinarily succeed to positions of leadership in Church and State, or, as Gell ingenuously expressed it in a memorial of 30th September 1842 to the Colonial Secretary, for securing "to the colony an enlightened and liberal order of gentlemen sprung from those who had been the first to lay the foundations of prosperity in this country".

The argument, as the advance of the broad and diverse curriculum of "modern" studies showed, carried little weight with colonial parents, who, in spite of the pretensions of some of their number, were not comparable as a class with the English landed gentry, high state officials and higher clergy. The manner in which the latter derived its income enabled it to live apart from the hurly-burly of competitive business and to conduct the nation's affairs untroubled by the ceaseless activity and carking cares of commercial life. The colonial middle class had no lack of land and wealth but its land and wealth were not hereditary acquirements. Effort and risk had been involved in their acquisition, in natural conditions that were rude and rough. Its typical member was not a gentleman of graces and aesthetic sensitivity. His background—sometimes a convict background, sometimes that of a member of the lower English gentry whose fortunes had suffered as a result of the economic depressions following Waterloo—and the circumstances in which he had amassed his fortune had made him militantly practical and aggressive. And he was well aware that in the pioneer society of the Australian colonies neither the service of the Church nor the service of the State were likely to offer much opportunity of eminent and lucrative employment. The biggest and surest rewards were in commerce. Of seventy scholars who graduated from Sydney College between 1834 and 1839 five went on to British universities and sixty entered what in contemporary parlance were called "situations", in industry and commerce. The basic social circumstance which had made the classical curriculum articulate in England was wanting in Australia. Hence the inability of its apologists to prevent its decline in the face of the decisive development

[1] W.T. Cape in *Report of Sydney College*, 1838.

which at once varied the range of humane studies and reduced them to a rough equality with several groups of utilitarian studies.

Humane studies in colonial secondary schools had been partly classical and partly "modern", and had been but one group of studies in a fairly diverse curriculum for upwards of fifteen years when, in 1852 and 1855, the universities of Sydney and Melbourne opened for teaching and instituted matriculation examinations governed by regulations that were calculated to restore the classics to something like their earlier importance. The Sydney regulations required candidates to present for examination in Greek and Latin, also in Mathematics; there were no optional subjects. The Melbourne regulations, which had to be read in conjunction with the rules governing admission to degrees, required candidates to present in Greek and Latin, in Mathematics, and in one of English, History and Geography. The authorities in Sydney were convinced that "modern" humanities like English and History were unfit to rank as intellectual disciplines, while those in Melbourne were of the opinion that they were unfit to rank equally with the classics or with Mathematics and should therefore be included in the matriculation examination as optional subjects. The new regard for Mathematics and the mild respect for two of the "modern" humanities and Geography in Melbourne showed the universities to be unwilling to return to the almost exclusively classical curriculum of the early penal settlements. An increasingly forceful body of middle class criticism of the traditional classical predominance in England in the course of the first half of the nineteenth century had apparently not been without its effect on the ideas of colonial educators. The omission of most of the numerous "modern" subjects—including most of the "modern" humanities—that had made their way into the curriculum between 1826 and 1851 meant, on the other hand, that the schools were being asked to retrace their steps a considerable distance. To speak in this way of the universities' regulations governing their matriculation examinations is to use no mere figure of speech. The control of the school curriculum, in the universities' view, was one of their natural rights. "The functions of the university," said Sydney's vice-chancellor, the Hon. F.L.S. Merewether, at the university's commemoration celebrations in 1857, "practically invest it with the direction and control of the studies pursued in every school of literature of the higher class." [2] The schools, indeed, were not being asked to restore Classics to some of their former eminence; they were being directed to do so.

The schools for their part knew that they were obliged to accept the matriculation examination as one of the proximate objectives of their teaching. A heterogeneous group, they could not, of themselves, devise

---

[2] Press cutting enclosed with *Minutes of the Senate of the University of Sydney University*, 1st April 1857.

any impartial and authoritative assessment of the quality of their teaching which an increasingly pluralist colonial society would accept, and until such an assessment could be devised colonial secondary education could not be related effectively with the world that lay beyond it. A few attempts had been made to prepare pupils for the entrance examinations of English and Scottish universities but they had been desultory. The English and Scottish universities were geographically remote, and even if colonial parents still thought of England and Scotland as home, the remoteness was such as to place these universities beyond the normal reach of colonial calculations. There was never more than the merest trickle of colonial students to English or Scottish universities. The matriculation examinations of Sydney and Melbourne provided a means of articulation between the secondary school and colonial society which headmasters knew could not be ignored.

Willing as the schools were to organize their curricula to suit the requirements of the matriculation examinations, they were yet unwilling to be bound entirely by them. They provided special "upper school" or "Classical" courses in which Greek and Latin were compulsory, but they also provided "lower school" or "commercial" courses from which Greek or Latin could be omitted in favour of French or, in a few instances, German. And in addition to these subjects they provided a range of "modern" subjects as wide as had ever been taught by the schools of the late thirties and the forties. The schools, in brief, had rejected the demand to restore Classics to the position where they comprised at least half the curriculum and the whole of a pupil's training in humane studies.

The schools were responding to a set of realities which differed significantly, if not entirely, from those which the universities had in mind. The universities had in mind a secondary school population of which all, or nearly all, would proceed to higher education, a school population of secure financial background, in other words, which would "go up" to the university as a matter of course. The schools, by contrast, had in mind a secondary school population, a large section of which felt it had no use for the type of education prescribed by matriculation requirements, and did not, in any case, stay long enough at school to complete it. Just what proportion of pupils entered the universities and what proportion took "modern" courses of study and left school before completing their education it is impossible to say. One would expect the establishment of colonial universities to have caused an increase in the proportion of pupils proceeding to higher studies, but it is doubtful if it effected any marked increase. Headmasters like W.T. Stephens of Sydney Grammar School, Dr Alexander Morrison of Scotch College, and the Rev. J.R. Buckland of Hutchins School assured their constituencies that the proportion leaving school early to enter industry and commerce was too large for them to ignore. The consequence of their refusal to ignore it was the "commercial" course, which brought the "modern" humanities prominently to the attention of all concerned. In the fifties, however, it appears to have done little more for the humanities than strengthen the position of English and History. The day of the modern foreign language was not yet.

It was some years before the universities became aware of the existence of the non-matriculant and convinced that he was an enduring feature of colonial secondary education. The phenomenon was brought sharply to their notice towards the end of 1859 in the course of two parliamentary inquiries: an inquiry by a Select Committee of the New South Wales Parliament into the state of Sydney Grammar School and an inquiry, by royal commissioners appointed by the Tasmanian Parliament, into the state of "superior and general" education in Tasmania. But a few more years were to elapse before they were ready to consider the education of the non-matriculant as a problem separate from that of the education of the potential matriculant, and to assume responsibility for solving it. The first attempt at a solution was made by a quasi-university corporation set up in Tasmania in 1858, called the Tasmanian Council of Education, which instituted an examination for a qualification known as Associate of Arts. Candidates for this examination were given a choice of the two classical languages; five "modern" humanities—English (including History and Geography), French, German, Italian, and Drawing and Architecture; Mathematics and five branches of science—Natural Philosophy, Chemistry, Zoology, Botany and Geology. A preliminary test in the elements of language and number was demanded, but no subject of the main examination was compulsory. At about the same time the Governor of South Australia, Sir Richard MacDonnell, set up a board called the Board of Competitive Public Examinations, which conducted a similar kind of examination. Both plans were borrowed from a scheme of public examinations instituted by Oxford and Cambridge universities in 1858 for pupils, mainly of middle class parentage, who were not destined for university studies.

The University of Melbourne studied the Oxford and Cambridge scheme but, instead of introducing new examinations for the non-matriculant, contented itself with making its matriculation examinations more acceptable to him. To the three "modern" subjects—English, History and Geography—that had been made subjects of the matriculation examination in 1855 it added in 1862 French and German, allowing candidates to present in one or the other but not in both. The University of Sydney in 1867 followed the Oxford and Cambridge plan almost to the letter by instituting two public examinations, a junior and senior examination, the latter containing a variety of "modern" subjects even more numerous than those offered for the Tasmanian A.A. degree. The Sydney plan became the model for public examinations instituted by the University of Adelaide in 1882 and 1886, and by the University of Tasmania, which in 1890 superseded the Tasmanian Council of Education.

The changes made in the examination system in the interests of the non-matriculant gave a new dignity to the "lower school" or "commercial" courses, in which one or both of the classical languages could be omitted in favour of French and other "modern" subjects. The almost immediate result was a precipitous decline in the proportion of pupils taking Greek, a moderate decline in the proportion taking Latin, and an abrupt rise in the proportion taking French. In 1861, at the Melbourne matriculation examination, for example, Greek was presented by 83% of candidates but in 1866 by only 51% and in 1873 by only 13%. The falling off in the numbers taking Latin, by comparison, took place gradually, yet by 1874 the proportion presenting it had fallen as low as 55%. Within a year of French becoming a matriculation subject the proportion of candidates presenting it rose from 36% to 60%. In 1866 it superseded Greek as the second language in "popularity" in Victorian schools and by 1875 it superseded Latin as the first language in "popularity". In New South Wales the position of French relative to Latin was slightly less favourable but in the other colonies it was the Victorian story over again. The great casualty among the humanities in this period of formal provision for the education of the non-matriculant was undoubtedly Greek; Latin suffered considerably but not to such an extent as to warrant classification as a subject of minor importance. The great success of the period was French.

The position of the humanities, as a group, was not affected. The so-called "English" subjects in the group, English language and History, were common to the "classical" and the "commercial" courses and held firm, losing no more support than would have been expected when an increasingly wide range of subjects was made available to an increasingly large number of pupils. There was, in the language of statistics, a drift from concentration to dispersion, but it was without serious effect on the relative importance of both subjects.[3] English and History, with Latin and French, comprised half the basic curriculum; the other half consisted of Geography and the three fundamental branches of mathematics, which were also common to "classical" and "commercial" courses.

Outside the basic curriculum was a motley host of "extras" and occasional subjects: German, Italian, Drawing, Music (both vocal and instrumental), various branches of applied mathematics like Trigonometry, Mechanics and Land Surveying, several branches of natural science, Book-

---

[3] History suffered a decline between 1871 and 1874, but in 1875 began to recover. The decline, however, was peculiar to Victoria.

keeping, Shorthand, Elocution, Dancing, and a variety of competitive sports, games and drills. To these was now added Greek. Among this varied collection of subjects only German showed any sign of becoming a subject of consequence, and this was only in South Australia, where a large minority of German immigrants raised the proportion of pupils presenting the subject at the examinations of the Board of Competitive Public Examinations in the early sixties to as high as 35%. Typically, however, the colonial preference for a modern language as against a classical language worked to the advantage of French.

It is difficult to account satisfactorily for the decline of Greek and the rise of French other than in the terms already indicated. Greek was the classical language generally omitted from the "commercial" courses taken by the utilitarian majority but why Greek in particular was marked down for sacrifice is not clear. The Melbourne professors in the fifties expressed the view that it was of no great antiquity as a liberal study and had no virtues as a mental discipline which Latin did not have in greater measure. This may hold a clue to the answer. There may have been a tendency to place Greek second to Latin in estimates of the relative disciplinary value of the two languages, but the value of classical studies as mental disciplines was not generally argued with reference to Latin alone. John Conington, who occupied the Chair of Latin Language and Literature at Oxford from 1854 to 1869, believed that it was difficult to teach Greek properly. Just what was meant by teaching it properly can only be guessed. One would wonder, however, if Greek was any more difficult to teach than Latin. The lack of enthusiasm for Greek was general in Western education at the time; it was not colonial in origin, even if it may have been more decided in the colonies than elsewhere. The preference for French instead of German or Italian may also have had non-colonial origins. French, it is true, had certain initial advantages: it was taught more widely in the secondary schools of the first half of the century, and it was taught in the national and denominational elementary schools. But here, again, there is evidence that the colonies were reproducing certain conditions prevailing in England. Too much confidence can be placed in the view that it was a simple reflection of the nineteenth century's estimate of the relative importance of the life and literature of France, Germany and Italy. The modern languages were not as a rule valued for their humane interest, and French, quite as much as German or Italian, was known to colonial parents as one of the "languages of commerce".

The essential contribution of the universities and quasi-university corporations to colonial secondary education in the period from 1852 to 1875 had been a system of matriculation and public examinations which provided a means of articulation between the schools and worlds of learning and business that lay beyond. The two types of examination were derived from different conceptions of the type of secondary education appropriate to the sons of the English aristocracy and the English middle class. The type of education prescribed by the regulations governing matriculation was considered appropriate for the sons of privilege and position who would enter the ancient universities, while that encouraged by the regulations governing public examinations was considered appropriate for the sons of middle class parents who would take up careers in commerce and industry. But the class structure of colonial society was not, of course, the same as that of English society. Colonial society, broadly speaking, contained in its traders, bankers, professional men, and its few industrial capitalists, a fairly typical middle class. But it contained no real aristocracy. Its class of pastoral proprietors was not a typical leisured class, nor was it a typical socially and politically privileged class. It had to accept a strenuous and somewhat rough mode of life, and it had to accommodate itself to a ruggedly democratic society that was careless of precedence and position. It had, as a consequence of the constitutional provision for upper house legislatures with a property franchise, an assured place in government, but the centres of power were the popularly elected lower houses. The pastoral proprietors, notwithstanding a few with aristocratic pretensions, constituted a rural branch of the middle class. Thus the particular social class that would ordinarily have supported the type of education prescribed by the regulations governing matriculation examinations was not to be found in the colonies. It was unlikely, therefore, that the matriculation examinations would survive indefinitely in their traditional form. Sooner or later they were bound to be modified by educational ideas in harmony with middle class opinion. A start had been made in 1862 and 1866 with the addition of French and German to Melbourne and Sydney's lists of matriculation subjects, but radical changes were not made until the late seventies.

In 1876 the recently inaugurated University of Adelaide instituted a matriculation examination in which candidates were required to present in Latin, Mathematics, English, History and Geography, and in one of a group of six optional subjects comprising Greek, French, German, Natural Philosophy, Chemistry and Natural History. This examination had three novel features: the exclusion of Greek from the group of compulsory subjects, the inclusion of three "modern" subjects—two of them humanities—in the compulsory group, and the addition of several branches of science to the group of optional subjects. In a middle class or public examination these features might have been expected; they would not generally have been expected in a matriculation examination. This new style of matriculation examination reflected a point of view that was not yet wholly acceptable in Sydney and Melbourne. Sydney added three branches of science to its list of matriculation subjects in 1876, though it reduced them to two in 1882, and in 1881 Melbourne added four branches of science. These adjustments brought the matriculation examinations, in the range and diversity of their subjects, a few steps nearer to the public examinations. The next step was the addition of Music and the various branches of Drawing to the circle, and the creation of more opportunities for the study of these subjects by easing the regulations governing matriculation and admission to degrees, which had been designed to protect Greek and Latin. The universities whittled away the compulsory status of Greek and Latin in subsequent years until, at the turn of the century, the only compulsory Greek retained at the undergraduate stage was in courses for the Arts degree in Melbourne and Adelaide and the only compulsory Latin retained was in courses in faculties of Arts, Law and Medicine. More respect was shown to Mathematics, which was generally compulsory in undergraduate courses except in the courses for degrees in Arts and Law in Melbourne, and for Music in Melbourne and Adelaide. All this was in marked contrast to the preceding twenty-three years, during which time the regulations protecting Classics and Mathematics were undisturbed, and additions to the range of subjects few.

Behind the succession of adjustments to the matriculation regulations was a new conception of liberal education. Instead of being conceived as a training in linguistic excellence and a discipline of the intellect, obtainable only from the study of Classics and Mathematics, liberal education was conceived as a varied mental discipline, obtainable from the study of a diverse group of subjects. It was now asserted, as the Governor of South Australia, Sir Anthony Musgrave, observed at the inauguration of the University of Adelaide, that there were "more means than one" of ensuring the cultivation of a disciplined intelligence. There were subjects other than Classics and Mathematics, notably the various branches of science, that could be studied with benefit in the training of the mind. Their value in mental training was not the same as that of Classics and Mathematics; it was quite distinct, inasmuch as they afforded a "peculiar and characteristic discipline", which was but part of a "complete" liberal education.

The basis of the new conception was the idea of the mind as composed of a number of primary powers, or faculties, and for a statement of it one can do no better than turn to the writings of C.H. Pearson who, at the time of his greatest concern with education in Australia, was successively Lecturer in Modern History at the University of Melbourne, Principal of Presbyterian Ladies' College, Melbourne, a Royal Commissioner inquiring into the state of public education in Victoria, a member of Council of the University of Melbourne, and Minister of Public Instruction.[4] According to

---

[4] His chief educational writings are: *Report on the State of Public Education in Victoria*, P.P. Vic. Legis. Ass., 1877-8, No. 105; *The Higher Culture of Women*, Melbourne, 1875; and his first report on the Presbyterian Ladies' College, Melbourne, 1875.

Pearson, the faculties of the mind were reason, memory, attention, observation and imagination. Each faculty had to be trained if a pupil's education was to be "complete", and for the training of each faculty there was a group of studies that was peculiarly appropriate. The reason, memory and attention could be trained by the study of Mathematics, English, French, German and Music, as well as by the study of Classics; the faculty of observation could be trained by the study of Geography, Botany, Chemistry and Drawing, and the faculty of imagination by the study of History, preferably that of the British Empire since 1700 and of Australia. It was thus possible to add a considerable number of "modern" subjects to the curriculum of liberal education, and all in the name of the traditional liberal ideal of the disciplined intellect. "Banausic" subjects like Bookkeeping and Shorthand were excluded.

Pearson was not, however, heedless of utilitarian motives; neither were his spiritual counterparts in Adelaide and Sydney, men like Sir Anthony Musgrave and Sir William Manning. The faculties, Pearson was ready to say, should be trained, but preferably by the study of those subjects that imparted "useful knowledge". The study of mathematics was a valuable mental discipline, and of considerable "practical use in common life, and in many professional and scientific pursuits".[5] French was an excellent mental discipline and one of the "languages of commerce". Greek, on the other hand, while it afforded an excellent mental discipline, was of little use to anyone but the occasional theological student. Nor was he heedless of the criticism of classical teaching that had recently been voiced in England. The disciplinary value of Greek was obtained only by those who mastered it, and mastery was not generally gained until after four or five years' study. Much of the teaching in grammar schools was given "at an extravagant cost of time"[6] that could be more effectively used in the study of "modern" subjects. By the same reasoning he rejected Latin composition. "Not even the most perfect scholar" could so "completely master a dead language as to compose in it"; he could "only string together old phrases that will serve to express new thoughts", which was like "a man trying to write Tennyson again in the language of Shakespeare".[7] A "young country" such as Australia could not afford to "throw away the thought of its youth upon the most artistic of Chinese puzzles".[8] The new conception of liberal education was clearly not born simply of a desire for a broad and substantially "modern" intellectual discipline. Its essential recommendation to the educational world, however, was its concern with mental discipline, even if understood in different terms from those which the pioneer professors had inherited.

[5] *Report on the State of Public Education in Victoria,* 1877-8, p. 96.
[6] ibid., p. 89.   [7] ibid., p. 91.   [8] ibid.

E

The new conception of liberal education and the changes in regulations governing matriculation and admission to degrees were generally well received by headmasters and headmistresses, who quickly reorganized their "classical" courses. Those who benefited were the prospective matriculants, the pupils who were uncertain of their future and who, as a precaution, usually elected to take the "classical" courses, and the non-matriculants in many small schools which, for want of enough teachers to enable them to provide an alternative course, drafted all pupils into one. The effect of the reorganization was to confirm the trends that developed under the stimulus of the formal provisions made for the education of the non-matriculant in the sixties. The "modern" humanities continued to make headway, while the classical humanities continued to lose ground, if slowly. English—well established as the first subject of the curriculum—History and French were confirmed in their position as subjects of the basic curriculum, while Music and Drawing were raised from the ruck of "extras" to become subjects of some consequence, if not of major importance. Only German and Italian failed to make significant progress. Greek became a very minor subject, being taken mainly by small classes of senior pupils in the large church schools. Latin disappeared from the curriculum of the small private schools and lost a little support in the church schools, but it could still fairly have been classified as one of the major subjects of the curriculum. In face of the utilitarian pressures of colonial society Latin had proved remarkably resistant. Humane studies, nevertheless, had become overwhelmingly "modern". They had also become more varied, embracing artistic as well as linguistic, literary and historical disciplines.

The position of the humanities as a whole in the curriculum was undisturbed, in spite of the fact that there had been continuing support for the various branches of mathematics and a decided growth of support for science, which by 1900 had become almost a major discipline. Though the cause of science was proclaimed with evangelical fervour in the closing years of the century, colonial secondary schools still regarded an education that was not basically and predominantly linguistic and literary as unsound.

So long as secondary education in Australia was a privilege of the middle classes it was conceivable that the favourable position of the overwhelmingly "modern" group of humane studies in the curriculum would not, other things being equal, be seriously challenged. But in the last two decades of the nineteenth century and the first decade of the twentieth century Australians tended increasingly to regard secondary education as a right of all classes, and to agree that it was the duty of the state to provide it for those unable to afford it. There grew up, as a result, a system of state high schools and higher elementary schools. The earliest growth was in New South Wales where by 1900 there were four high schools and 263 schools of the higher elementary type.[9] Tentative beginnings were made in other states soon after the turn of the century, and enabling legislation followed quickly. The period from 1905 to 1939 saw the steady growth of comprehensive systems of state secondary schools throughout the country, making the government the largest single agency in secondary education. In the thirteen years since the close of the second world war the number of high schools has more than doubled.

The state, having become an important agency in secondary education, had to be conceded a voice in counsels affecting the secondary school curriculum. Typically this was effected by amendments to university legislation or the state education acts which provided for representation from the state school systems on boards charged with responsibility for making regulations governing public examinations. The first boards were set up in New South Wales and Victoria in 1912. The New South Wales board, called the Board of Examiners, consisted of four officers of the Department of Public Instruction and not less than four teachers from the University of Sydney. No representation was given to the independent, middle class schools. The Victorian board, called the Schools Board, consisted of eight representatives from the Department of Public Instruction, ten from the University of Melbourne, eight from the independent middle class schools and two from the business world. Representatives from the independent schools, as well as those from the respective state school systems and universities, were included in the boards of public examinations set up later in other states,[10] and when, in 1937, the Board of Examiners in New South Wales was superseded by a new body called the Board of Secondary School Studies, a small representation was accorded the independent schools. The proportionate representation of the three main sections of the educational world varied from state to state, as did the powers of the boards themselves, but in each case it clearly expressed the fact that the state had entered the field of secondary education.

It is impossible, in the absence of any systematic research,[11] to indicate precisely the peculiar part played by the State in the evolution of the secondary school curriculum, and particularly in the developments taking place in the field of humane studies. It may be said, however, that the rise of the state secondary school has brought the problem of the education of the non-matriculant more insistently to the attention of educational legislators.

[9] The term used in reference to these schools was Superior Public Schools.

[10] The constitutions of the Queensland and Tasmanian boards were altered in 1941 and 1946, and their titles changed respectively to Board of Post-primary Studies and Examinations and Schools Board.

[11] Such work as has been done has been incidental to other purposes, and confined to New South Wales and Victoria.

The nineteenth century educationalists had perceived this to be both a vocational and an educational problem; so also have those of the twentieth century. The latter, however, have felt obliged to recognize the increasingly insistent demands of a highly industrialized society for skilled and semi-skilled workers—demands made trenchantly in the first decade of the century in a series of royal commissions of inquiry, which gave special attention to technical training, and voiced repeatedly in subsequent commissions over the last forty years. At the time these trenchant demands for technical training were first made experimental psychology began to throw doubts on the psychological foundations of the nineteenth century conception of liberal education as a diversified mental discipline. It criticized the validity of the psychology of faculties and the idea that there was any significant transfer of the various kinds of intellectual discipline. The form and direction of the criticism have since suffered several changes and the idea of intellectual discipline and its transfer have been stated in terms more acceptable to psychological theory, but the loss of confidence in the old propositions weakened the theoretical opposition to the advance of an insistent industrial and commercial utilitarianism. Attempts to oppose the advance with appeals to absolute educational values were met with the pragmatic argument that values were discoverable only in experience, and were relative to time and circumstance. Those which had informed educational thinking in an age when the nation's economy was mainly pastoral and agricultural were bound to be inappropriate in a period distinguished by the growth of an increasingly diverse economy more and more dependent on manufacturing, mechanization and scientific knowledge.

The way was thus open for the addition of essentially utilitarian subjects to the lists of public examination subjects. The first to be added were the commercial skills of Business Principles and Practice, Shorthand and Typing. The University of Tasmania led the way by making Shorthand a subject of its junior and senior examinations in 1903. The universities of Adelaide, Melbourne, Western Australia and Queensland set up special commercial public examinations at which pupils could present in several commercial subjects. The practice was continued by the respective public examination boards, but by 1930 all the commercial examinations had been merged with the ordinary public examinations. Following hard on the commercial skills came the practical science subject of Agriculture, first made a public examination subject by the University of Tasmania in 1907. A little later there appeared a variety of technical subjects like Technical Drawing, Metalwork, Woodwork, Woolclassing and Domestic Science. These last were either made subjects of the examinations controlled by a public examination board, as in New South Wales, or subjects of special technical school examinations controlled mainly by the technical branches of the state education departments.

The proliferation of avowedly utilitarian subjects was a source of uneasiness to the educational conscience, which was partly satisfied, however, by arguments that the more practical utilitarian subjects would give the pupil of inferior intelligence an opportunity to succeed, with benefit to his morale as well as his prospects of employment. The high hopes thus encouraged were somewhat modified by experience, but there were enough evident improvements to the morale of the pupils of inferior intelligence to cause those who were uneasy about the practical utilitarian subjects to withdraw their opposition. They were the more ready to do this when it was suggested that there might be positive creative value, also a certain artistic value, in the study of these subjects. Behind this suggestion was a growing feeling that the extent to which intellectual values could be realized in the schooling of many non-matriculants was definitely limited, and there might be wisdom in trying to increase its educational value by an appeal to the pupil's capacity for appreciation. From this realization grew a successful movement for the revision of the disciplinary courses in Drawing, leading to a general replacement of the term "Drawing" by the term "Art", and the addition of Craftwork and Musical Appreciation to some of the lists of public examination subjects. And teachers of Mathematics, Science, History and Geography who were concerned to increase the educational value of their disciplines for the non-matriculant began to see in the "appreciation movement", as it was called, a source of support for their attempts to devise general courses of study in their respective fields. The result was the addition in the 1930s and 1940s of General Mathematics, General Science, and Social Studies to the lists of public examination subjects. In 1900 the numbers of subjects listed for the junior and senior public examinations of the University of Sydney were respectively seventeen and twenty-four; the numbers listed for the intermediate and leaving certificates conducted by the New South Wales Board of Secondary School Studies in 1957 were respectively thirty-five and forty-two. This was a typical result of the efforts of the public examination boards to provide for the non-matriculant.

The utilitarian and educational motives which had increased the range and diversity of subjects that could be taken at public examinations also brought an increase in the range and diversity of subjects that could be taken at matriculation. At the insistent call of commerce and industry such subjects as Commercial Principles, Commercial Practice (Accounting), Economics, Agriculture and Domestic Science were added to the lists of matriculation subjects, and, at the suggestion of teachers anxious to increase the educational value of the matriculation examination for students who regarded it simply as a terminal secondary school qualification, subjects like Musical Appreciation, General Mathematics, various forms of general science, and Social Studies were added to the lists. The universities tended to be sceptical of the claim that these subjects should be regarded as coherent, basic and rigorous disciplines, but were ready to accept them if they were included among the optional subjects. In the last twenty-five years a combination of educational, political and economic motives brought additions to the foreign languages that could be taken at matriculation; these were Japanese, Chinese, Dutch, Spanish and Russian. And to render a service to a growing minority of Jewish pupils and nonconformist theological students Hebrew too was added.

The doubts which experimental pyschology had cast on the psychological foundations of the nineteenth century conception of liberal education, and which had weakened theoretical opposition to the further addition of utilitarian subjects to the lists of public examination subjects, also weakened the general university conviction that the foreign languages and mathematics were the fundamentally important liberal disciplines. It was said that there was no conclusive evidence that the study of these subjects imparted a general intellectual training that was noticeably superior to the training imparted by a study of many other subjects. It was admitted that they each might afford a unique intellectual training, but that this did not necessarily justify their retention as compulsory subjects for all matriculants. It was said also that there was doubt about the conditions under which transfer of training occurred and the extent to which it took place, if it took place at all, and that it was therefore unwise to be dogmatic about what subjects were fundamental and what were not. To the many heads of university departments who, over the years, had seen intelligent students lost to higher studies because of an inability to meet the foreign language or mathematics requirements the rise of these uncertainties seemed heaven sent. Academic specialization thus found common cause with experimental psychology, and there ensued a long series of attempts to obtain a relaxation of the requirements which made a foreign language and a branch of mathematics compulsory for all contemplating a course at a university.

The first moves were made in the University of Sydney soon after the turn of the century, when proposals were brought forward making Latin optional at matriculation for all students except those contemplating courses in Arts. The move failed, but a second, made in 1911, succeeded. In the course of the next forty years increasing respect was paid in the Australian universities to the practice of allowing each faculty to name its own special requirements for matriculation. There was a consequent paring down of the protection given to foreign languages in the regulations, and fewer and fewer faculties named them as prerequisites. Lately the universities have tended simply to require all potential matriculants to take English and to select three or four additional subjects from two or three groups, the range of groups being typically: "foreign languages", "social studies", among which History may be included, "mathematics", and "science". A foreign language is still required by the faculties of Arts in Melbourne and Adelaide, and by the faculties of Arts and Law in Queensland. It is only in Queensland that the technical faculties still require a foreign language; they require it, however, only at the junior public examination.

The combination of increasing numbers of public and matriculation examination subjects and a progressive relaxation of regulations making a foreign language and mathematics compulsory for matriculants gave the schools more and more opportunities to provide suitable courses for the many different types of pupil that crowded into their classrooms. By 1915 in New South Wales, for example, 20% of the state school children whose primary education had been completed the previous year were receiving a post-primary education; forty years later the proportion had risen to 98%.[12] As the numbers increased so the range of mental capacity, social background and vocational interest represented in the classrooms widened. The state education departments responded typically by establishing "multi-lateral" high schools, which allowed pupils a choice of several courses variously designated "technical", "commercial", "general" and "professional". In the "technical", "commercial" and "general" courses humane studies were represented mainly by English and History, in the "professional" course by English, History and one or two foreign languages which were usually French and Latin. In recent years they have also been represented in three of these courses by Art and Musical Appreciation. In the cities these courses were often made the responsibility of separate schools, called Technical High Schools, Home Science High Schools, Modern Schools, Commercial High Schools, and simply High Schools (the latter concentrating on courses leading to the university and the professions), thereby adding a variety of refinements to the types of course provided in the typical multi-lateral school.

In the "non-professional" type of high school the refinements that were devised did not as a rule involve any increase in the number of humane subjects that were taught or any change in their status. There were instances of enterprising principals who, after detecting among their pupils a significant minority with a capacity for higher studies, made successful attempts to provide for the teaching of a foreign language, and such other subjects as were required for university matriculation. But this sort of action, if fairly common, was not general. In the "professional" type of high school the refinements involved an increase in the number and variety of humanities that were taught, but a certain reduction in their status. The increase in the number and variety of humane studies resulted from the addition of German,

---

[12] Derived from statistics in the *Report of the Committee appointed to Survey Secondary Education in New South Wales, 1957*, Government Printer, 1957, p. 24.

sometimes Greek, and in rare cases Italian and Japanese, to the lists of foreign languages that might be chosen, also from the addition of such branches of history as Ancient History, Modern European History, Pacific History, and, in recent years, such subjects as Art and Musical Appreciation. The reduction in status took place in courses heavily loaded with mathematics and science which, beyond the junior or intermediate stage, did not necessarily contain any humane study apart from English. In the "professional" course of the typical multi-lateral high school of the outer metropolitan areas and country districts the chances were that the great majority of students would take at least three humanities to the leaving certificate or matriculation stage; in the "professional" type of high school in the cities the chances were, as time went on, that a large section of the student body would take no more than two humanities, and often only one.

In addition to the various types of high school the state education departments developed in country districts a junior or intermediate type of secondary school, usually a four-year institution, which provided a type of course significantly different from the courses given in high schools. Its curriculum was designed to give a common general education in humanities, social studies, mathematics, and science, and a substantial technical training adapted to the peculiar industrial requirements of the respective districts which it served. The particular humanities included in this common general education have been English, Art, and, when not merged with broad environmental studies under the banner of social studies, History. Perhaps the best known examples of this type of school have been the Tasmanian and South Australian Area Schools.

The independent schools for their part introduced several refinements of the "classical" and "commercial" courses, that had been devised in the nineteenth century. They became, in effect, secondary schools of the multi-lateral type. But they differed from the multi-lateral state high schools inasmuch as they tended to make *ad hoc* arrangements for technical training and to provide more refinements of the "professional" type of course. The Catholic teaching orders, in some instances, established technical schools in the metropolitan areas, and a few of the Protestant schools in country districts made substantial provision for training in agriculture and farm mechanics. The independent school's typical response, however, to the widening range of intelligence, background and vocational interest in its enrolments was a multi-lateral organization which made slight provision for technical training and detailed provision for various kinds of "professional" courses.

The progressive increase in the number of courses containing a great variety of subjects, in which humane studies other than English had a minor or uncertain place, meant a progressive dispersion of pupils over the whole

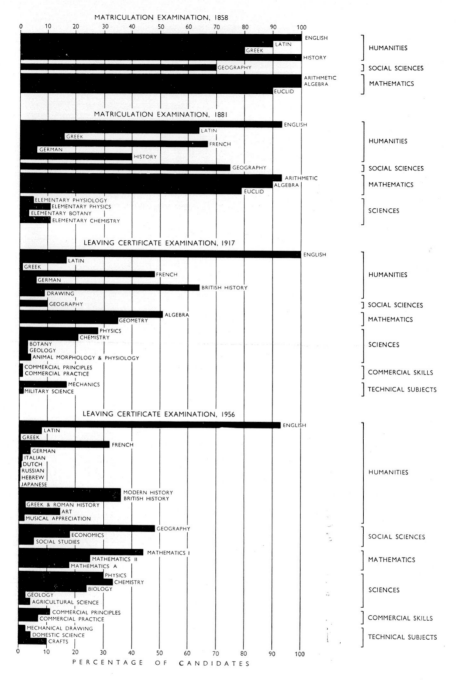

Percentage of candidates sitting for various subjects at the University of Melbourne Matriculation examination, 1858 and 1881, and the University of Melbourne Schools Board Leaving Certificate examination, 1917 and 1956.

arena of the secondary school curriculum and a decline in the proportion of pupils receiving a secondary education which was to a large extent a training in the humanities. As pupils were drawn to the various branches of science, the various commercial skills, social studies, home sciences and crafts, the humanities as a group tended to suffer. At the Adelaide intermediate certificate examinations in 1956, for example, the only humane study which was presented by a greater proportion of candidates than presented for Mathematics (53%), Physics (40%), Chemistry (39%) and Geography (37%), was English, the compulsory subject. Below Geography came History with 32% of candidates. As for the other humane studies, Latin (29%) was presented by the same proportion as Bookkeeping; French (25%) by only 2% more than Typing; Drawing (17%) by the same percentage as Shorthand; Music (8%) about the same percentage as Woodwork, Home Science, Physiology, Social Studies, General Science and Needlework; German (2%) by 2% less than Agricultural Science, and Greek (1%) by the same proportion as Geology and Sheetmetal work.

A similar picture was presented by the statistics of the leaving certificate examination of the University of Melbourne. At the top of the scale stood English with 94% of the candidates; below it Geography and Mathematics I with respectively 12% and 8% more than Modern History, which attracted 36%; French with 32%, the same percentage as Chemistry; Art with 15%, well below Physics, Mathematics II, Biology, Mathematics A, and Economics; Latin with 8%, slightly below Commercial Principles and the crafts; German with 3%, a little below Commercial Practice, Social Studies, Agricultural Science and Domestic Science; and Greek and Roman History, Italian, Musical Appreciation, and Greek more or less on a par with Geology and Mechanical Drawing. The statistics of leaving certificate examinations which served the dual purpose of school leaving and matriculation examinations tell substantially the same story, though they show in a few instances one or two of the humanities a little better placed. History in the leaving certificate examinations of the universities of Sydney and Western Australia, for example, in 1956 fared noticeably better than Geography, and in the Sydney examination better also than General Mathematics, which attracted 49% of candidates. The less "popular" languages, German and Greek, fared a little better by comparison with typically less "popular" subjects like Agriculture and Domestic Science and the trade subjects. French and Latin, on the other hand, showed no significant improvement by comparison with Physics and Chemistry.

The decline in the proportion of pupils taking courses which were largely a training in the humanities was mainly at the expense of the foreign languages. Early in the twentieth century French and Latin ranked a little lower than History, Geography and Mathematics in the hierarchy of secondary school subjects. In recent years Chemistry and Physics have occupied this position, French generally ranking a little below Chemistry. Latin, except in South Australia, has shared a comparatively humble position with the commercial skills, the arts and the crafts. With the exception of German, which improved its position in Western Australia, none of the other languages made any compensating gains. Hebrew and the Oriental languages have not been studied by more than a handful of pupils, and these have been collected only in the large metropolitan areas.

The expense to History was by comparison small, smaller even than the expense to Mathematics in several states. At a time when large numbers of pupils were attracted to the sciences and more deliberate provision was made for the teaching of the commercial skills and technical subjects, the position of History in the hierarchy of secondary school studies may be counted by humanists as highly satisfactory. In the light of the fact that Australia is one of the youngest Western countries some may even count it an achievement, especially since History has not in the last fifty years been a compulsory subject of either the public or the matriculation examinations. An immediate cause of History's fairly successful resistance to the erosion of the nineteenth century's hierarchy of studies was the practice of including it as the second humane study—English being the first—in the various "commercial", "general", and "technical" courses, and often in the "professional" courses which were heavily weighted with science and Mathematics. Why, among the humane studies, History should have been so included is not clear. There is some evidence that it was thought to present to the teachers of "non-professional" classes fewer pedagogical problems, and more returns, in terms of educational values, in proportion to the amount of effort expended. There is evidence also that it was vaguely felt to be a basic discipline, which stood in much the same relation to the social sciences and certain humane studies as did Mathematics to the physical sciences, and ought therefore to be preferred to other humane studies. Whatever the reasons, it has continued to be one of the major subjects in Australian secondary schools.

The fine arts, with one conspicuous exception, failed to improve their position. The exception was Art, earlier called Drawing, which had been a subject of some consequence in the latter part of the nineteenth century but had subsequently lost ground. In 1956, however, the proportion of candidates that presented it at junior public and intermediate certificate examinations varied from 13% to 42%; in Victoria, Western Australia and New South Wales the proportion was little lower than that which presented in French. Its place in the curriculum of the most senior classes, as revealed by the statistics of leaving certificate and matriculation examinations was, by comparison, a minor one. Yet even here it has received more support than has customarily been given to the less "popular" foreign languages. Art, like History to some extent, has not presented to the teacher of "non-professional" courses any insuperable difficulties which prevent some of its inherent educational values from being readily realized, and it is probably this which, more than anything else, has enabled it to gain support while continuing as an optional subject at public and matriculation examinations.

The decline in "popularity" of the foreign languages and the marked support given to History and Art has meant a significant change in the nature of the discipline imparted by humane studies. At the turn of the century the discipline of humane studies was predominantly "modern", literary and linguistic. In the course of the last fifty years, while continuing to be predominantly "modern" and literary, it has become less frequently linguistic and more often historical and artistic. This is a change which must give humanists in general, and especially those in universities, cause for considerable thought. What, it must surely be asked, is to be the future of foreign languages in Australian education? Is there a prospect of French and Latin declining until, as in the United States, they are studied by less than 10% of pupils?[13]

If there is such a prospect, with what concern should it be regarded? With what satisfaction, if any, can the present position of such important Western languages as German, Greek, Dutch, Russian, Italian, Spanish and the Scandinavian languages be regarded? What also, of the Oriental languages—Chinese and Japanese, and others not yet introduced, like Hindi, Indonesian and Tagalog? How satisfactory is a secondary education in which the only training given in humane studies to the great majority of pupils is in English and History? How satisfactory are the present positions of Art and of Music in the curriculum? What, also, is to be said of the slight study made of Religion in many independent schools, and of recent oecumenical efforts to put it on a sounder footing? These, and the many related questions that arise, can only be answered in the light of a comprehensive examination of the tasks and problems that face the Australian secondary schools in the mid-twentieth century. The last ten years have seen three notable attempts, in South Australia, New South Wales and Western Australia, to make such an examination. But we are as yet some distance from formulating a comprehensive theory of secondary education and a statement of national policy, which could be a guide to the Australian educational leadership in the years of decision that are upon us.

[13] Arthur Bestor in *The Restoration of Learning*, Knopf, New York, 1955, p. 44, gives the proportions for 1949 as Latin 7.8%, French 4.7%. The accuracy of Bestor's figures has been challenged, but his view of the state of foreign languages in the U.S. must be regarded as at least substantially true. See his discussion of Professor Boyd Carter's figures relating to foreign languages in Nebraska schools, and of the figures of the U.S. Office of Education in "The Education Really Needed for a Changing World", *Harvard Educational Review*, Winter 1957, pp. 4-6.

CHAPTER IV

The University Faculties

By A.G. Mitchell

The General Picture

DIFFERENCES AMONG THE FACULTIES OF ARTS IN THE AUSTRALIAN universities are explained by their history. The oldest of them was founded in 1851 and the youngest in 1953. Sydney alone has separate chairs of Greek and Latin, partly because the university was founded when Greek and Latin were still the central subjects of a university education, partly because men of distinction and strong personality have occupied the chairs, partly because the view in a period of flight from the classics that the two chairs should be amalgamated into a single Chair of Classics, has been firmly resisted within the university. In a younger university like Western Australia the position of the classics is weak both within the university and in the schools. In the younger universities English as a separate subject is found from the beginning. In the older universities English developed independence comparatively late. In Sydney, for example, English was taught originally as part of the Department of Modern Literature and it was not until 1921 that the two chairs of English were established.

Certain developments are common to the history of all the universities, as, for example, the separation of Psychology from Philosophy. The establishment of chairs in Education, the development of subjects like Geography and Anthropology to full departments, are comparatively late developments, and in some universities have not yet appeared. Two chairs in a subject are found only in the older universities.

The differences among the faculties of Arts are also reflections of the resources that the states have been able or willing to devote to the universities, of endowments and of the influence of strong personalities. It would be unrealistic to expect that the state of Western Australia could devote as much to its university as the state of Victoria, even leaving out of account the briefer history of the University of Western Australia. The Nicholson Bequest provided Sydney with a collection of antiquities which has developed into a teaching museum for archaeological studies of high standard and made possible the existence of a Department of

56

Archaeology. In all the faculties the influence of men like Badham, Tucker, Wood, MacCallum, Murdoch, Scott and others is still felt.

There are some departments that are unique in their respective universities. Melbourne alone has a Department of Fine Arts and of Russian. Sydney alone has departments of English Language, of Greek and of Archaeology. Queensland alone has a lectureship in Phonetics.

Local conditions sometimes explain interesting differences. The German community in the Barossa Valley maintains Lutheran seminaries from which many able students come to the study of German in the University of Adelaide. In Queensland the vast area of the state has meant that external studies have been organized on a larger scale than in the other states, and with the exception of the new development in the University of New England, pursued with more serious purpose.

In Australia members of faculties of Arts have often felt themselves struggling harder for support of their work than seemed necessary to scholars in England or America. Australia has neither the strength of long tradition in humane studies that England has nor the resources for education that America has. In Australia humane and cultural studies are apt to have a harder time of it when competition with studies of more direct practical utility appears. We may feel some satisfaction that not very long after the beginning of the colony the foundation of a university was thought of, but in the comparatively brief history of Australia a very large proportion of the nation's fund of effort has had to go into the task of establishing organized social and commercial life. The amount that could be spared in time, informed interest and money on the things of the mind has been limited. But there are encouraging signs just now of an increase in interest and support that can be spared and that people are anxious to spare for these things. Support for music and serious theatre has increased remarkably even in the last ten years. The state and federal governments have accepted the report of the Murray Committee on universities, and the universities for the first time in their recent history see a hope of fulfilling their manifold obligations in the community. Australian governments and the community generally were obliged to realize that the needs of the universities had far outgrown the resources that they had felt was all Australia could or needed to devote to them. Australians are becoming increasingly aware that the Australian way of life of which they like to talk will be a poor thing if humane learning is not flourishing in the universities and spreading its influence through the community.

Though there are many encouraging signs just now to make the humane scholar in Australia more hopeful of the future, it is still true that for some subjects it is harder to gain interest and support than in Europe or America. In a country as remote as Australia from the European background it is harder to create a feeling of reality and living interest in the learning of languages. The study of remoter periods of history and of history in distant settings has probably a harder time in the contest with the study of what is more recent and near at hand. The long and the comprehensive view so necessary in humane studies is likely to lose to the shorter and narrower view that has a more readily understood bearing on matters near at hand. When the monuments of the past are accessible, and indeed part of the pattern of contemporary life, or where a newer country like America makes the past of Europe its own past in ways made possible by great national resources, university scholars may assume an interest that the Australian must first work to create.

The Australian student, however, is quick to respond to thoughtful efforts to arouse interest. The number of classical scholars and archaeologists that the Australasian universities have produced is in itself a remarkable sign. There is reason to believe that we are finding more and more people in Australia who need no convincing and fewer and fewer people who are hard to convince that national life, particularly in a technological age, would, without the influence of a flourishing humane learning, be dreary and shallow, however comfortable and prosperous.

It is not easy to compare the faculties of the Australian universities on some common fairly meaningful basis. Age has great advantages in the accumulation of resources and the development of tradition, but the new start offers opportunities of originality and experiment. Size is important but smallness can be compensated for in many ways. The impression one has of the comparatively small University of Western Australia is of energy and vitality and a thoughtful use of limited resources.

Speaking generally, Australia has six universities of the traditional kind and three of a rather special kind. Of the six Sydney and Melbourne are very large and have a long tradition behind them. Queensland and Adelaide are, on the Australian scale, large universities, though markedly smaller than Sydney or Melbourne. Western Australia and Tasmania are the two smaller universities. The other three universities are the University of New England, the University of New South Wales and the Australian National University. The University of New England represents the first move towards university decentralization in Australia. It began as a college of the University of Sydney in 1938 and was granted independence in 1953. It sees its development as a rural university, supporting arts and the basic sciences but with a special interest in developing rural studies. It has an opportunity of becoming a residential university. The University of New South Wales was founded with the purpose of training technologists, but it was decided that some part of every student's time should be spent in the study of the humanities and social sciences, an educational principle of which humanists cannot but approve. It is expected that the University of New South Wales will soon proceed to establish a faculty of Arts. The National University is at the moment an organization of research schools with a fine centre of academic community life in University House. The humanities are not officially within the pattern of the National University but they have distinguished representation in scholars in Philosophy, History, Oriental Studies and some other subjects.

A particular mention should be made of the Canberra University College, whose position has been somewhat uncertain, but which it now seems is to become an independent university. A remarkable thing about this small college has been the high quality of its academic staff, in which the humanities are well represented.

The only comparison that seems meaningful is of the subjects in the faculties that have the status of full chairs. The following is the picture given by this comparison:

Sydney: Greek, Latin, English Language, English Literature, French, German, Oriental Studies, History, Philosophy, Moral and Political Philosophy, Psychology, Education, Anthropology, Music, Geography.

Melbourne: Classical Studies, English, French, Germanic Languages, Semitic Languages, History (two chairs), Philosophy, Psychology, Education, Fine Arts, Music, Geography.

Adelaide: Classics, English, French, History, Philosophy, Music, Education, Geography.

Queensland: Classics, English, French, History, Philosophy, Psychology, Education, Geography.

Western Australia: Classics, English, French, History, Philosophy, Psychology.

Tasmania: Classics, English, Modern Languages, History, Philosophy, Psychology.

New England: English, French, History, Philosophy, Psychology.[1]

In Australian universities the members of the faculty are ordinarily the permanent members of the academic staff. The faculty is presided over by an elected dean who has a fixed term of office. In Sydney and Melbourne the dean's task has become so heavy that sub-deans are elected and in these universities the possibility of full-time deans of the faculties has to be envisaged.

The faculties have the responsibility of advising the council on academic

[1] New England has advertised a Chair of Geography; Adelaide a Chair of Education, and New England Chairs of Classics and German.

matters and they have the day-by-day task of administering by-laws and regulations as set down. Within the faculties the cohesion of departments is loose. There is considerable variation in the matters that must be submitted to and determined by the faculty. In general only matters that affect by-laws are determined by the faculty. Awards, standards, and courses are matters for the individual departments. Progress through the degree course is not by single years whose requirements are laid down, but by the accumulation of passes which satisfy a general pattern. This means that, so long as he keeps within the by-laws and does not become a borderline case, the individual student is not particularly the concern of the faculty.

It is generally felt that decision about awards, courses and standards must always be in the hands of the individual departments. But some have remarked that more serious attempt might be made to exchange views on standards and requirements and on such measurable problems as the bulk of written work required by departments. In some universities it is felt that there is not enough common understanding among departments about what constitutes, for example, the difference between master's degrees at the honours and pass standard.

As between universities variations in standard are pretty clear. An honours degree does not mean at all the same thing in all the Australian universities. In recent years there has been a certain exchange of ideas about standards through the appointment of external examiners. But this has been desultory and on a very small scale.

MATRICULATION

Most Australian universities accept for purposes of matriculation subjects passed at a school leaving certificate examination. Generally the universities have considerable influence in the framing of the syllabus for this examination and in the determination of results at the examination. It is common practice for the university to conduct a matriculation examination some two months after the final school examination. The matriculation examination usually serves as a post to the school leaving examination or gives a chance to those unable to sit for the school leaving examination.

The system has its advantages and disadvantages from the point of view both of the schools and the universities. The universities have abundant opportunity to influence the syllabus of the schools and the contributions that the universities can make in showing the way to educational application of advances in science and scholarship are to the advantage of the schools. The schools sometimes complain that under the system the programmes in the schools are tied too much to university requirements, particularly in view of the fact that only a comparatively small number of pupils go on to the university. The universities sometimes complain that the leaving examination has to try to do too many things at once. It has to be a means of determining fitness to enter the university and it has to certify a reasonable standard of performance at the end of a secondary school course attained by pupils who plan to enter industry, commerce or the public service. Only one university, Melbourne, differs from this pattern. For matriculation to the University of Melbourne the candidate must pass certain subjects at a school examination and then, after one or two years' further study with matriculation in view, pass the university's matriculation examination. A somewhat similar system for New South Wales is recommended in the recently published report on secondary education.

The general aims of matriculation in the Australian universities are fairly clear. They are mainly: (a) to ensure a satisfactory standard of intellectual competence; (b) to ensure as a basis for specialized study at the university a satisfactory general education in subjects of basic importance.

There has been a good deal of stocktaking in which the uncertainties of the examination system and the possible vagaries of standards have been pointed out. Investigations have been made in the spirit of wisdom after the event to test the success and failure of the matriculation examinations as means of predicting success at the university, and much anxious thought has been given to ways of improving examination methods in the light of these findings. In the University of Sydney it was once suggested that the standard of matriculants might be raised if an "A" pass were required in some subjects at the leaving certificate examination. Investigation showed that so many "A" passes would have to be required to make any appreciable difference that the device could not be entertained. Some university people, on the other hand, feel that the pass mark fixed in an examination serving many purposes is not really adequate for university entrance. But, while all these uncertainties and difficulties are constantly in the minds of examiners, it is generally thought that a student who cannot pass in five subjects at a respectable though not exacting standard has little hope of success in university studies.

Though there is argument in detail about the subjects in which a student should be required to pass for matriculation, there is surprising agreement among the Australian universities. This may be made clear in a very brief synopsis of the requirements:

Sydney: The student must pass in English and four other subjects chosen from at least two of four groups. The groups are: A—English, B—History and Economics, C—Foreign Languages, D—Mathematics, Music, E—Sciences. Under the new matriculation requirements, to come into force in 1959, candidates must pass in either Mathematics or a foreign language.

New England: The requirements are at present the same as for Sydney.

Adelaide: The candidate must pass in five subjects, selected from four

F

groups. He must include one subject from each of groups B (Languages, History, English) and C (Sciences and Mathematics). He must include either Mathematics or a foreign language. He must either pass in English Literature or satisfy the examiners of his ability to use the English language as a vehicle of expression.

Queensland: The candidate must pass in English, a foreign language, and in two subjects selected from two of the groups c, d, and e. (The groups are c—Mathematics, d—Sciences, e—History, Geography.)

Western Australia: The candidate must pass in English and four subjects chosen from at least three of the groups ii, iii, iv, and v. (The groups are ii—Languages, iii—History, Geography, Economics, iv—Mathematics, v—Sciences.)

Tasmania: The candidate must pass in one of the subjects English Literature, English Language, Modern History, Ancient History; in one of the subjects French, German, Latin, Greek, Mathematics; and any other three subjects.

University of New South Wales: Candidates must pass in five subjects, which must include English, Mathematics, and three other subjects from groups A and B, one of these three being from group A. (Group A contains all subjects except English, Mathematics and Music; Group B is Mathematics and Music.)

Melbourne: A candidate must have passed in four subjects at the school leaving examination, and must then pass in one examination at matriculation level in English Expression and three other subjects.

Generally the Australian universities recognize one another's matriculation passes, and recognize for matriculation purposes educational standards reached at other post-secondary educational institutions such as the Royal Military College, the Royal Naval College, and various technical colleges and agricultural colleges. Most universities are very liberal in recognizing the matriculation passes of overseas universities. Most universities have an adult matriculation, admitting candidates over twenty-five years of age on more elastically determined educational qualifications. Most universities have a system of provisional matriculation, in which a candidate may be provisionally admitted to matriculation and have his matriculation confirmed if he copes satisfactorily with his chosen university courses. In the universities of Melbourne, Adelaide, Queensland, Western Australia and Tasmania there are provisions for the passing of the matriculation examination at more than one sitting. In the other universities the examination must be passed at a single sitting.

In the universities of Melbourne, Queensland and Adelaide certain prerequisites are laid down for entry into particular faculties. In the universities of Sydney, Western Australia, New England, Tasmania and the

University of New South Wales a matriculation pass admits to any faculty. Those who favour the principle of specific faculty matriculation argue, for example, that there is no point in allowing a student to take Engineering who is weak in Mathematics. Those who favour the general matriculation will argue that such matters may be left to the good sense of the students. A student who cannot pass in Mathematics knows that he would be unwise to attempt Engineering. There is also the general principle that a student should not be obliged to choose his speciality too early.

Generally the universities guard the status of "matriculation subject" with some care. Certain subjects are basic or central. Some are subjects, or types of subject, that everyone should be required to pass. Subjects that are too specialized or technical are not felt to deserve the status "matriculation subject" and in all states there are subjects which may be taken for the school leaving examination that are not matriculation subjects. There are some basic subjects of a certain difficulty which it is felt, rightly or wrongly, may be neglected in the schools if the universities do not insist upon their importance in matriculation. Mathematics and Foreign Languages are examples.

There seems to be general agreement that matriculation should be proof of a balanced and reasonably wide general education in basic disciplines. The point has been made that account should be taken of subjects done satisfactorily for the first three or four years of secondary education, though not actually passed at the matriculation examination. From the point of view of the humanist it has been worrying to see the number of narrow matriculation passes which contain English alone as a humane subject.

Some hold the view that from the final school year to first year university is a steep jump rather than a gradation. Some think that the universities should not expect the schools to do the whole job of bringing students to matriculation standard, but should be prepared to do part of this work themselves, as by the establishment of junior colleges on the American pattern. Some would say that in the past Australian universities have been admitting students on moderate requirements and then selecting them by serious university standards at the end of the first year. As against this many would say that we ought to have a more reliable method of selection at matriculation level so that an unduly large number of students should not have to suffer failure after a year's efforts at the university.

Matriculation is a perennial subject of discussion in Australian universities, and its complexities are generally recognized.

PASS COURSES

The aim of the pass course is a general education without very much specialization, to achieve both spread and concentration, breadth and depth.

The hope is to achieve spread without shallowness and depth without narrowness. Different devices are used to achieve this difficult aim.

Sydney in its general B.A. degree courses has probably the freest system, allowing freest choice to the student. Let us, then, take *Sydney* as a basis because this is convenient for developing comparisons.

Nine courses are required for the degree and these must be chosen from two of three groups:

1. Language and Literature.
2. Historical, Legal, Mental and Social Science.
3. Mathematics, Music and Natural Science.

The sequence of courses chosen by a student must include either three sequences of three courses, two sequences of three courses plus a sequence of two courses plus a single course, or three sequences of two courses plus a sequence of three courses. These patterns are perhaps more easily remembered in the form of figures: 3 3's, 2 3's + 2 + 1 or 3 2's + 3. Not more than three courses may be taken from the group including Geography and Physical Sciences.

There are then certain concessions—e.g., Law students are allowed to count certain of their first year Law subjects towards their Arts degree.

There are a number of restrictions aimed at preventing undesirable concentration on a narrow range of allied subjects, or the taking of too many courses that are not central to an Arts faculty. For certain subjects there are qualifying courses. Archaeology may not be taken until two other qualifying courses have been taken. Anthropology may not be taken until two other courses have been completed. Candidates are not permitted to take the course in Education until they have completed two other qualifying courses, including either Philosophy I or Psychology I. Candidates are not permitted to take the course in Government until they have completed two courses, one of which must be Philosophy I.

These are the devices by which the faculty seeks to reconcile breadth and depth in a very wide variety of possible courses open to the student. The regulations ensure that a student must pursue three subjects in two subject-groupings and that he must do one subject to third year level.

New England, allowing for certain subjects not taught, has the same grouping of subjects as Sydney. The principles of concentration are the same, and so are the preliminary requirements for subjects like Economic History and Education.

Adelaide and *Tasmania* rely little on grouping of subjects, and seek to ensure the balance by a combination of positive directions and prohibitions. In *Adelaide* the subjects that may be taken are listed in sequences. The usual form is Economics I—Economics II—Economics III. But one may also have forms like these:

History I (A or B)—History II (A or B)⟨↗ History III
⟨↘ Politics IIIB

Pure Maths I⟨↗ Pure Maths II → Pure Maths III
⟨↘ Statistical Methods→ Mathematical Statistics

Ten courses must be taken for the degree; the ten courses must include:

(a) two of the sequences listed;

(b) at least one course in a language other than English;

(c) at least one course in a science subject or Philosophy I, and not more than four courses in science subjects;

(d) not more than five of what looks at first sight like a miscellaneous group, but which are clearly chosen to reduce narrowness of range.

Tasmania makes a simple grouping of subjects into two groups. Section I contains the usual run of Arts subjects. Section II consists of—"All subjects which form part of the qualifications for the degree of B.Sc., Education I, Economic History, Descriptive Economics, Statistical Method, Public Administration I and II, Music." The rules then provide:

(1) Ten subjects are required for the degree.

(2) Not less than six are to be taken from Section I.

(3) Two three-year courses must be included.

(4) At least four first-year subjects must be included.

These arrangements are simple and clear. Rule (2) prevents the taking of too many courses in subjects away from the centre of Arts; rule (3) is to ensure depth and rule (4) breadth.

Adelaide is the only Australian university which in its pass degree has two such specific directions as that a student must do a language other than English and either a science or Philosophy I. Queensland and Melbourne have the language requirement. Western Australia expresses a good intention but leaves it to the individual schools to decide whether it will be taken seriously.

Melbourne and *Queensland* may be conveniently taken together as using a more elaborate grouping to ensure a wide spread of subjects. It is probably true to say that whereas in the other universities quite as wide a spread may be elected by the student, more is done by this device in Melbourne and Queensland to prevent a restricted range of subjects. In *Melbourne* there are four groups of subjects fairly elaborately subdivided: Group 1 (a) Foreign Language and Literature, (b) English, Fine Arts, Music; Group 2 (a) History, (b) Economics, (c) Political Science, (d) Criminology; Group 3 (a) Philosophy, (b) Pure Maths; Group 4 (a) Applied Maths, (b) Psychology, (c) Science. While groups 1 and 2 are generally consistent through the affinities of the subjects, groups 3 and 4 are diverse. The regulations provide:

(1) Ten subjects must be taken for the degree.
(2) Two majors (three courses) plus one sub-major (two courses) must be taken.
(3) The student must at some time during his course pass in at least one subject from each of groups 1 (*a*), 2, 3 and 4.

The mixed character of groups 3 and 4 is clearly designed to provide that a student may cover both groups by doing Philosophy and Psychology or by doing Pure Mathematics and Applied Mathematics.

In Melbourne no fewer than twenty subjects have prerequisites. Modern History, Australian History, American History, Social History, Economic History Part I and International Relations may not be taken by any candidate who has not already passed in at least *one* subject in the Arts course.

In *Queensland* subjects are grouped in six divisions:
(*a*) Foreign Language and Literature;
(*b*) English;
(*c*) History, Political Science;
(*d*) Philosophy;
(*e*) Mathematics, Sciences, Economics, Psychology;
(*f*) Miscellaneous—Ancient History, Australian History, Economic History, Public Administration, Music, Education, Physical Education, Legal History.

The regulations provide:
(1) Ten courses must be taken for the degree.
(2) Not less than five subjects must be taken.
(3) The course must include two subjects in three parts and one subject passed in two parts, or one subject passed in three parts and at least two subjects passed in two parts;
(4) Subjects must be taken from four different groups, including Group (*a*) and three of (*b*), (*c*), (*d*), (*e*).

In Melbourne and Queensland a pass degree in three subjects would not be possible as it is in Sydney and New England. Melbourne, Adelaide and Tasmania demand a spread over at least four subjects, Queensland over at least five. We may put it in two ways. (1) Sydney and New England as against the rest make possible a greater concentration. (2) Melbourne, Queensland, Tasmania and Adelaide as against Sydney and New England do more to prevent a narrow range. It is clear that the Australian universities agree and differ among themselves about the most effective way of striking the desired balance.

The University of *Western Australia* differs from all the rest. Western Australia requires nine courses for the degree. The student does at least four subjects in the first year and then enters a school. The subjects that he takes in the last six terms of the usual degree course are determined by the chairman of the school that he enters. The schools vary in the extent to which they ask students to do courses outside the environs of the subject. They invariably allow students a free choice to the extent of two or three units. On the whole it is probably true that the system in operation is not as restrictive as it looks at first sight. Some of the schemes of courses are quite interesting. There are, for example, five schemes for courses in History:

(a) History with Constitutional emphasis;
(b) History with Economic emphasis;
(c) History with Geographical emphasis;
(d) History with Literary emphasis;
(e) History with Political emphasis.

In some cases universities will, without going against the general principle and directing students to choose particular subjects, nevertheless draw attention to the relevance of certain other subjects for students who want to do a full course. In Western Australia a student's course is laid down for him by the school in which he enrols, though a good deal of free choice is left him. In Melbourne an honours student has his course laid down for him, though here again a good deal of free choice is allowed him.

In Sydney there is an Arts degree in the School of Social Sciences. This is not a different degree, but merely a particular way of taking the Arts degree. The courses that may be taken in the School of Social Sciences are laid down and certain subjects are compulsory. The school is under the direction of a Board of Studies. This is the only example of a strict pattern laid down for the Arts degree.

In the survey of the humanities in Canada there is evidence of a great deal of close examination of the principles, aims and content of a liberal education in the faculty of Arts. There is some dissatisfaction with the traditional system. In Alberta a new scheme has been worked out by a committee of the staff, and it is based on two assumptions: "that the elective system as a way of providing for general education has been definitely discredited" and that the aim of a general education is "some familiarity with every important field of modern culture", combined with "a more intimate or competent knowledge of at least one particular field". There is also a feeling that more should be done by the lecturers to integrate for the student the courses he chooses to do.

If it is accepted that "the most elementary precaution is to see to it that the principal disciplines, literature, language, philosophy, history, the social sciences, mathematics and the natural sciences, shall each receive some representation in the pass student's course", then the courses in the Australian universities would fall far short. They do not profess such an aim. The difficulty is to find a way of covering such a broad field of knowledge. The survey course seems the only device that will serve, and the survey course has obvious dangers and disabilities. It obliges (and tempts) the student to rest content with absorbing opinions at second-hand. There is no time for training in the examination of primary materials or for the thorough scrutiny of different approaches and points of view. It is in the best academic tradition that in university education the student as he goes must both acquire knowledge and become acquainted with the foundations upon which knowledge of the subject rests and the constant criticism and reassessment to which knowledge is subject. Most Australian scholars would probably reject a scheme in which the same subject was taught both in the survey style and in the traditional style. Most would feel that literature courses based on "great books", or a course in Political Science which simply outlined the main political systems, would be sub-university work.

If we set ourselves against the survey course and against a programme of bits and pieces full of part-courses, and if we see no reason for revising our estimate of the standard that a pass student should reach, then it seems that nothing can be done to ensure a broader spread of subjects in the Arts faculties of the Australian universities. It is doubtful whether much thought has been given to these matters. The feeling has been expressed that too little attention is given to the arts of music, painting, sculpture, architecture and theatre in the Arts faculties. In all universities a good deal is done in informal extra-curricular activities to foster such interests, but there is widespread feeling that the faculties themselves should give some consideration to these subjects. There has been some discussion in the universities of New England and Western Australia on the basic question—what constitutes a liberal education?

Another question that deserves consideration is the integration of knowledge for the student. There is, of course, profit in pursuing a number of disciplines along their separate lines. But unless the student learns to make connections between them and glimpse the interdependence of traditionally independent segments of knowledge, a great benefit of liberal education is lost. In an age when everyone deplores the splitting of knowledge into separate specialized subjects, if the Arts student is not going to make some attempt at integration, who is? We are not suggesting that the student should be taught the interconnections as so much information, but rather that he should be led to an attitude of mind that actively seeks the unity of all the spheres of knowledge with which the student can become familiar. We might well assume that the serious student well taught in the traditional way would develop this attitude of mind. We might assume that if subjects are well taught, the historian, for example, using literature as evidence, the lecturer in literature bringing in the historical background, the importance of such integration would be constantly before the student.

But it is not to be doubted that many students simply follow their separate disciplines and make no attempt at integration. This suggests that at least in the teaching of the subject, and in thinking of the general attitude of mind that the student is encouraged to develop, closer attention might be given to this problem. In some universities there is a certain amount of organized association between subjects. There are combined seminars of related subjects, more often at honours than at pass level. When a course is being done in one subject and part of a course in another subject is specially relevant to it, students are sometimes asked to attend some lectures in a subject that is not being taken ordinarily by them. A lecturer from another subject may be invited to deliver certain background lectures. Lectures on classical drama have, for example, been delivered to English students in the University of Sydney, and in the University of Melbourne the departments of Classical Studies and Fine Arts combine in courses on classical art.

An experiment was begun in the University of Sydney some years ago which has proved interesting enough to continue. In order to provide lectures that might be attended by second year students present at the university while their fellows were away doing national service training, a course of lectures on general topics was organized. The response, inside and outside the university, was encouraging enough to make these lectures an annual event. The tradition has developed that scholars of the highest repute in Australia give lectures on topics from their own subject that are related to a particular theme. The theme for the 1958 series, for example, was "Modern Views of Man". The lectures were: "The Biological Uniqueness of Man", "The Neuro-physiological Basis of the Mind", "Man and Culture", "The Mind of Man as Mechanism", "The Authoritarian View of Man", "Man from Within", "The Nature of Man in Contemporary Christian Thought".

These are some of the devices now used to bring together and relate specialized areas of knowledge. The making of such connections is a particular responsibility of faculties of Arts. If Arts faculties cannot discharge the whole responsibility of integrating knowledge, they should, at any rate, give the lead to the other faculties in the universities.

If the effectiveness of the traditional system of free election is seriously called in question as a means of ensuring a true liberal education, then we shall find ourselves engaged in an inquiry of some magnitude into fundamental principles. Perhaps we ought at least to decide whether such an inquiry is called for.

PART-TIME STUDIES

Evening Students

All the Australian universities admit part-time students—evening students and external students. There is considerable variation in the number of subjects available for part-time study.

The system of evening lectures serves various purposes. It gives anyone who has to work during the day a chance of a university education. It gives the day student who has to give up his course through failure a chance to complete a degree. In most universities, a good many of the evening students are teachers. Some of these would have failed their day courses, would then have completed professional training in the Teachers' College and would have been appointed to schools. They are later brought back by the Department of Education to the city and given the opportunity of completing their degree. Some of them would not have been selected for university training on their matriculation and are taking the opportunity of graduating while they are working. In Adelaide the Government awards a number (not very great) of evening studentships as an encouragement to students to undertake evening courses.

The industry and determination shown by evening students is wholly admirable. No concession is made to them. They are expected to sit the same examinations and reach the same standard as day students. One can only admire the strength of purpose that enables them to reach the required standard while carrying out a full-time job. A suspicion is sometimes felt, however, that the evening student's examination pass is not proof of the amount of thought and reading that is desired. On the face of it it is hard to see how a pass at the same examination can be proof of the same mastery of the subject in a full-time and a part-time student. Because of the pressure of time an evening student is more likely than the day student to cut down reading, to select in a way that he thinks meets the bare requirements of the examination. The evening student more than the day student asks the question that lecturers most dislike being asked: What may be safely left out?

It is felt by some that the presence of part-time students has an insidiously demoralizing effect upon the work of departments. There is a tendency to trim requirements, as of reading, according to the amount that the part-time students may be expected to cope with.

In the University of Sydney it is true that in some subjects the failure rate among evening students has been higher than among day students. But examinations do not necessarily reveal this deficiency in reading and this abbreviation of time for thinking. There is only one solution to this problem of the student necessarily in a hurry and only one circumstance that may make it less serious than it appears. The solution is that the student should take longer over his course or be obliged by regulation to do so. It is probably true that most evening students take longer over their course than day students but whether by design or through failures in examination it would be difficult to say. In some universities proposals to oblige evening students to take at least a year longer than day students have been discussed. The fortunate circumstance is that on the whole evening students are older and more mature and have a stronger feeling of purpose than day students. These enable them to cover work and acquire mastery that one might have feared, considering their difficulties, to be beyond them. Evening students appear pretty regularly in the honours lists in some universities. In one university, at least, fourth year honours seminars and lectures are held at a late hour so that evening students may attend. Two professors have been evening students.

In Melbourne and Sydney evening lectures were at one time separate from day lectures and were given by separate lecturers. It is a good many years now since this system was abandoned. The lectures given to evening students are the same as those given to day students and are given by the same lecturers. If there are tutorials given to day students they are given also to evening students.

Attempts have been made to bring evening students into the life of the university, to encourage in them the growth of an *esprit de corps* and to break down any inclination on the part of the day student to regard the evening student as an intruder and an inferior sort of student. There are in the Australian universities quite strong evening students' associations. These look to the interests of evening students and by organizing social and cultural functions make possible some corporate life for students. In one university at least the evening students publish their own journal.

Attention to evening students is a considerable additional burden on university departments. All lectures have to be repeated for their benefit. There are some who feel that it would be less expensive of effort and no more expensive of money if evening students were subsidized so that they could do their courses as day students. But, impatient as they understandably are of the added burden of evening lectures, most lecturers see general benefits in the system of evening study that are important in Australian conditions. They would in principle not like to see any disproportionate increase in the number of evening students but they would not press for the abolition of the system. The main weakness already pointed out could be removed by regulation.

External Studies

There are weighty arguments of principle against external or correspondence studies at university level. There is a special value in the presentation of the subject through the living voice which transmits personality and enthusiasm with great effect. Direct contact of lecturer and student has a value for which there is no substitute. Some subjects, for example the oral side of language, cannot be taught at all satisfactorily by correspondence. The external student is denied a specially valuable part of university activity in which undergraduates educate one another through discussion. The external student who has not free access to a university library must rely on a small book-box selected by someone else, and has no chance of learning the art of exploring a subject for oneself. If this art is not learned then what the student gets may be instruction—it is not a university education. Cyclostyled notes once made are for reasons of economy and convenience kept in use for an unduly long time. Changes cannot be made in them when changes are dictated by changing points of view in scholarship.

These are some of the objections that spring to mind when one thinks of external studies. Correspondence courses are a poor substitute for a regular university education. While we are sympathetic to the student who can get a university education in no other way we suspect that often this substitute university training is forced upon students by government departments for reasons of administrative convenience.

Some people have spoken feelingly about the disabilities of external courses. In any subject where the object is some kind of critical thinking the method cannot apply. To attain even moderate success the students would need to do a multiplicity of exercises which would have to be commented upon without delay and in great detail by a very able tutor. If the student is to become acquainted with many points of view he must be supplied with a large number of books. In other words, there is really no possibility of good work in this field except at costs so high that it would be better to give the students scholarships.

State departments of education seem to have a great deal of responsibility for the scale of external studies. In Western Australia, for example, 90% of the students enrolled externally in 1957 were teachers. This is regrettable if only because it is not a good thing to be doing two jobs at once. Teaching and scholarship are both exacting and the student should be enabled to give his whole energy and mind to one or the other. Yet one must understand the problem that faces departments of education. Taking Western Australia again as an example, we are told that the secondary school population has trebled in recent years. The department has a most pressing need for a large number of highly qualified graduates and it needs graduates in the field teaching as soon as possible. It cannot really have both but it has a desperate problem to which some sort of solution is demanded. Australia's educational needs in recent years have far outgrown the resources in human qualification and physical facilities that we have built up to meet these needs. The whole educational effort, from school to university, is under great strain.

The Australian universities vary greatly in their attitudes to external studies. The University of Sydney has always resisted them on principle for the sort of educational reasons we have suggested.

In the University of Tasmania there are no external students so named. But there are "exempted students", that is, students who are exempted from lectures but who may sit the examinations. These are in fact external students. They get no help at all in their studies. There is a certain disquiet about this situation and a feeling that if external students are allowed by the university then something should be done to help them.

In Adelaide it is the declared policy of the university to go on having external students, to examine them and to do nothing for them. They enrol, pay a fee, are informed of the curriculum and are in due course examined. They are given no help with their programme of reading or through criticism of work submitted. They are encouraged to enrol with the Technical Correspondence School, a state institution which relies upon printed lecture notes. Only about half the students enrol there. External courses have been abolished in Philosophy and they are not offered in the languages.

In the University of Melbourne external studies are fairly generally available but have been greatly reduced. External courses never amounted to more than permission to enrol, the circulation of lecture notes and the correction of exercises. In the last ten years some departments, because of lack of staff, have refused permission to enrol. All the work for external students has to be done within the department, and the departments complain that they are too understaffed to do the work properly.

In the University of Western Australia the work of external tuition must be done within the department. Departments that offer external courses generally have external tutors to attend to the work. These tutors are all part-time and poorly paid. Students may study by correspondence or at certain "affiliated institutions".

In two universities, Queensland and New England, external studies are taken seriously and conducted on a considerable scale. In both universities some attempt is made to reduce some of the inescapable disabilities of external studies.

In the University of Queensland there is a quite separate External Studies Department under the control of a director, having on its staff tutors in the subjects offered. The external student must satisfy examination standards set by the professor and he follows the courses laid down for internal students. The relationship between the internal staff and the external tutor varies from department to department. Often the external lecturer is invited to deliver lectures to internal students. The system tries to avoid any cramping of the work of the ordinary internal department by the problems of the external department.

A wide range of subjects is offered in the faculties of Arts, Law, Commerce, Divinity and Education. Certain residential qualifications are required and students are eligible from a wide area in the state of New South Wales, the Pacific Islands and Papua, in addition to the state of Queensland. The mechanics of management, such as dispatch of material and comment on assigned work, are very efficiently worked out. The student receives guidance and direction regularly and systematically. An interesting development in Queensland has been the establishment of "university centres" at Townsville, Rockhampton, Ipswich and Toowoomba. Each has a part-time officer in charge, usually the deputy principal of the local high school. In any subject for which there is a sufficient enrolment and when there is a suitable local tutor available there are evening lectures. In these lectures the tutor uses the external study notes as a basis. There are other devices for lessening the disabilities of external studies. Classes are arranged by travelling tutors, and a vacation school (attendance voluntary) is held every year.

In the University of Queensland it is felt that the great size of the state and the wide scatter of the population make a system of external studies appropriate. When the university was founded it was felt that external studies should be catered for but it was thought that they would dwindle. On the contrary, they have increased and are increasing. In 1959 there were 2961 day students in the university, 2219 evening students and 2220 external students. In Arts there were 363 full-time students, 662 evening students and 771 external students. That is to say, there were almost as many external as internal students and over three times as many part-time students as full-time students. This is surely not a healthy state of affairs.

In the University of New England some attempt is made to reduce the disabilities of the external student through the organization of vacation schools in the January, May and August vacations. For some subjects attendance at these schools is compulsory. The university proposes also to organize weekend schools in the larger country towns of New South Wales and where numbers of students are sufficient. New England has the advantage of being a residential university and so able to bring students for limited periods into association with lecturers and with one another.

In some Australian universities the part-time students (evening and external) have so increased that there is a disturbing disproportion between their numbers and the numbers of full-time students. Considerable anxiety is felt on this score in Queensland and Western Australia. The Queensland figures for 1959 have already been quoted. In Western Australia in the last six years the disproportion has been growing alarmingly. In 1951 there were 247 full-time students, 325 part-time students and 139 external students. In 1957 there were 232 full-time students, 565 part-time students and 251 external students. In other words, 80% of Arts students are part-time or external.

These figures are quite alarming. In two Australian universities 80% of the students enrolled in the faculty of Arts do their courses with very little or hardly any association with the university itself, with the lecturers, with the general corporate life of the university or with one another, without the opportunity of applying the whole of their time and energy to their studies free of the burdens and distractions of a full-time occupation. One consequence of this, which is probably not fully realized among the universities themselves, is that B.A. degrees awarded by Australian universities mean very different things. The variation in standard is greater than, taking a national view of university education, one would like to see.

It is dangerously misleading, however plausible, to point to the mature and able evening or external student and to what he can achieve and then to attribute such possibility of achievement to the system. The achievement is attributable to the individual student; the system merely provides him with the opportunity—under considerable difficulties. To assume that the mature and able students are coming forward in great numbers as evening students or external students is foolish and dangerous. In at least two Australian universities the number of part-time and external students is now so great as to make one fear some effect on the very life and work of the faculty of Arts and some danger to the standing of the degree.

TEACHING

In Australia only two universities, the University of New England and and the Australian National University, have been able to plan their work as residential universities. They are the only ones that are able to ensure a corporate life by regulation and organization. The other universities can do no more than use a small number of unrelated and inadequately supported means for encouraging a corporate life.

Ideally, a university is a community of learning—a community of scholars, a community of students and a community of scholars and students together. It is not merely that the lecturers teach the students. The lecturers teach one another, the students teach one another and the students teach the lecturers by responding to teaching. In the faculties of Arts in Australian universities the approach to such a desired community of learning has been remote.

The Australian universities have always suffered from inadequacy of staff, and ever since the first world war, at latest, from a serious disproportion of students to staff. In Sydney in 1932 there were 400 students doing English and two professors and one lecturer to teach them. In 1948 there were 1850 students doing English and five permanent members of staff and two young Teaching Fellows fresh from graduation to teach them. Recalling such conditions one wonders how such things could have been allowed to happen. Looking back beyond 1930 one is struck by the devoted service that the older generations of teachers gave to university education in this country and the great burdens of teaching they carried. Professor Fitzherbert in Adelaide at one stage conducted all the teaching in Greek, Latin and Comparative Philology himself. Looking back over his career he recalled a point at which he said things improved greatly. He was given one part-time lecturer! E.R. Holme of Sydney, in addition to a full programme of teaching in the day, lectured to evening students three evenings of the week, twice a week till 9.15. The Australian universities may look back with gratitude to the work of such men, but with little pride, most of them, in their parsimonious treatment of the faculties of Arts. Arts on the cheap has been the usual thing.

This general situation—small staff, large numbers of students, inadequate equipment—has forced the faculties to rely mainly on the formal lecture in teaching. In Sydney for many years almost all the written work of students and much of the examination work had to be farmed out to outside markers. Outside the formal lecture there was hardly any contact between members of the staff and their students. It is to be hoped that if, following the Murray Report, Arts departments are to be better staffed, means will be found to bring staff and students into a closer and more frequent association. The development of an adequate tutorial system is one of the most urgent needs in the Australian universities.

Various attempts have been made to introduce tutorial systems. In English in Western Australia there have always been regular tutorials during Professor Edwards's term. In Sydney various devices have been used in English to give students tutorial help. There have been voluntary tutorials (to which 300 students would turn up). In 1957 the staff in desperation decided that though not equipped to do it, they would provide students with tutorial help and each student was given two tutorials in the year in groups of ten. In the Sydney departments lack of staff has always prevented the development of an adequate tutorial system. This is true also, in the main, of the other Australian universities. The best off has been Melbourne where the staffing of Arts departments, particularly departments heavily burdened with students, has been better than in the other universities. As a result Melbourne now has and has had for some years a better developed tutorial system than any other Australian university. Melbourne might well be the model for the others. The tutorial system in History and English in Melbourne seems quite impressive. Students are divided into groups of ten and the groups meet for tutorials once a week.

Tutorial meetings of small groups conducted in conjunction with formal lectures have manifold advantages. They enable students to state and exchange views. Through the closer examination and discussion of written papers the lecturer is able to show students how to go about the exploration of the subject and how to set out their points of view. Students may see demonstrated through experience of discussion the important truth that differences in approach and conclusion are inevitable in almost any topic met in the Arts faculty. Difficulties that students meet in following the subject may be stated or discovered in good time so that such failure to understand will not then stand in the way of their progress in the subject. What is rightly stated in a general way in lectures may be followed up by practical exploration in tutorials. A part of a subject simply opened up in lectures may be pursued in greater detail in the tutorials. Practical criticism, as in the assessment of a poem, and practical exercises, as in phonetic transcription, may be done in tutorials. By exchanging views, students may educate one another and broaden one another's approach to include other possible points of view.

These are only a few of the benefits of a tutorial system. Two points must be made. First, tutorials are not coaching sessions. Their purpose is not to help students to get through examinations. Second, tutorials are not supplementary or additional lectures. They work in conjunction with formal lectures with different aims and different potentialities.

One would not suggest that tutorials should supplant formal lectures. The formal lecture has great benefit for both lecturer and student. For the lecturer the formal lecture requires the reading and consideration, a comprehensiveness and attempt at synthesis that makes it different in kind from the lesson or an hour given to the simple retailing of information. The formal lecture, prepared at a proper standard, keeps the lecturer's mind running at a proper scholarly level. It obliges him to try, at any rate, to keep to the principle that what he says should be backed by a reasonably comprehensive knowledge of the "literature of the subject". It keeps him on his mettle, and gives him an opportunity to expound in his teaching the breadth of knowledge which, as a scholar, he seeks by inclination and principle. The benefit of the formal lecture to the student is that it obliges him to keep his understanding and his background of knowledge at the standard where he can follow a formal lecture and pursue its implications when it is finished. It follows that in the economy of both teaching and learning in a university formal lectures cannot be unduly numerous.

The disabilities of the formal lecture are so obvious as hardly to need mention. The lecturer may not be able to judge when students are failing to follow him. The level at which lectures should be pitched is not always easy to decide, particularly to a large class (say of 400) which is known to include a wide variety of knowledge and ability. The lack of personal association between the lecturer and the students is a serious disability of the formal lecture. All of these disabilities may be removed by the tutorial system. It seems clear that a combination of formal lectures and tutorials

G

properly conceived and designed is the teaching programme best suited to the conditions in the Australian universities. It is to be hoped that the faculties of Arts may be adequately staffed to put it into effect.

In the History School of the University of Melbourne, in which the tutorial system has been developed furthest, there is a difference in principle between pass courses and honours courses. In the pass courses the formal lecture is central and the tutorial follows; in the honours courses the tutorial or seminar is central and formal lectures are of a rather special kind and not given regularly. When the aim is to treat a subject in depth the discussion method alone is effective. The subject must be explored from many points of view, and these points of view emerge only through an exchange of ideas that are produced by many different backgrounds of knowledge, different programmes of reading, different individual habits in weighting and distributing emphasis and different inclinations to follow certain lines of thought. The first step is to open up the subject; the second and more important step is to explore it in depth. The opening up may be done through a paper prepared by a student or through a course of lectures delivered by a member of the staff. This provides an opportunity for lecturers to prepare short courses of lectures (say six or eight) for which the preparation in assembly, arrangement, weighing and presentation of material, is more or less of the standard required for work that is designed for publication. Such a difference between the requirements of honours and pass lectures would help to maintain the difference in kind between honours and pass teaching to which we advert elsewhere.

The affiliated colleges of the universities have rendered a valuable tutorial service to students. Tutorials are available in most of them for the students in residence and in at least one college tutorials have been offered generally to students in the university. But tutorials in the colleges still leave most of the students uncatered for and would not necessarily be associated with lectures according to the academic principles we have outlined. Worthy as the efforts of the colleges are, they hardly reduce the need for tutorials organized and conducted by the university departments.

HONOURS

A B.A. degree with honours is awarded by all the Australian universities. It seems that honours work is done on a rather larger scale in Sydney, Melbourne, Queensland and Adelaide than in Tasmania and Western Australia. There are differences and similarities that suggest the following groupings in respect of honours work:

Sydney and New England with Melbourne;

Queensland with Adelaide;

Tasmania with Western Australia.

Sydney appears to have the freest system. The first year is an entirely pass year. At the end of it a pass with credit may be awarded and this is a necessary qualification for enrolment in the honours school. In the second and third years the distinction candidate does work additional to the pass work. In some subjects this means almost a doubling of the amount of work required for the pass course. At the end of his third year the student must have passed in seven subjects and must have passed with distinction in the subject in which he proposes to read for honours. He then does a fourth year which is ordinarily devoted entirely to his honours subject.

In Melbourne in his first year a student must read three subjects as prescribed for an honours school or approved as preparation for a choice among honours schools. The candidate is admitted to the honours school in his second year. The candidate must then in his second, third and fourth years pursue a course of study laid down by the faculty. The general pattern is the same as in Sydney. Additional work is required in the second and third years and the fourth year is given up to honours work. (One notable exception to this pattern is discussed below.)

Melbourne, Queensland and Adelaide agree in a fairly tight prescription of the courses that a student must do in the various honours schools. In these universities the student presents himself for examination in his final (fourth) honours year but there may be additional work required of him in his second and third year. In Adelaide the courses which the student must have completed before or during his final honours year are strictly laid down for each subject. For English, for example, a student must complete English I, II and III, Old and Middle English I and II and two additional courses, including one course in a language other than English. The requirement for English in the University of Queensland is: English I, II and III; six other parts of pass subjects including two parts of at least one subject, selected from the subjects Latin, Greek, Ancient History, French, German, History, Philosophy; honours and other work prescribed by the head of the department.

In Tasmania and Western Australia honours work is done by the simple addition of a fourth year. The student first completes his pass degree and then proceeds to honours in a fourth year. Both universities have certain prerequisites for entry upon an honours fourth year. The usual requirement is that the candidate must have done three courses in the subject for the pass degree.

In Tasmania and Western Australia, then, undergraduate honours work is on a smaller scale than in other universities. The common pattern is of a fourth year specially devoted to honours work and additional work required at least in the second and third years. In Adelaide and Queensland the courses required for the B.A. with honours are fairly strictly prescribed for the various schools. In Sydney and Melbourne the student's choice is much freer.

There are some other likenesses and differences among the honours systems that are worth noticing.

In Sydney and New England the common thing is for a student to take honours in a single subject. The taking of two honours concurrently in minimum time is not common. In Sydney and New England the student who wishes to take honours in two subjects may postpone the fourth year in one of the subjects to a fifth year. In Western Australia and Tasmania a candidate who has attained honours in a subject in fourth year may then proceed to honours in a second subject in a fifth year.

In Melbourne and Queensland there is a carefully designed system of combined honours courses. In general the courses are so designed that work for a combined honours degree would be about the same as for honours in a single subject. In Melbourne a principle kept in mind by many heads of departments is that the student really outstanding in a subject should do a single honours degree in that subject; a student who is not outstanding in any one subject but really good at two would be well served by the combined honours degree. There are five combined honours courses in the University of Queensland—Latin-English; Latin-French; English-French; English-German; French-German. The system of combined honours courses is specially characteristic of Melbourne where forty-six honours courses are at present approved and further combinations will probably be approved. In Adelaide there is general provision for a combined honours degree on the same principles as those followed in Melbourne and Queensland.

In Sydney, Melbourne and New England a candidate who follows the honours course to a certain point and wishes to abandon it, has a course laid down which he must complete to earn the pass degree. A student who fails to gain an honours classification may be awarded the pass degree if the work done towards the honours degree is regarded as sufficient.

In Sydney the principle is followed that once a student submits for examination and receives a classification, that classification is unchangeable. In Melbourne, Queensland and New England, on the other hand, a candidate who has obtained the ordinary degree may be admitted as a candidate for the degree with honours.

In Sydney provision is made for the candidate who is admitted to the pass degree of B.A. and who then wishes to become a candidate for an M.A. degree with honours. He may do additional work and qualify as a candidate for the M.A. with honours but cannot be awarded the B.A. with honours.

Australian universities for the most part have not honours schools as such. Honours work is either simply an addition to pass courses in a fourth honours year, or consists of additional work done in the second and third year and a concentrated final fourth honours year. In Melbourne and Queensland students may be required also to do some additional work in the first year. Generally the honours student is not separated from the pass student. For two years he is a pass student with additional work to do, and then becomes an honours student for one year. In his second and third year there is a difference in scope (sometimes the honours student has to do twice as much as the pass student) and some difference in kind between honours and pass work. But there is no thorough-going separation between the ordinary degree and the honours degree.

The reason for this is without doubt the understaffing of the Arts departments. So much time has been necessarily absorbed in the management of pass courses that not as much time as desired can be spared for honours students. In the training of honours students Australian universities have probably done better than might have been expected, considering the conditions under which they have had to work.

There have been some exceptions, mostly in Melbourne, to the general situation that we have outlined and separate honours schools are now being developed in some subjects in Sydney. In particular the School of History in the University of Melbourne has for many years separated pass from honours students. Candidates must qualify in their first year examination for admission to the honours school in second year. Second and third year are then regarded as continuous. Students who make satisfactory progress in the second year are admitted to the third year; those who are not making satisfactory progress are given notice that they must take an examination at the end of the second year. The examination for the degree with honours is taken in two parts—Part I at the end of the third year and Part II at the end of the fourth year. From the time they enter the honours school, students are regarded as a separate group from the candidates for the ordinary degree. The honours courses are planned on a quite different basis from the pass courses with a clear idea of what constitutes the difference in kind, not extent merely, between pass and honours work.

This difference in kind between pass and honours work is worth some attention. In pass work the aim is to cover a certain amount of the subject and to cover it in the university style. The student is not merely given information. He is at the same time made aware of the way in which knowledge is won and made to see how knowledge is constantly subject to criticism and reassessment. He is made to see the changes in attitude and valuation brought about by constant conflict of views. While he is expected to acquire a body of knowledge of the subject (which in a three-year course must in any case be selective) he is trained to think about the subject and make some progress towards independence of thought and judgment in respect of it.

In the honours course the emphasis upon depth, penetration and independence of investigation and judgment assumes far greater importance. Indeed depth and penetration become the important things. It is no less necessary that the honours student should know a lot about the subject. The extent of his knowledge must be wide because without extent of knowledge independent thought and judgment may be cramped. But the difference between the pass student and the honours student ought to be that the acquisition of knowledge of the subject should be left largely to the honours student himself. Where the pass student needs to be led and directed in most of the stages of his study, the honours student, being trained in mastery of the methods and principles of scholarship through the study in depth of selected topics, has the means of making his own way in the exploration of his subject in extent.

It is not merely, then, that there are parts of the subject that, because of their difficulty or speciality, are felt to be honours material and not pass material, but that there is an honours way as against a pass way of treating any part of the subject. It might be felt that in any case Anglo-Saxon, Icelandic, Palaeography or Renaissance Literature are English honours topics rather than pass topics. But there is also one treatment of Shakespeare that is appropriate to pass students and another that is appropriate to honours students. Pass students, for example might be made generally aware of what is involved in comparing early printed versions of the plays. Honours students will need to know all the scholarly techniques involved in the editing of Shakespeare and they must learn to handle the documents for themselves. In honours work the comprehensive study of methods and approach in, for example, literary criticism, historiography and linguistic theory becomes both possible and significant.

In the final honours year it is common to conduct a good deal of the work by the seminar method. Students prepare papers in turn on set topics and these topics are then discussed. In the School of History at Melbourne the relation between lecture and tutorial in honours teaching is the reverse of their relationship in the pass teaching. In pass teaching the lectures are central and the subjects of the tutorials follow the lectures. In the honours school it is the tutorial that is central. The topics to be discussed are opened up by papers read at tutorials and these set the lines of the discussion. The subjects chosen are treated in depth, from many sides and from different points of view. Now and again brief courses of lectures are given. These are always on a subject upon which the lecturer, after wide reading and long thought, feels he has something to say. They would sometimes be quite up to the standard of publication. A great deal more reading and consideration would go into them than a scholar could afford to put into pass lectures.

The development of separate honours schools is something needed in Australian universities. One is inclined to expect that honours schools of highest calibre would develop, initially at any rate, in departments with large numbers of students and with a need, consequently, for a large staff. There can hardly be an honours school of high quality unless there is an ample array of specialized qualification among members of the staff. Ideally a department should be staffed so that at least each main special area within its scholarship is represented by at least one scholar of specialized training. On this basis of calculation no English department could be regarded as adequately staffed with fewer than eighteen people. But universities of the Australian tradition have to earn their living by teaching students. In the better days that we hope are now ahead of the universities a department with a thousand students might hope for a staff of at least thirty. If it were possible to choose this thirty so that the main fields in the scholarship of the subject were represented we should have a staff able to conduct an honours school and a post-graduate school of good quality. The inescapable fact, at the moment at any rate, seems to be that the array of specialized qualification necessary for honours and post-graduate teaching would appear where departments face a heavy load of undergraduate teaching. But it is to be hoped that it will not be long before Australian universities will be seeking scholars of distinction for honours schools of good reputation.

There is no doubt of the need to develop honours schools. The Australian universities are producing too few honours students in proportion to their numbers. In Melbourne in 1957, 1300 students were doing History and eighteen were doing honours in the final year. In Sydney in 1957, over a thousand students were doing English and of these seven graduated with honours. It seems that in recent years the number of students has been increasing while the number taking honours has remained stationary or has actually declined. In the School of History in Melbourne, the numbers for 1957 were:

First year   50
Second year   25
Third year   25
Fourth year   18

In English in the University of Sydney, the numbers were:

Second year   40
Third year   16
Fourth year   10

Some of this wastage is of students who do not reach honours standard and fall out. There is little doubt that the fourth year is an economic stumbling block for many. The fourth year is also a problem where education departments do not freely allow qualified students to take a final honours year. There is no doubt that many students are lost to the honours schools for a variety of other reasons. The relative decline in number of honours students in some schools may be due in part to the emergence of other schools. For example the emergence of strong schools of Psychology in Melbourne and Sydney has undoubtedly drawn off honours students from other departments.

Australian universities need to produce more honours graduates. They are needed in all the places where Arts graduates do a professional job or exercise an influence. They are needed, too, to enable the universities to staff their Arts departments adequately. All who are faced with the task of recruiting highly qualified staff know how hard it is to attract scholars from abroad, and how poor is the supply of adequately qualified local graduates. In a period when the demand for honours graduates is going to increase the development of honours schools will be vital. The situation may well develop in which the Australian universities will be looking more and more to a number of strongly developed honours schools for their lecturers.

Some academic people in Australia feel that Australian universities have done moderately well in the circumstances in their development of honours courses. Others have expressed the opinion with some emphasis that Arts departments in the Australian universities have far too small a top in proportion to their large numbers of pass students.

POST-GRADUATE STUDIES

The M.A. Degree

An M.A. degree is awarded in all the Australian universities. In all the universities except Sydney and New England preliminary qualifications equivalent to B.A. with honours are required. This means that a B.A. with honours may proceed directly to the M.A. but that a B.A. pass must pursue further courses or sit for an examination or both before he is accepted as a candidate. The qualifying examination is usually at about B.A. honours standard.

In Sydney and New England there is no qualifying examination. Pass graduates must have done three courses for their first degree in the subject in which they are candidates for an M.A. They are then eligible as candidates for a pass M.A. First or second class honours B.A.s are eligible as candidates for an honours M.A. but may be awarded a pass M.A. if their work is not of honours standard.

The method of examination for the M.A. varies only slightly. Honours students usually present a thesis only, the departments reserving the right to require a written or oral examination as well if this is considered necessary.

In Sydney, where there is a clear distinction between pass and honours students, the honours student submits a thesis; the pass student submits a thesis and, as a rule, sits for an examination.

In the universities of Melbourne and Queensland the course of work to be undertaken by the M.A. candidate is approved by the faculty. In the other universities, this approval is decided by the heads of the departments concerned. In Melbourne it is common practice to award students a research scholarship which enables them to complete their M.A. in one year as internal students. With this exception the M.A. degree in Australian universities is essentially an external degree.

In the University of Tasmania a candidate is required to submit regular reports on his work. But for the most part the amount and kind of supervision that the candidate gets is decided by the department. A good deal is done by correspondence with students working outside the cities and by interviews at the odd times when the candidate is free to come to the city, as, for example, school vacations. In the Department of Psychology at Sydney regular seminars for M.A. candidates have been going on now for some time. In the Department of English at Sydney they are to begin in 1959.

It is certain that in the Australian universities the M.A. will continue to be a valuable degree testifying to further progress made in the scholarship of the subject. There is bound to be a large number of candidates for it, since there will always be many able candidates who will be unable to undertake the full-time course for the Ph.D. The tradition now firmly established in Australia is that the M.A. is an earned degree that is proof of further supervised yet largely independent work and proof of considerable advance in the study of the subject. There seems no inclination to desert this principle. Post-graduate work for the M.A. might, however, be made more effective by the provision of more regular supervision and the conducting of seminars on general scholarly method and approach. In universities where the propriety of undertaking Ph.D. work is dubious the strengthening of the M.A. should be regarded as the chief means of extending post-graduate studies, a development to which the faculties of Arts will need to give more and more serious thought.

The Ph.D. Degree

In most Australian universities the M.A. degree, usually an external degree with wide variation in the kind and amount of supervision, has been a degree of good standard. The M.A. with first class honours in the universities that award it has been a rare and a worthwhile distinction.

But the Ph.D. degree has set some difficult questions, and in some universities has met with resistance until comparatively recently. There is first the widespread distrust of a degree which in some places has been allowed to fall to a poor standard. There is the suspicion that the Ph.D. may lead to narrowness and triviality in the students' preoccupation. There is the feeling that "research" as the scientists and technologists understand it is not quite the same thing as the Arts scholar understands by scholarship and original work.

Apart from all this there is the conviction that in most of the Arts subjects a Ph.D. ought to be done abroad, that no one should have a doctorate in German who has not studied in Germany, that no one should have a doctorate in English who has not studied in the great libraries of England and experienced English life and tradition at first hand. Apart from such reasons, which might be adduced for every subject, there is the general principle that a Ph.D. in Arts should be proof of first-hand knowledge of the European home of our civilization and traditions and of a scholar's exposure to other influences than those operating in his own university. At the Ph.D. level, it is believed, scholarship should operate and should be experienced at the international, cosmopolitan level. In many subjects, of which modern foreign and classical languages are obvious examples, a Ph.D. done entirely in Australia would, even if satisfying the accepted Ph.D. requirements, have a regrettable parochial limitation about it. If the Ph.D. requires an addition to knowledge and if such addition ordinarily demands search among documents, then research in English is narrowed down immediately on the language and the literary side to Australian subjects. Such narrowing would be intolerable. In History the scope of the Ph.D. would be narrowed immediately to research based on Australian documents. There are documents in plenty to keep post-graduate students busy for years to come in researches that will require the exercise of all the historian's techniques of research, but it is not heartening to think of droves of Ph.D. students confining themselves to the brief and recent history of Australia.

These are some of the difficulties in principle that many Australian scholars feel about the Ph.D. When we come to practical problems of Ph.D. work in Australian universities these are even greater. Two things are necessary if Ph.D. candidates are to be taken seriously. The first is an adequately stocked library and the second is a senior staff possessing the specialized knowledge necessary for supervising a Ph.D. candidate. As to the first requirement, the report on libraries in this survey is particularly relevant. There would not be more than two or three university libraries in Australia that could claim to hold adequate numbers of books and periodicals to make Ph.D. candidature possible, and even then only in selected fields. Even the best staffed of the Arts departments could not show a large group of scholars with the specialized knowledge necessary for supervising Ph.D.

students, and even so, much of their time is occupied in undergraduate teaching. The development of the Arts departments has been so minimal and so few resources have been made available for their full growth that they cannot now claim to be in a position to undertake full-time post-graduate work except by tentative stages.

If the Ph.D. in Arts in Australia is not to get a poor name from the beginning a great deal of austerity must be exercised. Universities in which staffs are inadequate even for the load of undergraduate teaching and in which library holdings are small should not even think of the Ph.D. University senates must be made to understand that if there is to be post-graduate development in Arts subjects the staffing of departments and the expenditure on books and materials must be very greatly increased.

In the regulations for the Ph.D. in some Australian universities, it is stated that candidates will be admitted only if the head of the department concerned considers that the work proposed may be effectively carried out with the facilities available. It is clearly necessary that this kind of restraint should be exercised.

In some universities it has been felt that the Ph.D. has been forced upon Arts by circumstances. Government (and university) funds are made available for research and unless Arts departments go in for "research" as their scientific colleagues do and unless they award the Ph.D. degree, the accepted seal upon a successful period of full-time post-graduate research, then they will be denied a share of such funds. Some have felt, too, that in the general growing up or reaching toward full status of the Australian universities, the stage has come when we ought at least to begin to stand on our own feet in post-graduate studies. Just as, after a long period during which the Australian universities looked abroad for their teachers, a stage came at which they began to appoint teachers who were originally their own graduates, so it seems to many that a stage has come when the universities should try to provide this post-graduate training themselves. If, in order to ensure the continuance of the academic tradition, the Australian universities will have to try to produce more honours and post-graduate scholars, this may well be a most important stage in their development.

In Australia there are two impediments to the development of post-graduate studies of which too little account is often taken. These are the isolation of the country itself and the isolation from one another of the universities within the country. American and Canadian students may find near at hand large American post-graduate schools with well-equipped libraries and highly specialized scholars of high standing. American students may find, for example, a renowned school of medieval studies at Toronto. But Australia in this respect is the most isolated of all countries inheriting the civilization of Western Europe. The nearest distinguished supervisor or adequate library outside Australia may require a long and expensive voyage and use can be made of the opportunity only through a single protracted stay. The Australian student has not the same opportunities within his own continent as the American and the Canadian student and he has to make a much longer and more expensive journey to get to Europe.

In recent years provision has been made for visits of scholars of high astnding from abroad. In the last ten years we have had visits from British and American scholars of the highest rank in Philosophy, History, Classics and Fine Arts, some of whom have lectured in a number of our universities while others have worked for extended periods in one or two departments. This has been possible through the aid of the Nuffield or Carnegie foundations, the Fulbright scheme, the British Council, or the Australian Vice-Chancellors' Conference. As yet, however, while funds can be found for visits from British and American scholars there is no provision for visitors from the great European universities and this is an urgent need, especially for the sake of our language schools. It is up to Australia to return the great generosity of France, Germany, Holland and Italy in finding grants for our graduate students.

Within Australia the isolation of the universities from one another was until comparatively recently almost complete. The earlier generation of Arts teachers hardly ever met or corresponded. Inter-university exchange within Australia is in its infancy. Some universities find funds for short visits and this practice has been growing. If extended it could be of the greatest benefit. The philosophers have set an example with their long-established annual conference which meets in the several states in rotation. The Australian Universities' Language and Literature Association has established biennial conferences. There is room for much more of this sort of thing. But again the cost is heavy when many of the delegates have to travel right across the continent and few travel less than 500 miles. Some universities meet some of the costs. The benefit of these conferences is so great as to justify a much more generous scheme of financing them.

Many scholars in Arts subjects did not really feel that they were getting to know one another and to exchange views until the exploratory meetings were held which led to the formation of the Humanities Research Council. There is no doubt that one of the great services that the Council will render Australian scholarship will be this breaking down of isolation. Even so the membership of the Council is only a small part of the body of Australian scholars and much more will need to be done to enable scholars to confer and to exchange ideas. It cannot be said with too much emphasis that a small university or university college, indifferently provided with books, is not at all the same thing in Australia as in Great Britain. In Great Britain there is no isolation from large centres of learning and big libraries.

In a young country, then, isolated from the great centres of humane learning, with its scholars and universities isolated from one another, its universities understaffed and under-equipped, there are great difficulties in the way of a vigorous development of post-graduate studies. How may they be overcome?

The position, in brief, is that some universities, because of the inadequacy of their libraries, are simply not equipped to carry out Ph.D. work. In such universities we may have the scholars with the specialized knowledge needed for the supervision of the Ph.D. students; but without the books and periodicals they cannot operate. In other universities the conjunction of the scholar and the adequate library holding will vary greatly from subject to subject. At a rough guess, a particular subject might be at best possible for Ph.D. in four universities. At the worst we should have to say that no Australian university would be equipped for it. One would commonly have to say that only one, possibly two, Australian universities would be equipped to supervise a given subject.

It is clear, then, that we must think nationally. While the larger universities might go ahead with the Ph.D. work within what they feel to be their capacities, it might be folly for *all* the Australian universities to proceed happily each with its own Ph.D. programme. It is necessary to use wisely the total national resources in scholarship and materials for research.

In spite of these difficulties, it is agreed that the time has come to develop full-time post-graduate work in the Australian universities and to do this in the Ph.D. way. How may this be achieved with proper safeguarding of principles and standards, without pretension and without undue timidity?

We are bound to reach the same general conclusions as those reached by A.S.P. Woodhouse in the Canadian survey of the humanities. We must find ways of consolidating the rather thinly spread national resources in specialized scholars and research materials while leaving the universities free to design their own requirements and to award the degree. There can be no interference with the right of a university to use its resources in its own way and to decide its own standards and requirements. But in this matter it is necessary to take a national view.

Various proposals for consolidating the national resources of scholarship are canvassed and dismissed in the Canadian survey. Though conditions in Australia are different there would be general agreement that such proposals would not find favour here either. We might briefly mention the proposals and the objections to them:

1. A national post-graduate school. The setting up of such a school would certainly not induce other universities to hand over post-graduate work. It would be most unlikely that such a school would be uniformly better staffed with specialized scholars than the other universities. Many would

feel that the association of post-graduate with undergraduate studies is important to both. There is general agreement that if such a school were set up, it would function as one of a number of post-graduate schools in the Australian universities, all of which are intent on developing their post-graduate schools. It is felt by many that in the humanities, more than in the other branches of learning, a post-graduate school without an under-graduate school would be pale and precious.

2. A plan for what Woodhouse calls "a devolution of specialization", a plan whereby the various universities would each assume responsibility for a particular discipline and prepare to offer training in it to all the students in the Commonwealth. The obvious objection to this is that it might involve a curtailment of the work of a university or of a scholar. What if the one discipline is well represented by specialists in different universities? Further-more the arrival or emergence of specialist scholars in the different uni-versities would cause a constantly shifting pattern.

3. A proposed national graduate university which would be simply an examining and degree-granting body. But universities would be very unlikely to agree that they should do the work of supervision and teaching and leave it to another body to award the degree. It seems desirable, too, that the Ph.D. should share the prestige of other degrees awarded by the universities.

One can imagine four sorts of circumstances:

1. When a university has a graduate of its own seeking enrolment as a Ph.D. candidate, and within the university there is a specialized scholar in the field of study and adequate materials for research, the university will enrol the student if it is satisfied about his quality.

2. A graduate of a university seeking enrolment as a Ph.D. candidate may have to be told that, though facilities exist in the university to start him off, they are not sufficient to see him through his study and that he would have to seek enrolment in another Australian university for part of his time. He might then take the degree of his original university.

3. A candidate may have to be told that there are not any facilities for his study in his own university A, but that there are facilities in another Australian university B. If he can gain admission as a candidate in university B he would take the degree of that university.

4. A candidate may have to be told that there are no adequate facilities for the pursuit of his subject at any Australian university and that he cannot expect to proceed with it unless he goes abroad.

Cases 1 and 4 are not problems. Cases 2 and 3 are problems that it should be possible to deal with on a national basis and by co-operation among the universities. A solution would require in the first place that a student should be assisted to proceed to another university for his study.

Apart from the needs of the particular cases it is a very good thing in principle that Ph.D. students should be exposed to the influences of more than one university. An extension of the Commonwealth scholarship scheme to cover students moving to another state for post-graduate study would meet the problem.

The second case, of a student who does some of his work or the greater part of his work in university B, but who takes the degree of university A, is already largely covered. The Ph.D. regulations in all the universities provide that part of the work may be done in another approved institution. It might be necessary for the universities to agree how much of a student's work might be done in the university whose degree he does not take.

The third case, of the student who must seek his degree in another Australian university, would require some form of Commonwealth scholarship and some agreement among the universities about the terms upon which they would accept as Ph.D. candidates graduates of another university.

So far we have spoken of the need to organize and assist mobility of candidates among the Australian universities. But there is need also to try to ensure mobility of scholars. It is bound to happen quite often that the outstanding specialized teacher and the best collection of research material in the field are not found together in the one university. The scholar may be in a university poorly equipped with materials, while the materials are in another university. This makes desirable a system of grants that would enable such scholars to spend a year in a university furthering their own reading and supervising post-graduate students.

All these proposals for co-operation and mobility among the universities aimed at a consolidation of the national resources in scholarship would be most effectively carried out if a National Committee on Graduate Studies and Research were set up to advise and to co-ordinate efforts. Such a committee might compile a register of library facilities, of the specialities of scholars, might keep a running record of abstracts of theses, acquire a library of the various guides to scholarship and so be in a position to advise students, scholars, universities and governments. It might recommend on the award of post-graduate scholarships and appointment to visiting professorships. It might become a guardian of the standard of the Ph.D. A sound development of post-graduate studies in the Australian universities requires co-operation and goodwill among them, made effective by some formal organization such as a national committee.

The regulations for the Ph.D. in the Australian universities usually make a special provision for members of the staff. The member of staff cannot in the letter of the law be at work full time on his Ph.D. Yet it is reasonable to recognize the fact that the whole of his time is occupied in scholarship. In various ways the universities make it possible for a member of staff to proceed to a Ph.D. In Melbourne, for example, the regulation states that a member of staff may be accepted as a part-time candidate for the degree and the Board will prescribe a minimum for the duration of the course. It is clearly desirable that members of staff who are constantly working at the university should be enabled to proceed to a Ph.D. It is particularly desirable that a younger member of staff should not be precluded from a candidature by being good enough for appointment to the staff.

Two interesting points of view are held about younger members of staff proceeding to a Ph.D. The head of a large department in Melbourne remarked that his experience was that the best of his students were quickly snapped up for teaching posts in their own or other Australian universities. It was the students of the grade below the very best that did a local Ph.D. The best would go abroad from their teaching posts and do a higher degree abroad.

Another point of view is that in some subjects no student should be awarded a Ph.D. who has not spent a year abroad. In the University of Sydney such a requirement may be enforced by the head of a department and in the Department of English, for example, this requirement is quite strictly enforced by the professors. This avoids the danger of parochialism. It ensures that the degree carries with it some guarantee of broadening experience and exposure to the influences of more than one university. It also fits rather well the condition of the young member of staff who has a fair chance of getting a year away but a much slimmer chance of getting away for the full two or three years needed for a degree abroad. He may begin his Ph.D. work in his own university, continue it abroad for twelve months and complete it on his return.

If it is desirable to require study abroad as part of the Ph.D. work in Arts subjects it will be necessary that the number of overseas scholarships be much increased.

PROFESSIONAL EXTENSIONS OF LIBERAL EDUCATION

The principle operates with few exceptions in the Australian universities that a liberal education in Arts should be pursued for its own sake, without any cramping considerations of professional applications. This is not to say, of course, that the Arts student should pay no heed to useful work that he may perform with the equipment of his Arts education. But the student who enters upon an Arts course with the idea of selecting for wholehearted application those parts of it that will have utility in this or that professional application is bound to falsify his education in Arts because of this limitation of his approach.

It is a good thing that the diplomas given in various professional applications of a liberal education in Arts are with few exceptions post-graduate diplomas. There is little point in teaching a librarian the techniques of storing and classifying books until he has an idea of the significance of books and some appreciation of their living contents. It is not good that a teacher should be preoccupied with the techniques of teaching method until he is master of the organized body of knowledge in a particular subject. It is important, above all, to know by first-hand experience what is meant by an understanding of a subject in breadth and depth, even if in the process of getting this experience the student acquires only part knowledge in some breadth and depth of one or two subjects. The free pursuit of a liberal education in Arts gives the student an attitude of mind and a principle of approach that is more important than the actual knowledge he has gained.

There is a variety of professional post-graduate diplomas awarded by the Australian universities. Of all these the one that bulks largest and has the biggest influence on the work of the Arts faculties is the training of teachers in the principles and methods of education. In general a large proportion of students in the Arts faculties (though not always as large a proportion as one might expect) are sent to the universities by departments of education. The policy of the Education Department and of the Teachers' Training College may have a considerable influence upon the work of the faculty. These policies differ greatly from university to university.

In some states there is serious interference with the student's opportunity to make full use of his university course and with the faculty's ability to regard the undergraduate as primarily its concern during his course. The best off are the universities in New South Wales and Victoria, the worst off those in Western Australia and Tasmania. Queensland and South Australia have quite serious problems.

In New South Wales and Victoria the Teachers' College student, once selected for university training, is for the most part left alone until he completes his degree course. In the advice that is given the student about the selection of his degree courses there is some thought of shortages of teachers in particular subjects, and some weighting of subjects that have a professional application, as for example Psychology. In Melbourne and Sydney there is sometimes conflict between the course that a member of the faculty would advise and the course that the Education Department thinks practically desirable. In both states it is generally the practice to leave a student who is making good progress undisturbed in his university studies.

In Melbourne there has been some conflict between the Secondary Teachers' College and the faculty. There has usually been a tug-of-war when a department in the faculty has tried to persuade the Teachers' College to let an able student do honours. The general policy of the Teachers' College is not to let students do some pure honours schools, for example Classics, Philosophy and Germanic Languages. This policy is having an

H

effect on the distribution of students in the faculty. The numbers taking Classics, Philosophy and some languages are being reduced.

There is a clear conflict here on principle and policy. The faculty feels that the teaching profession will be the loser if the really brilliant student is not given the chance to develop fully. It is grievous to see an able student allowed to develop only part of his capacity. The Teachers' College, on the other hand, takes the utilitarian view. The Department of Education wants its graduates out in the field teaching as soon as possible. Further, it does not seem to be convinced that the fully trained honours graduate is necessarily the best for them. A humane scholar (or a scientist) would never concede this point of view, and sees it as not only denying opportunity but in the long run causing loss to education.

Since about one-quarter of the students in Arts, Science and Commerce are Teachers' College students, the effect of such narrow points of view is serious. Even in a university of the size and standing of Melbourne it is necessary to struggle to get educational authorities to recognize the value of a liberal education carried to the highest honours level.

But in comparison with some other Australian universities Melbourne's cause for discontent is mild. In Western Australia it is common practice to take a student away from the university after he has finished a year or two years, to appoint him to a school and oblige him to complete his course as a part-time or external student. One has no desire to ignore the problem that administrators have in providing teachers. But this situation in Western Australia is disturbing.

Western Australia, it may be noted in passing, is the only university with a faculty of Education which awards a primary bachelor's degree. In the faculty of Education, the regulations provide that a student will commonly do no more than two courses in subjects in the faculties of Arts or Science.

In Tasmania there is a peculiar situation which must interfere with the work of the faculty. In Hobart there was once a separate Teachers' Training College. But this has been taken over by the faculty of Education in the university. Students do a two-year course in the university, four Arts subjects in the first year and professional training in the second year. Since a good many of these students are unmatriculated their results are appalling. In one year one passed out of twenty-three, while fifty out of sixty ordinary students passed. This is a hopelessly anomalous position in which both the students and the faculty are badly served.

In Adelaide there is another sort of problem. Members of the faculty complain that Teachers' College students are tied to a programme of useful teaching subjects and it is difficult to persuade the education authorities to allow students to do honours. But the worst part of the Adelaide situation is that Teachers' College students do their professional training simultaneously with their university course. Members of the faculty complain that the first loyalty of the student is to the college; he is only secondarily a university student. Apparently he attends the college more regularly than the university. He seems to be primarily a college student who now and then during the week goes off to the university for lectures.

In Queensland it is generally felt that far too few students are selected to do university courses. In Queensland, as in Western Australia, it is quite common to have students appointed to teaching posts after a year at the university and obliged to complete their degree as evening or external students.

In the universities of Adelaide and Queensland there are associateships which make it possible for unmatriculated students to obtain a certificate of the university. In Adelaide the student may become an Associate in Arts and Education, the courses being under the control of the faculty of Arts. In Queensland the student may become an Associate in Education and the courses are under the control of the faculty of Education. In both universities the students are expected to take certain subjects that are relevant to a professional training in education along with a number of Arts courses. In Adelaide the student must take English I and three other courses in the faculty of Arts. In Queensland likewise the student does, in addition to English I and educational subjects, three courses from a restricted list in the faculty of Arts or the faculty of Science or both faculties. It is not necessary for the student wishing to enter upon this course to have matriculated, but he must reach a matriculation standard if he wishes to have credit for the subjects he has done towards a bachelor's degree. An A.U.A. of Adelaide who becomes a B.A. is not entitled to call himself B.A., A.U.A.

Thus in three universities, Adelaide, Queensland and Tasmania, the provisions for teacher training bring into the university a number of unmatriculated students. In two universities, Adelaide and Queensland, a diploma is given on completion of five subjects in the faculty, in Adelaide, with the simultaneous completion of professional studies.

In the universities of Sydney, Queensland, Adelaide, Western Australia, Tasmania and New England a Diploma of Education is awarded. This is a strictly post-graduate diploma ordinarily requiring a year's full-time work. In Melbourne there is a two-year course following graduation. A student who successfully passes the first year is awarded a Diploma of Education. A student who goes on and passes in the second year is awarded a B.Ed. degree. In Queensland the B.Ed. is also a post-graduate degree. An M.Ed. degree is awarded in Melbourne, Sydney, Western Australia and Queensland. In Sydney the M.Ed. is the only degree in education. A degree in another faculty and the Diploma of Education are prerequisites. In

Western Australia and Queensland the M.Ed. follows the B.Ed. In Melbourne the M.Ed. usually follows the B.Ed. but there is provision for a graduate in another faculty to proceed to the M.Ed.

In addition to the diplomas and degrees in education, a few professional diplomas are awarded. In Sydney there is a post-graduate diploma in Anthropology. In Melbourne and Queensland there is a diploma in Journalism. A student may be admitted to the course in these universities when he has matriculated. In Sydney, Adelaide and Melbourne there is a diploma in Social Studies (called Social Work in Sydney). In Queensland there is a combined degree in Arts and Social Studies. This double degree is done by means of a combined course spread over five years.

The principle that we enunciated at the beginning must be affirmed with all emphasis. Training in the professional extensions of an Arts education, as in librarianship and social work and particularly in education, should come after graduation. The librarian who is skilled merely in the techniques of cataloguing, storing and issue of books cannot be more than a technician. Unless he has direct feeling for what books contain and what they say and mean and unless he has the habit of mental discipline and the breadth of view that an Arts education gives him he cannot reach full stature as a librarian. It is specially important that in educational training as much liberal Arts education as possible should be provided for teachers and for as many of them as possible. One does not deny the need for training in the principles and techniques of teaching. They are obviously necessary and important. But such training may be to a degree sterile if it is not preceded by a degree course. It has the professional danger as well that people who teach subjects of which they have not mastery will teach them dully, without real understanding, yet deceive themselves that they are teaching them well because they know they are using accepted methods skilfully.

It is important, too, that as much as possible of the values which an Arts training affirms and develops should be let loose in the schools. We probably have far too little of it just now. Many Australian academics, while not ignoring the practical problems that educational administrators face, feel that considerably more students who plan to become teachers should be given the chance of a university education.

It is everywhere felt (and it is a problem acutely experienced in Canada) that a vigorous effort must be made to persuade educational authorities of the value of an honours degree. This is particularly necessary in those states where departments of education are reluctant to allow students to complete a full four-year honours course. Nothing would be more likely to raise the stature and the status of teachers than the presence and activity in the teaching service of men with the scholarship and the breadth of view of the honours graduate. The teaching services have too few of them and cannot have too many of them. The demands of universities and teachers' colleges are going to make honours graduates hard to get. We can expect to see the teaching services leavened by the work of honours graduates only if the departments of education and the universities co-operate, the departments by encouraging their students to complete honours courses and by recognizing their value in the service afterwards, the universities by extending their honours schools.

While we would hesitate to describe the training of students with a vocation for the Christian ministry as a professional extension of a liberal education, yet there is an affinity between the two to which attention should be drawn.

In two Australian universities, Sydney and Queensland, a B.D. degree is available. In Sydney the course for the B.D. degree is controlled by a Board of Studies under the Professorial Board. It is a post-graduate degree, usually following upon a B.A. The University of Queensland also offers a diploma in Theology.

In all states the training of candidates for the ministry in the various churches in Australia is largely carried out within the several colleges established for that specific purpose by the major religious bodies. Theological students who are qualified to enter upon a course toward an Arts degree are commonly encouraged to do so. At least one college requires all its students to attend lectures in certain subjects at a neighbouring university.

In the courses laid down for theological students there are many subjects which are paralleled in the courses of the faculties of Arts. Ancient languages and their literatures, with the associated scholarly disciplines of textual interpretation and literary criticism, History, Philosophy and Psychology are obvious examples. Among studies which have a technical, professional content or treatment there is an area, too large to be ignored, where the humanities have an important place. It is claimed that these subjects are commonly done in the theological training colleges at a level that would justify their association with the work done in the university faculties.

The position of Music[2] in the universities has varied because there is both an academic and an executive or professional side to musical study. In the universities of Adelaide and Melbourne both sorts of study are included in the university. The first Chair of Music in Australia was founded in Adelaide in 1884. In 1898 Sir Thomas Elder bequeathed a permanent endowment for the chair, together with funds to establish the Elder Conservatorium. The second Chair of Music was established in Melbourne through the generosity of Francis Ormond in 1891.

[2] The section on Music is based on material supplied by Mr John Horner, F.R.C.O., L.R.A.M.

In New South Wales the pattern has been different. The New South Wales State Conservatorium was established by the New South Wales Government in 1915. This is a large institution which has had some very distinguished directors and has taken responsibility for executive training in music and singing. A Chair of Music was established in the University of Sydney in 1945 and within the university the study of music has been academic.

In Western Australia the university has a readership but no conservatorium or practising school. In Queensland there is now a State Conservatorium but, as in New South Wales, it has no connection with the university which has a senior lectureship in music. In Hobart the university has had a lecturer in music but the course failed to attract full-time students and in 1938 was discontinued.

The practical executive side of musical study is supervised in all states by a number of independent teachers, for whom standards are set by the Australian Musical Education Board. This Board unites the universities of Melbourne, Adelaide, Tasmania, Queensland and Western Australia and the State Conservatorium of New South Wales in the conduct of public examinations in music and speech.

In the past this sort of private teaching under an examining board has been the usual pattern. But in recent years music has received more attention from some state departments of education. Emphasis has been placed upon education in musical appreciation and understanding as distinct from training in practical musicianship.

It is not surprising, then, that the universities approach the teaching of music in different ways according to local conditions and facilities. Melbourne and Adelaide offer a B.Mus. and a doctorate. The universities of Melbourne, Queensland, Adelaide and the State Conservatorium of New South Wales offer a diploma in Music. The Queensland State Conservatorium offers an associateship and licentiateship. In the University of Sydney musical studies are available within the framework of the courses for the Arts degree, but the institution of a B.Mus. degree is under consideration. Suggestions have been made that the Professors of Music and the directors of the conservatoria form an Australian music committee and that money be made available for youth camps and orchestras.

CHAPTER V

The University Libraries

BY G.H. RUSSELL IN COLLABORATION WITH A. GRENFELL PRICE

Introduction[1]

DISCUSSIONS OF THE PRESENT STATE AND FUTURE PROSPECTS OF university libraries in Australia are to be found in a number of reports analysing the general situation of Australian libraries though, understandably, the subject receives for the most part a quite summary treatment. Thus the famous Carnegie ("Munn-Pitt") Report of 1934 bestowed more of its rare praise and less of its frequent criticism on certain universitiy libraries which it judged to stand above the general backwardness of the Australian library system.[2] Unfortunately, the section of the report devoted to university libraries is quite brief, largely because the greater part of the surveyors' attention was directed primarily to the state of public and municipal libraries. Further, in assessing the state of academic libraries, they concentrated most of their attention upon questions of administration and housing. One has the impression that their investigations were rather hastily made, and in particular a balanced judgment upon the crucial question of the nature and value of the holdings of the libraries seems to be wanting.

Again, the Price Report on libraries in South Australia, published in 1936, paid a tribute to certain good features of the Barr Smith Library in the University of Adelaide. It noted, for example, that throughout the depression of the nineteen-thirties, the university had refused to reduce library services or purchases but added that the respective expenditures on their libraries by the universities of Sydney, Melbourne and Adelaide were then only £8466, £6363 and £3709. The Commissioner, however, criticized, both in the Barr Smith Library and in the libraries of other Australian universities, certain fundamental weaknesses. He thought, for example, that the amount spent on books was very small, that book lending policies

[1] In the compilation of this chapter the authors have received valuable assistance from the librarians of the Australian universities, from the Librarian of the Commonwealth National Library and from the librarians of the public libraries of the various states. In particular they acknowledge their debt to the Librarian of the Barr Smith Library, University of Adelaide.
[2] R. Munn and E.R. Pitt, *Australian Libraries: A Survey of Conditions and Suggestions for their Improvement*, Melbourne, Australian Council for Educational Research, 1935, pp. 89-102.

99

were illiberal and that library staffs were too small and too poorly paid. It was apparently in spite of these things that he saw the "library becoming more and more the heart of the University". [3]

Ten years later, in 1946-7, Mr L.R. McColvin, City Librarian of Westminster and honorary secretary of the Library Association of Great Britain, conducted an inquiry and prepared a report for the Commonwealth and state governments. Since his main objective was the improvement of public library services, particularly the free lending system, he devoted small space to academic libraries. Nevertheless, so apt were his appraisals, so trenchant his criticisms and so relatively little does his account vary from present conditions, that we think it worth while to quote at length from his account. Mr McColvin wrote:

> Despite the strictures of the Munn-Pitt Report—and perhaps because of them— the University Libraries of Australia, with one exception, form the group of which it would be least fair to be critical and derogatory. The exception is the University of Queensland, which is shockingly housed in "temporary" premises, with its stock dispersed in a variety of unsuitable rooms—even in corridors. It is true, on the other hand, that only two—those of South Australia (which created a most favourable impression not only with regard to housing) and Western Australia—are properly housed. And, speaking of favourable impressions, may it be noted that at the latter library, too, one was conscious of the potent if indefinable way in which expert librarianship, that has gained by contact with the wider horizons of extra-Australian experience, can inspire a service—an impression all the stronger because nowhere else in this great State was a similar atmosphere to be found.
>
> In the University Library at Melbourne good work is being done in totally inadequate and somewhat gloomy premises—but it is useless and inappropriate to criticise these because the need is well recognised; plans are afoot for a new library; an able architect, with a wide knowledge of University library architecture abroad, has been appointed—and the University Librarian himself is, as I write these words, enjoying the opportunity to study American and British university library services.
>
> At Sydney there is no immediate prospect of new premises; indeed, the existing ones, if not ideal, are reasonably suitable; every effort is being made to utilise the accommodation to the best advantage and already the main criticism of the Munn-Pitt Report—the lack of reasonable open access facilities—has been met. Here, as at Melbourne, the standard of librarianship is to-day no longer open to criticism.
>
> In Tasmania, too, the best is being made of very inadequate accommodation— and new premises are being planned. And, here, too, the librarianship is good.
>
> If that is all I have to say about university libraries, may it be regarded as the expression of reasonable satisfaction. There is, however, one matter with which

[3] A. Grenfell Price, *Libraries in South Australia. Report of an Inquiry Commissioned by the South Australian Government*, Adelaide, 1937, p. 81.

one cannot be satisfied—the staffing of university libraries both as regards numbers and remuneration. On the whole, university library staffs are not paid satisfactorily even in relation to the not over-remunerated staffs of State libraries. For example, in one State (where the University Library is the much more efficient and effective institution) the University Librarian receives only 61% and the Deputy only 66% of the salaries of the not over-paid State Librarian and his Deputy, and certain of its juniors get as little as £2 a week (inadequate, even though they have facilities for studying for a degree). [4]

These sentences of praise or criticism give us valuable background information on the state of the Australian university libraries in 1947—a decade ago. Unfortunately, the intervening years have not witnessed any spectacular change. On the accommodation side, for example, Melbourne is has only just occupied the new library which the report envisaged. Hobart has not yet acquired the accommodation planned in 1947; the "not ideal" but "reasonably suitable" premises of the Fisher Library in Sydney have become totally inadequate, while the Queensland library remains "badly housed", although no longer in temporary premises.

Finally, in 1957, the Report of the Murray Committee on Australian universities devoted a part—a disappointingly small part—of its space to a discussion of the present situation as the members of the Committee saw it. Their assessment is as follows:

It should be unnecessary to stress the importance of the library to the whole framework of university education. In arts, law and social sciences the library fills the place of the laboratory, with its technical equipment and practical exercises, in the sciences and technologies. The library must be found by the student to be a place where he is welcomed and encouraged to pursue a personal and independent search for knowledge and understanding, where his capacities for independence of thought and judgment are enlarged, and where, above all, he is treated as a scholar to be provided with peaceful and uncrowded conditions conducive to scholarly work.

While the importance of the library is recognised in all universities, there is a wide disparity in the standards of library service offered. The most urgent need for substantial new provision for library accommodation and facilities was found in the Australian National University and the Universities of Sydney, Melbourne and Tasmania. In the Australian National University the library is housed in a wooden building which is already fully taxed and which represents a most serious fire hazard. The library of the University of Sydney, once its pride, was planned to meet the needs of a student body but a fraction of that of to-day and has had no appreciable increase in its reading facilities for many years. It is now quite unsuited to its purpose and so grossly overcrowded that students are discouraged from attempting to use it. In view of the situation which will arise during the next ten years, its immediate replacement becomes a

[4] L.R. McColvin, *Public Libraries in Australia: Present Conditions and Future Possibilities*, Melbourne, Australian Council for Educational Research, 1947, pp. 64-5.

matter of the greatest urgency. The University of Melbourne is already building a new library so that it is needless to stress the deficiencies of the existing library which rival those of the University of Sydney. The library of the University of Tasmania is in keeping with the other accommodation of that institution; no more need be said, except that, for the sake of its energetic librarian, the staff and students, a new library must be provided as perhaps one of the highest on a lengthy list of urgent priorities. The University of New England needs a permanent library building.

For the rest, library facilities are not unsatisfactory in the other universities, but accommodation for books will become critical in Adelaide in another two years and extension of general library facilities in the University of Queensland must be related to the expected increase in the student body in the next five to ten years. [5]

In the light of this assessment, it is not surprising that later in the same report we learn that, in addition to other obstacles, "inadequate reading accommodation in many libraries has led to some students abandoning all hope of consulting books and benefiting from this most important part of university life". [6] It is, perhaps, unfortunate that the Committee did not see fit to offer its estimate of the value of the book collections of the respective universities since it would then, we believe, have been even less flattering in its estimate of the "facilities" offered to staff and students.

It will be seen that almost all of these quotations, largely as a result of the nature of the reports from which they are taken, stress problems of administration and accommodation. While we should not wish to question the importance of this aspect of the present plight of Australian university libraries, we think it wise, at the outset, to insist that in the more important aspect of the adequacy of their holdings, these libraries are similarly deficient. This we hope to demonstrate later and, for the present, we content ourselves with quoting the opinion of the United Kingdom University Grants Committee on the situation in British universities between 1947 and 1952, which is, we think, an important reminder of the centrality of this last problem. The picture here outlined will serve to give, in brief, some hint of the seriousness of the position of the Australian universities in 1958 since these are, in almost every respect, greatly inferior to their British counterparts:

The pressure on university libraries is very much heavier than it was before the war, and is constantly increasing. Not only has the number of undergraduate students greatly increased, but the habit of purchasing books for personal use seems to be on the decline, with the result that the undergraduate of to-day

[5] *Report of the Committee on Australian Universities,* Canberra, 1957, p. 51. It is a significant addendum to this judgment that in the "Recommended Building Programme" for the years 1958-60, seven of the existing universities are described as needing substantial expenditure on library building.
[6] ibid., p. 108.

leans more heavily than his predecessor on the university library. Libraries have also of course to serve the more exacting needs of scholarship and research, and these also have greatly increased. The number of academic staff has more than doubled, and that of full-time advanced students is between three and four times as great as it was before the war. At the same time the price of books and periodicals has risen by leaps and bounds; and the rising output of the universities in works of scholarship and research increases the number of publications of the type which university librarians feel that they must have on their shelves. In these circumstances it is not surprising that, although the expenditure by university libraries on the purchase of books and periodicals has risen from £87,802 in 1938-39 to £321,269 in 1951-52, we are constantly told, on our visits to universities, of the inadequacy of library allocations and the difficulty of meeting the legitimate demands of students and staff. Moreover, as periodicals increase in number and in bulk, and as stocks of books rise, pressure on space develops from these causes as well as from the increased number of readers to be served. There is room for great expansion and improvement, and it is a matter for regret that, owing to the many pressing claims on the resources at our disposal, so little has been possible to meet the almost universal need for better library accommodation.[7]

(a) University	(b) Number of volumes in university library	(c) Number of volumes available in supplementary libraries— National, State, Municipal, Parliamentary and Teachers' College	(d) Specific nature of libraries listed under (c)
University of Sydney	387,213	1,062,000	Parliamentary, Public, Municipal and Teachers' College libraries
University of Melbourne	225,183	1,186,000	Parliamentary, Public and Municipal libraries
University of Adelaide	202,000	465,000	Parliamentary and Public libraries
University of Queensland	147,665	366,780	Parliamentary, Public and City libraries
University of Western Australia	137,365	214,000	Parliamentary and State libraries
Australian National University	127,000	450,000	National Library
University of Tasmania	92,000	287,000	Parliamentary and Public libraries
University of N.S.W.	51,285	1,062,000	Parliamentary, Public, Municipal and Teachers' College libraries
University of New England	35,000	28,000	Teachers' College Library
Canberra University College	13,177	450,000	National Library[8]

[7] Great Britain. University Grants Committee—*Report on the Years 1947-52*, p. 48. We have to thank Mr W.A. Cowan, Librarian of the Barr Smith Library, Adelaide, for drawing our attention to this passage.

[8] These figures may be compared with those for similar institutions in Great Britain, United States and Canada given in Appendix A.

Gross Statistics

It may be useful in opening this discussion to set out a statement of the holdings of the Australian universities, as supplied by their librarians, and to place alongside these corresponding figures for those libraries which might reasonably be regarded as supplementing their collections. (Table p. 103.)

These figures may be further broken down into the following approximate figures for subject collections within the humanities, to which we have added, for purposes of comparison, the figures given by the Canadian survey for three of the universities of Canada. [9]

1. *English:* Toronto 36,000; McGill 32,400; Adelaide 25,000; Melbourne 14,420; British Columbia 12,500; Western Australia 7735; Queensland 6950; Tasmania 4250; A.N.U. 3500; New England 3500.

2. *German:* Toronto 14,000; McGill 5150; Melbourne 4200; Adelaide 3000; Queensland 2630; Western Australia 1742; British Columbia 1825; New England 1300; Tasmania 1000.

3. *French:* Toronto 22,000; McGill 9275; British Columbia 7800; Melbourne 6500; Western Australia 5363; Adelaide 5000; Tasmania 2656; New England 1550.

4. *Italian and Spanish:* Toronto 15,200; McGill 3180; Adelaide 1300; Melbourne 930; Western Australia 831; British Columbia 400.

5. *Latin and Greek:* Toronto 16,000; Adelaide 7000; McGill 5965; Melbourne 5800; British Columbia 2500; Queensland 2480; Tasmania 2350; New England 1850; Western Australia 1488.

6. *Philosophy:* McGill 7248; Melbourne 7050; Toronto 6000; Adelaide 3600; British Columbia 2380; Western Australia 2311; A.N.U. 1500; Tasmania 1500; New England 1400.

7. *History:* Toronto 68,000; McGill 37,468; Melbourne 24,140; Adelaide 15,000; A.N.U. 11,500; British Columbia 10,390; Queensland 8100; Western Australia 6886; Tasmania 4600; New England 4000.

8. *Oriental Languages:* Royal Ontario Museum of Archaeology 50,000; A.N.U. 23,500.

9. *Fine Arts and Music:* McGill 19,536; Toronto 8000; Melbourne 7850; Adelaide 7600; British Columbia 2900; Western Australia 2605; Queensland 1050; Tasmania 1000.

10. *Religion:* Laval 42,078; Melbourne 3420; Adelaide 3000; Queensland 1850; Tasmania 1000; New England 500.

11. *Australiana:* Adelaide 4806; Western Australia 2351; Melbourne 2270; Queensland included in "History"; New England 200.

We are not unaware that gross figures, and even the break-downs of these figures in terms of holdings designed to meet the needs of particular

[9] The Australian figures are based on information supplied by university librarians. The Canadian figures are derived from Kirkconnell and Woodhouse, *The Humanities in Canada*, Ottawa, 1947 and are for the year 1945. It is unfortunate that the largest of the Australian university libraries, that of the University of Sydney, was not able to supply these details. It estimates that some three-sevenths of its total holding is devoted to humanities.

departments, are notoriously misleading. It is at once obvious that a newly-founded or newly-resurrected university library now undertaking an informed and vigorous buying programme may be cited as possessing only a small collection, but this may well prove to be a carefully selected collection without accumulation of rubbish and may be admirably adapted to the needs of the type of student using it. There is strong evidence that this is true of some of the newer Australian universities. Conversely, the older libraries may very well have relatively larger gross holdings which, in some cases, will belie their apparent strength by including a good deal of outmoded material of small value and by being inferior to their newer rivals in their holdings of modern current material. It is, however, probably true to say that gross numerical characterizations of those sections of university libraries devoted to the humanities will be less misleading than would be the case in the sections devoted to, say, the physical or social sciences where material quickly dates and where older material frequently has slight value. Anyone who has been confronted with the task of building up a neglected collection in one of the humanities will know very well just how much material of a primary or secondary character cannot be obtained by a library entering late into the field and how much the strength of a humanities collection depends upon its holding a large body of material published long ago and no longer easily available.

We feel that, with special cases left aside, it remains true that a valuable initial impression can be gained from gross figures and their break-downs and that this impression is usually borne out by close inspection of the quality of the holding in question. It also remains true, of course, that this confirmed strength or weakness may appear in quite a different light when the question of the pressure of the number of users is considered. This alone is capable of rendering a strong collection relatively useless for some purposes and, as we hope to demonstrate, this is an important aspect of the present situation of Australian university libraries.

Book Collections and Research Holdings

Our evaluation of the strength of the humanities sections of the libraries which we studied was based upon the assumption that, broadly speaking, they should seek to provide material to meet three basic demands— (a) equipment for the teaching programmes of the individual departments concerned and, in particular, an adequate provision of that primary and secondary material directly used in the study of prescribed curricula; (b) a reasonable provision of material and equipment to meet the needs of the research activity of staff and students; (c) the provision of a collection of what we may crudely call "civilized reading" for the whole body of university staff and students.

Our examination of the collections of the Australian universities in the light of these three demands has left us with the clear impression that they are, even at their best, completely inadequate, except in quite limited fields. Indeed it is only towards the first of the three demands that any really satisfactory progress has been made, and even here the situation is very far from encouraging. Although the adequate provision of material for undergraduate teaching purposes would seem to be a very modest goal, few Australian universities have been able to approach it and fewer still are at all happy with their present provision. We found no university librarian who was prepared to describe his collection as more than "reasonably adequate" and many heads of departments were greatly disturbed at the effect upon their teaching of the chronic shortages of accommodation and books, in face of the ever-increasing numbers of students.

It seems clear that through the greater part of their history the book-buying programmes of most universities have been quite inadequate. They have, for the most part, not enabled their librarians adequately to keep up with current purchases of an appropriately ambitious kind, with the result that "bread-and-butter" buying has been the target imposed upon them and there has been no real opportunity of filling the large gaps which exist from the past. It is consequently questionable whether it would be possible to find an Australian academic library whose holdings are adequate across the whole range of undergraduate needs.

For this several reasons may be adduced. Primarily it is a question of finance and the conclusion seems inescapable that library grants have, in general, been too low. Evidence for this abounds and, at this point, it is perhaps sufficient for us to record that it is a not uncommon experience of heads of departments to discover that they have exhausted their departmental library votes before half the year has passed—and this even when they are buying unambitiously and when their collections are disfigured by palpable weaknesses. While it would be unrealistic to demand that Australian libraries should buy on the scale of the large libraries of the United States and that our buying should be other than generously selective, it remains true that, on present grants, few academic libraries in Australia are able to keep abreast of the current production of books and that they are, as a result, reduced to a rigid selectivity in buying, in terms either of fields of interest or needs of curricula. Either process is unsatisfactory and each leads inevitably to the present situation. In particular, it explains the alarming gaps found in almost every collection once one leaves those areas of study directly covered by courses taught or research pursued within the departments of the university concerned.

We feel, then, that even leaving aside the question of current pressures, library expenditure has been far too low and that the existing state of undergraduate holdings is a true reflection of earlier and present parsimony. It is, of course, true that not all the libraries are equally defective. The collections at Melbourne, Sydney and Adelaide, especially if one adds the good collections held and good services offered by the respective public libraries, are adequate undergraduate holdings. Those at Brisbane, Armidale, Canberra, Hobart and Perth can scarcely be so described. Each of these has very bad gaps and each has total holdings which only a most unexacting scrutiny could pass as adequate.

It is, perhaps, proper at this point to recall the very considerable strength of the collections held by some of the public libraries in Australia. It is no part of our task to survey these, but an inadequate view of the situation may result from a failure to realize that the public libraries of Victoria and New South Wales hold collections in the humanities which are superior to those of many of the universities. That of South Australia, too, contains a very useful collection, while that of Western Australia is rapidly gaining strength. Since the Munn-Pitt Report the six states have legislated for the improvement and development of their libraries, and today, along with the Commonwealth National Library, appropriate increased sums for their support. These libraries have thus been able to maintain, if not always increase, the relative strength of their sometimes significant research collections. In 1956 the reference collections of the state libraries in Melbourne and Sydney and of the Commonwealth National Library in Canberra, together numbered about 1,600,000 volumes. Despite the increase in their appropriations these libraries, which supplement the resources of university libraries, and because of their responsibilities to the public, need further financial support in much the same way as academic libraries.

These public libraries can lay claim to notable research strength in certain fields. For example, advanced studies in Australian literature and history as a whole can be effectively conducted only in the Mitchell Library, which is a constituent part of the Public Library of New South Wales, and in the Commonwealth National Library in Canberra. Mention might also be made of the Shakespeare collection in the Public Library of New South Wales, the incunabula and fine modern printing and the fine arts collections in the Public Library of Victoria, and the history, especially United States history, and Asian collections of the Commonwealth National Library, all of which contain an increasing number of works unlikely to be duplicated elsewhere in Australia.

A closer study of the situation reveals yet another weakness in any dependence upon a mere check of holdings to the exclusion of the wider question of demands made upon any collection by the body of its users. It is clear that at the present time the enormous pressure of undergraduate use turns all of these libraries, good and bad, into something much worse than would appear as a result of a survey of their holdings. It is equally clear that this situation will worsen quickly and drastically within a few years. Here again, heads of departments and librarians are almost unanimous in agreeing that as teaching instruments Australian undergraduate libraries are deficient. For this the chief reason is that grants do not allow the purchase of substantial numbers of multiple copies of essential reference books. This can be effected only at the cost of paring down to a dangerous level an already restricted buying programme. As a result it is difficult to see how, in the larger universities at least, an appropriate amount of collateral and supplementary reading can be demanded by lecturers. No matter how extensive a bibliography on a given subject is drawn up, and no matter how great the good-will and co-operation of the state librarians (and these are ordinarily very great), no more than a quite small fraction of students in large classes is able to compass even a modest amount of reading. In certain large departments, such as those of English and History at the University of Sydney, the situation is extremely serious. Short of a very large increase in the amount allocated for library purposes, heads of such departments find themselves faced with the dilemma of either building up large numbers of duplicates (and so whittling their grants away) or of reluctantly refusing to meet the situation. Either policy is damaging to the teaching efficiency of the university in question. Indeed, in certain situations, it is questionable whether adequate instruction at university level can be given.

These are central problems urgently demanding solution, but lack of finance is not entirely responsible for the present state of collections. It seems clear that the whole method of buying for a university library is filled with difficulties. Readers of the Munn-Pitt Report will recall that a good deal of attention was there devoted to this subject and that the authors were roundly critical of the results of the procedure of departmental buying which is the norm in Australian university libraries.[10] We have no wish to give our opinion in this difficult and delicate matter beyond saying that, while the problem is much more complex than Munn-Pitt would suggest, it seems clear that some at least of the weaknesses in the collections examined are the result of the perversity or lack of interest shown by the heads of departments concerned. We found evidence of whole sections of the libraries being allowed to fall below minimal standards simply because the men to whom the task of stocking them had been committed had, for one reason or another, failed to meet their responsibilities. We found cases, too, where the head of the department was apparently unaware of the deficiencies of his collection, while the librarian who saw the situation for what it was, was unable to do very much about it. Certainly the patchiness of most

[10] op. cit., p. 89.

collections in the humanities is very obvious and there seems to be no effective machinery available for meeting the problem.

Another very obvious and probably unavoidable way in which this buying procedure adversely affects library collections is the great weakness so often displayed in those sections serving areas of study not actually included in the curricula. Usually we found the librarian trying to do his best with the relatively small "general grant" at his disposal, but the result was frequently most depressing. One would discover large areas of human knowledge and endeavour left almost unrepresented and works of international repute missing simply because the "subject" in question was not "taught" at that university. If, as we believe, a university library is to be much more than an aid to "studies" in the narrowest sense, there is an urgent need to populate these desert areas. Many examples of this kind of deficiency could be cited, but it is, perhaps, most apparent in fields like music and fine arts where these form no part of the curriculum of the university in question. Here, we felt, was one striking illustration of the damaging effects of the utilitarian approach to library stocking, which has for so long been imposed upon Australian academic libraries.

With these important and perhaps damaging reservations, it seems reasonable to claim that, on present holdings, undergraduate teaching at pass level is moderately well catered for. Strains and deficiencies are often painfully apparent, notably in those universities whose collections are numerically strong, but the general situation, though by no means a matter for satisfaction, is tolerable. With honours courses the problems are much greater and the deficiencies much more obvious. Indeed, most departments appear to face very real difficulties in their honours teaching since, with the more elementary levels of study left behind, their library resources now begin to be fully tested, and demands which are not simply routine are made upon them. This fact is widely recognized and many departments have obviously bought carefully, within their resources, and some at least claim success in building up adequate holdings. Unfortunately this is by no means generally true, and a great many collections could hardly be used successfully with honours students, especially when a thesis is part of the requirements of the course. Here, particularly, the inter-loan system seems to be a very useful, if rather clumsy, way of overcoming many of the difficulties and, by one shift or another, the departments appear to manage to their reluctant satisfaction. But we should like to stress here that "shift" is the operative word. A good deal of ingenuity and makeshift is called for in all departments except those blessed with local resources. Here again, we should wish to distinguish among the universities. Adelaide, Sydney, Melbourne and Canberra (in one or two cases) are more fortunately placed than the other universities and one cannot but wonder how some of the

I

smaller institutions manage work at this level in face of the distressingly obvious weakness of the holdings of their libraries.

There seems to be one final difficult question raised by any consideration of library collections as media for undergraduate teaching. It is that of departmental libraries. These are not normally maintained in Arts departments in Australian universities and the objections raised against them, notably those of dispersion of resources with resulting duplication and of difficulty of adequate supervision, seem validly based in view of the overall situation. While librarians and teaching staff are rightly dubious of the wisdom of their introduction, the question might well be raised whether a system could not be devised which would give students some kind of focal point for their work in a given department (as is common in universities overseas) and which would do something towards providing the necessary multiple copies of essential, much-used and much-needed texts and reference books.

Most librarians agree that to provide large numbers of multiple copies is no part of normal library stocking policy and is, in any case, impossible and even improper under present circumstances. Nevertheless, the reality and seriousness of the problem raised by the existence of ever-increasingly large classes cannot be ignored and teaching staffs in general believe that some form of solution is urgently needed, which will enable them to provide adequate reference resources for their large classes and will allow of some attempt to break down the inhumanity of present mass-production methods. This is a problem of large dimensions whose solution is not simply one of expansion of library services. Yet it seems clear that such an expansion may prove to be an important element in any final solution.

As we turn from considering the adequacy of our libraries as undergraduate collections to study their provision for post-graduate and general research purposes, we leave a situation of relative sufficiency for one of almost total inadequacy. The research holdings of Australian academic libraries are, in our view, extremely weak and it is clear that, with rare exceptions, advanced work in the humanities in Australia can be carried out only under great difficulties. Even our best collections—such as those of the universities of Sydney and Melbourne, in association with the public libraries of New South Wales and Victoria, are, in this respect at least, inadequate.

While we advance this as a generalized view we must, of course, distinguish. Most of the libraries seem to be relatively strong in the field of Australian or local state history, where holdings in both primary and secondary materials appear in general to be good, and the pooling of the resources of the university, the state library, the archives, and various collections in Canberra normally allows scope for advanced work in these fields. Something of the same is true in the fields of Australian literature and language.

Apart from these rather special categories, few librarians were prepared to describe their libraries as even remotely equipped to meet the needs of research workers. It is clear that one of the most difficult academic problems facing heads of departments in Australia is that of the provision, from available library resources, of material upon which advanced students may be trained and to which they themselves and their staffs may profitably give their attention in order to carry out the duty of research imposed upon them. Here the glaring weaknesses of our collections are embarrassingly apparent. In fact, we believe that it is true to say that, with occasional exceptions such as those cited above, advanced work is hardly possible without frequent reference to overseas collections.

It would, of course, be unrealistic to expect that research in the humanities, so much of which is based upon the culture of Western Europe, could be carried out without difficulty so far from the sources and repositories of that culture. To take an elementary example, it would be foolish to expect Australian libraries to be rich in manuscripts and incunabula illustrating the history, thought and culture of Western Europe, when we recall that even the wealthy American collections are frequently quite weak in holdings of this kind, and that to attempt any adequate equipment of Australian libraries would involve an unthinkable and indefensible expenditure upon material which, as we shall see, may be obtained in other ways. And yet, while this important reservation is to be made, it seems clear that the legitimate complaints to be made against our collections are complaints which take full account of this fact and which are based upon the total inadequacy of holdings in periodical,[11] secondary and edited material generally—that is, in that material which is or has been available and can still be purchased at a reasonable price. If this material were provided, the rare primary material could be made accessible by means of reproductions of various kinds.

Into this question, again, the problem of finance enters and the principal explanation for our disturbing weaknesses is to be found, as usual, in the persistent inadequacy of library grants. It is the almost unanimous view of both librarians and teachers that, on present budgets, it is impossible to buy adequately to meet research needs. The common experience of these men is to find themselves forced to buy carefully any material primarily used by undergraduates and to leave aside, however reluctantly, the more esoteric material which is essential to good research. It is true that grants made from research funds do something to meet the more serious deficiencies, but

---

[11] It should, in justice, be pointed out that most universities seem now to be subscribing to a good range of periodicals and that those departments seriously interested in research are well provided with current journals. The serious deficiency referred to lies in the absence of complete sets of less obvious but important periodicals. We might also add that the Union Catalogue of Non-Scientific Periodicals has proved a valuable aid to research.

these grants are rarely large enough to permit any adequate buying pro-gramme and, since they are normally *ad hoc* grants, they will not, in any case, help towards remedying the absence of periodical runs, great printed collections of sources, series of monographs and such other basic research tools. At best, they will permit the purchase of more or less isolated items of a primary or secondary character and photographic reproductions of material.

After so much neglect, any remedial policy becomes difficult to imple-ment. It is clear that much more money is needed and that when this is provided, both librarians and heads of departments will be called upon to shoulder a very heavy responsibility in analysing their own situations and setting about to remedy them in face of the long-term research plans of staff and students. Clearly, no library can or should—at least in the fore-seeable future—attempt to make itself into a collection which would rival the great and ancient (or wealthy) European and American collections. It seems very doubtful whether any Australian collection can now hope to be all-sufficient. There must, it seems, be selection and some form of rationalization. There will be need for specialization upon lines laid down by the academic policies of the various departments and for consequent heavy buying to produce collections upon which Australian scholars may work with some approach to satisfaction. As the numbers of post-graduate students rise, the undertaking of this task becomes increasingly urgent. Few will deny that Australian universities need stronger post-graduate schools but, in the humanities at least, this is hardly possible with present library resources.

In other respects, too, our libraries are ill-equipped to make reasonable provision for research workers. In particular, a surprisingly large number of them lack adequate facilities for handling microfilms, microcards and micro-prints. These must, for the future, be accepted as an essential part of the material which scholars will use, and serious efforts will be needed to make their use as effective as possible. At present, as will appear later, many Aus-tralian academic libraries are able to make only makeshift provision for their use, with the result that they are deservedly unpopular and scholars have come to regard their use as excessively burdensome and unpleasant. It is true that, at best, they will never be more than an expedient, but they are a necessary expedient in our situation and one which must be made as effective as possible. It seems likely that it will be necessary for certain departments to embark upon large-scale projects of photographic reproduction in order to have on hand the essential raw material for research. But these, unless they are accompanied by major alterations in library accommodation and services, will remain an inconvenient and unpleasant makeshift.[12]

[12] Other questions of accommodation and services are discussed below.

On the third function of a university library, that of providing a body of "civilized reading" for the whole academic body, there is relatively little that needs to be said. In some ways, the libraries are already doing this quite effectively and most tastes and interests are reasonably well catered for. But always the system of departmental buying and the relatively small amount of discretion allowed to most librarians have left our libraries with many weak sections. It is common experience, as we have already remarked, that where a "subject" is not "taught", the appropriate section of the library will be very weak. It is easy to find a defence for this and there is justice in the claim that a university library cannot, and should not, attempt to usurp the functions of a central reference library, traditionally carried out in Australia by the public libraries, or of a lending library. While this is a valid position, it remains true that the task of education in the broadest sense is the basic mandate of the university and that the humanities, in all their breadth, have an indispensable role to play. Once more, the desperate husbanding of resources which is so characteristic and necessary a part of our buying policies has meant that the broad aim has had to be sacrificed in face of the realities of our plight. It was distressing to look in vain in one library for a copy of Camoens's *Lusiads* and to realize that the explanation for its absence was that "Portuguese" was not "taught" in that university. It was perhaps the more distressing to realize, after a study of the library's collection as a whole, that since "Portuguese" was not taught, it was probably wise to attempt, with the meagre resources in hand, to do something to fill the enormous gaps which revealed themselves at every turn, before providing a copy of one of the classics of Western literature.

To conclude this section, we give a brief summary of what, in the light of the assumptions which we have been discussing, seemed to be the condition of the collections in each of the university libraries.[13]

Adelaide: The Barr Smith Library is a sound undergraduate collection providing, according to our information, a very reasonable coverage for most of the pass, and some at least of the honours' courses offered by the university. This relatively advantageous situation is further improved by a close collaboration with the Public Library of South Australia, which clearly affords very considerable assistance to staff and students. In the higher reaches of scholarship the collection is, inevitably, inadequate, but even here, in some subjects at least, there is evidence of an attempt to provide for the advanced worker by quite ambitious buying. This seems to us to be an example of a library which would respond well to increased financial

---

[13] It is hardly necessary to say that these remarks are recognized to be crude generalizations rather than accurate characterizations. At particular points they may seem to be misleading but they are intended to represent our general impressions of the overall strength of each library.

assistance and which could well become a collection of true university standard if even reasonable financial provision were made.

Canberra University College: As reference to the figures will show, this is a very small library serving the needs of a small institution. In most sections there is evidence of careful buying along the lines of courses offered and of a resultant tolerable undergraduate collection. As it stands, it is a fair utility collection whose resources may, in some subjects, be easily supplemented from the other larger libraries in Canberra. Assisted in this way by good neighbouring collections and serving only a small body of students, it appears to give good, if unambitious, service. To bring it into line with more stringent requirements would, however, require a great deal of effort and expenditure.[14]

Melbourne: As the size of its holding would indicate, this is in general a reasonable undergraduate collection against which the undergraduate teaching of the university would proceed satisfactorily were it not bedevilled by the problem which besets all the larger Australian universities— that of accommodating and serving a large body of students. It would appear that, under existing circumstances, its resources are far from adequate to meet this task. As in Sydney and Adelaide, considerable help is afforded by the very good collection held in the Public Library of Victoria, which is a most valuable source of material at both undergraduate and post-graduate levels. It is, inevitably, an unequal collection but one which reflects, in general, sound buying policies of a necessarily rather unspectacular kind and which, thanks in part to the variety of courses offered in the faculty of Arts in the University of Melbourne, has an unusually broad spread of interest.

New England: The Dixson Library is a small collection, begun only twenty years ago in what was then a university college, with access to the library of the University of Sydney. Its development appears to have been slow in its early years and only since the granting of autonomy to the University of New England does the attempt to raise the quality of its holdings seem to have been seriously made. As it stands, it is a useful though slender undergraduate collection, which contains many gaps and would appear to be inadequate for honours work. It has the advantage of holdings which are carefully selected and well up-to-date, but is seriously deficient in a great deal of the standard earlier material. The prospects for its progressive improvement seem to be good, but much money will have to be spent upon it. The present buying policy is very vigorous and the realization of the need to overcome past deficiencies gives hope for the future. Yet it

---

[14] We have not included the library of the Australian National University in this survey since, as reference to the departmental figures given earlier will show, it does not have large holdings in the humanities, except in Oriental languages, philosophy and history.

remains true that the gap between its present state and any ideal condition is very wide and the problem of its bridging is a serious one.

Queensland: This, once more, is quite a weak collection which appears to have suffered badly from inadequate buying during a large part of the history of the University of Queensland. In most areas of the humanities, it is barely adequate as a collection for pass undergraduates. Honours work is made very difficult by its manifold deficiencies and these are made the more burdensome by the serious weakness of the holdings of the Public Library to which one might otherwise have looked for amelioration. Fortunately, it is an improving collection (as, indeed, is that of the Public Library), but it will need a great deal of strengthening before it becomes fully adequate even for undergraduate teaching. It is hardly necessary to add that, for research work, it is negligible, but the great improvement of the last eight years again gives some reason to hope that future development will enable its librarian to begin to overcome its more serious deficiencies.

Sydney: By local standards, the Fisher Library is a rich collection and, in general, possesses the most adequate resources in the humanities to be found in Australia. In both books and periodicals the undergraduate body is well served (subject, of course, to the inevitable reservation in face of the large number of students seeking to use it) and both pass and honours work and even, in selected cases, post-graduate work, can be carried on with the aid of its resources. If its grants could be increased to a reasonable level, one could look forward with confidence to its becoming, by international standards, a good collection. Scholars who use the Fisher Library are further helped by the excellent holdings and efficient services of the Public Library of New South Wales which, in certain fields, is, in its own right, a most important reference and research library.

Tasmania: The state of the holdings of the library of the University of Tasmania is that normal to smaller Australian universities. It possesses an undergraduate collection which is patchy and which is, at best, adequate for undergraduate needs, though even here its weaknesses are perhaps more obvious than its strengths. For all the more advanced demands traditionally laid upon a university collection it is quite inadequate. Its future prospects, however, seem brighter since it is making a serious and consistent attempt to remedy the results of earlier starvation.[15]

University of New South Wales: More than any other library in Australia, that of the University of New South Wales (along with that of its constituent college at Newcastle) is in need of large-scale expansion. At present, only ten years after its establishment, it is to be expected that it is in urgent need

[15] Some idea of the extent of this starvation may be obtained from the Munn-Pitt Report, pp. 100-1.

of a great deal of basic material and cannot be described as reaching minimum standards. The presence in Sydney of older and larger collections does a great deal to alleviate the position for the staff of the university, but it is obvious that even the undergraduate collections are in great need of expansion.

Western Australia: Once again, this is a reasonably adequate undergraduate collection of an unambitious kind. It reaches minimal standards for such undergraduate teaching as is done within the university and leaves the impression of being a well-chosen and very well-managed collection. But much more than this is needed, and to meet the legitimate demands laid upon it by staff and students, the collection will need wholesale enlargement and strengthening. The impressive development of the services of the Library Board of Western Australia suggests that these will be an ever-increasingly important auxiliary to the university library, while the policy of integration of library services within the state seems to promise a most intelligent use of available resources.

Accommodation

Following the publication of the report of the Murray Committee, there is little need to stress here the seriousness of the accommodation problem faced by university libraries. This Committee was struck, as all observers must be, by the wretchedness of the conditions in which many members of library staffs and many students are called upon to work, and how the neglect of the libraries, so obvious in the state of their collections, is publicly proclaimed by the comparable, or even worse, state of their accommodation. It is, however, encouraging to learn that the governing bodies of several universities are likely soon to make long overdue attempts to improve the situation.

Thus, in September 1958, the University of Melbourne began to move from its present totally inadequate accommodation to a substantial new central library building, the plans for which make good provision for both present needs and future expansion. It is expected that much of the accommodation made available will be devoted to the housing of the humanities collection, as most other subjects, with the exception of pure science, will continue to be housed in branch libraries. The University of Adelaide, too, is following immediately the Murray recommendation to extend. The present library building, constructed twenty-five years ago, has served student needs very well but is now inadequate; extensions costing £190,000 have been built. The Australian National University, upon whose accommodation the Murray Report commented so unfavourably, is about to spend £500,000 on a permanent building. The universities of New England and Tasmania have plans in hand. In two of these cases, present accommodation is very bad, while the University of New England's library is housed in temporary quarters which meet present needs but which were never designed to provide a long-term solution of that university's problem. The Fisher Library in the University of Sydney which also attracted the unfavourable comment of the Murray Committee is to be rehoused in a new building. Its present accommodation and facilities are totally inadequate for undergraduate and post-graduate purposes. In the University of Queensland practically the whole of the humanities collection is housed in the main library which repeats some of the weaknesses of its earlier accommodation. The result of this is a relatively new building which is functionally most disappointing. It is, in many ways, ill-designed and inconvenient and is already approaching the limits of its accommodation. It seems clear that additions and modifications will be needed quite soon, and it is perhaps unfortunate that the Murray Committee made no recommendations in this matter. In the University of Western Australia which, surprisingly, was also exempted from the criticisms of the Murray Report, the situation is not encouraging. The general facilities are by no means good and expected increases in the size of book holdings and in student numbers will soon create a very difficult position. Canberra University College will presumably implement the recommendations of the Murray Committee. Here a suitable library building is badly needed. The small collections of the University of New South Wales and its college at Newcastle are both in need of good permanent accommodation and it is hoped that this will be provided before long.

In all, the present situation is a depressing one. Reference to existing and projected buildings overseas merely serves to underline our present poverty. Students, research workers, academic and library staffs are frequently called upon to endure conditions which are as bad as can be imagined. At present, few Australian universities provide more than a fraction of the seating accommodation required by undergraduate readers, with the result that it has become needlessly difficult for students to work unhindered in these libraries. If we add this limitation to that caused by weakness and inadequacy of holdings, it is not hard to see what damage is being done to the teaching and research efficiency of many Australian universities.

Since undergraduates are so restricted, it is not surprising that our libraries are able to offer almost no facilities for advanced students. The equipment necessary for the use of microfilms and other reproduced material is usually quite inadequate and, even if available, it is rarely accommodated in such a way as to make its use pleasant or convenient. In face of the general acceptance of the necessity of photographic reproduction of overseas and local research material, this is certainly a serious shortcoming. Similarly, the provision of carrels and small studies, so common in modern libraries overseas, has in the past been ignored. It is to be hoped that the inclusion of these and similar amenities for research workers in newly-planned libraries will stimulate all Australian university libraries into making similar provision. Modern practice accepts these as being necessities, not luxuries.

Finally, we draw attention to the difficult conditions under which library staffs are asked to work. It is in line with the generally shabby treatment given to the staffs of university libraries that the conditions under which they are compelled to do their important work are frequently excessively poor. The generally high level of efficiency shown by these staffs in such circumstances is a tribute to their ability and their sense of vocation. They, too, must have greatly improved facilities in the newly-planned and newly-renovated library buildings that are so urgently needed.

Finance and Organization

It is, we trust, clear from what we have written that we regard the present financial provision made for Australian academic libraries as being completely inadequate, and the present weak state of many of their collections is directly referable to this inadequacy of financial support.[16] Our libraries made late starts and have had, from the outset, a great deal of leeway to make up. Yet the size of early grants did not allow their librarians to undertake this process and, with one or two fortunate exceptions, no serious attempt has yet been made. As we have seen, the moneys available have rarely been substantial enough to provide more than a working undergraduate collection—and too frequently not even that. It is regrettably obvious that, in the past at least, many of our universities have failed in an important responsibility.

If we bear in mind that, in addition to this disability, Australian scholars are without the advantage of the great collections held in non-academic libraries overseas and that, with the partial exceptions of New South Wales and Victoria, no public library is, leaving aside one or two specialized collections, yet capable of substantial supplementation beyond the undergraduate level, the real gravity of the situation is seen and the academic effects of past and present financial starvation begin to appear. For example, it is estimated that in 1953 the amount spent on libraries in the United Kingdom represented 3.9% of total university expenditure. This figure is in spite of the fact that the libraries of the universities of Oxford and Cambridge received a free copy of every publication appearing in the United Kingdom, though it is also true that the figure is inflated by the fact that the new University College of North Staffordshire allocated 6.6% and the London School of Economics 10.1% of their respective expenditures

---

[16] For convenience, we have tabulated the details of financial provision made for university libraries at Appendix B.

for library purposes. In the same year, the average for seventy universities in the United States was the same though, again, some of the individual figures were much higher.[17]

The Australian figure for 1954 was 4.3%, a figure again somewhat inflated by the much higher expenditure of several universities and not eked out by any substantial intake of free material. In our present circumstances, this rate of expenditure is far too low. While it remains at this low level it is clear that there can be no substantial improvement in the quality of our holdings and that Australian universities will persist in refusing to supply their staffs and students with the library resources upon which good research work might be based. While it is true that library grants have been rising steadily in universities, it is also true that costs, too, have been rising and that even at the present increased level little can be done to make good the deficiencies of the past. There is unanimity among librarians and teaching staff that greatly increased grants are needed and that the intellectual future of Australian universities is bound up with a full recognition of this fact.

It would seem that, confronted with the present situation, universities will need to undertake large-scale expenditure and will need to plan carefully for the future.[18] Each university will continue to provide for the needs of the undergraduate body, buying in the light of its curricula and the demands placed upon it by the students working for its degrees. This, along with full and careful attention to general buying appropriate to a university library, is the first and basic task. But there is need for much more and it is in moving to the higher stage that the need for planning is seen. So great are the deficiencies to be made good that, with foreseeable resources, it would seem impossible and impracticable for any single university to build up for itself a respectable research collection across the whole range of the humanities. Obviously the nature of collections made will depend upon the policy and direction of the research schools functioning in the university concerned and material will be amassed in accordance with the needs of these. Inevitably this will lead to some duplication and, in the case of less esoteric material, this duplication is necessary. Past this point, however, there seems to be a case for some rationalization in buying and for some agreement amongst the departments of various universities that where one university has bought and is buying extensively in a field for the purposes of building up a research collection, other universities should, if possible, turn their attention elsewhere.

[17] For example, the University of California at Los Angeles spent 8.8%, the University of Oregon 7.9%, the University of Virginia 7% and the University of South Carolina 6.6%.

[18] We do not, of course, wish to suggest that such planning is not already in hand. A good deal of what we are examining in these pages is already under active and informed discussion —some, indeed, is in prospect of realization.

Clearly any such plan is fraught with every kind of difficulty and, in some cases, such an agreement may not be possible or even desirable. Nevertheless it seems to offer the only practicable way of eking out resources which will certainly be inadequate for the great expansion needed. The urgency of the problem would seem to call for the utmost co-operation among the universities of Australia and while it would be undesirable, on merely bureaucratic principles, to define the area of work to be undertaken by particular universities, it seems to us that our real hope of building up adequate total national collections lies in the acceptance of the principle of one university supplementing another's research holdings by buying heavily and judiciously in one major area in each subject while leaving the intensive cultivation of other areas to sister universities. For example, it is known that the University of Adelaide is strong in English literature, especially fiction, of the nineteenth century, while the University of Sydney is strong in Elizabethan and Jacobean drama and the literature of the seventeenth century. If it is at all practicable, the obvious course would seem to be that each should further develop its speciality and seek to attain really first-class standards while going slow in the field known to be well developed elsewhere.

Doubtless any such plan would not be easy to implement. In particular it is quite properly urged that a research collection is built up in the light of the research activity of the staff and students concerned and that it is most undesirable to force upon unwilling students a programme of work conceived solely in the light of library resources. While admitting the force of this objection, we feel sure that, if the field chosen is both significant and extensive, and if adequate research funds are available for travel and specialized *ad hoc* buying, there should be no need for harmful forcing. Again, the maintenance of a full-scale inter-loan system, modified to meet circumstances, would go a good distance towards obviating many of the disabilities that would otherwise be suffered.

The question of the nature and organization of such an inter-loan system is clearly one of great moment. To have some such system seems inevitable, though most librarians and scholars naturally find it irksome and inadequate, while the costs involved are so heavy that it is certainly wasteful to use it for inexpensive material. And yet it is difficult to see what other satisfactory alternative presents itself. If finance is available to enable all universities to build up good undergraduate collections, their inter-loan demands at this level should almost disappear and will be made only for some rare and esoteric material. This should mean that the cost of the system would be kept reasonably low, though all its other disadvantages would remain.

Another desideratum of the present Australian academic library system, which is very relevant to this discussion, is a union catalogue of books. Once more, librarians and scholars are, in general, agreed upon its value and if there is to be any measure of rationalization of buying, its existence would be a necessary condition of successful co-operation. As usual, the financial aspect of the proposal is important and it is manifest that if the work of compilation is to be properly done a considerable recurring expenditure will be necessary, since the planning and execution must be placed in the hands of a competent librarian, supplied with an adequate trained staff. But, once again, it must be insisted that, if we are ever to have healthy research schools, such expenditure is unavoidable and will, in any case, absorb only a fraction of the money which should have been spent on our libraries over past decades.

Both this and the preceding item might well be amalgamated into something along the lines of the Farmington Plan operated in the United States and to this might be added consideration of the question of central deposit collections. These are technical matters fraught with difficulties upon which we should not choose to pass an opinion beyond saying that practice in the United States suggests that some kind of workable plan is possible. In these and allied matters, we feel certain that if Australian librarians and university teachers are given the necessary resources, their realization of the urgency of the problem and the seriousness of the issues involved will enable them to evolve workable solutions to even the most complex situations.

In 1956 a further improvement in organization was made towards the comprehensive survey and recording of Australian library resources as a basis for intelligent policies for developing further strength and remedying known weaknesses. This was the establishment of the Australian Advisory Council on Bibliographical Services and of the Australian Bibliographical Centre, within the Commonwealth National Library, with a present full-time staff of four. The Council itself is composed of representatives of the Commonwealth National Library, state libraries and library boards, the universities, the Commonwealth Scientific and Industrial Research Organization, and the Library Association of Australia. Its functions include planning and recommending to appropriate authorities measures for the better co-ordination and the further development of Australian bibliographical services. It has completed, and will shortly publish, a survey of Australian bibliography and bibliographical services, and a union list of newspapers in Australian libraries. These will supplement existing union catalogues, such as the Commonwealth National Library's *Union List of Serials in the Humanities and Social Sciences*. After preliminary inquiry, the Council is actively examining the need for, and the possibility of, compiling a national union catalogue of current monograph accessions. An outline survey of the library resources and types of holdings of major libraries is to be completed within the next year, along with a plan for a wider survey. Meanwhile several *ad hoc* surveys are in progress to meet immediate needs. In all their work the Council and Centre co-operate with other interested institutions and agencies to assist co-ordination and ensure the efficient and economical control of bibliographical information.

Staffing

It is apparent to all who use Australian academic libraries that university authorities have been as parsimonious in their provision of staff as they have in their allocation of funds for accommodation and purchase of books. It seems to us almost miraculous that such a high standard of service is provided with such inadequate staffing and that such a standard exists is a notable tribute to the devotion, skill and unremitting effort of our library staffs. It is rare to find any adequate provision of senior staff and most universities appear to proceed on the assumption that highly specialized and complex organizations, such as university libraries have become, may reasonably be expected to function with a handful of senior staff and a large number of junior assistants amongst whom there is only exceptionally much continuity of service. Here, as elsewhere, there is a marked contrast between our policies and those of enlightened overseas libraries. There are, it is true, hopeful signs of improvement both in staffing and in facilities for the training of staff, but much remains to be done, and it seems clear that only when our present overworked and frequently underpaid staffs are given substantially improved conditions and significant relief, can we hope to progress beyond our present stage. This we should regard as a matter of urgency.

Staff Training

In the early days the supervision of an Australian university library was frequently added to the duties of a professor or the registrar. With the growth of the libraries and the development of standard technical processes the need for full-time and trained librarians was recognized, but even as late as 1935 the Munn-Pitt Report stated that Australian universities had not yet accepted the idea that a librarian should be a man "with both general scholarship and expert knowledge of bibliographial processes and research, and should take a leading place on the professorial board and in the life of the university". The report went on to say that university library staffs were small and poorly paid and that they were recruited largely from boys and girls who, starting as cadets, were trained in the libraries, sometimes earning degrees.

In 1937 the Library Association of Australia was founded under the title of the Australian Institute of Librarians, and in 1944 held its first examinations under the Board of Examination and Certification. The minimum requirement for admission to the preliminary examination is matriculation; the preliminary certificate is the prerequisite for the registration examination taken after two years, and after a further two years the candidate, if possessing a university degree, can sit for the association's diploma which is secured by examination and thesis. Although the association conducts examinations at these three levels it does not prepare the candidates. There are, however, library schools attached to the National Library in Canberra and the public libraries of New South Wales and Victoria. Training classes are conducted by the public libraries in several other states, while the association itself has proposed the establishment of library schools within the universities.

As university librarianship requires a blend of academic, technical and administrative qualifications, opinions vary as to training, even in the United States where thirty-four accredited library schools are attached to institutions of higher learning, and require degrees as qualifications for admission. There is no unanimity about the best qualifications for university librarianship. Nevertheless all authorities would agree with the statement of the University Grants Committee that no qualifications can be too high, and it is a tragedy when they are too low. We strongly support the efforts of the association to improve professional standards, but point out that it rests with the universities to offer adequate salaries and status to those who have qualified. Books are essential to a library, but unless that library is in the hands of a trained, adequate and enthusiastic staff, it cannot play its essential part in stimulating the work of the university.

Archives

Essential to research on Australian topics are the National and State Archives, a system which originated in part from the pioneering work of Professor G.C. Henderson, Professor of History in the University of Adelaide. Under the Australian system the archives are in most cases managed by the Commonwealth and state public libraries and housed in buildings under their supervision. The National Library at Canberra and the Mitchell Library in Sydney already contain famous collections both of documents sent in by government departments for preservation and of private papers, and other states are pursuing the same aims. While there are at present conflicting views as to whether or not librarians rather than specially trained archivists should control archives, and a committee set up by the Prime Minister has just recommended the separating of the National Library and Archives, the fact remains that the assistance given by the various archives to research scholars has already proved incalculable and that, for the future, the question of their accessibility and management is central to the problems of research within the universities.

Conclusion

This study by the Humanities Research Council seems to lead to somewhat the same conclusions as those of the McColvin Report. Comparatively speaking, the university libraries form one of the stronger links in the weak but improving Australian library system but, in general, they seem notably inferior to academic libraries in the United States, and they have not yet reached Canadian standards in size and facilities. Much the same can be said of the humanities sections of these libraries as these are, in most subjects, inferior when judged by reasonable academic standards. It is also clear that the needs of the vitally important collections of books and periodicals will continue in competition with essentials such as accommodation and salaries, unless there is a stronger and wider appreciation of the importance of these libraries, both for the humanities and the sciences. This is a grave matter for, although most of the librarians consider that they can, with some difficulty, meet the demands of the undergraduates, the provision for staff requirements is in many cases weak and that for research, in most libraries and subjects, hopelessly inadequate. The two outstanding needs are increased assistance from the university councils and senates, that is directly or indirectly, from the Federal Government, and for closer co-operation between the universities themselves, so that, while each library provides the general collections required for teaching and undergraduate reference, it also builds up for advanced research special sections of material which will be available to scholars throughout the Commonwealth.

It is, perhaps, appropriate to close this chapter on Australian university libraries with a few words from the reports of that experienced and successful body—the British University Grants Committee. That Committee states that some years ago the inadequacy of many of the British university libraries was "grave and glaring", and adds that although great advances have been made, "we are by no means satisfied that the true status of the library in a university is really appreciated. Many university institutions have still to give evidence of being conscious that their quality and standing as instruments for the advancement of learning may to a great extent be gauged by their libraries, and by the policy pursued for the maintenance and development of them."

If this was the considered judgment passed on the British universities by so responsible a body as the Grants Committee, we can only speculate on what would have been their verdict on Australian universities whose meagre resources compare so poorly with those of many countries overseas and with those of some of the state libraries in our own country.

APPENDIX A

Statistics are available in Australia for a comparison of the number of volumes in the university libraries of Australia (1956) with those of British universities (1957), United States libraries (1956) and Canadian libraries (1955):

Title of institution	Country	Number of volumes
Harvard University	U.S.	6,085,761
Yale University	U.S.	4,073,946
University of California	U.S.	3,302,529
Oxford University	G.B.	2,104,000
Cambridge University	G.B.	over 2,000,000
University of Chicago	U.S.	1,925,754
Princeton University	U.S.	1,407,179
University of Texas	U.S.	1,166,295
Trinity College, Dublin	Eire	800,000
McGill University	Canada	751,260
Edinburgh University	G.B.	700,000
Manchester University	G.B.	650,000
University of Toronto	Canada	606,560
Glasgow University	G.B.	455,000
University of Sydney	Australia	387,231
University of British Columbia	Canada	300,000
Queen's University	Canada	278,000
Laval University	Canada	275,201
University of Melbourne	Australia	225,183
Queen's University, Belfast	G.B.	225,000
Bristol University	G.B.	216,000
University of Adelaide	Australia	202,000
University of Alberta	Canada	157,250
University of Queensland	Australia	147,665
University of Western Australia	Australia	137,365
Reading University	G.B.	133,000
Australian National University	Australia	127,000
University of Tasmania	Australia	92,000
University of N.S.W.	Australia	51,285
University of New England	Australia	35,000
University of New Brunswick	Canada	30,000
Newcastle University College	Australia	24,460
Canberra University College	Australia	13,177

Average holding of 70 large U.S. universities 1953–4:   551,166 volumes
Average holding of 70 small U.S. universities 1953–4:   148,267 volumes

U.S. statistics are derived from *College and Research Libraries*, vol. 18, No. 1 (Jan. 1957); Canadian statistics from the *Commonwealth Universities Year Book*, 1956.

To these may be added, as a more or less random sample, the following table setting out the position in various U.S. and Canadian cities when the resources of the leading ancillary libraries are added to those of the university library:

K

(a)	(b)		(c)
University	University Library, Volumes	Total Volumes	Supplementary resources— National, State, Municipal, Parliamentary and Teachers' libraries
UNITED STATES			
Washington			
(Washington University)	650,000	7,877,002	Library of Congress
New York			
(Columbia)	2,164,652	4,449,192	New York Public Library
Chicago			
(University of Chicago)	1,925,754	1,993,604	Chicago Public Library
Cambridge, Mass.			
(Harvard)	6,085,761	1,714,910	Boston Public Library
Detroit (Wayne)	560,579	1,054,984	Detroit Public Library
CANADA			
Toronto			
(University of Toronto)	606,560	682,730	Toronto Public Library
		175,000	Ontario Parliamentary Library
Montreal (McGill)	751,260	143,600	Bibliothèque Saint-Sulpice
Ottawa (Ottawa University)	260,000	{ 196,126	Ottawa Public Library
		525,000	Parliamentary Library

Statistics derived from W. Kirkconnell and A.S.P. Woodhouse, *The Humanities in Canada*, Ottawa, 1947.

The Canadian Survey (p. 158) gives even larger figures than these for it notes that in various libraries the students have available 1,700,000 volumes in Toronto, 1,500,000 in Montreal and 1,400,000 in Ottawa. Nevertheless we should not care to press too closely the detailed implication of these figures. It is, however, fair to point out that no Australian university approached in 1956 the figure achieved by the average of seventy large U.S. universities in 1953; that in 1956 only Sydney, Melbourne and Adelaide had passed the size achieved in 1953 by the average of seventy small U.S. universities; that the library of the University of Sydney alone was comparable in size with those of McGill and Toronto, and that in Canada there were five university libraries larger than that of the University of Melbourne.

APPENDIX B

The following table sets out the total revenues of each Australian university in 1954 (other than revenues secured for special purposes); the percentage spent on the university libraries; and the expenditure of each library in books, periodicals, and binding, both in the humanities and in other sections.

Several librarians warned the Council against using these figures for comparative purposes, and such a warning is fully justified unless they are set against a very detailed knowledge of local conditions.

(a) (1954) University	(b) (1954) Total revenue	(c) (1954) Expenditure on libraries	(d) Per-cent-age	(e) (1956) Expenditure on books, periodicals & binding of humanities sections	(f) (1956) Similar expenditure on other sections	(g) (1956) Total books, periodicals & binding
	£	£		£	£	£
Sydney	1,664,898	53,026	3.2	no record		33,234
Melbourne	1,414,940	54,317	3.8	10,140	20,994	31,134
University of N.S.W.	1,122,063	39,580	3.5	records not comparable		
Queensland	794,576	37,184	4.6	4277	19,375	23,652
A.N.U.	763,704	40,857	5.3	records not comparable but recent expansion great		
Adelaide	722,761	39,852	5.5	5735	9975	15,710
Western Australia	504,378	23,725	4.7	1861	9939	11,800
New England	263,775	8465	3.2	records not comparable but recent expansion great		
Tasmania 1955-6	245,046	17,420	7.1	895	4850	5745 *Books only*
Canberra University College	73,288	9273	12.8	records not comparable		
	7,569,429	323,702	4.3	—	—	—

Compiled from information supplied by university librarians and from *University Statistics*, Commonwealth Bureau of Census and Statistics, Canberra, 1954.

CHAPTER VI

University Research

CONTRIBUTED BY H.A.K. HUNT IN COLLABORATION WITH THE CONTRIBUTORS
OF THE SEVERAL SECTIONS

THE RIGHT SPIRIT OF APPROACH TO RESEARCH IN THE HUMANITIES is joy and enthusiasm, aided by imagination and inventiveness. Now there are certainly material difficulties in the universities which impede that sort of approach, and a man must be fresh rather than jaded, with days enlightened by intervals of freedom and not overcast by details, if he is ever to achieve the mood for resourcefulness and originality. Towards the end of this chapter we shall mention some of these difficulties and discuss also the possibility of overcoming them. But we shall start by surveying what research has been done and is going on in the several humanities. It may be an encouragement to see in this way that in the past our colleagues have made original contributions to learning while at present a great number of projects are being tackled with vigour and enthusiasm.

The scholar in the humanities in Australia has several tasks which, if not peculiar to him, demand special attention. He must maintain his grasp of an intellectual inheritance whose main centres of learning are remote, in lands which he can visit only at long intervals. He must detect the relevance of this inheritance to the life of a nation which cannot continue in the Pacific as an isolated piece of Europe; which means that an increasing number of scholars must start to find out about the languages and civilization of our neighbours. And he must stimulate enthusiasm for scholarship in a community whose predominant interests are immediately practical and where the spirit of improvisation, so necessary for coping with material problems in a new land, is matched in education by the ambition merely to "qualify" rather than to lay the foundations of broad scholarship.

Research is what will help the scholar in his tasks. It will help him to win respect by his accomplishments, to preserve his keenness for his subject —to keep his mind lively and his influence vital. The broad conception of research we can describe: it is to explore things thoroughly and for oneself, and it is the essential function of a university and an essential activity of university teachers. But about its processes it is not easy to generalize for they differ in different subjects. In some, such as some forms of historical investigation, the systematic survey and arrangement of material, which is familiar in scientific method, may be in evidence. In literature it is very much a matter of wide reading and study of meaning, development of individual taste and of powers of criticism. For long periods a philosopher, when he has read the relevant books, may need no apparatus except his own mind. What is needed is the opportunity to examine things thoroughly by studying the material wherever it may be and by discussing it with other scholars working in the same field. All this requires time free for independent thinking, travel to meet colleagues, to see the places and study the material, facilities for offering one's theories for criticism in the periodicals and for publishing them in books when they have crystallized—books and again more books.

So much for the importance of research in the humanities, its varied nature, its needs. The particular purpose of this chapter is to describe in a general way what has been done and what is going on in the various disciplines and to consider tasks that are waiting to be tackled. It is not possible to attempt more than a general sketch, for a detailed account of what has been written even in one of the sections, for example history, would absorb the whole space available for this Survey. Accordingly in the account of past work we do not attempt to do more than pick out examples in order to show the sort of research that has been found possible in Australia. Similarly we must confine ourselves to the work of university men except where a broad acknowledgment of research done outside the universities is necessary to put things in perspective, as in English and history where a lot of scholarly studies have naturally been made by non-university men, or in art history, because of the recency of the establishment of its first university department. Moreover in certain subjects we have had to limit the scope of our interest. Thus historical investigation extends beyond the humanities as they are generally understood. Accordingly we omit mention of important work in such fields as legal and constitutional history and economic history of a technical kind which lie within the province of our sister body, the Social Science Research Council. Anthropology too we have felt to be beyond our project except those parts of it which deal with primitive art. Again there are writers on education whose interests are certainly humane but we have felt that information about research in education is adequately presented by the Australian Council for Educational Research.

Research grows out of good teaching. A full account of the development of research in each discipline would show the sort of teaching attempted at first, the standard of scholarship it produced and the stage at which the men trained in it began to write for themselves. For reasons of space again we are not able to attempt so detailed a survey, but here and there in this chapter we make mention of the teaching to explain some critical effect of its impact on the growth of research.

At the present moment we stand at the end of a phase of great development in teaching methods in some of the universities: it is not too much to describe what has occurred in the last twenty years as a revolution. It has created in the students of the humanities a general sense of the importance of research and of its methods which a generation ago in Australia was but dimly perceived. Opportunities for the young graduate have improved tremendously. Teaching staffs have grown. There are many more research projects on hand than there were before the war. Of course we face a rising tide of students which may create a challenge to their continuance. But the interest in scholarship is there. It may have the strength to stand above the flood and it will certainly inspire and strengthen the determination to meet the task.

CLASSICAL STUDIES AND ARCHAEOLOGY
BY H.A.K. HUNT

When the older Australian universities were founded Classical Studies, being then pre-eminent in Europe, were among the first to be established. It was the great period of textual criticism. There was some doubt whether this would be possible in places so remote from the main centres and when Charles Badham accepted his chair in Sydney in 1886 keen regret was expressed in England at the probable loss to active scholarship of a man regarded as one of the most brilliant textual critics. But in Badham's Australian Postscript to his second edition of the *Philebus* published after twelve years in the chair we find this tribute to his working conditions: "And this edition of one of the most interesting dialogues of Plato is a specimen of the manner in which a great part of my leisure time has been occupied for many years and as I owe this leisure (by which I mean not only spare time, but health and comparative freedom from care) to the position which I have had the honour to fill in this Colony, a very natural feeling has prompted me to add a few pages more immediately addressed to Australian scholars, in order to show that I am not . . . insensible of my obligation to this land which has enabled me to dedicate myself to my favourite pursuit."

Badham's example was followed. The editions of several of the plays of Aeschylus brought out by T.G. Tucker of Melbourne early in this century were considered by the reviewers "to represent Cambridge scholarship at its very best" and he gave us too a splendid edition of the first book of Plato's *Republic* (1900). G.P. Shipp's edition of Terence's *Andria* (1938) is the main one for university classes and J.E. Powell, who joined the armed forces after occupying the Chair of Greek at Sydney for the year 1938, published on Herodotus in 1939 and would undoubtedly have produced a lot more at Sydney had he remained there.

Of course the man who edits texts in Australia faces difficulties. Only at long intervals can he see the manuscripts or talk with colleagues in Britain and Europe. Most of the printing, especially of Greek, has to be done abroad and here Badham's Postscript touches on a problem: "Had it been possible I should have made Sydney the place of publication and the book would have been the gainer—for I have never seen any of the sheets as they went through the press, until it was too late to introduce any improvements. Yet it is precisely at that period, when the general drudgery is over and you are at leisure to fix your attention upon particular points that the happiest observations suggest themselves. It is also at that time, when an author knows that this opportunity for revision is his very last, that he is unusually quick in detecting his own inadvertence or in checking his own precipitation."

However the air mail now mitigates this sort of handicap, and photostats and microfilms assist the study of manuscripts. Thus A.H. McDonald when in the chair of Ancient History at Sydney carried on his work on the text of Livy which he is now continuing at Cambridge, while several other men have work in progress. At Sydney A.J. Dunston is working on the manuscripts of the *Punica* of Silius Italicus and A.P. Treweek is almost ready with an edition of the *Collectio* of Pappus of Alexandria. In general it may be said of textual criticism and editing that there has been a moderate output and that with the diminution of material difficulties there are improved opportunities, so that for texts which still need editing a scholar may make himself an authority as well in Australia as elsewhere.

Aided by the increase in the size and number of classical departments, which has been quite striking in the last ten years, and in keeping with contemporary trends, research has been moving more to problems of literary criticism and historical re-interpretation. Here there are precedents of successful publication in Woodhouse's *Composition of Homer's Odyssey* and his books on King Agis and Solon which attracted attention in the 1930s. Tucker again, who was the most prolific writer we have had in classics, brought out a number of short works on literature; e.g., his *Judgment and Appreciation of Literature* (1925) and two detailed studies of life in Athens and the Roman world. F.A. Todd of Sydney, who made a mark towards the end of his career with articles on the wall-inscriptions of Pompeii, wrote a discerning study of early fiction in his *Some Ancient Novels* (1940). More recent works of literary criticism are the books on Virgil and Sophocles by F.J.H. Letters of New England, who is also making a study

of Roman satire. Among those who have literary studies well advanced
are G.H. Gellie, who has worked for some time in Melbourne on Greek
drama, and K.F. Quinn of the same university who is offering a fresh
interpretation of Roman personal poetry. At Sydney J.J. Nicholls is working on the *Poetica* of Aristotle and the later development of Greek aesthetic
theories, while J.H. Quincey has special interests in Menippean satire,
Seneca and Pindar, and W. Ritchie is examining the authenticity of the
Rhesus of Euripides.

Historical study received a great impulse by the presence in Sydney
together in the 1940s of A.H. McDonald and R.E. Smith who have both
gone on to important posts in classics in England. Here the main evidence
of activity is in articles rather than books. The lack of an Australian classical
journal is a handicap which is overcome in part by the generosity of the
British and American journals in giving space. As in literature there is a
great diversity of interests. J.J. Nicholls has published on the Roman
assemblies and R.StC. Johnson of Melbourne on classical education and
rhetoric. A. French of Adelaide has published several articles on Greek
history and economics. H.A.K. Hunt of Melbourne has produced articles on
population problems and this may be the place to mention his book *The
Humanism of Cicero* (1954) which fills a gap in the history of philosophy by
linking the Stoicism of the Roman Republic with the post-Aristotelian
schools. Among historical studies in progress there are topics as diverse as
the Athenian constitutional development, the historiography of Attica and
the Roman tribunate.

The distance of Australia from the classical lands is a handicap in
historical study in that it is hard to get a clear view without knowing the
terrain. Hence the need of sabbatical leave and travel. There is perhaps one
slight advantage: the vegetation and agricultural life in some parts of
Australia are fairly close to Mediterranean conditions. Hence in the field of
ecological and economic history lies the possibility of a commonsense view of
society and the rural economy which may be more difficult to achieve in
the typical British or European background.

Of necessity there has been a good deal of writing on the justification
of classical studies and on means of making them interesting and adapting
the teaching to changing conditions. This was a topic which engaged the
pen of Tucker; e.g., his *Foreign Debt of English Literature* (1907), and similarly
Leeper wrote a *Plea for the Study of Classics* (1912). More recently C.G.
Cooper of Queensland has produced a number of articles on the value of
classical studies while H.A.K. Hunt's *Training through Latin* (1948) is an accepted text-book in teacher training. Notable work has been done in
several universities in devising courses for starting Greek at the university
for students deprived of the opportunity to study it at school, particularly

by A.P. Treweek at Sydney, M.N. Austin in Western Australia, and the classical staff at Melbourne.

The interest in philology which was predominant in the great days of textual criticism has persisted. Early in the century Tucker followed up his highly-regarded editions of Aeschylus by venturing on some original suggestions on the development of language in his *Introduction to the Natural History of Language* (1902). His successor in the Chair of Classical Philology, C.A. Scutt, though he did not publish while at Melbourne, maintained a strong philological interest among his students. In Sydney at present G.P. Shipp has established himself as our leading philologist by his studies in the language of Homer and other studies in phonology in which his interests are shared by A.P. Treweek and J.H. Quincey. In the same general area of scholarship fall K.C. Masterman's *The Power of Speech* and C.G. Cooper's *Introduction to the Latin Hexameter*.

The fine collection in the Nicholson Museum developed by W.J. Woodhouse and expanded by A.D. Trendall and J.R. Stewart gives Sydney special advantages for the study of the art and archaeology of the classical lands and of the ancient Near East, whence it has had recent acquisitions from the work of J.R. Stewart on Cyprus, noted below. Around this museum and Stewart's establishment at Bathurst, which serves as headquarters for the Cyprus expedition, could be built a training centre for all Australia in archaeological methods.

Writing by A.D. Trendall and by J.R. and Dorothy E. Stewart makes archaeology one of our most prolific branches of study at present. Trendall, well known before he came to the chair at Sydney for his books on Paestan and early Italiote vases, has recently made a major contribution in his publication of the South Italian red-figured vases in the Vatican collection. He has to his credit a considerable number of articles in learned journals, and is so closely in touch with current developments that he edits the Archaeological Reports on Sicily and Magna Graecia for the British Society for the Promotion of Hellenic Studies.

J.R. Stewart directed an expedition in Cyprus in 1955, sponsored by the University of Melbourne, which examined early Bronze Age sites at Vasilia and Ayia Paraskevi. Another expedition, sponsored jointly by the Ashmolean Museum at Oxford and the Department of Archaeology at Sydney, excavated at Pighades and Stephania in Cyprus in 1951. While full publication of material is prevented by reasons of finance, a summary of the Stephania material prepared by P. Åström of Lund (Sweden) under Stewart's supervision will appear in the Final Report of the Swedish Cyprus Expedition and has already been published as a doctoral thesis. The Melbourne Cyprus Expedition has already produced *The Coinage of Tiberius in Cyprus* by Michael Grant formerly of Edinburgh and an article by Aström on a fourth century tomb group is ready for publication. As an offshoot of Stewart's research on ancient Cyprus may be mentioned here an extensive work on the Lusignan coinage of medieval Cyprus still in manuscript but about to be used in part in a chapter of the Pennsylvanian History of the Crusades.

During Trendall's tenure of the chair Sydney was a strong centre of study and research in the art of the ancient Near East, Greece and Rome. Since his move to Canberra some reorganization has become necessary for the continuance of a branch of teaching which is essential for developing scholarship capable of research in classical art and Western art as a whole.

ENGLISH

BY I.R. MAXWELL

It was in 1911 that R.S. (now Sir Robert) Wallace came to Melbourne to occupy the first independent Australian Chair of English Language and Literature. At that time Sydney still had its Chair of Modern Languages (French, German, and English) on much the same pattern as had obtained in Melbourne from 1882 to 1902; and in Adelaide English Language was linked, not as it once had been with Mental and Moral Philosophy, but with Modern History. The creation of separate departments of English was a good as well as an inevitable thing, but no doubt something has been lost as well as gained by it. Sir Mungo MacCallum worked in Sydney with a small but highly gifted group of colleagues in an atmosphere of comparative literature; in Melbourne Walter Murdoch, who was later to be the first professor of English in Western Australia, took charge of English studies from 1902-11 with the co-operation of a distinguished professor of Classical and Comparative Philology, T.G. Tucker. Such connections are favourable to a broad and humane culture, and we are now uneasily aware that some links have been broken that should be forged anew.

It will be convenient to begin by sketching the work of our English departments under the heads of Language and Literature.

The fortunes of Language have been various. In Melbourne two holders of the general Chair of English, Sir Robert Wallace and Professor G.H. Cowling, were specialists in it; and in Sydney, from the time when an independent department was first established, there has been a Chair of Language as well as one of Literature. In Queensland, Language was strongly developed during the tenure of the Chair of English by G.H. Russell; and in Tasmania the study of modern structural linguistics has a representative of some standing in F.W. Harwood, whose work on the structural patterns of English using mathematical techniques has attracted the attention of distinguished linguists in America. In Adelaide, on the other hand, Language has never been taken seriously; and in Western Australia it has lapsed with the death of H.S. Thompson, though W.A. Edwards has persistently advocated the establishment of a Language chair.

The earliest research work on the Australian vocabulary is embodied in E.M. Morris's dictionary *Austral English* (1898). Sir Mungo MacCallum contributed a section to Funk and Wagnall's *New Standard Dictionary* (1913), and E.R. Holme to the *Merriam Webster Dictionary* (1935). Holme's work is the latest to be published on this subject, but research is being carried on in the English Department of the University of Sydney where the archives are being assembled for a dictionary of Australian English. The most important non-academic contributions to the subject in recent times have been S.J. Baker's *The Australian Language* and *Australia Speaks*.

The first publication on Australian pronunciation was Ruby Board's *Australian Pronunciation* (Australian English Association Pamphlet, No. 4). Investigation was carried further and the subject was presented in the light of modern scholarship by A.G. Mitchell in *The Pronunciation of English in Australia* (1946). Later, Mitchell wrote a general book on phonetics, *Spoken English* (1957), designed for Australian students and taking as its basis the educated speech of Australia. Other Australian scholars are now working on Australian pronunciation, in particular Elizabeth Liggins of the University of New England (who has done some valuable work on Old English syntax), A. Delbridge of the University of Sydney, and G.R. Cochrane of the University of Queensland.

The study of the older literature of England, and of the related literature of Scandinavia, is being carried on mainly in the University of Sydney and at Canberra University College, where G.K.W. Johnston is using new manuscript materials to prepare a text of *Hávarðar saga Isferðings*. A.G. Mitchell and G.H. Russell of Sydney are preparing a critical edition of the C-text of *Piers Plowman* and a general critical work on the poem. Mitchell recently published *Lady Meed and the Art of Piers Plowman* which had been delivered as the third Chambers Memorial Lecture. Russell is working on the aesthetic and conceptual traditions of Middle English religious literature and on the transmission of the classical heritage through Middle English vernacular literature. In Melbourne Icelandic studies have been eagerly pursued for the last few years but have not yet led to publication.

In Literature we may point to some works by authors no longer living that have given standing to English studies and shown that it is possible to do valuable and substantial work at the far end of the earth. Sir Mungo MacCallum's *Shakespeare's Roman Plays* is still the chief authority on its subject; T.G. Tucker's edition of Shakespeare's Sonnets was long the standard one; Sir Archibald T. Strong's *Short History of English Literature* is a manual of critical quality: A.J.A. Waldock's books

on Shakespeare, Milton, and Sophocles are of high recent repute. Alfred
Hart's important work on Shakespeare's quartos represents fruitful research
not emanating from a university.

To pass to the present state of affairs: some Australian universities tend,
by tradition or policy, to concentrate on certain fields. Thus Sydney is
especially strong in Elizabethan and seventeenth century studies, whereas
Adelaide now tends to favour the nineteenth and twentieth centuries,
and since 1951 this policy has influenced its book buying. In Melbourne,
on the other hand, there is no specially favoured period among members
of staff, and students are encouraged to study what interests them most.
In Western Australia there has been a strong and continuing interest in
the study of drama, but on the whole the tendency has been towards
practical criticism and original work rather than scholarship of the more
conventional sort. In the University of New England, which has only
recently become independent and has an opportunity of working with
comparatively small classes, the policy is to favour topics which span two
literatures or relate literature to the history of ideas or the life of society.

Our best opportunities for research are obviously in Australian or in
comparatively recent English and American literature. Our libraries,
especially the Mitchell Library in Sydney, are the best for Australian subjects; and the research worker will have the background of local life in
addition to the local records. In nineteenth and twentieth century English
and American literature we may hope to gather the necessary materials,
whereas we are never likely to rival older libraries in earlier periods.
Microfilms, however, will help to fill the gaps; and it would be most undesirable to limit the interests of research workers to a few fields in which
special opportunities exist. The aim of all literary study should be to enrich
our knowledge of great literature.

Australian studies are in good health. Morris Miller's Bibliography has
now been revised by F.T. Macartney; and the former librarian of the
Fisher Library (Sydney), H.M. Green, is now publishing the first large-
scale history of Australian literature to appear in this century. In addition
to these essential works of reference, there is a growing body of critical
and historical work. Many articles and some books—for example, the
critical work of F.T. Macartney and Nettie Palmer, or Vance Palmer's
recent *The Legend of the Nineties*—come from outside the universities.
Our main academic specialists at present are Brian Elliott (Adelaide) and
T. Inglis Moore (Canberra University College). A.R. Chisholm (Melbourne)
and the late J.J. Quinn have brought to the verge of publication a definitive edition of the works of Christopher Brennan. The published critical
work of R.G. Howarth (late of Sydney) and A.D. Hope (Canberra University College), H.J. Oliver and G.A. Wilkes (Sydney), C.H. Hadgraft

(Queensland), and Vincent Buckley (Melbourne) illustrate the interest taken in Australian letters over the last few years; and in many Australian universities members of staff are working on Australian themes. G.A. Wilkes is preparing a full study of Brennan's poetry, a subject on which he has already published substantial articles.

The literature of the sixteenth and seventeenth centuries is receiving more attention in Sydney than elsewhere in Australia. W. Milgate is working on his edition of Donne's Satires, Epigrams, and Verse Epistles; and H.J. Oliver has edited *Timon of Athens* for the New Arden Shakespeare and writing a book on the life and work of Robert Howard. His book on Ford has recently been published. G.A. Wilkes is preparing a study of the poetry of meditation about 1600 in addition to studies of Fulke Greville and Thelma Herring and K.G.W. Cross are working on Jacobean drama and seventeenth century drama respectively. In Melbourne, S.L. Goldberg has recently published articles on Sir John Hayward and seventeenth century historiography, and is working on sixteenth and seventeenth century poetry; T.B. Tomlinson is writing a critical study of Jacobean drama. In the University of New England, C.H. O'Brien is writing a book on the rogue literature of the seventeenth century. In the University of Western Australia, David Bradley is working on music in Jacobean drama, and Philip Parsons on the Baroque theatre.

The eighteenth century attracts little research attention, though W.A.G. Scott (Melbourne) is working on this period, especially its fiction, and L. Burrows (Western Australia) is preparing a critical edition of Edward Young's satires. The nineteenth century is somewhat better represented. F.M. Todd (Tasmania) has published articles on the early Romantics, and lately a book on Wordsworth, *Politics and the Poet;* H.W. Piper (New England) is studying the history of ideas in the English Romantic period; G.A. Wilkes (Sydney) is writing on Meredith. The work of S.L. Goldberg (Melbourne) on James Joyce and of E.H. Flint (Queensland) on some aspects of modern verse drama represents the modern period. It is interesting to observe, within the field of modern literature, a tendency to fasten on Australian themes. The question whether "Aust. Lit." should grow up in an overcrowded English course may soon become a pressing one. Only in Canberra University College where it is directed by T. Inglis Moore has it the status of an independent subject, although in Melbourne it will be an optional subject in the honours course in 1959.

This summary would give an imperfect view of academic interests in literature. It happens, for example, that at the moment no specific research work is being done in our departments of English on American literature; but there is much interest in the subject both in Sydney and Melbourne where Kathleen Fitzpatrick (Department of History) has completed a critical study of Henry James. There are, moreover, certain types of work that are easily passed over in a survey of this kind. In Western Australia Alec King's *Writing*—to mention his latest book—fits neither of our conventional Language and Literature categories and is perhaps not "research" in the usual sense of that word. It is, however, an original contribution to a very important subject.

In the circumstances, perhaps, this record is not a bad one. In most Australian universities the obstacles to research are formidable. English departments are large; teachers meet classes ranging from two or three to as many as five hundred[1] and examine droves of undergraduates and legions of matriculation candidates. In most universities the average weekly number of teaching periods for one member of staff is about eight or nine. This might not be excessive if one were teaching one's own special subject to small groups of co-operative students, but in fact most of them have to do a great deal of general teaching. To pass in one day from *Islendingabók* to *Paradise Lost*, from T.S. Eliot to Chretien de Troyes, demands much time if one is to speak with any intimacy and not simply read last year's lecture; and, though the example given is extreme, there is much to be said for range and variety, whatever the cost may be.

Teachers share with students certain inevitable limitations. Despite the beginning made by the Elizabethan Theatre Trust, they can seldom see the classics of the theatre adequately presented. Good music is popular among educated Australians, and concerts can be supplemented by records; but in painting, sculpture, and architecture—despite the notable acquisitions of, for example, the Felton Bequest in Melbourne—Australians have comparatively poor opportunities for familiarity with the masterpieces of the past. It is these limitations, as well as those of our libraries, that make experience abroad so important for members of staff and post-graduate students. In one sense there is no reason why a Ph.D. student, working on an Australian subject, should not begin and end his inquiries here; but most of us would feel that there were strong objections to awarding the degree to a candidate of purely local experience. In Sydney the policy is to insist that candidates should spend a year abroad; in Melbourne, that they should take the degree abroad, if they take it at all.

The last half-dozen words may indicate a certain misgiving, shared by not a few university men, about our present obsession with publication and higher degrees, and in general with a type of research which is modelled perhaps too closely on the sciences. Research in some sense is of course essential, and a university that has become a mere teaching institution has

---

[1] e.g., 1100 undergraduates study English at the University of Melbourne; 11,000 candidates present English at the leaving certificate examination in New South Wales.

ceased to be a university—or even an efficient school. On the other hand, the exhaustion of a special subject is not necessarily more profitable for academics than the selective inquiry that good teaching requires; and certainly the practice of thesis writing has its dangers for literary studies. The thorough combing-over of a limited "field" to the examiner's satisfaction is not always the best way of encouraging gifted graduates to write for the delight and instruction of intelligent readers. It would perhaps be generally agreed that this delight and instruction should be the object of books that comment on literature, though not of course of all valuable works of scholarship, and that, if the doctoral thesis is to be the literary pilgrim's only wicket-gate, he may find the way to the Celestial City somewhat roundabout.

MODERN EUROPEAN LANGUAGES
BY R.H. SAMUEL

The late founding of independent departments postponed the development of research in modern languages, their teaching in most universities being for a long time a mere appendage of the English departments.

There was some growth of independent teaching early in the century, but the decisive change came when G.G. Nicholson, a Sydney and Oxford graduate in both Modern Languages and Law, was appointed Assistant Professor of French and German in Sydney in 1913, having already been a lecturer there for some years. After making a name for himself in Britain and Europe with his *Introduction to French Phonetics*, he now introduced into Australia strict discipline in language teaching and exacting philological methods. The Nicholson school has come in for some criticism in recent years because it did not perhaps give adequate attention to French life and letters, the literary and social development of France and French culture generally. But its stress on a high standard of spoken French, on stylistic grace and above all exact linguistic knowledge based on historical study was particularly valuable for those who were unable to visit France. He was certainly instrumental in starting modern language studies in Australia. Nicholson trained whole generations of scholars, many of whom have ably filled teaching posts in Australian and overseas universities.

In 1921, the year in which his *Recherches philologiques romanes* appeared in Paris and made his work known among Romance scholars all over the world, Nicholson was appointed Professor of French in the University of Sydney. In the same year, Nicholson's pupil, A.R. Chisholm was appointed Lecturer in French in Melbourne where, without departing from Nicholson standards, he developed a school not only noted for literary research but also as a training ground for future university teachers. In Melbourne also, Augustin Lodewyckx, a first-class philologist in all the Germanic languages, starting as lecturer in 1915, subsequently as associate professor directed for over thirty years Germanic studies with the same scholarly precision as had characterized Nicholson's teaching and research. Thus in the early 1920s in Sydney and Melbourne there were strong influences for the development of scholarship in the modern languages. Nor can an account of this period be complete without acknowledgment of the influence in Sydney of C.J. Brennan who, while a brilliant student of language, was also distinguished by his critical studies of Romantic and Symbolist literature. Even so, the establishment of chairs was a slow and tardy process. Of the nine chairs in Australia only one was established before 1938 and four started in the present decade.

Australia has been slow in developing academic teaching in modern European languages other than French and German. There has been a fully developed pass and honours course in Dutch language and literature within the Department of Germanic Languages at Melbourne since 1943. Perth has taught Italian since 1927, Sydney since 1935, and Melbourne will start teaching it in 1959. Russian has grown in ten years to the status of a full honours school of Language and Literature at Melbourne; it has also recently been established at Canberra University College, and is planned for Sydney from 1961.

There is no doubt that more Russian, Italian and Dutch should be taught in Australian universities, and that attention also be given to the study of Ibero-Romance languages and literatures.

Because of the late establishment of independent teaching and because in the early phases such practical problems had to be solved as the development of adequate competence in the languages by pupils so remote from the countries concerned, the recruitment of skilled staffs and the development of honours courses—problems discussed more fully at the end of this chapter —it is only recently that an appreciable flow of research work has started. But among the ninety members of modern language staffs of the Australian universities (as compared with less than thirty in 1938) it would be hard to find anyone who has no research project on hand, while there are many who have already made significant contributions to learning.

Before Nicholson's work there were few publications of note, an exception being *Studies in Low and High German Literature* by Mungo MacCallum (Sydney) published as early as 1884. A.R. Chisholm's contributions to the interpretation of the French Symbolist movement are well known. Among his studies of Australian literature, which are mostly outside the scope of this chapter, his critical edition of Christopher Brennan's works, soon to be published, includes Brennan's long study of European

Symbolism which has never previously been published or evaluated. I.A. Henning of Sydney has written a remarkable study on the reception of Mme de Stael's work in Germany. L. Tauman of Perth has made a name for himself through his well received work on Marcel Proust and he has completed the first volume of a comprehensive work on *Le langage de l'art*. K.J. Goesch of Sydney has broken new ground in his biographical studies on Raymond Radiguet which he interspersed with unpublished material. Lodewyckx's research has not only embraced the Austrian writer Franz Grillparzer, Dutch linguistics and the history of the name of Australia, but he also wrote the standard work on the Germans in Australia, and published, in his eightieth year, a much discussed book entitled *People for Australia*.[1] R.B. Farrell of Sydney published an incisive study of Stefan Georges' relations to English literature; he has nearly completed a book on Mörike's poetry, and his *Dictionary of German Synonyms* has become a standard work since it appeared in 1953. L.A. Triebel of Tasmania and D. Van Abbé of Adelaide have shown by their researches into German and Swiss literature of the sixteenth century that even this comparatively remote field is well represented in Australia. Triebel's *Rasser of Alsace* is a painstaking work of minute scholarship, the harvest of decades of research. D. Van Abbé's forthcoming edition of Eckermann's *Gespräche mit Goethe* commissioned by he Deutsche Akademie der Wissenschaften promises to be the definitive work on this example of "truth and imagination". Under Triebel's direction there has been a study of documents relating to the French exploration of Australia and with Jean C. Batt he has recently published a volume which includes translations from the originals.

The novel as a form of art has attracted a number of scholars. R.T. Sussex, now in New Zealand, wrote on the origins of the novel while he was at Melbourne. Christine Morrow of Perth has developed the theme of the "irrealist" nature of the novel in French and English literature where it is set up as a mirror of the problems of particular historical periods. In Melbourne H. Wiemann has adopted a similar attitude in his study of the German novel of the decade 1945-55. K. Leopold of Brisbane has completed a penetrating study on the "first person" novel and E. Koch-Emmery of Canberra an inquiry into the style of Marcel Proust and Thomas Mann and how far it is reflected by their translators. R.H. Samuel of Melbourne has published on the German Romantic period, in particular on the poet and philosopher Friedrich von Hardenberg (Novalis), on the critical edition of whose complete works he has been engaged for some time. His second major field of interest is the Expressionist movement. In Dutch studies at Melbourne J. Smit is a leading authority on the literary critic

[1] cf. the bibliography of Lodewyckx's works in *AUMLA* No. 5, October 1956, pp. 67-70.

L

and poet, E.J. Potgieter, and R.P. Meijer has completed a study of the contemporary poet Gerrit Achterberg. A recent appointment has brought to the Russian staff at Melbourne R.G.A. de Bray, already well known for his comprehensive handbook on Slavonic Philology, while Canberra has in J.J. Gapanovich an historian of Russian affairs who has many publications to his credit.

The edition of texts and handbooks is a special field of scholarship which may involve more research than is realized. *Cinq Maitres du Conte Français* by J.G. Cornell (Adelaide) went into its 4th edition in 1956. Twelve French short stories appearing under the title *La France d'Hier et d'Aujourd'hui* edited by H. Burger and R.L. James (Melbourne) provide a guide to the "evolution in matter and technique of the French story", as A.R. Chisholm testifies in his foreword. Lodewyckx's *Handbook of Dutch* covered a wide range and has been followed by a new Dutch handbook edited by J. Smit and R.P. Meijer on different lines. E.K. Horwood and Anita Rodgers (Melbourne) wrote a German Course for Science students which has many novel features, and the Department of Languages in the Faculty of Science in Melbourne is preparing a text book in Russian for Science students. Triebel, in his *Crocodile* and Van Abbé in his edition of *Manuel's Ablasskrämer* have produced texts for advanced scholars. Samuel's editions of Goethe's "*Urfaust*" and Kleist's *Der zerbrochene Krug* and *Prinz Friedrich von Homburg* aim at assembling the material around these plays in a handy way to promote further study of these works and their authors.

There is much more work in progress than can be mentioned in a brief survey. To show its range a few examples must suffice. R.F. Jackson of Melbourne is engaged on an aesthetic analysis of Baudelaire's *Fleurs du Mal*, D. Scales of Canberra on the novels of Alphonse Karr, and K. Sinclair of Canberra on studies in Old French literature. The spread of interest is shown by a few names from the long list of authors on whom work is being prepared, such as Lessing, Diderot, Hölderlin, Herder and Ugo Foscolo. The forthcoming publication of a detailed consideration of Hugo von Hofmannsthal's later dramas and essays by B. Coghlan of Armidale will show that Australia has in him an expert in the interpretation of this writer who, apart from Rilke, is the most eminent of the modern Austrians.

Research into methods has made possible the development at Melbourne since 1949 of an effective method of teaching French, German and Russian to students of Science and Medicine which, while satisfying their material quest for a reading knowledge for scientific papers, also spreads the influence of the language schools in Arts by keeping in close touch with them. E.K. Horwood, who directs this work, has thus introduced a special humanities subject to students of Science.

In the present decade there has been a great extension in the range of post-graduate research in modern languages and literatures, and young workers for M.A. or Ph.D. have presented theses of high quality on a variety of authors and topics too wide to be mentioned in detail. The titles of these theses are to be found in the annual research reports of the universities.

PHILOSOPHY

BY J.A. PASSMORE

In the Australian universities, Philosophy is one of the more important subjects. In Sydney and Melbourne, in particular, first year undergraduate classes are very large: and in the later years the classes are much bigger than they would be in a comparable British university. Philosophy is as conspicuous in the newer, experimental Australian universities as it is in the older, traditional ones; thus it plays an important part in the School of Humanities at the University of New South Wales, and is one of the very few traditional Arts subjects taught at the Australian National University. The teacher of Philosophy, furthermore, very often includes amongst his students considerable groups of social and physical scientists.

The effect is that Philosophy colours a great deal of Australian intellectual life. Many of our leading jurisprudentialists, academic scientists, historians, literary critics and creative writers have had some contact—often a quite considerable contact—with Philosophy. (Although, perhaps naturally, this is less true of those Australian intellectuals, a growing number, whose eyes are fixed on the local scene than it is of those whose intellectual interests are predominantly European.) At the same time the teaching of such large and diversified undergraduate groups, to say nothing of the accompanying administrative responsibilities, absorbs most of the time and energy of Australian Philosophy teachers. Many of them are well known overseas for the quality of the students they send on to graduate courses, but their own work, for the most part, is of a somewhat insubstantial character.[1]

It is not suggested, however, that Australian philosophy is alive only as an undergraduate subject; if that were so, indeed, the Australian universities could scarcely turn out so many able graduates. The *Australasian*

[1] Passmore notes: "I am well aware that 'lack of time' is often used as an excuse by men who do not really wish to face the effort involved in continued scholarly work, or who have nothing to say, or who fear the shafts of critics. Perhaps I may be permitted to refer to my own case to illustrate the fact that the difficulty of finding time is, in Australia, a perfectly genuine excuse. In the fifteen years I spent as a lecturer at the University of Sydney I wrote nothing except a few articles and pamphlets; in five years as a quite busy Professor of Philosophy in New Zealand I completed a book and wrote the major part of another one, in addition to a number of articles. This comparison speaks for itself; the difference was that in New Zealand a staff of five coped with one hundred students, in Australia a staff of the same size had the responsibility for six times this number of students."

Journal of Philosophy is now in its thirty-fifth year; it has a longer history, that means, than any other Australian journal in the realm of humanities. Its reputation has steadily grown, and it is now widely regarded as one of the leading philosophical journals of the world. Regular conferences, for many years past an annual event, have long been a feature of philosophical life in Australia, whereas in other branches of the humanities they are still a novelty. In short, Australia has a vigorous philosophical life—but one that has not, during the last thirty years, issued in any large-scale contributions of world importance.

Articles in plenty there have been and the tide has risen in recent years. Quite apart from their contributions to the *Australasian Journal of Philosophy*, Australian writers have recently been prominent in all major philosophical journals; several of their contributions have been selected for republication, as articles of more than passing interest, in collected volumes of philosophical essays. Australian philosophers have written small books and pamphlets, too, for the general reader or for the undergraduate, but there have been in recent years no works comparable in magnitude with those produced by Sir William Mitchell—such as his *The Structure and Growth of Mind* (1907)—in the first decade of the present century, nor with the many contributions to scholarship which appeared up to the early nineteen-thirties (when the Australian universities experienced for the first time a great expansion in student numbers). Certainly no one writing in Australia has produced a work of the same order as the Australian-educated but British-resident Samuel Alexander's *Space, Time and Deity*.

In part, of course, what has happened in Australia reflects what has happened in Great Britain. This is not a period notable for its large metaphysical constructions, but rather for its essays on specific topics. At the same time, the contrast with New Zealand is striking. Between 1950 and 1956 no less than eight substantial books were published by New Zealand university philosophers; no comparable work was produced by a philosophy teacher in Australia.[2]

There is one special reason for the silence of Australian philosophers which deserves comment, a comment which will at the same time provide a background to the understanding of what has been happening to philosophy in Australia. During the earliest years of the century a Christian Idealist tradition was firmly implanted in Australia by such teachers as Sir William Mitchell, Sir Francis Anderson, W.R. Boyce Gibson; Australian philosophy departments were dominated by them and by their former students. The new trends in philosophy represented by men like Moore and Russell at Cambridge, Cook Wilson and Prichard at Oxford,

---

[2] The Bibliography may suggest otherwise, but only because D.H. Monro and J.A. Passmore have now taken up university posts in Australia; their books were published from New Zealand.

passed Australia by, although there was a considerable interest—finding expression in a number of books and articles—in such Continental philosophers as Bergson, Eucken, Hartmann and Husserl. Of course, the new movements in philosophy, which tended to be grouped together under the name of "realism", were in some measure discussed and criticized, but they had no outstanding representative in Australia until John Anderson arrived in 1927. He combined an original version of realism with revolutionary views about ethics, aesthetics, the State, and religion, which created a considerable stir. In the thirties the dispute between Anderson and his pupils on the one side and Idealist critics on the other was the main centre of interest in Australian philosophy, as is very apparent in the files of the *Australasian Journal of Philosophy* for those years. From 1938 onwards, however, the position was complicated by the intrusion of a new element; the ideas of Wittgenstein were brought to Australia by George Paul and D.A.T. Gasking and controversy began to take a different form.

The philosophical atmosphere in Great Britain, as we said, was no longer favourable to the construction of Idealist systems; this fact may have discouraged Idealists in Australia from publishing major works—although Mitchell's *The Place of Minds in the World* appeared as late as 1933. Anderson himself wrote little, and his pupils did not feel that they ought to write his books for him; Wittgenstein, too, was silent, and his admirers were affected in the same way. So the philosophical situation in general was discouraging to the production of major works. These considerations no longer apply with quite their old strength; and new men have come to Australia who stand outside the competing groups. It is no coincidence that there is now in so many quarters a greater willingness to write. The record of the ten years 1956-66 ought, unless university teachers are completely submerged by the new wave of undergraduates, to be very different from the record of the last twenty years. Perhaps one can risk a prediction in a number of different areas of philosophical activity.

In logic one can distinguish three main tendencies. Modern "symbolic" logic, never strongly represented in Australia, has come to the fore in recent philosophical congresses, and should shortly appear more prominently in the record of Australian publications. Already a number of articles have been published, mainly by Sydney philosophers, on the connection between recent and traditional logic. A Sydney lecturer, T.A. Rose, is writing a lengthy critical study on the rise of symbolic logic in the nineteenth century; and essays on logical themes are promised from I. Goddard of New England and C.F. Presley of Adelaide. There is a great deal of interest, too, in the Ryle-Wittgenstein "informal" logic; a considerable book, working out in detail a logic of that general type, is now being prepared by D.A.T. Gasking of Melbourne.

Philosophy of science is much cultivated in Australia; and it is of particular importance as the area within which misunderstandings between the humanities and science—physical and social—can most easily be resolved. At the moment great attention is being paid to the construction of undergraduate courses in the philosophy and methods of science; Australia's experiments in this field—especially at the University of Melbourne and the University of New South Wales—are being watched with interest overseas. Many articles on such topics as the nature of physical theories and the role of "imaginary entities" in physical science have appeared in the *Australasian Journal of Philosophy* and elsewhere. These are questions with which J.J.C. Smart of Adelaide, C.F. Presley of Adelaide, and J.B. Thornton of the University of New South Wales have particularly concerned themselves. At Canberra—both in the Canberra University College and at the National University—substantial work on the methodology of the social sciences is in progress. The philosophy of history, too, has recently attracted considerable attention in Australia; such themes as the nature of historical explanation and the degree to which history can achieve objectivity have been explored in a number of articles.

In aesthetics interest is perhaps less widespread. All the same, it probably plays a larger part in Australian philosophical life than it does in Great Britain. Once again, one has to point with regret to the absence of any large-scale contributions. But Anderson's pamphlet *Some Questions in Aesthetics* aroused a good deal of discussion in the thirties, and provoked a number of subsequent articles. There has been a continuous interest in aesthetics at the University of Melbourne where aesthetics is an honours course in Philosophy; and a more recent arrival in Australia, Denis Grey of the University of New England, has also contributed to aesthetic theory.

Ethics has been more extensively cultivated. Once again, Anderson's ethical views were widely discussed in the thirties; but they have never been systematically expressed, and in recent years interest has shifted rather to the exposition and criticism of recent Oxford ethical theory. Articles by D.W. Falk of Melbourne and K. Baier of Canberra University College have already aroused considerable interest in Australia and overseas, and Baier's views are more fully expounded in his recently published *The Moral Point of View*. Criticism has mainly come from D.H. Monro, of the University of Sydney. A.K. Stout of the University of Sydney, A.C. Fox of Western Australia and A. Boyce Gibson of Melbourne have concerned themselves, in their different ways, with the traditional problems of right and duty; J.J.C. Smart has been defending, and hopes to expound in detail, a version of utilitarianism; J. McCloskey of Melbourne has completed a considerable study in deontological ethics.

In the history of philosophy Australia began well with a number of works on Continental philosophy. Latterly—and this again reflects a British trend—there has been considerably less interest in historical studies. But, as in Great Britain, the wheel may be turning. In 1957 there appeared, from the National University, a lengthy study of British philosophy over the last hundred years; and a number of other works are ready for publication. At the University of Queensland there has been a continuous concern with the eighteenth century British moralists, to whom D.H. Monro and J.A. Passmore have also devoted some attention. There is a good deal of interest in Greek philosophy; but (apart from H.A.K. Hunt's treatment of the later Greeks in his book on Cicero, noted under Classical Studies) that has so far been reflected publicly only in two small books, Anderson's *Education and Politics* and Gibson's *Should Philosophers be Kings?*.[3] Work on the history of philosophy is in many respects very difficult to undertake in Australia; the scholar suffers from the fact that Australia has not a single large library. Australian libraries are particularly defective in their coverage of what are perhaps the two most interesting periods in the history of philosophy— the seventeenth and eighteenth centuries. Of course, the classical writers are well represented, but not those minor writers who are so essential to the historian.

If we use the expression "metaphysics" to refer to discussions of the central issues in Kant's *Critique of Pure Reason*, then we have again to point out that no systematic metaphysics has been published in Australia since the works of Sir William Mitchell. During the thirties a number of articles by John Anderson stimulated some controversy on metaphysical issues— particularly on causality and free will. G.F. Stout, who spent his last years in Australia, considered afresh his metaphysical ideas—especially in relation to the ideas of Alexander—in a number of articles; Boyce Gibson has re-examined the nature of metaphysical theories; there has been some discussion of the logical positivist criticism of metaphysics; and a number of Australian philosophers have published essays on the philosophy of religion. But there is no sign of any work of major importance.

This then is the story. It is not an impressive one in terms of books published. Yet a good deal has been achieved. Australia's reputation as a nursery of philosophers stands, I should say, higher than it has ever been. From the Australian philosophical ferment something of the first importance may yet be produced, particularly if some means can be found of ensuring for university teachers those periods of quietness and ease which are certainly essential for the construction of major works in Philosophy. Australian professors of Philosophy have, in general, been extremely active in the

---

[3] It will be observed that the emphasis in these pamphlets is on political philosophy; issues in political and social philosophy have been a good deal discussed in Australia. What has been achieved can be discovered in the reports of the Social Science Research Council.

affairs of their university and of the community at large; men such as Anderson, Stout, Gibson and Fox have played a part in shaping the cultural life of Australia which is only in slight measure reflected in their writings. As well—and this has borne fruit—Australian Philosophy teachers have taken very seriously their responsibilities towards the very many undergraduates who have passed through their hands. But the time has certainly come when these burdens are too heavy to be carried by a few men. Only if there are large increases in staff, and more adequate provisions for study-leave, can the work in progress described in this document ever come to full fruition.

HISTORY

By R.M. CRAWFORD

For reasons stated at the beginning of this chapter we must limit the account of historical writing and research in the Australian universities to a general sketch. In the first place, work on the history of Australia has always had a good deal of interest for the general reader, who is likely to be better informed about it than about that done in other fields of the humanities. In the second place, the volume of work is relatively very large. Histories of a sort were being written within a few years of the arrival of the first fleet in 1788, and a detailed account of past and present historical writing would absorb this Survey. And in the third place, much historical investigation extends beyond the humanities as they are generally understood and is better discussed elsewhere. Important works which lie primarily within the province of the Social Science Research Council, for example, are barely mentioned here.[1]

In short, since a detailed discussion is impossible in the space available, it will be wise not to attempt it, but to sketch in its place the pattern of change in the conditions and character of historical writing in this country. Given this limited purpose, there will be no attempt to assess the work of individual historians who are still occupying positions in the Australian universities and whose contributions to learning will be apparent in the Bibliography.

University research in history comes late into this story. The foundations of historical writing in Australia were laid outside the universities by amateurs, by men of affairs such as W.C. Wentworth, by clergymen such as John Dunmore Lang and John West, by Henry Gyles Turner, a banker, by civil servants such as G.W. Rusden and T.A. Coghlan, by school-

---

[1] e.g., A.C.V. Melbourne's *Early Constitutional Development in Australia* (1934), S.J. Butlin's *The Foundations of the Australian Monetary System* (1953) and N.G. Butlin's studies of *Capital Formation in Australia, 1860-1900* (1954-5).

masters such as James Bonwick.[2] In this regard, the Australian colonies were not peculiar; in England, university research in history scarcely vied with that done outside the universities until the days of Stubbs, Tout and Vinogradoff.

The writing of history in Australia began at its first settlement with the journals and narratives of those who took part in it, such as W. Tench's *Narrative of the Expedition to Botany Bay* (1789) and D. Collins's *Account of the English Colony in New South Wales* (1798). It continued in the ever-growing quantity recorded in the volumes of Mr Justice J.A. Ferguson's *Bibliography of Australia*. But for the century after the first settlement in 1788, the very large amount of writing which can in some sense be called "historical" contained little historical research. For the earlier writers the span of colonial history was short and they were writing from personal recollection, hearsay, newspapers and private official documents, what was for them contemporary or near-contemporary history, and often enough history in which they were personally involved and about which they held strong views. If their histories were not, like the *Official History of New South Wales* (1883) or J. Fenton's *History of Tasmania* (1884), colourless chronicles of events dated by the reigns of those Lilliputian sovereigns, the governors, they were tendentious, being either large-scale pamphlets, such as J. Macarthur's *New South Wales: its present state and future prospects* (1837), intended by interpretation of the past to influence the course of controversy, or recollections but not in tranquillity. In such works as Henry Gyles Turner's *History of the Colony of Victoria* (2 vols, 1904), natural resentments had neither cooled nor been disciplined into calm judgment.

The historian of today is more apt to use these nineteenth century histories as illustrations of attitudes of the time than as reliable accounts or interpretations of events. This is true of what was probably the most ambitious work on Australian history published in the later nineteenth century, G.W. Rusden's *History of Australia* (3 vols, 1883), a lengthy work based on a good deal of miscellaneous reading of published official documents, pamphlets and earlier books together with the writer's own highly personal knowledge. It has the appearance of serious history and was so in intention; but the author imposed his almost ludicrously conservative bias on everything he related. Much the same is true of Henry Gyles Turner, his contemporary, though Turner was a man of larger mind than Rusden.

[2] W.C. Wentworth, *Statistical, Historical and Political Description of New South Wales* (1819); J.D. Lang, *Historical and Statistical Account of New South Wales* (2 vols, 1834, and four later editions); J. West, *History of Tasmania* (2 vols, 1852); H.G. Turner, *A History of the Colony of Victoria* (2 vols, 1904); G.W. Rusden, *History of Australia* (3 vols, 1883); T.A. Coghlan, *Statistical Account of the Seven Colonies of Australasia* (1894), and *Labour and Industry in Australia 1788-1901* (4 vols, 1918); J. Bonwick, *Discovery and Settlement of Port Phillip* (1856), *First Twenty Years of Australia* (1882), *Port Phillip Settlement* (1883), *Romance of the Wool Trade* (1887).

Greatness of mind could to some degree counter the cramping effects of colonial circumstance, as in John West's *History of Tasmania* (2 vols, 1852) a work which out-topped in style and breadth of vision the other historical writing of our first century. But colonial circumstances were indeed unfavourable to mature historical writing. The shortness of span and the colonial preoccupation with questions of immediate practical progress and utility did not normally encourage the asking of questions of universal significance or the discovery of themes greater than expansion of wealth or the justification of the author's personal viewpoint. And not only was the spiritual condition of mature writing absent, but even practical means were lacking until scattered sources were gathered together and catalogued in libraries and archives, and until documents, once confidential, were made public.

Spiritual maturity could be left to time and to the inevitable growth of Australian society in complexity, in experience, and in exposure to the dangers and the stimulus of the world. About the practical needs of historical writing something could be done meanwhile. Paradoxically, the man who did more than anyone else to help the transition from the miscellaneous chronicle or the highly personal interpretations that were called history was not himself a notable historian. The modest long-lived schoolmaster, James Bonwick (1817-1906), wrote vastly on many subjects from 1856 when he published his *Discovery and Settlement of Port Phillip*; but he was a chronicler rather than a historian, one to whom every detail was equally important. He was, however, a chronicler with a passion for records, for the original documents. It was he, almost alone, who recognized that much of the material for early Australian history lay, inaccessible to Australian writers, in the public records in London. In his later years in England he patiently began the transcription of these originals as archivist for the Government of New South Wales, the first fruit being the unfinished *History of New South Wales from the Records* (2 vols, 1889-1894) by G.B. Barton and A. Britton, and the more important consequence the publication between 1893 and 1901 of the seven volumes of the *Historical Records of New South Wales*.

The publication of these dispatches and other documents marked an epoch in Australian historical research because it showed the nature and volume of the evidence that had to be examined before reliable judgments could be made, even about the early history of the colony. Sixty years later the documents transcribed by Bonwick and edited by F.M. Bladen represent only a fraction of the material even for their short period, the first twenty years of the colony of New South Wales; but the seven fat volumes in which they were embodied were in themselves sufficient to demonstrate that Australian history must be based on serious research.

The opening of the Mitchell Library in Sydney in 1910 made such research both attractive and possible by providing a rich and well-catalogued collection of Australiana, manuscript and printed, which both attracted additions to itself and stimulated the opening of similar collections elsewhere. Genuine research could occasionally be carried out before this development. T.A. Coghlan's position as Government Statistician of New South Wales from 1886 to 1905, and as Agent-General for New South Wales in London thereafter, enabled him to achieve work which was, despite its neglect of scholarly conventions, the result of massive, faithful and penetrating research.[3] But in general historical research had to wait for the opening of libraries and archives sufficiently extensive to serve it, and in this development the opening of the Mitchell was of the first importance.

It was at this time that university teachers were beginning to exercise a direct influence on indigenous historical research. University scholars of an earlier generation such as William Edward Hearn[4] had written works which owed all to their European education and nothing more to Australia than the accident of their being written here. Their influence had been great, that of men of wide culture and independent mind; but it had not been an influence directed towards stimulating scholarly work in Australian history. In any case, the study and teaching of History had been merely part, and sometimes a subordinate part, of their multiple functions. In Melbourne Hearn had been appointed in 1854 as Professor of Modern History and Literature, Political Economy and Logic. A generation later, professors were allowed to be less versatile; but apart from the Challis Chair of Modern History established in Sydney in 1890, professors of History were still expected to profess Politics, Economics or English as well as History. More important, they taught alone, or at most with one assistant, until quite recently, and were therefore compelled to profess all History, or at least all branches of it offered to their students. George Arnold Wood in Sydney had no assistant from his arrival as Challis Professor in 1891 until the appointment of J.F. Bruce in 1916 and no more than one assistant until his death in 1928, although students' essays were sometimes farmed out to external examiners. Ernest Scott, Professor of History and Political Science in Melbourne from 1913 to 1936, had one assistant in History at his appointment. They—and those who succeeded them were like them in this —were bound to spread their study over wide ranges of history, a scattering of effort which limited the time allowed for specialized research.

<hr/>

[3] Sir Timothy Augustine Coghlan (1856-1926), *Labour and Industry in Australia. 1788-1901* (4 vols, 1918), etc.
[4] 1826-88, Professor of Modern History and Literature, Political Economy and Logic, University of Melbourne 1854-73, Dean of Faculty of Law 1873-88, author of *Plutology* (1863), *The Government of England* (1867), *The Aryan Household* (1878), *Legal Duties and Legal Rights* (1883).

It was, however, as much a matter of belief as of circumstance. The generation of Wood, Scott, Henderson and Shann[5] did much for Australian historical research, but were teachers first. They did not think of themselves as turning out historians, except as an acceptable by-product of their teaching; all of them thought of themselves as persons occupied in giving a liberal education to people intended for a variety of callings. This was above all true of Arnold Wood, the nonconformist liberal from Manchester and Balliol; but it was also true of Ernest Scott, who, lacking a university background and appointed to his chair because of his research, might have been least expected to conform to the usual pattern. Scott was widely read in several languages and not only in history; and the teaching of Australian history in which his research was done, fell into its place as merely one of the wide range of histories which he taught, supporting his teaching by continuous reading in medieval and modern European history, in the history of British and European colonization, and in the history of England as well as the history of Australia. If he insisted that his students must go to the documents this was not done in order to turn them into worthy writers of theses, but to show them the interest and to teach them the discipline of their subject.

These men valued research and did much to stimulate it; but they could not make a god of it to which their other functions must bow. Consequently, the organization of historical research in their time continued to be somewhat casual and their own research to be what wide general study left time for. They valued historical research and enagaged in it, and did a good deal to encourage their students to do so; but on the whole they talked about it less than has become fashionable.

Nevertheless, they and their immediate successors transformed the state of original historical writing in Australia. They increased the facilities for scholarly research, left the universities dominant in it, and, indeed, may be said to have prepared the way for the replacement of the amateur by the professional in Australian historical writing.

Their own work remains impressive. It is easy enough for the student of the 1950s to correct errors and omissions in the published work of Wood and Scott and Shann; it is more difficult to remember the wide scatter of their interests and duties and their more limited facilities, or to remember that the triumphs of correction may be small beside the humanity of Wood, the vigour of Scott and the insights of Shann.

[5] George Arnold Wood, 1865-1928, Challis Professor of History, University of Sydney, 1891-1928; (Sir) Ernest Scott, 1867-1939, Professor of History, University of Melbourne, 1913-36; George Cockburn Henderson, 1870-1944, Professor of Modern History and English Language and Literature, University of Adelaide, 1902-24; Edward Owen Giblin Shann, 1884-1935, Professor of History and Economics, 1913-31, of Economics 1931-34, in the University of Western Australia, and Professor of Economics, University of Adelaide, 1935.

Wood, long preoccupied with contemporary affairs, published only two books in the last years of his life, *The Discovery of Australia* (1922) and *The Voyage of the "Endeavour"* (1926), the latter being a superb book for children. He also left the manuscript of a third book on the early history of New South Wales, much of which is represented by articles in the *Journal* of the Royal Australian Historical Society. Immediately after his arrival in Sydney in 1891, he had served on the committee which recommended the publication of the *Historical Records of New South Wales*, was later much concerned, often to his own frustration, with advising about the *Historical Records of Australia*, and encouraged many generations of students to use the new opportunities provided by the opening of the Mitchell Library. Scott had already published two books[6] when he was appointed to the Chair of History in Melbourne, and thereafter published eight more, as well as acting as adviser for the Australian volume of the *Cambridge History of the British Empire* (vol. vii, Part I) to which he contributed three chapters and a section of a fourth. Scott's encouragement of his better students to engage in original work in Australian history was constant, and its fruits are evident in the work of Hancock, Roberts, and Kathleen Fitzpatrick, to name only some of them.[7] In Adelaide G.C. Henderson made the work of future historians of South Australia possible by working for the establishment of the South Australian Archives, an ambition finally achieved in 1920. How important such provision was soon became evident in the publication in 1924 of A.G. Price's *The Foundation and Settlement of South Australia*, a work which carried the study of South Australian history from reminiscence to scholarship. In the young University of Western Australia, E.O.G. Shann, while Professor of History and Economics, wrote a small book, *Cattle Chosen* (1926) and a larger book, *The Economic History of Australia* (1930) which, written far from the main collections of documents, remains an Australian historical classic for its wise humanity, its writing and its insight.

These men and others working at the same time transformed Australian historical research. The Australian volume of the *Cambridge History of the British Empire*, published in 1933 but largely written in the closing years of the preceding decade, could not have been a work of scholarship adequate for that series when Scott was appointed to Melbourne in 1913. Two decades had made possible a substantial volume which adequately expressed the state of Australian historical scholarship in 1930 and gave evidence of the increasing accessibility of documents and of the growing interest in

---

[6] *Terre Napoleon* (1910) and *The Life of La Pérouse* (1912). After his appointment, Scott published *The Life of Captain Matthew Flinders* (1914), *A Short History of Australia* (1916), *Men and Thought in Modern History* (1920), *History and Historical Problems* (1926), *Lord Robert Cecil's Goldfields Diary* (1935), *Australia during the War*, vol. xi of the *Official History of Australia During the War* (1936), *Historical Memoir of the Melbourne Club* (1936), *History of the University of Melbourne* (1936).

[7] See Bibliography under W.K. Hancock, S.H. Roberts and K.E. Fitzpatrick.

Australian history in the universities. It was during those two decades that the Commonwealth Government had published thirty-three volumes of the *Historical Records of Australia*, a series begun in 1914 and suspended, incomplete, in 1925.

None could be more aware than the contributors to the *Cambridge History* of the difficulties which still beset Australian historians. In certain fields and for certain areas they might find excellent bibliographies; but for the most part they had still to be their own bibliographers, while official documents in manuscript still remained for the most part in government departments which could rarely, however well-disposed, provide adequate conditions for study.

Moreover, the student who had surmounted all these obstacles still found great difficulty in publishing the results of his work. Some aspects of it, read as a paper to one of the historical societies, might be published in its *Journal* or *Proceedings*; but overseas publishers were at that time little interested in Australian work and local publication of scholarly books was still very limited. Wood, who could find no English publisher for his own *Settlement of New South Wales*, went to great trouble to find a publisher for Miss Myra Willard's *White Australia Policy*, the first book published, in 1923, by the Melbourne University Press. "I have an excellent research scholar (Miss Willard)," he wrote to Tait in Manchester in January 1922, "who has spent 3 years in working in the most thorough way at 'Immigration into Australia'. I got her to re-write part of her work in the form of an essay on *The Policy of White Australia* which I hoped might grow into a small book. It would be by far the best historical account of the central Australian idea. I had thought of sending it on spec. to Macmillan. But what they say and what you say makes me think this would be useless."

Nevertheless, historical works were being published at a gathering pace during the 1920s. The appearance of Miss Willard's book in 1923 was followed in 1924 by J.S. Battye's *History of Western Australia* (Oxford), A.G. Price's *The Foundation and Settlement of South Australia, 1829-45* (Adelaide) and S.H. Roberts, *The History of Australian Land Settlement* (Melbourne) all of them the results of serious research. This steady increase in the substantial knowledge of Australian history continued throughout the decade, to reach something of a culmination in W.K. Hancock's *Australia* (Benn's Modern World Series, 1930) and E.O.G. Shann's *An Economic History of Australia* (Cambridge, 1930), books in which narrative was tamed in the service of reflective discussion, and in the Australian volume of the *Cambridge History of the British Empire*.

Much of this work had been made possible by grants to university graduates enabling them to spend a year or more in research. Such grants were fewer and smaller than they are now and they were not so systematically organized as they have come to be. They were the product for the most part of private endowments such as the Frazer Scholarship (1890) in Sydney and the Tinline Scholarship (1907) in Adelaide, and not until the recent war did government grants come to be the main source of research funds. In Melbourne, however, individual endowments were supplemented after 1920 by the use for research scholarships of some of the money raised by a public appeal of that year, and the encouragement of good graduates with research grants showed its fruits in such works as S.H. Roberts's *History of Australian Land Settlement*. But in most Australian universities at this time, including Melbourne, endowments which could be used to support research seem to have been often used as travelling scholarships to help young graduates to undertake further courses in Oxford, Cambridge and London; and many who benefited from this policy would not question its wisdom for that time.

The depression of the 1930s, if it stirred the minds of those who lived through it, brought some check to this steady growth of historical research. Meanwhile the university schools of History were changing. Wood of Sydney had been succeeded by S.H. Roberts in 1929. W.K. Hancock had succeeded Henderson of Adelaide in 1924, to be followed by G.V. Portus in 1934. In Western Australia, History had been separated from Economics in 1931 under F. Alexander. In Melbourne Ernest Scott, the doyen of Australian historians, retired in 1936, to be followed by R.M. Crawford. In a world that had been shaken by the Depression and was watching the gathering clouds of a second world war, the pleasing art of historical narration was at times elbowed out by the insistent demand that the past must somehow illuminate the present, that history must find answers to the problems that beset and bewildered us. Analysis and discussion came more and more to replace the telling of a story, and the historian for various reasons to look more and more to the economist as his most promising companion. This had its dangers. Shann and Hancock, brought up on narrative history and deeply interested in problems, managed to unite narrative and discussion without loss to either; but it often happened that the emphasis on analysis produced a neglect of the art of narrative or even a blindness to the existence of such an art. This was not always so, and one of the most important works of the late 1930s, E. O'Brien's *The Foundation of Australia, 1786-1800: A Study in Penal Colonisation* (1937), written as a doctoral thesis in the University of Louvain, was a distinguished piece of writing. This work and another work written at the same time and published in 1939, B.C. Fitzpatrick's *British Imperialism and Australia, 1783-1833*, had this in common, that both sought to illuminate Australian history by setting it in the wider context of British history. Fitzpatrick's book and its sequel, his *British Empire in Australia, 1834-1939* (1941) owed their approach to the impact of the Depression. Pioneer works in their exploration of the bearing of economics on the political history of Australia, they stimulated, often by provoking dissent, a great amount of research which is still continuing in this field.

The war at first inevitably checked and later stimulated the growth of historical research in this country. *Historical Studies, Australia and New Zealand*, planned during 1939 and first published, despite the outbreak of war, that year, offered the student not only the opportunity to publish, but also many useful bibliographical aids, such as details of accessions of manuscripts to libraries and archives. It also offered more serious reviewing than could be found in the press, and the critical review is a prerequisite of sound research. In 1941 appeared the first volume of Mr Justice J.A. Ferguson's *Bibliography of Australia*[8] a work which has now reached 1850 with volume iv.

The path was not always smooth. Not even the combined efforts of the Public Library, the Victorian Historical Society and the university's Department of History could prevent or cancel a Victorian Chief Secretary's instruction of 1941 to local court houses ordering the dispatch of old documents for pulping, although at the same time the Chief Secretary in Tasmania had given a friendly reception to an informal report written by the Melbourne Professor of History on the state of official document collections in Hobart. The destruction of local records in Victoria was the last instance of an official obscurantism which has widely given way to a friendly and at times lively interest in the proper care of records. This has been evident in the more systematic organization of archives departments in both Commonwealth and states, in more thoughtful policies governing the preservation and destruction of records, and in a general readiness to make records available to students. The years immediately following the second world war were years of great activity in this field.

By this time the state of historical research in Australia had radically changed. Numbers of students in the universities increased so rapidly at the end of the war that it was necessary to expand teaching staffs to a degree without precedent in Australia. This need could be met in some measure because the Commonwealth Government, recognizing that its scholarship and rehabilitation schemes imposed new burdens on the universities, began to supplement the state endowment of the universities, while the state grants were at the same time greatly increased. Although inflation kept needs in advance of these increased means, new conceptions of what might be considered adequate endowment of university teaching and research gained

[8] vol. i, *1784-1830* (1941); vol. ii, *1831-1838* (1943); vol. iii, *1839-1845* (1951); vol. iv, *1846-1850* (1953).

acceptance in the post-war years. The university teacher is no longer expected to spread his efforts over a great diversity of fields as in pre-war years and, with the possible exception of those burdened with the administration of large departments, he has found it easier to specialize. It is not clear that production has kept pace with the increased opportunity. Meanwhile, the way was made immensely easier for the good graduate. In all universities he could now expect a research grant which would enable him to study full-time for a higher degree, while the continuing expansion of university staffs held out good hopes of academic preferment to cheer him on. Although the proportion of Australian university students who work for a higher degree in History is said to be low compared with the proportion doing so in England, the proportion of better honour students who went on with research in History for a higher degree did show a sudden increase after the war. Of 310 research theses on historical subjects listed by *Historical Studies* as held in Australian universities in 1956, all but fifty-eight had been written since the end of the war.

The research student's path has been made easier in other ways. If rising costs still keep the possibility of publishing his book in doubt, the number of historical books published since the war seems to have risen in fair proportion with the rising number of those engaged in serious historical research. Endowment and subsidy have in many cases overcome the publishers' natural fears. In any case, the historical scholar now finds no difficulty in publishing in Australia an article that is worth publishing. To the journals of historical societies in several states and to *Historical Studies, Australia and New Zealand* (from 1940) published by the University of Melbourne, has been added the *Australian Journal of Politics and History* (from 1955) published by the University of Queensland, *University Studies in History and Economics* published by the University of Western Australia, and the *Papers and Proceedings* of the Tasmanian Historical Research Association; while the Australian Humanities Research Council has begun to publish longer articles in its Monograph Series. In the initial labours of research, moreover, the research worker has been helped by a great deal of work done in recent years in discovering, listing and preserving collections of official and private papers. One may illustrate a story not exhausted in these illustrations by referring to A.G. Serle's systematic combing of Victorian country districts for documents, to Miss Margaret Kiddle's use of sabbatical leave in the British Isles to seek, very successfully, letters written home by Victorian pioneers, and to F.K. Crowley's monumental labour in listing the records of Western Australia.[9]

In the encouragement of research in Australian history, C.M.H. Clark's

[9] *Guide to the Principal Documents and Publications Relating to the History of Western Australia* (1949) and *The Records of Western Australia*, vol. i (1953).

publication of selections of documents[10] has played an important part in offering the student an imaginative sample of the rich records available. It is, of course, true that all these aids to research would matter little if the stimulus to undertake it, and above all the stimulus of inspiring teachers, were lacking. It will be for the future to judge if Wood and Scott have found their successors.

The more plentiful provision of scholarships, the more certain hope of academic preferment, the expanding services of libraries and archives and journals, have bred a race of research students whose pre-war predecessors were few and scattered. The historian working independently of the universities (although fortunately in increasing association with them) remains, it is true, an honourable part of the scene. Australian biography would be immensely poorer without M.H. Ellis's studies of Macquarie, Greenway and Macarthur, and Marnie Bassett's *The Hentys*, while the scholarly and devoted labours of Philip Brown in editing the Clyde Company Papers would grace any university which had the wisdom to endow them.[11]

But academic historians now dominate Australian historical research. Excluding economic historians, the dozen, more or less, who taught history full time in the Australian universities in 1937 had jumped seven-fold to eighty-four in 1957; and in Australian history, in place of the small handful of university teachers outnumbered by the Bonwicks and Turners and Coghlans, there are now many scores of university teachers and research students engaged in an intensive study of Australian history. This has its dangers here as elsewhere. It is possible to specialize too narrowly too early. Except where the drive of a passion or an idea outweighs all else, specialization needs a basis of general history more extensive than an undergraduate course allows; and much work now being done would be richer and more penetrating if minds more richly and diversely stocked were brought to it. But this is no peculiarity of the Australian scene or of research in history; and its excesses provoke sound although not necessarily successful reactions.

It has been inevitable that Australian historical research should be overwhelmingly devoted to the study of Australian history, with excursions into the Pacific. Its sources are at hand, its unexplored tracts more obvious, and, one is bound to add, its linguistic demands are less exacting. Distance from the great collections and the difficulty of ploughing a lonely furrow

[10] *Select Documents in Australian History, 1788-1850*, and *1850-1900* (2 vols, 1950 and 1955) and *Sources of Australian History* (1957).

[11] M.H. Ellis, *Lachlan Macquarie: His Life, Adventures and Times* (1946), *Francis Greenway* (1949), *John Macarthur* (1955); Marnie Bassett, *The Hentys, An Australian Colonial Tapestry* (1954); P.L. Brown, *Narrative of George Russell of Golf Hill* (1935), *Clyde Company Papers*, vol. i, 1821-35 (1941), vol. ii, 1836-40 (1952). This essay cannot attempt to list distinguished histories, but some reference should be made to H.V. Evatt's studies of Bligh (*The Rum Rebellion*, 1938) and of W.A. Holman (*Australian Labour Leader*, 1940) and to G. Mackaness's biographies of Bligh (1931) and of Governor Arthur Phillip (1937) as examples of serious historical research undertaken outside the universities before the recent war.

far from the helps and useful provocations of fellow-workers have kept
very low the number of those attempting serious historical research in
non-Australian fields. Nevertheless, the universities have been teaching a
diverse range of histories in their undergraduate courses, which have
stimulated some teachers and students to undertake research in non-
Australian fields, much of it, it is true, carried out overseas. Further, the
old-established schools of classical studies have a record of research in Ancient
History which lies outside the scope of this section. Research in other than
Australian history has been further diversified by the growing interest in
Asian history, one important expression of which has been the foundation
of the Research Department of Far Eastern History in the Australian National
University, a school devoted to the study of Chinese and Japanese history.
More generally, as teaching staffs grow larger and those interested in research in non-Australian history more easily find companions, the obstacles
to such research lose their terrors; while the recruitment in larger numbers
since the war of British and European scholars whose interests in research
have already been determined has further added to the variety of historical
research in this country.

It remains true, however, that most research in other than Australian
and Pacific history is being carried out by scholars who suffer from isolation,
from, that is to say, their distance both from the records and from other
scholars in their field; and the prohibitive cost of the frequent short visits
overseas that are necessary to continuous progress in non-Australian research does not allow that isolation to be readily broken down. The help
given to Australian scholars by the great foundations, Carnegie, Rockefeller
and Nuffield, has been invaluable in countering this difficulty; but it still
needs to be supplemented by much greater local endowment. No other
Australian universities approach the favourable conditions offered for study-
leave by the Australian National University and the University of
Adelaide. Meanwhile, the deficiencies of local collections can be made good
to some degree by means of microfilm and microcards. What could be
done in this way for other fields of study has been shown by the combined
effort of the National Library, Canberra, and the Mitchell Library in microfilming all documents in the Public Records Office which are relevant to
Australian history.

Historical research has not yet become in Australia the large-scale
business which it is in Germany, the United States and even England.
Nevertheless, a growing number of people live by it and for it. Does this
mean that historical study has reached maturity in Australia? Perhaps all
one can say is that many more people are doing it and that they have much
better facilities than their predecessors. If maturity were marked by technical
competence, one could claim it in fair measure for Australian historical

study. In bibliographical studies, source-criticism, the competent employment of "ancillary sciences" as they become relevant, it reaches proper standards. But maturity connotes something more than that. It suggests an ability to see the particular *sub specie aeternitatis*, and yet to do so without flaunting the eternal verities as though they have been newly discovered. It means a combination of vision and urbanity, of what Sir Keith Hancock has called "span", with the ease which comes of having an established civilization behind one. We tremble on the brink of the promised land; but that we have yet displayed these qualities more than rarely, no Australian historian will feel confident.

UNIVERSITY RESEARCH IN THE HISTORY OF ART

By F.A. PHILIPP

Research in the history of art has an even shorter history in this country than that of other disciplines of the humanities, and the cultivation of the different fields of the history of the visual arts has not altogether developed in step. Thus they must be treated under separate sub-headings: the art of the Near East and of Greece and Rome will be treated in the section on Classical Studies, while this section will be concerned with research in (1) primitive and prehistoric art, (2) the art of Europe from late antiquity to the present day, and of its colonial and post-colonial expansion (particularly in Australia) and (3) the art of the Far East.

It must be emphasized that the future of research in the history of art depends on its sound establishment on the level of undergraduate teaching. Connoisseurs and antiquaries of acumen and enthusiasm have often overcome the handicap of the lack of a sound training in the methods, standards and traditions of academic art historical research, which have developed with reference to the special nature of the monuments concerned. But amateurs have not always been able to avoid the pitfalls caused by a lack of such training.

Primitive and Prehistoric Art

Research undertaken has been very markedly focused on the art of the Australian aboriginal, the study of rock painting and bark painting being given predominant attention. Research centres have been either the universities (especially Sydney, the Australian National University, Melbourne and Adelaide) or museums with important collections in the field (especially Adelaide and Sydney).

Of scholars holding university appointments, or associated with public collections, the following have made important contributions to the study of Australian aboriginal art:

(a) in general: L. Adam, F.D. McCarthy, C.P. Mountford;
(b) on rock painting and engraving: L. Adam, A.P. Elkin, F.D. McCarthy;
(c) on bark painting: L. Adam;
(d) on the art of Arnhem Land and northern Australia: R.M. and C.H. Berndt, and D.F. Thomson.

The work of other scholars not directly connected with universities or museums, such as L. Black, R. Etheridge, F. Rose, S. Kenyon, E.A. Worms ought to be mentioned, though it may not be included in the Bibliography.

While most of this work has concerned the primitive art of the Australian continent, an important contribution to the study of the art of Oceania and especially of New Guinea has been made by R.W. Firth, Professor of Anthropology at London, a New Zealander who was acting professor at Sydney for a short time in the early thirties and more recently was advisor to the Research School of Pacific Studies at the National University. Of course his work has mainly been done outside Australia. Among resident scholars, L. Adam, who retired from a lectureship at the History School of the University of Melbourne in 1957, has made contributions also in the wider field of primitive art. He came to this country in 1940 with a background of European scholarship, and before settling here had contributed to the study of primitive and oriental art. Already before his arrival here he had published a brief general survey of primitive art (Pelican, 1940) which has subsequently revised and enlarged (3rd edition, 1954) and also translated into other languages. Adam is at present completing the volume on primitive art for the Pelican History of Art. He has also built up a small but fairly comprehensive teaching collection for the University of Melbourne.

Post-classical European Art and Australian Art

Some important contributions to the study of Australian art had been made before the foundation of the Herald Chair of Fine Arts at the University of Melbourne in 1947 and such studies have continued independently of university research during the last ten years. Amongst lasting contributions W. Moore's *Story of Australian Art* (1934) and R.H. Croll's edition of Streeton's letters to Roberts (*Smike to Bulldog*) are still indispensable. In the field of architectural history only a few can be mentioned: the various volumes of that devoted antiquary C. Nesta Griffiths, and Hardy Wilson's *Old Colonial Architecture in N.S.W. and Tasmania* (1924) with its careful and loving drawings and its deep-felt appreciation, which started a growing interest in the early architecture of Australia. This has found fruition in the recent work of another architect, Morton Herman, whose *The Early Australian Architects and their Work* is the most important publication in this field. The same author's *Victorian Sydney* (1956) is a valuable book of illustrations but lacks the thorough historical documentation of the earlier work. An important contribution to the study of colonial architecture is the monograph on Francis Greenway by the Sydney historian M.H. Ellis (1949, 1953) though its method and approach have been severely criticized. *Australia's Home* by Robin Boyd, a former part-time lecturer at the School of Architecture, University of Melbourne, views for the first time analytically the whole architectural development of the country. It is a work of brilliant presentation and provocative argument with some sound documentation also.

Some of the works mentioned suffer from some historical isolationism, which prevents the author from taking full account of the decisive links with the European tradition; others suffer from a lack of familiarity with the methods which the nature of art historical material demands. The only attempt to write the history of Australian art in a critical and historical manner, with awareness of its genetic links with European art, is Bernard Smith's *Place, Taste and Tradition* (Sydney, 1945). Smith, now senior lecturer in the Department of Fine Arts, University of Melbourne, has subsequently focused his research on the investigation of the early phase of the interplay between a European vision and the new physical and social environment of Australia and of the Pacific region. Apart from one publication relevant to the whole field of Australian painting, viz. his *Catalogue of Oil Paintings of the Australian School in the National Art Gallery of N.S.W.* —the best critical catalogue yet published by an Australian collection—two articles, "European Vision and the South Pacific" and "Coleridge's Ancient Mariner and Cook's Second Voyage" have been published in the *Journal of the Warburg and Courtauld institutes*. The author is at present preparing for print (O.U.P.) his doctoral thesis on *A Study of European Art and Related Ideas in Contact with the Pacific, 1768-1850.* He is also preparing a catalogue of original drawings and paintings of artists who travelled with Captain Cook, for the Hakluyt Society's publication of the Cook Journals.

Important research into a later phase of Australian painting, the Impressionist Heidelberg School, has been carried out by Ursula Hoff of Melbourne, Keeper of Prints and Drawings at the National Gallery of Victoria, who has also published articles on the work of Frederick McCubbin. She is now preparing for print an evaluation and catalogue raisonné of the work of Charles Conder during his stay in Australia. Another important contribution to the study of one of the leading figures of the Heidelberg School is the critical essay by R.M. Crawford of Melbourne on the unpublished correspondence between Tom Roberts and Alfred Deakin to be published (together with the full text of the Roberts's letters) in a volume of studies in honour of Sir Daryl Lindsay.

This volume, under the editorship of F.A. Philipp, will contain a number of contributions by eminent scholars from Australia and overseas.

European Art

Research in the history of European art in this country has been carried on in three main fields:

(1) It has been closely related to the respective scholar's work in the field of Australian art, cf. Bernard Smith's research on Captain Cook's draughtsman, William Hodges, in his contact with the strange geophysical environment of the Pacific, i.e., generally to the theme of the European vision and the Pacific.

(2) It has continued or branched out from studies initiated or explored in outline by the various scholars during their previous European training or academic activities.

Thus the research of J.T.A. Burke, the first occupant of the Chair of Fine Arts at the University of Melbourne, is centred on British eighteenth century art and continues in a field to which Burke had made contributions before his arrival in this country: (*Hogarth and Reynolds: A Contrast in English Art Theory* and *A Classical Aspect of Hogarth's Theory of Art*). Both Burke's critical edition of Hogarth's *Analysis of Beauty* and his volume for the *Oxford History of English Art* (vol. ix, 1714-1800), which is nearing completion, illustrate this continuation of studies which have grown out of a European background and training. Another work in progress, based on previous studies at Yale University, is concerned with Benjamin West and the revival of history painting in Britain and America. A study of seventeenth century iconography (*Archbishop Abbott's Tomb, a Problem of Carolean Iconography*) must also be mentioned for it points to that link with a great European research centre, the Warburg Institute, to which all members of the staff of the Melbourne School of Fine Arts are deeply indebted.

Other instances of research following up earlier work abroad are the article *Goethe and the Dutch Interior* by Ursula Hoff, who had previously specialized in the study of transalpine seventeenth century art and the art of Rembrandt (Ph.D. thesis, *Rembrandt und England*); and the same scholar's research on the Flemish primitives in the National Gallery of Victoria, to which reference will be made later, also continuing earlier fifteenth century studies. The study of sixteenth century Italian portraiture (with special emphasis on the emergence of new portrait types) and of the art of Italian Mannerism by F.A. Philipp is also based on research interests initiated during a period of European training.

(3) The National Gallery of Victoria has been and always will be a main focus of art historical research in this country. The cataloguing of the

various branches of the collection, and especially—in this context—of those sections containing masterpieces of post-classical European art, will indicate the standard of Australian scholarship in this field.

At present Ursula Hoff is preparing a critical catalogue of the paintings in the gallery. A selective volume, *Masterpieces of the National Gallery of Victoria*, was published in 1949 under the editorship of Ursula Hoff, who was also the main contributor. The quarterly *Bulletin* of the National Gallery of Victoria, under her editorship, has published a considerable number of shorter articles on new acquisitions of the gallery and on other individual works or groups of works. The more important of these articles are listed in the bibliographical section of this Survey under the names of the authors. More extensive essays on important works are to be published in the volume of studies in honour of Sir Daryl Lindsay.

Research on works in the National Gallery of Victoria has recently been linked with an important scholarly publication abroad. At the request of Dr Paul Coremans (Brussels, editor of the *Corpus de la peinture flamande*) Ursula Hoff has prepared material on the Flemish primitives in the National Gallery for inclusion in the *Corpus*.

Art of the Far East

No formal courses in this subject are at present given in Australia, though it forms part of the general teaching in the School of Oriental Studies at the Canberra University College, and research in the field has been undertaken at the Australian National University, especially by Dr. Noel Barnard, who has recently published some important articles on early Chinese inscribed bronzes. A catalogue of the Oriental Collection in the National Gallery of Victoria is being prepared by Dr. Leonard Cox, Honorary Curator, and by Gordon Thomson, Assistant Director of the Gallery.

Research Facilities and Needs

It is obvious that research facilities in such fields as Australian aboriginal art and Australian art generally are far more favourable than in European art. In the former, main desiderata are: (*a*) Specialized research libraries and archives of the type of the Mitchell Library in Sydney. (*b*) A topographical and photographic survey of the main surviving monuments, the number of which is continually diminishing; the foundation of National Trusts in some states has considerably advanced the prospect of such surveys being undertaken and finally integrated. In Victoria the preliminary work on such a survey has in fact been started. (*c*) An index of private collections of Australian paintings.

When we turn to research in European art, very much greater difficulties have to be faced. Firstly there is the factor of remoteness, "a crippling factor" in the words of one correspondent. European and even American scholars can visit sites, monuments, collections and relevant archives, if not every year at least frequently. Scholars working in Australia are clearly under a very severe disadvantage since transport expenses make shorter and more frequent visits to Europe practically impossible at present.

The second great impediment is the sad insufficiency of libraries. The most extensive art library in the country—the Public Library of Victoria— has very large gaps, not only in the history of art itself but in many other adjoining and related disciplines of the humanities, to which reference may often be indispensable. Important reference works, much of the older literature and periodicals and learned journals (especially in foreign languages, the latter an absolute necessity for serious scholarship) are often not available in any Australian library. The Public Library of Victoria is the only library in the country where at least fragments for a research library of European and Oriental art can be found. The art section of the library of the University of Melbourne, built up in the last ten years, while a fair reference library for undergraduate study, lacks many of the large serial reference works. For the study of art in Australia as a whole the systematic building up of at least one research library is an overriding need. There is also need of co-operation between the more important libraries in establishing a planned purchasing policy by which certain libraries, by building up sections in which they are already relatively strong, may be the acknowledged centres for certain studies. As for the development of university research in art it might be possible, just as Canberra is the agreed centre for the main concentration on Oriental studies, to concentrate the main effort in one place. If so, then Melbourne, with a university department already established, and access to the only art collection in Australia in which the sequence of Western art can at least be traced, seems to qualify as the natural centre of university research provided it can be strengthened in the fields not yet academically represented in Melbourne, mainly classical and Oriental art.

Finally there is need of a comprehensive photographic study collection, indispensable to any research in a field where the primary material is visual, and even more vitally important in a country as remote from the original monuments as Australia.

ORIENTAL AND PACIFIC STUDIES

BY H.A.K. HUNT FROM INFORMATION SUPPLIED BY H. BIELENSTEIN AND G.P. SHIPP

Awakening of interest in the languages of the primitive peoples and of the large nations which are in Australia's part of the world has given scope for enterprise in research. This is a field where progress has been quick. It has been achieved first by the adventurous spirit of discovery in men willing to go out among the native tribes, then more recently by exploitation of the new science of linguistics, and more recently still by inspired imagination at the level of public policy in the establishment of a strong centre for Oriental Studies in the national capital. Work on the aboriginal languages has gone on for a long time. There has been strong recent development in Oceanic Studies. Oriental Studies in Canberra are in their first phase: the idea is to gather a group of distinguished scholars at whose feet will sit students from all over the continent. In this section also we include Semitic Studies which have been established for a dozen years at Sydney and in Melbourne have just had a severe blow in the death of their brilliant founder, M.D. Goldman.

Oriental Studies

Sydney was the only university with a Department of Oriental Studies until 1951, when a start was made at Canberra. J. Murdoch, the first occupant of the chair at Sydney, published a history of Japan. His successor, A.L. Sadler, who was professor for a quarter of a century until his retirement in 1947, published studies such as *The Art of Flower Arrangement* and *The Japanese Tea Ceremony*, as well as descriptions of architecture and literature and *A Short History of Japan*. The present professor, A.R. Davis, has in progress a translation with commentary of the works of T'ao Yüan-ming of the fourth century.

There was no other significant research in Oriental Studies in the universities until the establishment of two important departments in Canberra early in the present decade. The Department of Far Eastern History at the National University developed from the appointment of C.P. Fitzgerald as visiting Reader in Oriental Studies, which led to the establishment of a chair five years ago. Fitzgerald has attracted to his department a group of scholars well equipped for the study of Chinese and Japanese history and contemporary trends. The titles of two of his own topics for research: "The development of the Chinese revolution since the Communist party came to power" and "The life of the T'ang Emperor Hsüan Tsung" and N. Barnard's study of the forgery of archaic Chinese bronze inscriptions illustrate the diversity of historical periods which interest this school.

The School of Oriental Languages at Canberra University College began its activities in 1953 after the appointment of H. Bielenstein as professor. Its name has now been changed to School of Oriental Studies because of the widening scope of its activities. The subjects currently taught are the Chinese, Japanese and Bhasa Indonesian languages and Oriental civilization. While considerable effort had has to be given to development of teaching methods in the language, Bielenstein and his staff, like Fitzgerald's group, have been starting research into various aspects of Chinese and Japanese history and civilization. The diversity of interests is shown by these titles of work in progress: "The restoration of the Han Dynasty", "Population development in China from the T'ang Dynasty to the present" (H. Bielenstein), "The administrative system of the Ming Dynasty" (O.B. van der Sprenkel), and "A history of women's emancipation in Japan" (Joyce Ackroyd). Considerable encouragement has been given to Oriental Studies by the Morrison Lectures founded by Chinese residents in Australia and arranged since 1948 by the Australian National University.

It is clear that the plan of assembling a number of Oriental scholars in one centre and of building up a good library is stimulating a volume of research far exceeding anything previously achieved. The problem of gathering a respectable body of students for the scholars to teach and inspire by their research is the next problem to be solved.

Indonesian Studies, which had made a little headway when several university departments at Melbourne embarked on what they called an "area survey", were given strong encouragement in 1955 by grants from the Commonwealth Government to the universities of Melbourne and Sydney and to Canberra University College. The teaching of Bhasa started at Canberra and Melbourne in 1956 and more recently in Sydney. The main work going on is not what we should call research but rather development of teaching methods. However, there are some research projects in progress in Melbourne as a result of the area survey.

Semitic Studies

Semitic Studies have been directed at Sydney University by E.C.B. MacLaurin as lecturer in the subject since 1945, and at Melbourne by M.D. Goldman, who during his twelve years in the chair, until his untimely death last year, developed a department with a small staff but a high reputation and himself did important research. Naturally a fair amount of work also goes on in the various theological institutes and colleges outside the universities, some of which is noted in the Bibliography. Textual criticism of classical Hebrew texts is handicapped by lack of access to early manuscripts, just as similar work in Greek and Latin is handicapped. But publications like Kittel's *Biblia Hebraica* or Ginsburg's Massoretic Text render possible textual criticism of a secondary kind. Theological research is possible by closer analysis and cross-indexing of the Biblical text but not without the handicap of shortage of literature published overseas. Carefully planned co-operation between the libraries of the university and the various colleges in Sydney as well as private orders have remedied gaps in the supply of the main journals, although a severe shortage remains. MacLaurin has worked on an analysis of the theological concepts of the historical books of the Old Testament, which he recently published, and has prepared commentaries on the Hebrew texts of various books in the Bible. Goldman's interests were wide and varied. He did a good deal of work on methods of teaching. Examples of his more serious work in philology were his project to study the place of Ugaritic in the family of Canaanic languages and to write an account of the semasiology of the Semitic languages. He had in hand an examination of parallel passages on the Old Testament and their importance for textual research. In his last few years he took a great interest in the historical significance of the Dead Sea Scrolls and, with his strong philological bent, was embarking on a comparison of the Isaiah Scroll with the Massoretic Text. One of Goldman's helpers, J.A. Thompson, has done a lot to establish in Melbourne an interest in the archaeology of the Biblical lands and is doing research into the significance of Transjordan in the history of Israel. N. Milne, who has been directing the department since Goldman's death, had started work on "the use of the Old Testament in the New Testament and the Qur'an" before his fairly recent arrival in Australia.

The present political and strategic significance of the Muslim world suggests various topics for research and here E.C.B. MacLaurin has started a work, part of which has appeared in an article entitled "*Oman and the Trucial Coast*".

Aboriginal and Pacific Languages

A large part of the work on aboriginal languages started outside the universities among men whose interest was awakened by work at the missions. Thus Rev. R.M. Trudinger was a teacher with the Presbyterian Mission when he started to study the language of the Pitjantjatjara, whose territory extends from the Petermann Ranges in the south-western corner of the Northern Territory across the South Australian border into the Musgrave Ranges. In 1942 he published a grammar of their language. Another missionary, the late J.R.B. Love, became the authority on the language of the Worora (a tribe on the north-western coast, about a hundred miles north-east of Derby) and published a grammar in 1938. Father E.A. Worms of the Pallottine Order conducted extensive ethnological and linguistic research in north-western Australia. In 1935 he was joined by his great teacher Dr H. Nekes who taught African linguistics, especially Bantu, at the Oriental Seminary of Berlin University until the first world war. These two scholars worked together on *Australian Languages* published on microfilm by Worms in 1953 after the death of Nekes in 1948. Worms has many publications to his credit. N.B. Tindale of the Adelaide Public Museum has compiled vocabularies of aboriginal dialects from many parts of Australia.

That South Australia has been an important base for such work has been due not only to propinquity but also to encouragement by J.A. Fitzherbert, Professor of Classics. Classical philology and also the philological interests of the departments of modern languages extended the university's influence to systematic research into the aboriginal dialects. It is interesting to observe the estimate of one of our most scholarly workers in the primitive languages, T.G.H. Strehlow, of the value of traditional philological training in approaching the task. Such training, in his experience, is valuable because it develops the ability to detect and systematize significant language forms, gives an appreciation of rhythms together with some experience of their functions in poetry and legend and creates an awareness that, just as Greek drama used a vocabulary different from colloquial speech, so primitive men in their ceremonies will have special forms of vocabulary and the patterns of formal recitation. Adelaide's appointment of Strehlow in 1946 as Research Fellow and subsequently as Reader in Australian Linguistics has proved a major contribution. He has worked mainly on the Aranda dialects. His collection of over a hundred myths, almost four thousand verse couplets, and thirty-two hours of recordings affords a satisfactory basis for serious linguistic studies of a more detailed nature than those attempted in Australia so far. He has already published accounts of the phonetics and grammar of the Aranda dialects. He hopes next to publish a large volume which deals with the grammar, the rhythmic measures, the music, and the specialized poetic diction of the Central Australian songs under the title of *The Songs of Central Australia*. In Strehlow's studies linguistic research is treated as the study of the speech and the oral traditions of men and women living as an organized community in a cultural environment that influences not merely their actions but also their language. His research accordingly seeks to show also the links existing between language studies and such other modern disciplines as psychology, anthropology and music.

In other states too the work on aboriginal languages goes on. G.N. O'Grady of Sydney has published notes on a secret language used in the rites of initiation in north-western Australia and has in preparation a study of the language of the Njangumada, a tribe living some distance inland from Port Hedland, Western Australia. O'Grady has also gathered remnants of a language formerly spoken in south-western Australia. S.A. Wurm of the National University, whose general project is mentioned below, has plans for work on the aboriginal languages of north-western New South Wales and south-eastern and southern Queensland.

Anthropologists also have collected native songs, but a description of their work is beyond the scope of this survey.

A large part of the research mentioned above has been done by men who have gone out to live with the natives in their natural conditions. For example, Strehlow collects some of his best material by going out alone for three months at a time in the winter. Such men have gathered a mass of linguistic material which is much more extensive than the scanty list of publications suggests. Such material exists largely in manuscript form or on untranscribed recordings. There is ample work in linguistic research waiting to be done if only funds can be found for training re-searchers and for supporting the fascinating expeditions from which new information is derived.

Publications on the aboriginal languages have mostly appeared in the series of *Oceania Linguistic Monographs* which were started by the Australian National Research Council. When this Council dissolved after the founding of the Academy of Science the *Oceania Monographs* were continued by Sydney University. They are giving a great service also to research into the Pacific languages which is strongly based at Sydney. An important stage in its development was marked by the publication of *A New Approach to Australian Linguistics* by A. Capell of Sydney who is the driving force behind a projected linguistic survey of the Pacific and is preparing for publication a text-book for the linguistics courses at Sydney University. As part of the general scheme *Oceania Monographs* are to include accounts of the languages of New Guinea (e.g., *Middle Wahgi Phonology* by Rev. J. Luzbetak) and a volume on Philippine linguistics by various authors. Capell is preparing grammars of the languages of the south New Hebrides in terms of present-day structural linguistics and, by means of tape re-cordings and phonetic studies made during special expeditions, he is having material collected from other areas of the Condominium.

A researcher who, working outside the universities, has made a scholarly study in this area is Rev. Frank Paton who was awarded the Doctorate of Letters at Melbourne for his account of the language of Ambrym in the New Hebrides. In Canberra several scholars have concentrated on the lan-guages of northern Australia and New Guinea. W.E.H. Stanner has published on the Marithiel language of the Port Keats area in western Arnhem Land and R.F. Salisbury on the Siane language of the eastern highlands of New Guinea. S.A. Wurm has in hand a programme of research embracing languages not only of New Guinea, but of Australia and the islands with the broad purpose of surveying the state of knowledge of the New Guinea and Australian native languages as a whole.

Our survey of research completed and in progress in the various disciplines ends with the languages and civilizations of the East, from Israel to the islands. It is a field of tremendous possibilities and urgent needs. There are serious gaps. Thus nothing significant has yet been done about the great Indian sub-continent, although in our area as a whole the influence and wisdom of its leaders may be of the utmost importance. The languages and history, civilization, philosophy and art of our neighbours great and small must be studied. It is some encouragement that we can record the progress just described in this section. The task will be aided in part by the new sciences like linguistics but above all by the scholarship forged in Europe and here continued, as it is hoped has been shown, not without distinction.

FACTORS AFFECTING RESEARCH

By H.A.K. Hunt

Overseas Sabbatical Leave

As has been shown, research in Australia is to a large extent an offshoot of European scholarship and many of the projects are a continuation of work started overseas. Much of the information lies in other lands and in the libraries of the great European and American centres of learning. It is there that the scholar must go to meet his colleagues in their gatherings, to compare notes and to find out what is going on in his subject. Even where there are strong local opportunities for research into topics crying out for investigation, such as the Oceanic languages, the probability is that the men whose help is most needed live in the other hemisphere. Or if there are several experts in Australia they may live two thousand miles apart. Now, if the aeroplane cuts down the time of travel, the cost remains. If a married lecturer who visits Europe takes his family with him or provides for it at home he will need in the one year about twice the amount of his annual salary.

The universities all recognize the need for travel and it is the usual thing that a university teacher may obtain sabbatical leave with full salary. His problem is to meet the cost. There are various schemes among the universities for helping him. The best is that of the National University which, as a research institution, has a system of generous grants. Among the other universities there has been a variety of schemes. With one or two exceptions these have been inadequate but recently there has been an improvement.[1]

[1] These are the provisions for financial assistance for study-leave overseas in several of the universities—Note that special provisions may be made also for short periods of leave at shorter intervals.

Australian National University: Professors—one year's leave on full pay every four years, together with return tourist air fare to U.K. and up to £1000 for other costs. Other ranks have leave at longer intervals with smaller allowances; e.g. a Fellow may have leave on full pay every seven years with return tourist sea fare and up to £600 for other costs. Such leave is regarded as a legal right provided for in the contract of appointment.

The other universities mostly provide for leave with full salary every seventh year with the following grants for travel (which are reduced, of course, if outside assistance is given):

Adelaide University: Any member of staff may apply for a grant not as of right but according to needs and merit consisting of £A600 for fares, *plus* a daily allowance for married men for the time spent in countries overseas up to a maximum period of 300 days. A married

However, the Rockefeller and Carnegie foundations, the Nuffield Trust, the British Council and the Fulbright fund all give generous help. It may reasonably be said that since 1946, with the exception of some whose obligations have been insuperable, nearly every university teacher whose turn for study-leave has come around has been able to go abroad to Europe or America. Whether increased numbers of staff and rising costs will allow this to continue, unless some extraordinary effort is made, is doubtful and there is little reason for complacency.

Now even supposing the material difficulties are met and the scholar can go abroad every seventh year, he will have to use that year in collecting a mass of ideas and information on which he must work for the next six years with little chance of a quick visit to check up or refresh his mind. He is much less favourably situated than his colleagues in Canada or America who can afford a visit to Europe in the vacation. There is a case for shorter periods of study-leave at more frequent intervals.

Leave in Australia

Within Australia the increase in university staffs, the maturity of some departments and the founding of new universities, particularly the National University, are offering increased opportunities. Although most staffs are small in relation to the number of students, nevertheless a staff of half a dozen teaching several hundred students is better able to release one of its members from teaching duties than the typical staff of thirty years ago, which might have been no more than a professor and one assistant. So some departments do manage to give a man a term free from teaching and this is invaluable when he has a subject ready for writing up or needs uninterrupted reading. A system of visiting fellowships has just been

professor or reader may claim per day 26/- *plus* 5/- for each child. A married lecturer may claim 15/- *plus* 5/- per child daily.

Canberra University College: A new scheme (August 1958) provides for an unmarried man £150, for a married man £300 *plus* provision for travelling expenses for wife and children, the maximum grant being £1000.

Queensland: No allowance for single men but for a married man an amount based on family responsibilities and ranging from £100 to £300.

Western Australia: An amount of up to £500 for a married man and £300 for a single man with a special scale for members awarded grants to visit U.S.A. and for those who spend their time both in U.S.A. and Europe. Thus a married man without outside assistance could claim £375 for five months in U.S.A. and £250 for five months in U.K.

University of New South Wales: Half normal salary plus a grant for expenses not exceeding the balance of the normal salary together with provision for additional financial assistance. A professor may apply for six months' leave every three years.

University of New England: There is no established system of grants but they have been made from time to time to members of staff of considerable seniority.

University of Melbourne: A full year's leave with pay is granted at the end of each six years of service if the needs of the relevant department permit. At present a travel grant of £200 is made for study-leave overseas. Recently proposals have been made to increase this amount.

University of Sydney: A grant is made once in each seven years of service, provided the leave approved is for at least six months. This grant is £400 for a married member of staff, £250 for an unmarried member.

established in the National University under the terms of which a scholar who has brought a piece of research to the stage when he needs freedom for writing will be able to work in superb conditions.

The Teaching Load

In all the universities it is provided in the conditions of appointment to the staff that a proportion of time shall be spent upon research and this is generally fixed roughly and optimistically at 50% of the time. In practice the research has to be done by men busily engaged in teaching and examining and, in the case of senior men, in administration. In general the average number of teaching hours is eight to ten per week. By comparison with our colleagues in Canada this may not seem unduly heavy. But the present size of classes requires a tremendous time for correcting exercises, essays and examinations. In this post-war period the increase of staff has brought relief and the annual research reports do show an increase in scholarly writing. Whether this can be maintained will depend largely on the ability to maintain an expansion of staff commensurate with the predicted growth of student numbers. Already this year (1958) has brought a sharp increase in the latter; it can be quite serious to find yourself faced with a prose composition class of fifteen instead of ten. If you have to split the class, teach for two hours instead of one and spend an extra half-hour on correction that is so much less time and vigour for research.

Some subjects have special problems as this statement on modern languages by R.H. Samuel shows:

Independent research in the field of modern languages, i.e., in the field of foreign cultures and in particular of foreign literatures, and their social, historical background on which their aesthetic character is so dependent, meets with many difficulties in a country so far away from these foreign civilizations and their resources. Compared with other humanities the basic difference is found in the fact that the student of modern languages has first of all to acquire an additional tool—a command of the foreign language itself. In order to lay the necessary foundation for academic work, university departments have to pay particular attention to the teaching in schools and to the standard of matriculation. One important task of university departments is the training of teachers. In spite of growing possibilities of sending post-graduate students overseas, few students can avail themselves of such an opportunity, and most language teachers in Australian secondary schools have never been overseas. This affects the standard of teaching and necessitates a large amount of elementary language work during the first two university years at least. Conditions in Australia vary in many respects. On the whole, language courses are built upon "matriculation" standard, i.e., freshers are supposed to have had some four or five years' language instruction in school before they begin an academic course. In some languages, this is not possible as they are not taught in schools. This applies to Italian, Russian, Dutch

N

and Oriental languages, although matriculation examinations are held in these subjects in some states. However, the majority of these students embark upon a course without sufficient knowledge, and universities attempt to train them in summer schools (Dutch, Russian and Hebrew in Melbourne). In Sydney a preliminary year for Italian attempts, in an intensified course within the university, to bring students to matriculation standard in one year; the same applies to German in New South Wales, Queensland and Canberra for students without sufficient knowledge for the academic course. Of necessity, the courses in Dutch, Russian and Italian have to begin on a lower level than those offered in the two main foreign languages.

In short, the staffs of the modern language departments have to do a great deal of extra-curricular work in order to stimulate the practical use of the living language. The largest burden in this respect is active work in the schools which is by no means restricted to the setting of the school syllabus and the holding of examinations, but includes visits and lectures to schools, organization of lectures for matriculation students, of plays, special afternoons and evenings for school children and refresher courses for modern language teachers. All this cuts down the time for research.

Staff Recruitment and Research Posts

Our sister body in its Survey "The Humanities in Canada", aware of the danger of "academic stagnation due to inbreeding" gave considerable attention to the variety of training among the university staffs. It found that a high proportion had been trained in other countries and that the multiplicity of foreign contacts was a desirable thing. Australia's remoteness creates a greater danger of inbreeding. That this has been resisted so far has been due to the willingness of men to come here from the British universities and to our ability to send our graduates to do advanced work there, as well as to a welcome accession of European scholars just before and after the last war. Without analysing the composition of our staffs in such detail as the Canadians employed we can see from the lists in the calendars that there is a healthy mixture at present, and this is confirmed by the variety of gowns in our academic processions. More recently, however, there has been a dwindling in the number of young British graduates willing to come out, while within our own country the pressure to early vocational specialization, the premature bonding of students to secondary teaching and similar factors are creating a shortage of recruits suitable for appointment to university staffs. This shortage may become quite serious as student numbers rise. The need for cross-fertilization is great. There is danger in taking local graduates on the staff immediately after graduation in minor posts from which they hope to rise step by step. Their initial energy goes into teaching because, naturally, they are worried as to whether they know enough to teach. The first years are hard in this respect and often they may not be encouraged to research or have little energy left for it. They need the stimulus of being with other post-graduate students and usually there are not enough of these about, as in English or American universities. It is desirable for our young graduates to go abroad to get further training in research and, if possible, teaching experience in an English university. But at present it cannot be said that we have the scholarships available to send a large enough number of graduates abroad. If we cannot do something about this quickly things may become serious. The general problem is well expressed in this statement on the recruitment of staff for modern languages:

> Appointment of graduates of English universities is becoming more difficult because there is a shortage of university modern language teachers in Great Britain on the one hand; on the other hand Australia has few attractions for those younger scholars from overseas who feel they should not forgo the possibility of going frequently to the country of their study and interest. It is therefore the aim of the larger departments in Australia to train their own university teachers and they have been doing so with increasing success. A standing rule adhered to as much as possible is that no Australian trained person will be appointed to the rank of Tutor or Teaching Fellow and above without having spent at least one year of intensive study and research in the country of his field (or, for Russian, at an Institute of Slavonic Studies abroad).

One suggestion for increasing the supply of recruits from Britain is that instead of requiring the new lecturer to wait for the full six years he should be guaranteed study-leave after four years. This is done in some of the universities in Africa and, though we should hope that a young Englishman would not expect the way of life in Australia to be just as it is in Africa, it seems reasonable to provide a period of trial so that he may not seem so thoroughly committed to a career here as an initial period of six years suggests.

While the majority of the staff is heavily engaged in teaching duties some posts have been created in this generation which do show that concentration on research is respected as an ideal, although the posts in which it is fulfilled may be few. At Sydney G.P. Shipp, as Reader in Classical Philology for many years before he accepted the Chair of Greek, and in Adelaide T.G.H. Strehlow, as Reader in Australian Linguistics, have been able to pursue research in freedom from teaching duties. More recently in Sydney and Melbourne others have been appointed as readers who, though they may have extensive teaching duties, are more free from administration than the associate professors of equivalent rank and accordingly are expected to find more time for research. The National University, founded mainly as a research institute for medical, physical and social sciences, touches on the humanities, particularly on the side of History and Philosophy which, within its structure, fall within the province of the social sciences. Other fairly recent foundations such as Canberra University College and the University of New England have been developing strong staffs in the humanities and conditions which favour the steady pursuit of scholarship. In general it may be said that since the last war the conditions for research and the general appreciation of the desirability of doing it have been improved tremendously.

In recent years the creation of various junior teaching posts, some of them tenable by graduates working for the M.A. or Ph.D., has provided further financial aid for research workers. Thus Melbourne has tutors and Adelaide has research assistants who normally are working for a further degree and whose appointment does not entail heavy teaching duties. Similarly the teaching fellowships at the University of New South Wales provide a moderate salary at the beginning of an academic career while providing the opportunity to improve one's scholarship.

Obstacles in the Schools

The increased "research consciousness" is largely the product of teaching methods adopted in the universities these last twenty years and designed to foster it. But success is achieved not without obstacles at the undergraduate level and also in the schools.

Secondary education in each state is conducted partly by a great public department and partly by a large number of independent schools, many of which were founded by the churches. They all train pupils in courses of studies decided by an approved authority which also holds great public examinations to mark the completion of the several stages of the school course. This authority in some states is the public department, in others the university acting in consultation with secondary teachers. The system is elaborate, orderly and capable of spreading general education of a high standard while giving splendid opportunities to the excellent. The danger is, as always when a large number of people have to reach some standard, that the standard which is fair to the average may not provoke the really good to make the best use of their opportunities. There is no doubt that throughout Australia there is a tendency to regard the passing of these examinations as the goal of secondary education and that in choosing their subjects for them many children consider just what is necessary to satisfy the regulations rather than what is the wisest choice for giving full scope to their abilities. In short, in the choice of school courses there is grave danger that the dead hand of mediocrity may suppress the appreciation of intrinsic values and high ideals. The remedy should not be an attack on the general organization, which has many excellent features, but rather an attempt to find some means of inspiring the good pupils—and this, we must admit, is not entirely neglected as things stand. The problem which concerns us is that many pupils come up to the universities without having done subjects which they should have done. This particularly affects the languages. Although language study has been traditionally and rightly an important part of the humanistic tradition in European education, the influence of America on our educational theorists and the temptation to choose the easier course provided it "satisfies the regulations" has created a resistance to language study. The result is that in states where a language is not compulsory for entry to the universities language study drops off while elsewhere pupils who might have benefited tremendously by doing two or more foreign languages confine themselves to one, the minimum which the regulations prescribe.

The Humanities Research Council is seriously disturbed at the threat to language studies. It considers the study of languages and civilizations an essential part of education. It regrets that too many pupils cease their studies at school without any training in foreign languages, while such studies of other civilizations as they attempt are deprived of much of their value because they are done without any knowledge of another language.

Obstacles to the Flow of First-class Graduates

Apart from the premature specialization which deprives great numbers of science pupils of any serious introduction to the humanities, the pressure to produce an adequate supply of secondary teachers causes both at school and undergraduate level restriction of the choice of subjects by students who bond themselves to a state department and are consequently directed to certain studies in which the shortage of teachers may be acute. Again, at the university the state department may prefer its trainees to do a wider range of what it regards as "teaching" subjects at pass level rather than an honours course and it may not accept the university's assurance that a man will be a better thinker—and accordingly a better teacher—if he achieves personal integration in a coherent discipline at the more serious level of study offered by the honours course. In short there is a danger that some trainee teachers may be directed to the pass course who would benefit by the honours course. And although in fairness to the state departments we must admit that there is quite a lot of enlightenment in their administration, so that trainee teachers are in fact allowed to attempt the honours course in certain "teaching" subjects, the barring of the honours course in certain Arts disciplines (e.g. Classics, Philosophy, Psychology and Political Science) does mean that a number of students who could do well in these, and whose ability implies that they should do them, are diverted away from them.

This could cause a serious threat to the perpetuation of various disciplines through the insufficient production of graduates of the quality needed for university teaching and free to undertake it. Unless some vigorous effort is made to increase the number of first-class graduates who at the end of their first degree course find themselves free of any bond and able to commence higher training for university teaching, then, because of the impending need of greater staffs, we cannot hope to avoid a serious predicament.

Financial Aid for Research

However there are some encouraging factors, namely the Commonwealth Scholarship scheme, an improved system of grants at the M.A. stage and increased aid for graduate study abroad, although this is the field where most remains to be done.

The Commonwealth Scholarship scheme, because of its stringent means test, for the majority of scholarship holders gives little more than relief from fees. Most of the holders have to find their own living costs which may well amount to more than £300 per year. Hence the preference of many for the grant of the Education Department which because it provides living expenses without a means test may be worth just about £300 more per year. Among these many there will be some who would benefit intellectually by being perfectly free from non-university direction both during their course and at the end of it. Perhaps some system of more generous Commonwealth grants for special students might preserve the flow of potential tertiary teachers. The present age limit also debars some who after some years of junior teaching or some other work discover a real aptitude for higher study and should be helped to do a university course.

The M.A. year is coming to be treated as a valuable preparation for advanced study abroad for those who devote their full time to it. They are aided in several universities by grants from the research funds of about £500, a sum which, though it falls below the basic wage, yet does make full-time study possible.

In recent years M.A. students of modern languages have been helped by grants from foreign governments. Since the last war France has given about fifteen scholarships of about £300 per annum with fares, for further study in French universities. The German Academic Exchange Service since 1953 has given thirty-two scholarships worth about £450 to £480. The Italian Government and the Government of the Netherlands also give scholarships. It is possible in this way for a student to continue working for his Australian degree while living in the country of the language. Some Australian universities, such as Melbourne, are able to supplement these foreign scholarships by sums from their own research funds. The benefit to the students from these prolonged studies overseas is, of course, very great. Not only do they become completely conversant with the language but they are also introduced into the methods and ways of continental research while enjoying the better research facilities overseas. It is therefore only natural that the Australian Humanities Research Council should express in this Survey its appreciation for the assistance these foreign governments offer to Australian students in their training for research, also for the considerable help they offer to language departments with regard to material in books and teaching aids. The Dutch Government, for instance, has for some years past given the University of Melbourne an annual grant of £575 to build up a research library and to assist members of staff when they are on study-leave in Holland.

Financial aid has started at the Ph.D. stage in those universities which have this degree. Thus Melbourne makes grants of £625 for the first year and £700 for the second year of the full-time Ph.D. course and candidates are allowed to earn an additional amount of up to £300 per annum by a limited amount of teaching. Since the report of the Murray Committee the Commonwealth Government is understood to be bringing out a scheme for granting scholarships for post-graduate study in Australian universities worth something more than £700 per year.

As for financial provision for post-graduate study abroad, this is our greatest need. Conditions vary in the different states. Sydney, with its greater private benefactions, can offer a fair number of scholarships. At Melbourne there is always a waiting list, with many disappointments. At Adelaide the number of scholarships meets the demand only because there are few honours graduates to compete for them. Most universities have a small number of travelling scholarships for research but these are not available for many of the courses which graduates in the humanities such as Classics, English and Philosophy may want to do at Oxford or Cambridge. What we need is a greater number of unrestricted travelling scholarships so that a first-class man can count on getting abroad after the M.A. stage. Without that we shall continue to lose to vocational courses a number who could become first-class scholars and university teachers.

Research Funds

During the present decade the universities have been able to make research grants to the departments in the humanities. These are used for paying young research workers at the M.A. or Ph.D. stage, for material aids to staff members such as photostats and microfilms, sometimes for special books, for travel or research projects and for part of the cost of attending academic conferences.

This is much better than anything attempted twenty years ago and it is making a lot of work possible. Nevertheless, in most of the universities these grants are said to be inadequate. It is said that the distribution of them suffers by lack of a clear policy and by the overwhelming claims of the sciences. Moreover in some universities, such as the University of New South Wales, there is no such fund for the humanities. In any case they do not extend to certain large projects which might reasonably be considered the concern of the universities but have to look elsewhere for funds. It does seem reasonable to urge that a member of a university staff who develops a project for important research in connection with some branch of the humanities should be able to get financial support from his own university's research funds. His project is bound in any case to be much less costly than most projects in the sciences.

Libraries and Publications

The inadequacy of most of the Australian academic libraries for research except in regard to various special or local subjects is fully dealt with in the chapter on Libraries. Mention should be made here of the similarly inadequate provisions for publication.

A small press has been started at each of the universities of Queensland and Western Australia but so far Melbourne is the only possessor of a university press with a permanent publishing programme and fully organized facilities for production and distribution of books. Even there the author of a scholarly book with limited prospects of sale may have to find a large part of the cost of publication. Some universities do have publication funds but these are of negligible size. Adelaide has one of £300 per annum and for many years the Melbourne fund stood at £140. But such funds have to serve the whole university, are used for scientific papers and for articles in learned journals and can give no serious aid to the publication of a book. The Melbourne University Press, by boldly taking risks (which have built up a heavy overdraft at the bank) and by a policy of retail trading from which the profits have subsidized publication, has been able to publish about twenty books a year, some of them for authors in the other universities, and has thus done a notable service to Australian scholarship. Moreover its affiliation with the Cambridge University Press assures world-wide attention for its publications. But the unhappy fact remains that no scholar in Australia has a substantial publication fund to back his book. It is well known that several of our colleagues have manuscripts of high standard and based on years of scholarly work, which cannot be printed because the cost would be about £1500 or £2000 each.

Within Australia there are periodicals in philosophy, history, and literary criticism while in modern languages and classics the newly founded journal of the Australian Universities' Languages and Literature Association has come to fill a need. But there is little or nothing available for fine arts, music, archaeology, linguistics and Oriental languages. The generosity of our colleagues in Britain, Europe and America provides some outlet for articles in their learned journals. But the lack of Australian periodicals is a handicap which cannot be overcome without the generous provision of finance.

CHAPTER VII

University Finance

BY A. GRENFELL PRICE

THE REPORT OF THE COMMITTEE ON AUSTRALIAN UNIVERSITIES IN September 1957, and the general adoption of its recommendations by the federal and state governments, have greatly improved prospects for the development of the humanities in Australia, for, although the weaknesses of the existing position were well known, the Committee opened the eyes of the Australian governments and people to the way in which they had allowed their universities to fall behind owing to inadequate finance. Although this Survey must approach the subject with considerable caution, as the universities have only recently begun to collect adequate statistics and to present them on a uniform basis, several chapters show that the humanities have been amongst the worst sufferers from this financial neglect. Chapter V, for example, indicates that the Australian academic libraries and their Arts sections compare unfavourably in size and financial outlay with those in Canada and still more with those in the United States.

That Australian academic leaders were aware of the increasing gravity of the position was shown by the statistics which were prepared in recent years for the Australian Universities Commission and Commonwealth Bureau of Census and Statistics, by an important pamphlet *A Crisis in the Finances and Development of the Australian Universities* published by the Vice-Chancellors' Committee in 1952, and by the various cases submitted to the Committee on Australian Universities (the Murray Committee) in 1957.

An analysis of the various documents shows that in the opinion of Australian university educationists (1952-7):

1. The Australian governments were failing to spend sufficient sums on their universities as was shown by a comparison with the universities of the United Kingdom (Table A).
2. The staff-student ratio in Australia was very poor, again as shown by a comparison with Britain, and this poor ratio had serious effects both on teaching and research.
3. Partly as a result of there being no effective selection of students entering Australian universities (all local candidates who satisfy the minimum

entrance requirements are admitted), and partly because of inadequate staffing, the Australian rate of student failure was unduly high, particularly in the first year, as was again demonstrated by a comparison with British universities.

4. The Australian university expenditure per student was particularly low in some of the faculties and subjects of Arts, and this low ratio involved the staffs in an amount of administration and teaching which was highly deleterious to research.

5. Predictions of experienced demographers as to the trend in student numbers in the immediate future indicated an increase of 60% or more in the next ten years, and even an increase of perhaps 100% by 1970. An analysis of numerical trends over recent years, indicated that the number of Arts students had increased, while student numbers in some other important faculties had shown a slight decline; it is therefore not unreasonable to infer that the expected increase would apply in no small measure to Arts.

Table A presents a comparison of expenditure of representative Australian and United Kingdom universities (Australian 1956, United Kingdom 1955-6):

TABLE A[a]

	Full-time equivalent students [b]	Total expenditure £A	Expenditure per student £A
Sydney	6949	2,400,330	345
Melbourne	6005	2,334,387	389
Queensland	3386	1,236,410	365
Adelaide	2974 [c]	1,137,918	383
University of N.S.W.	4358	1,618,446	371
Western Australia	1606	813,553	507
Tasmania	673	390,714	581
Total: Australian universities	25,951	9,931,758	383
Birmingham	3281	1,997,918	609
Bristol	2890	1,657,990	574
Leeds	3690	1,976,375	536
Manchester	4296	2,078,864	484
Nottingham	2301	941,288	409
Sheffield	2230	1,182,996	530
Edinburgh	5359	2,191,053	409
Total: U.K. universities	24,047	12,026,484	500

(a) Source of Australian figures: Commonwealth Bureau of Census and Statistics, *University Statistics* (Parts I & II), 1956. Source of U.K. figures: H.M.S.O. Cmd. 211, Returns from Universities and University Colleges in receipt of Treasury Grant (academic year 1955-56).

(b) For Australian figures one part-time student is counted as one-half, and one external student as one-third. For U.K. figures, one part-time student is counted as one-half.

(c) Students at the Elder Conservatorium, Adelaide are excluded.

The Vice-Chancellors gave in 1952 "a further indication of the extent to which the scale of university expenditure is lagging behind other countries":

TABLE B

	United Kingdom (1950-51)	United States (1946-47)	Canada (1950)	Australia (1951)
Total running costs of universities	£Stg24.3m.	$1,000m.	$40m.	£A4.7m.
Amount per head of population (Australian currency)	12s.	£3	£1.5s.	11s.
Percentage of national income	.21	1.36	.31	.15

From the Vice-Chancellors' *A Crisis in the Finances and Development of the Australian Universities*, 1952, p. 15.

EXPENDITURE ON ARTS

Turning to the expenditure on Arts, we present in Table C a statement of the number of students, total costs and costs per student in the faculties of Arts and Education, as compared with other major faculties—Science, Engineering and Medicine—in the universities of Adelaide, Melbourne, Sydney and Western Australia.

Table C seems to present a number of valuable facts, although comparisons between even these four universities are dangerous and must be carefully safeguarded.

There is, at the outset, the problem of how the total cost per faculty is to be calculated. On this question the Registrar of Sydney University wrote: "In this Survey it was assumed that the whole of the normal running expenses of the University, as set out in the General Account of the University for 1954, should be included in considering the costs of the faculties. Hence faculty costs were calculated by adding together the following figures: Salaries and Wages Votes; Maintenance and Equipment Votes; Library Votes; Research Votes; Other Special Expenditure Votes. Overhead was spread over each faculty *pro rata* in accordance with the total of budgetary expenditure for each faculty. Overhead includes the expenses of administration, the library, building maintenance, and such expenditure which cannot be charged specifically to a faculty. The total faculty costs were then redistributed somewhat because of students who enrolled in one faculty with a view to proceeding to a degree in that faculty, taking courses which normally belong to other faculties. For example, Veterinary Science students take Chemistry I, Physics I, Botany I, and Zoology I, which are Science subjects, and Physiology I, Biochemistry I, Histology and Pharmacology and Toxicology in the Faculty of Medicine."

In contrast to this, the University of Adelaide did not attempt in its analysis to redistribute faculty costs on the basis of students of this type,

TABLE C

UNIVERSITIES OF AUSTRALIA, 1954

Number of students, total costs, and costs per student in the faculties of Arts and Education, as compared with those in Science, Engineering, and Medicine in the universities of Adelaide, Melbourne, Sydney and Western Australia.

	Arts and Education			Science			Engineering			Medicine			Total of all faculties		
	No. of students	Cost £	Cost per student £	No. of students	Cost £	Cost per student £	No. of students	Cost £	Cost per student £	No. of students	Cost £	Cost per student £	No. of students	Cost £	Cost per student £
ADELAIDE	749	87,048	116	334	250,567	750	398	92,702	233	507	104,485	206	2713	718,274	265
MELBOURNE ARTS	1572	310,077	197	867	306,728	354	365	166,099	454	911	307,387	337	5557	1,423,269	258
EDUCATION	325	41,354	127												
SYDNEY	1726	251,221	146	520	168,241	324	473	267,222	565	1437	352,740	245	6199	1,627,221	262
WESTERN AUSTRALIA ARTS	548	110,670	202	345	185,525	538	232	78,139	337	—	—	—	1437	469,687	327
EDUCATION	140	31,577	226												

From statistics forwarded by the registrars of the above universities; originally sent to the Australian Universities Commission for the year 1954.

Some universities include a number of Education students in their figures for Arts; others have separate faculties of Education.

In all of these universities the number of students includes a "full-time equivalent" for part-time students.

which accounts for the fictitiously high cost of a Science student and for the unrealistically low costs of Engineering and Medical students. Second, there is the problem of evaluating full-time, part-time and external students. The Universities of Adelaide and Western Australia calculate each part-time student and each external student as half a full-time student. In the University of Sydney "an attempt was made to estimate the number of equivalent full-time students in the Faculties of Arts, Law and Economics . . . in these Faculties . . . the gross sum of subjects taken by pass students was divided by three and in the case of Arts only, the number of honours students added." The Murray Committee counted a full-course student as one, a part-course student as a half, and an external student as a quarter, but noted that the University of New South Wales was not comparable since a number of its full courses were designed for part-time students (Report, p. 23).

The figures presented by the University of Adelaide illustrate another difficulty referred to above, that of allotting to the faculties concerned students who take one or more subjects in these faculties as part of their de-gree courses in their own faculties. Thus in Adelaide, as noted above, the ab-normally high cost of £750 for each Science student is largely due to the fact that students in Engineering, Medicine, Dentistry and Agriculture take a considerable number of Science subjects in their earlier years, while every student must pass in one Science subject to gain the pass degree in Arts. These difficulties are sufficiently serious to make any scholar who may attempt to compare Australian university statistics proceed with the utmost caution. Unfortunately, however, when this Council approached the Vice-Chancellors' Committee on the subject the secretary replied that no steps were being taken to improve matters.

Even admitting these difficulties, however, we can conclude that in all four universities the total expenditure on the humanities ranks fairly high. In Melbourne the highest expenditure on any faculty is that on Arts. In Western Australia the expenditure on Arts is second to that on Science. The position in Sydney seems less satisfactory as the expenditure on Arts is below that on either Medicine or Engineering, but even this is superior to the situation in Adelaide where Arts trails behind all three Science-type faculties—Science, Medicine and Engineering—although it exceeds the cost of the smaller faculties such as Economics, Dentistry or Law.

While the total expenditure on the humanities ranks high in all four universities, the outlay per student presents a very different picture, even when allowances are made for difficulties in calculation.

It is clear that in 1954 in the universities of Adelaide, Melbourne, Sydney and Western Australia, the expenditure per Arts student was, in general, considerably lower than the expenditure per student in many other faculties.

In Western Australia the cost of Arts—£202 per student—was seventh after Science, Dentistry, Agriculture, Law, Engineering and Education; in Melbourne the cost of Arts—£197 per student—was eighth to Agriculture, Dentistry, Engineering, Science, Medicine, Social Studies and Architecture; in Sydney the cost of Arts—£146 per student—was eighth after Veterinary Science, Agriculture, Engineering, Dentistry, Science, Architecture and Medicine; in Adelaide the entirely inadequate expenditure of £116 per Arts student limped far behind the expenditure per student in Science, Dentistry, Engineering, Economics, Medicine and Law until substantial staff increases were made in 1958.

It would require a very detailed study of the position in each university to determine exactly how far those low expenditures throw light on certain important points in the submission made by the Australian Vice-Chancellors' Committee in July 1957 to the Committee on Australian Universities, but it seems probable that they are highly relevant. The Vice-Chancellors stated that whereas eleven English "red-brick" universities had an average staff ratio of 1 to 6.7 students, and four Scottish universities had an average of 1 staff to 7.1 students, the staff-student ratios in the four Australian universities examined in Table C were: Adelaide 1 to 14.4; Melbourne 1 to 11.2; Sydney 1 to 15.8; and Western Australia 1 to 13. In Sydney these figures were based on full-time staff and full-time students. In the other three universities weight was also given to part-time staff and to part-time and external students. Although the Murray Committee published rather different rates which they took from "University Statistics, Part I, 1956" (i.e. Adelaide 1 : 11.3; Melbourne 1 : 12.6; Sydney 1 : 11.6 and Western Australia 1 : 10.5) they admitted that "the older Australian universities are not well staffed, and would require a staff increase of about 60% to bring them up to the standard in Great Britain". The Committee noted further that the eight departments which carried the heaviest teaching loads were English, History, Philosophy, Psychology, Mathematics, Physics, Chemistry and Botany, five of which fall in the category of Arts, and that in 1956 in the University of Sydney, thirteen full-time staff were teaching English to 1143 students and ten full-time staff were teaching history to 1248 students (Report, p. 40).

It may also be suggested that the comparatively low expenditure on Arts plays its part in the high failure rate in the Australian universities. The Vice-Chancellors wrote in their submission: "All Australian universities experience in their most crowded departments" (and these include many Arts departments such as English and History) "the failure in half or more than half of the first year's work of 30 to 40 per cent of students. After the first year the failure rate is less objectionable." The University Grants Committee of Great Britain in its report of 1953 wrote: "A certain wastage of students at the end of the first year is inevitable, and we did not regard it as unsatisfactory to find that over the whole university field the casualty rate in the summer of 1951 was between 8 per cent and 9 per cent."

In its submission to the Committee on Australian Universities, the University of Adelaide stated: "When one turns to the teaching given to students, it is disturbing to find how poor is the ratio of staff members to students. In the large departments the ratio of staff to enrolments in individual subjects is sometimes much worse—1 : 100 for first year students. For them there is virtually no teaching by tutorials and seminars. They hear lectures and write essays or perform practical work, and are otherwise left to their own reading and devices. For a mature student this is not enough; for the immature it is grievously insufficient." The university urged strongly that the staff should be strengthened. If the size of the full-time academic staff was increased by about 40% it would provide a staff-student ratio of about 1 to 10 or 11 students. Even this ratio is only about half the ratio of universities such as Leeds in England, which has a ratio of 1 : 5.6, while the ratio in Reading is as high as 1 : 3.9.

A study of the examination results in 1955 made by the University of Adelaide gave the following failure rate for first year students in various faculties—Economics 41%, Arts 37%, Science 33%. The failure rate for all years other than the first were—Arts 22%, Science 21%, Economics 16%. The Adelaide submission to the Murray Committee does something to explain these failures when it states: "In the big departments of the Faculty of Arts little tutorial help can be given." It may be noted that in a number of instances the university residential colleges which, as in Melbourne and Adelaide, provide special tuition in most university subjects, have a considerably lower failure rate than that of university students as a whole.

Research

The expenditure of the various Arts faculties covers, in addition to administration and teaching, a certain amount of outlay upon research. In the University of Adelaide conditions of appointment allot 50% of time to administration and teaching and 50% to research. In the large departments, when student numbers soared after the war, such an allotment of time proved impracticable for many university staff people, who found it increasingly difficult to spare time from student duties. The Adelaide submission states: "Research in the Humanities and Social Sciences depends on the possession of time free from routine teaching. In some fields the provision of research fellows and graduate assistants is likewise necessary. In all fields, the existence of good library facilities is of first importance." The University of Adelaide considered that its disabilities would be much relieved if the staff was increased, library facilities improved, and provision made for a number of research fellowships and graduate assistants. It may be noted that, for the year 1956-7, only fifteen out of thirty-three members of the Australian Humanities Research Council distributed throughout the Australian universities were able to publish research, although several others reported that they had work in process of publication. It must be remembered, moreover, that these members were elected to the Council for their successful research, and that the thirty-three members possibly rank above the average in their publications.

Study-leave and Travel

Included in the costs of the various faculties is the expense of study-leave, which is important to the members of all university departments and vital to those whose research objectives lie overseas. On this subject the Vice-Chancellors wrote in their submission to the Committee on Australian Universities: "It is hardly necessary to labour the argument that knowledge of what is being done and thought by other scholars and scientists in their own fields is of incalculable value to university staff members. The stimulation to teaching and research of meeting fellow workers is of special importance to staff members of the Australian universities. The continent's geographical isolation is a severe obstacle and even within Australia itself the distances make travel between universities a costly and infrequent undertaking. Not all universities in Australia have satisfactory schemes for enabling staff to travel for this purpose and it is desirable to emphasize the need. It extends primarily to travel overseas, but also includes financial assistance for those who wish to attend appropriate conferences within Australia. Evidence will be given upon this matter in the individual submissions of the universities. Special attention, however, is drawn to the scheme of the University of Adelaide. The Adelaide scheme does not treat the need as one to provide 'sabbatical' leave. The sum annually earmarked for the scheme is awarded by a committee of academic staff members to applicants who show that their current work will be substantially assisted by personal contact with university departments or persons overseas. Rules for administering the scheme are kept to a minimum and the guiding principle is the strength of the applicant's need for the purpose of his work."

The Murray Committee supported this submission realizing that in an isolated country with widely scattered universities, travel both at home and overseas is "essential". For this reason the Committee thought that the universities should receive sufficient funds to enable them to grant their staffs adequate study-leave overseas, and to make it possible for them to meet at conferences of learned bodies within Australia. Study-leave is perhaps particularly necessary for those Arts people, who like the students of

o

languages, art or history (other than Austrâlian), have their research
resources overseas.

THE FUTURE

Increasing Number of Arts Students

Great as are the financial requirements of the Australian universities as
outlined above, they are likely to be magnified in the immediate future by
an expected increase in the number of students, not least in the number of
Arts students. Thus the Vice-Chancellors submitted the estimates of Professor W.D. Borrie, of the Research School of Social Sciences in the National
University, Canberra, that under the most modest assumptions the number
of students enrolled would increase by 60% in the next ten years, and might
double by 1970. The Murray Committee accepted (pp. 81-2) the detailed
predictions of the Commonwealth Office of Education that the student
numbers of 36,465 in all universities in 1957 might increase to 70,785 in
1965 and 80,000 in 1967, the latter figure showing in ten years a growth of
120%.

The Committee did not distribute this growth amongst the various
faculties, possibly because it felt that in future "the key must be judgment
of national requirements". While admitting the probable importance of
changing the present trends in view of these national needs, it is worth
while considering the actual distribution of students in Arts and the other
principal faculties from 1952 to 1956.

TABLE D
UNIVERSITIES OF AUSTRALIA

Student numbers in the faculties of Arts, Science, Engineering and Medicine, together with
the total number of students in all faculties, 1952-56.

	1952	1953	1954	1955	1956
Arts	5609	5684	6115	6748	7579
Science	2504	2431	2382	2686	3108
Engineering	2483	2428	2360	2384	2564
Medicine	3850	3586	3446	3516	3608
All Students	29,641	28,792	29,374	30,792	34,406

This table, which is taken from University Statistics, Part I, Commonwealth Bureau of Census and Statistics, 1956 presents some very important
information bearing upon the future number of students in the humanities,
although this information must be examined most carefully, particularly
in view of possible underlying facts.

Thus it seems that between 1952 and 1954 the number of students in
Arts registered an increase, while the number of students in Science, Engineering and Medicine and the total number of students in all faculties showed
a decline. The expected advance in numbers appeared in all four faculties
and in the total number of students in 1955, and developed strongly in 1956.

Preliminary figures for 1957 presented by the universities to the Murray Committee indicate a continued growth. The Adelaide figures show a marked increase in Arts. Two qualifications should, however, be made. First the decline of numbers in the science-type faculties from 1952 to 1954 was due to the fact that ex-service people were completing their university courses. Second, if the case of the University of Adelaide is a fair example, the continued rise in the number of Arts students is due almost wholly to an increase in the number of Education Department students. Indeed, in Adelaide, the number of Arts students entering the university from other sources is showing a slight decline. Again, however, if Adelaide is a fair example, the demand for teachers is so heavy that the pressure on the faculties of Arts from this source will probably grow in strength.

Effects of the Murray Report

A situation of deep gloom was lightened by the action of the Menzies Government in appointing the Murray Committee, by the illuminating frankness of that Committee's Report, and by its general acceptance by the political leaders in the Commonwealth and states. It can now be said without exaggeration that the Report is likely to have fundamental effects upon the Australian universities and their services to the humanities in the Commonwealth.

The Committee found that the university staffs were seriously underpaid, and that the provisions of superannuation, research, study-leave, teaching accommodation, equipment and libraries were inadequate, all of which deficiencies were impeding the progress of the Arts. There is now little doubt that the adoption of the minimum professorial salary of £3500 recommended by the Committee, together with consequential adjustments in the lower salaries, should improve recruitment, personnel and scholarship. This is particularly important to the humanities where staffs very often work at the lowest rates in the universities, as they cannot supplement their incomes by the "private consultation" which is so often permitted in the cases of Medicine, Engineering or Science officers, an important point that the Murray Committee did not stress. It is true that some Arts people can slightly augment their incomes by such means as tutorial class lectures, broadcasts to schools and the correction of university matriculation and other school public examinations. While many university folk claim that they engage in such work in order to maintain school standards, as is indeed important, some frankly admit that they undertake the work from financial pressure, although these extra-university activities seriously impede research. Whereas most staff members avoid these tasks or reduce them to a minimum, instances occur when even professors and departmental heads draw cheques for the correction of very large numbers of matriculation papers. When at the end of a year weary university people spend some weeks in such elementary work, research may suffer considerably. The position is remarkably like that in certain American universities where one finds that staff "teach summer school", sometimes from a sense of duty but usually because they receive inadequate salaries paid over only nine or ten months of the year. One hopes that in Australia the implementation of the Murray Report will raise university salaries sufficiently for Arts people to avoid such unhappy expedients.

A final point, and one which the Murray Report omits, is the vital question of the provision of staff housing as close as possible to the various universities, for such provision is becoming essential both from the aspects of staff recruitment and stability, and in the saving of time and energy for academic work. This question, and others that lie outside the scope of this survey, the Committee left to an "Australian University Grants Committee" which the Federal Government has now appointed. On the capacity of this body to obtain adequate finance, and on the liberality of its attitude to the Arts, the future of the humanities in Australia will largely rest.

CHAPTER VIII

Aids and Facilities

THEOLOGICAL COURSES AND COLLEGES

BY W.F. HAMBLY AND H.A.K. HUNT

Courses of Study

IN ANY VOLUME DEVOTED TO A SURVEY OF THE PLACE OF THE HUMANITIES within the scheme of Australian education, it would be improper not to include at least some outline of the work done in the field of religion by a group of competent teachers, responsible for the professional training of more than a thousand students who profess a vocation for the Christian ministry. The training of candidates for the ministry of the various churches in Australia is largely carried out within the several colleges established for that specific purpose by the major religious bodies of the Commonwealth.

It seems a fair generalization to say that all the churches—particularly as they speak through their theological teachers—regard the standard of the university matriculation examination as the ideal minimum academic qualification for entrance to a course of theological training. However, just as some Australian universities provide a special matriculation test for persons of mature age who desire to read for a degree or diploma, so the theological colleges generally provide some equivalent preliminary examination for those who seek admission to their courses in similar circumstances.

In the large majority of cases, students qualified to enter upon a degree course in Arts are encouraged to do so. At least one college requires all its students to attend lectures in some subjects offered by the faculty of Arts at a neighbouring university. In addition to the courses of study given within the several denominational colleges, two Australian universities offer, as noted in Chapter IV, facilities for teaching and examination in certain subjects of a normal theological course. The University of Sydney prescribes a post-graduate course in Divinity leading to a degree; the University of Queensland offers a diploma course in Theology as well as the option to read (within the faculty of Arts) some theological subjects as part of the course for a B.A. degree.

Two other examining bodies figure prominently in the Australian theological scene: the Australian College of Theology, an institution governed by the Church of England in Australia, awards to successful candidates the degrees of Th.L., Th.Soc., and Th.D.: the Melbourne College of Divinity was constituted in 1910 by an Act of Parliament in Victoria, and includes representatives of all the major non-Roman churches. By its charter the college is empowered to award a diploma in Theology to all candidates who pass the prescribed examinations. It is also authorized to confer degrees in Divinity on graduates of any recognized university who fulfil the requirements for this "second degree". The college has just made a significant move by adding to its list the degrees of B.D. with honours, and Master of Theology. The latter will require a thesis, as do many master's degrees in the universities. This will mean an advance in original research and a corresponding demand for supervision and guidance in the teaching of the theological halls.

In the brief space of this Survey it is impossible to do more than indicate in outline the place which the disciplines of the several humanities hold in the courses mentioned below.

Language and Literature

In nearly every course there are biblical studies which involve a study of the Bible in English translation—generally an introduction to the several books, together with an exegetical study of at least some of them.

Most examination courses prescribe a study of the New Testament, calling for some knowledge of the grammar and syntax of koine-Greek as well as for a general grasp of the principles necessary for the textual, historical and literary criticism of the documents. In examinations for degrees, as distinct from diplomas a knowledge of Old Testament Hebrew is generally required. In some advanced courses, opportunity is given for the study of Aramaic and Syriac and the Greek of the Septuagint Version of the Old Testament.

Latin is introduced particularly in the study of the Vulgate Version of the scriptures, and in those courses which require students to study the writings of the Latin Fathers in the original tongue.

Patristic studies when undertaken lead also to a study of Greek documents belonging to the second and subsequent Christian centuries.

History

Ecclesiastical history is common to the curricula of all courses. Generally speaking, the tendency seems to be to study especially those periods of its history when, in the crisis of controversy, the doctrines of the church were challenged with resulting formulation or revision. Some consideration is given in most colleges to at least some aspects of the history of Christian missionary enterprise. The attention of those who teach the history of the Christian Church is at present directed towards a consideration of this problem. Is not this study more effective as a true historical discipline when the prime emphasis is laid upon the church as an active and developing organism rather than upon the minutiae of the debates which determined the shape of the Christian creeds? This may well be only another aspect of the changing pattern of the humanities under the constraint of the emerging discipline of social science as an independent discipline in its own right.

Philosophy

The study of theology as such has never been able properly to divorce itself from the discipline of philosophy. The study of philosophy of religion is imperative if religion is to have a consistent "world-view". It is not surprising to find that scholastic philosophy is taught as one subject in the theological group offered by the University of Queensland. Courses given in most non-Roman theological halls deal with the works of some of the Greek philosophers as well as with the thought of medieval and modern philosophers. It is universally recognized that any worthy Christian apologetic demands the discipline of philosophical study. The significant fact that many Australian theological students who read for an honours degree do so in the school of philosophy must not be overlooked.

Social Science

The use of the study of the various social sciences has affected the professional training of theological students as surely as it has challenged the traditional structure of the departments of the faculties of Arts within the universities. The comparative study of religions is no longer merely a historical survey of the growth and development of one or more of the various religions of mankind along with some more or less detailed examination of the system of ideas which inheres in a particular religion. It is now a sociological discipline involving some understanding of the structure of community and the nature of man in society.

The development of psychology, in which the experimental investigation of the "body-mind" relationship has superseded the earlier armchair speculations of philosophers on the subject, makes it more and more difficult to continue to combine the teaching of psychology of religion with the philosophy of religion. Here as elsewhere psychology still seeks to live within the family of the humanities, but in its own right as a social science and not as a mere subsidiary philosophic discipline.

The theory and practice of education have come more and more to be recognized as essential parts of the training of the ministry. If education is a discipline in its own right, it also belongs to the experimental group of the social sciences.

It is always easy (though, of course, quite proper) to offer criticism of the content and balance of subjects in any specialized curriculum. Suffice it to say that in the Australian scene there is, as elsewhere, an area too large to be overlooked where the humanities occupy an important place. Here, in fields largely ignored by those whose work must be done within the framework of the secular university, a group of teachers and students is making a contribution which, in many instances, can stand with proper dignity in company with the excellent work carried out by their colleagues whose studies are controlled by the same basic disciplines.

THE WORK OF THE THEOLOGIANS

Whereas the main object of this survey is to discuss the state of teaching, scholarship and research in the humanities in the universities, no account of the humanities in Australia as a whole would be satisfactory without some mention of the writings of scholarly men in the ministries of the various denominations, and a broad description of the nature of advanced studies in the theological colleges and seminaries. A detailed account is beyond our purpose and resources but a general statement, supplemented in the Bibliography by the book lists of a selected few of the contemporary scholars, will give an idea of the work that is going on.

As was natural, some of the most serious writing during the formative years of the country came from the churches. For example, an important work in the middle thirties of last century was *Horrors of Transportation Briefly Unfolded* by W.B. Ullathorne, Vicar-General of the Roman Catholic Church in New South Wales and subsequently Archbishop of Birmingham, who was noted also for his writings on the state of religion in the colony about 1840. A generation later Archbishop R.W.B. Vaughan, of the same church, found time, amidst strenuous efforts for the development of schools, to publish the *Life of St Thomas of Aquin*, 1871.

In the early years of this century Father G. O'Neill wrote distinguished works on the pioneers of the church in Australia, including the *Life of Mother Mary McKillop* and a work of scientific interest on Tenison Woods.

Very distinguished research in native languages by missionaries has been noted in the section on Aboriginal and Pacific Languages, while the linguistics section of the Bibliography includes a number of names of members of the ministries of the churches who are still working in this field. Some important studies remain unprinted. At the Drysdale River Mission founded by the Benedictine Order in 1908, the monks systematized the Pela language and wrote about it, but the results remain in one or two typed copies. In this same area Don Theodore Hernandez, who was a missionary there for years, made copious notes which mostly remain unpublished, on aspects of native life, although articles by him on the social organization of the native tribes were published in *Oceania*, 1941. There is a very old work published in 1851 in Rome, in Italian, and subsequently translated into Spanish and French, entitled *Memorie Storiche dell' Australia* by the founder of the famous Benedictine Mission at New Norcia (W.A.), Monsignor D. Rudesindo Salvado, which deals, among other things, with the customs of the aboriginals and contains a dictionary of native words.

The Methodist Church had a distinguished scholar and writer in the person of E.H. Sugden, Master of Queen's College, who, among other works, wrote *A Topographical Dictionary to the Works of Shakespeare and his Fellow Dramatists* (1925) and other studies such as *Israel's Debt to Egypt* (1928) and *John Wesley's London* (1932). History and religion were included in the works of W.H. Fitchett of the Methodist Church who wrote *How England saved Europe* 1793-1814 (1900) and *The Unrealized Logic of Religion* (1905).

One who attracted great attention a generation ago was S. Angus, Professor of New Testament and Historical Theology at St Andrew's College, Sydney, highly respected as a scholar, although a centre of controversy in the Presbyterian Church. His *Truth and Tradition* (1934) and other minor works express his views on current controversies, including those surrounding his own person. His more scholarly works on the Hellenistic background of the New Testament, include *The Environment of Early Christianity* (1914), *The Mystery Religions and Christianity* (1925), and *The Religious Quests of the Greco-Roman World* (1929).

The late Professor N. MacLeish published a study in *The Sinlessness of Jesus* which attracted a good deal of attention overseas. More recently a most distinguished Presbyterian theologian, John McIntyre, now of the Chair of Divinity of Edinburgh, made important contributions to theological thought during his period in Australia, with his *Anselm and his Critics* (1954) and *The Christian Doctrine of History* (1957). In Melbourne L.L. Morris, Vice-Principal of Ridley College, has recently published a number of valuable contributions to biblical studies: *The Apostolic Preaching of the Cross* (1955), and commentaries on *I and II Thessalonians* (1956) and *I Corinthians* (1958). E.F. Osborn of Queen's College has published an important study on *The Philosophy of Clement of Alexandria* (1957).

In Church of England scholarship one of the most important of recent contributions has been that of the Rt Rev. T.T. Reed, now Bishop of Adelaide. Bishop Reed gained the D.Litt. degree of the University of Adelaide by his definitive edition of the life and writings of the poet Kendall, a work which he is now arranging for publication.

Other work in progress by recent graduates in the Presbyterian Church includes a book on *Semitisms in the Book of Acts* by M. Wilcox, to be published by the Oxford University Press, and one by J.M. Owen on *Luther's Doctrine of Grace*, based on research in Germany.

The Redemptorist Fathers, based on Australia, extend their work into a number of areas. One of their members, Rev. Leo English, is working on a dictionary of the Tagalog language, the principal dialect of the Philippines, but since this requires prolonged residence in the Philippines, he is hardly to be considered a worker in the Australian field. Another of the same order, Rev. Francis Sexton, temporarily based in New Zealand, but mostly engaged in Australia, has been working on the development of Gregorian Chant (plainsong) and has made some discoveries of importance on which he has a work nearly ready for publication in England. A work accepted for publication in America is a translation with introduction and notes of *The Commentary of St John Chrysostom on the Gospel according to Saint Matthew* by Father J.S. Kelly of Corpus Christi College, Werribee. This is a translation from the Greek text in Migne's Patrology and its magnitude may be judged from the fact that it will appear in three or four volumes, each of 300 or 400 pages. Father J.P. Kenny of Canisius College, Pymble, has in progress a major work *The Deification of Man*, involving a study of St Cyril of Alexandria and other Fathers of the Church and the reflections of modern theologians; fifteen chapters have been published in *Sursum Corda* in 1956-7, but a large amount of work remains to be done. He is also preparing a work on the Sacrament of Confirmation with chapters on the liturgy of it, the scriptural basis, patristic evidence and a theological essay on its meaning.

On quite a different subject is a work in preparation by Rev. C.M. Churchward of the Methodist Church, who from his studies of the Rotuman, Fijian and Tongan languages has turned his attention to English grammar, and after having articles on English language teaching published by the British Council in London, is bringing out a new exposition of English grammar entitled *Let English Speak for Itself*. Father A.A. Snell of the Society of the Sacred Mission has in the press an explanation of the Epistle to the Hebrews entitled *New and Living Way*, and Father A.G. Hebert of the same society has with the printers *God's Kingdom and Ours* and *When Israel Came out of Egypt*. At the Lutheran Seminary in South Australia Rev. Hermann Sasse has in process of publication *This is My Body: Luther's Fight for the Real Presence in its historical context*.

THEOLOGICAL INSTITUTIONS

A large part of the credit for the standard of scholarship in the churches belongs to the theological colleges and the houses of studies of the various religious orders. Of these, some are closely associated with the universities in the undergraduate training of candidates for the ministry. The position at Melbourne may be cited as an example of their relation to the university. Within the grounds of Ormond and Queen's, colleges of the university conducted by the Presbyterian and Methodist churches, there are theological halls staffed by professors. Many of their students attend the undergraduate courses as part of their training for the ministry, as do some students of Trinity (in which some theology is taught by the chaplain and by visiting lecturers), and Newman College, which has no theological teaching. Less closely connected geographically with the university are Ridley College of the Church of England and Campion Hall, the Jesuit House of Studies, whose students take the university courses in addition to instruction within their own institutions. This system is followed by others, for example, the Baptist College of Victoria, the Christian Brothers' Training College, St Paschal's College (Franciscans) and the Carmelite Order, to name a few. That is to say, the training schools of the churches, while maintaining their own instruction, send some of their young men to the universities. The same system prevails in other states.

Quite apart from the work done in and around the universities, the various churches have their own institutions which give opportunities for studies in the humanities at senior levels, either by the members of their staffs or by selected graduates. Such are Morpeth College and Moore College of the Church of England in New South Wales, and the Immanuel Theological Seminary conducted by the Lutherans in South Australia, which has on its staff first-rate theologians with an international reputation, or again St Michael's House, the college of the Society of the Sacred Mission in the South Australian hills near Adelaide, a community containing scholars of the highest rank under whom candidates for the priesthood of the Church of England undergo training. At St Patrick's Ecclesiastical College at Manly the Roman Catholic Church has a complete theological faculty of senior and highly qualified scholars: similarly Corpus Christi Ecclesiastical College, situated at Werribee and Glen Waverley (Victoria), has comprehensive faculties well equipped for guiding research in a wide range of studies; and again the Jesuit Order has at Canisius College at Pymble in New South Wales a community of distinguished scholars who instruct a select group of young graduates. Then there are houses of theological studies maintained by the various religious orders such as the Franciscan Fathers, the Redemptorists, the Benedictines, the Capuchin Franciscan Fathers and others. These are not specifically research institutions, but since various members of their staffs have done post-graduate work in universities, there are some who continue to work in their specialities. The number of theological and ecclesiastical colleges, houses of studies and similar institutions throughout Australia is considerable, and the number of highly qualified scholars in them is large. From these scholars come numerous publications on theology and related questions and there are some distinguished names. From these institutions there is a steady flow of graduates for work at doctoral level in places like Louvain and the Angelicum and the Gregorian University in Rome.

A most promising venture for the encouragement of higher studies is the opening by the Church of England of St Mark's Collegiate Library in Canberra. Its purpose is to promote advanced theological studies and research in related fields, especially in Australian church history. It has commenced a series of St Mark's Library publications.

A senior society which encourages research among its members is the Fellowship for Biblical Studies, founded in recent years by Rev. Professor Hector MacLean and M.D. Goldman. Its membership includes all faiths. Its yearly bulletin contains many articles and studies.

Overseas Studies

Opportunities to go abroad for further study which the best of our students have had in recent years have been shared by the graduates of the theological colleges. Thus, although lack of finance for fellowships and libraries may limit the extent of research by young graduates within these colleges themselves, they are interested in advanced study and trained for independent research; since the second world war they have shared the general impetus to go overseas and many of them have achieved distinction in higher studies there. A note from one theological hall reports the research abroad of some nine recent graduates in places such as Edinburgh, Glasgow, Oxford, Cambridge, Heidelberg and U.S.A. with various successful doctoral theses and publications. Similarly in the Roman Catholic Church many candidates for the priesthood, after undergraduate and special theological studies in Australia, go overseas for further study and do a good deal of post-graduate work at doctoral level in Europe.

Conclusion

As will be seen from the Bibliography (which is selective and lists only a fraction of what is being published) scholars in the churches and church institutions are maintaining a very respectable output of books and articles in a wide range of subjects. There are works on general and moral theology, canon law and philosophy, studies in literature, in religious ethics and social criticism and in native languages and customs. Most of the humanities receive attention. A generous number of periodicals is available for the publication of articles. They not only print articles by professional theologians, but also fulfil an important service by providing a means of publication to laymen and accordingly are a valuable outlet for university writers.

In short, there is a great deal of scholarly writing of high standard going on. No comprehensive survey of it has been attempted, but it is hoped that this present sketch will serve to indicate its nature and to suggest that a detailed survey might be a worth while undertaking.

MUSEUMS AND GALLERIES

BY BERNARD SMITH

Museums and galleries reveal, at their best, the richness and variety of man's material culture as expressed in his inventions, arts and crafts. In a country like Australia, so isolated from the great centres of contemporary society and so lacking in material evidence as to the magnificence and glory of the past, museums and galleries have a most important role to play in education and the pursuit of the humanities. In a society which has always shown strong tendencies to isolationism they function as civilizers, providing links with other contemporary societies and with the past, revealing creative human achievement as something inextricably interrelated, essentially indivisible.

For the purpose of this Survey Australia's museums and galleries may be divided into five categories: Commonwealth, State, Provincial, Institutional (University, College and Library collections) and Private.

The Commonwealth Collections

The Commonwealth Government has not entered the museum and art gallery field to any great extent. It does, however, maintain the Australian War Memorial (1941)[1] which contains relics of all the wars in which Australia has participated and publishes the official war histories. The memorial also houses many works of art painted by official war artists and others relating to both the first and second world wars. A large mosaic by M. Napier Waller has recently been completed (1957) in the Hall of Memory. The memorial also contains the Shellal mosaic and other antiquities from Syria and Palestine.

The Commonwealth Government does not maintain a national gallery of the fine arts. However, a Senate Select Committee on the Development of Canberra (1955) strongly advocated the establishment of one in the Federal Territory. A new national collection would be a most welcome addition to Australia's cultural facilities and if conceived in the best tradition of the humanities, will be international in its scope and interests from the beginning. At the moment the Commonwealth National Library holds

[1] The date of the foundation of the institution has been placed after the name in each case.

two valuable art collections: the Gayer-Anderson gift of Indian paintings
and drawings (seventeenth to nineteenth centuries), bequeathed in 1954,
and the Rex Nan Kivell collection of paintings, prints and drawings relating to Australia and the Pacific. The latter collection, to which items
are still being added, is the most important collection of its kind assembled
since the formation of the Mitchell and Dixson collections.

The State Collections

The museums and galleries maintained by the state governments,
founded chiefly during the second half of the nineteenth century, include
most of the larger institutions. They may be subdivided into "natural
science" museums (devoted usually to the study of geology, natural science
and ethnology), applied science museums and art galleries. In this survey
the scientific work of museums has been mentioned only where it touches
to some extent—as in the case of anthropology, ethnology and archaeology
—upon the field of the humanities.

The Australian Museum, Sydney (1836), is the oldest of the natural
science museums. Its educational and research activities are extensive.
It possesses an outstanding collection of Australian and Pacific ethnology,
publishes scientific *Records*, occasional *Memoirs*, the quarterly natural
science *Australian Museum Magazine*, and a few special publications, such as
Australian Aboriginal Decorative Art. The National Museum of Victoria,
Melbourne (1854), contains the Baldwin Spencer and Lindsay Black
collections of Australian ethnology, publishes *Memoirs*, and is preparing
a series of handbooks to the collection, one of which has already appeared.
The Queensland Museum, Brisbane (1855), owes its existence largely to
the activities of Charles Coxon (1809-76), a naturalist and brother-in-law
of John Gould. It contains the Sir William MacGregor ethnological collection from New Guinea, and publishes *Memoirs*. The South Australian
Museum, Adelaide (1856), has a distinguished history of collection and
research, and publishes *Records*. The museum has specialized in the ethnology
and anthropology of the Australian aborigines and its Australian ethnological series probably surpasses any other similar collection. It has
extensive collections of the sacred symbols of the aborigines (waninga
and nurtanga, including more than 2500 carved and decorated wooden
and stone tjurunga). It has also large collections illustrating the anthropology
of New Guinea and the Pacific Islands. Its outstanding series of aboriginal
paintings and drawings are well known. Researches at the South Australian
Museum have by archaeological excavation established the existence of
four culture phases among Australian aborigines. Carbon 14 dates are
available which carry their existence in Australia back into the Pleistocene
Ice Age (over 10,000 years ago). The state governments of Victoria, New

South Wales and South Australia maintain museums devoted to science and technology. The Museum of Applied Science of Victoria, Melbourne (1870), provides exhibitions of primary and secondary industry, and of public health. It contains the Askew collection of clocks and watches, together with a good collection of fire-arms and a printed catalogue of them. Research is undertaken in dating ancient carboniferous objects by the radio-carbon method. The Museum of Applied Arts and Sciences, Sydney (1880), exhibits displays which seek to illustrate the industrial advance of civilization, the development of invention and the application of science to industry. There is an interesting collection of ceramics including the John Slater collection of Doulton ware. A *Guide to the Collections*, bulletins, and articles on technical subjects are published. The South Australian School of Mines and Industries, Adelaide (1893), functions as an applied science museum. The industrial section seeks to indicate the resources of the state and their utilization in industry. There is an extensive collection of fire-arms, but in more recent years the museum has sought to introduce the public to the nature of nuclear fission.

Each state possesses a "national" art gallery, the oldest and most important of which, the National Gallery of Victoria, Melbourne (1861), has been enriched by several important bequests, notably those of: James McAllen in 1903; Alfred Felton in 1905; John Connell (furniture and silver) in 1914; H.W. Kent (Oriental ceramics) in 1937; Howard Spensley (sculpture, drawings and Oriental ceramics) in 1938; and Colin Templeton (English ceramics) in 1939. The largest of these bequests, the Felton Bequest, has provided over one million pounds for the purchase of works of art since its inception. It has made possible the growth of a collection of international standing which includes in its scope classical, medieval, and Western art since the Renaissance. The seventeenth and eighteenth centuries are particularly well represented, and there are notable works by such masters as Nicholas Poussin, Rembrandt, Constable, Tiepolo, El Greco, van Dyck, Rubens and Reynolds. Four outstanding Greek vases were recently purchased, including an excellent example of Chalcidian black-figure and an early Attic red-figured cup bearing the signature of Pamphaios as potter. The print collection includes the Barlow collection of Dürer engravings, one of the finest Dürer collections in existence, thirty-six of Blake's illustrations to Dante, and drawings by such masters as Rembrandt, Claude and del Sarto, etc. There is a staff reference library of 1500 volumes of standard research literature; a quarterly *Bulletin* is published; and the latest catalogue was published in 1948, with appendices in 1950 and 1954. Questions of attribution concerning major works in the collection have been investigated by substantial overseas correspondence and local research. An active Gallery Society draws an average attendance of 500 of its members

to its monthly meetings. The Miss Mona McCaughey Prize valued at
£200 (for an Australian landscape and a genre painting in alternate years),
is awarded annually through the society and the prize-winning painting
given to the gallery to augment its Australian collection. The gallery,
however, suffers from some grave defects. Storage facilities are so cramped
and primitive as to endanger the preservation of invaluable works of art,
and the facilities available for photographing, cleaning and conserving works
of art cannot be compared with those of Sydney. There is no full-time
conservator. A gallery of Melbourne's size and importance requires a
well-equipped laboratory and a full-time professional staff for the physical
examination, cleaning and conservation of works in the collection. The
premises which the gallery shares with three other institutions are hopelessly
inadequate for the display of the collection. The Government of Victoria
recently enacted the National Gallery and Cultural Centre Act, 1957
which is designed to provide the gallery with a new building on a new site.
Nothing less will overcome the gallery's pressing problems, but the problems
of storage and conservation require immediate attention if the collection is
not to suffer. The educational activities of the gallery are vigorous, imaginative and sustained. Travelling exhibitions to rural centres are organized
each year in concert with the Council of Adult Education. A splendid
series of current exhibitions, tastefully presented, now continues throughout
the year, and frequent TV programmes are making the wealth of the
collection more widely known throughout the state. The gallery can claim
with justification to be an educational force of inestimable value to the
Victorian community and, like Sydney's Mitchell Library, has grown,
by attention to quality and service, from a state to a national institution,
known and cherished throughout the country by people of taste and intelligence, and has a growing reputation abroad. Such institutions are a
national responsibility and merit Commonwealth assistance and attention
should they need it.

The collection of the National Art Gallery of New South Wales (1876)
is essentially a painting collection devoted very largely to the Australian
(the largest and most representative collection in the country) and English
schools of the later nineteenth and the twentieth centuries. As an art collection it is, therefore, quite unbalanced and, both in range and quality,
unworthy of a city of nearly two million people. The great schools of
painting of Italy, France, the Netherlands and eighteenth century England
are unrepresented by all but a few modest or indifferent paintings acquired
more by chance than by policy, and several generations of trustees would
appear, on the evidence of their acquisitions, never to have heard of the
arts of Greece, Byzantium, or of the Middle Ages, or for that matter, of
the whole art of sculpture prior to its decline in the nineteenth century.

The poor quality of the collection as a whole is neither entirely due to a lack of important bequests—though it is true that for a city of Sydney's wealth benefactions have been few and meagre—nor to the modest purchasing funds provided by the state government. It is due mainly to the narrow range of the artistic interests and sympathies of the trustees who have been responsible for acquisitions since the gallery was founded. To take one example only: 213 of the 721 paintings in the Australian collection (or approximately 30%) purchased between 1876 and 1952 were all purchased from two local painters' societies—the Royal Art Society of New South Wales, and the Society of Artists. There can be no doubt at all that the purchasing policy of the gallery has been too greatly dominated by the sectional interests of local painters' societies to make the formation of an art collection of real distinction possible. There is no keeper of the prints, nor has there ever been any attempt to train one. A travelling exhibition scheme for rural centres, which provided a useful educational service and brought the gallery to country people, has been allowed to languish from a lack of adequate funds and officers to conduct it. The gallery has, however, one real achievement to its credit. In recent years it has assembled the best-equipped laboratory for the examination and conservation of paintings in the country. There is a Gallery Society, and a valuable collection of books, though they are still of small value to the staff and public owing to the lack of a trained librarian. The Archibald Prize for a portrait by an Australian artist, the Wynne Prize for an Australian landscape or a piece of sculpture, and the Sulman Prize for a mural or genre painting in alternate years, are awarded annually. A catalogue of the Australian paintings was published in 1953, but no general catalogue nor any other sectional catalogue has appeared since 1928.

The National Art Gallery of South Australia, Adelaide (1881), seeks to provide a token representation of the art of all periods. It possesses particularly good collections of Australian and contemporary British art, and there is an important collection of the colonial art of South Australia. The gallery is well lit and the exhibits pleasantly and unostentatiously displayed, the ample space given to prints and drawings being a feature of the presentation. Provision for the storage of pictures, including the use of sliding metal racks, is still superior to that in most Australian galleries, but more space is required to house the growing collection satisfactorily. The gallery has benefited from the fine public spirit of many South Australians. The Ragless, Elder, Morgan Thomas, Boxall, Murray, Melrose and Mortlock bequests together total over £126,000. The Melrose Prize for a figure composition or portrait is awarded every fourth year, and the Maud Vizard-Wholohan Prize each year for a landscape and a figure subject in alternate years. The gallery has published a quarterly Bulletin since 1939,

P

being the first Australian gallery to do so. A free lending service of reproductions of paintings is widely used by schools throughout the state. The collection contains a few Greek vases and some 33,000 coins, including 2100 classical (800 Greek and 1300 Roman) and 7000 German. The editor of the *South Australian Numismatic Journal* is employed full time as officer-in-charge of the collection.

The Queensland National Art Gallery, Brisbane (1895), is seeking to build up a representative collection of Australian art, a good collection of overseas contemporary art, and a special collection of art museum objects of quality. A *Bulletin* is published, gallery lectures held regularly, country loan exhibitions circulated, and a Saturday morning children's art class conducted. The Richards Memorial Prize is awarded annually for a tropical or sub-tropical landscape.

In Tasmania and Western Australia the museum and art gallery maintained in each case by the respective states is administered under a common trust. The Tasmanian Museum and Art Gallery, Hobart (1848), houses the library of the Royal Society of Tasmania. Research undertaken at the museum is normally published in the society's *Papers and Proceedings*. The collections—historical, scientific and artistic—are mainly of Tasmanian interest. A catalogue of the Australian paintings in the gallery was published in 1956. From 1911 to 1955 the Public Library, Museum and Art Gallery of Western Australia, Perth, was administered by a common trust, but the library was separated from the museum and gallery in 1955. A further separation of the museum and gallery may be desirable in the interests of both. The existing position, whereby the Director of the gallery does not attend the meetings of the trust to which he is responsible, is without parallel in Australia. The museum's work is mainly scientific and falls outside the scope of this survey. The gallery contains good collections of English and Australian art, the collection of nineteenth century graphic art being particularly noteworthy. Educational activities have been developed in recent years. With the co-operation of a commercial airline an art exhibition was flown to the far north-west of the state in 1956, and the venture will be repeated. There is, however, no gallery *Bulletin*, and no catalogue of the collection has appeared since 1929.

The Provincial Collections

Newcastle (1957), which possesses the Roland Pope collection, has recently opened an art gallery and appointed a full-time curator, and there are small collections at Manly (1924) and Broken Hill. But only in Victoria has the provincial gallery found an accepted place in the cultural activities of the state. There are seven of them: Warrnambool (1873), Ballarat (1884), Bendigo (1887), Geelong (1900), Castlemaine (1914), Shepparton (1936), and Mildura (1956). All contain collections of Australian art, varied in range and quality. Bequests of special interest include the Alan Currie Bequest of English furniture at Ballarat, the Neptune Scott collection of French paintings at Bendigo, and the R.D. Elliott collection of English drawings and paintings at Mildura. All these provincial galleries, however, lack funds. They receive from £150 to £350 per annum from state grants, supplemented in some cases by smaller municipal grants. A recent conference of the Victorian Provincial Galleries (1957) approached the state government for an annual grant of £1000 per annum for each institution—"the lowest possible sum within which a creative policy can be presented". These galleries require in almost every case professionally trained officers, more and better loan exhibitions, and local gallery societies to stimulate regional interest. The provincial gallery can play a vital role in the cultural life of Australian rural communities, and deserves far more attention than it has hitherto received.

The Queen Victoria Museum and Art Gallery, Launceston (1891), is administered by the local city council and obtains a subsidy from the state government. Situated in a delightful garden setting it is unquestionably the finest provincial museum in Australia, its interests and activities being in most fields quite comparable with those of the Tasmanian Museum and Art Gallery, Hobart. There is a good collection of Tasmanian aboriginal petroglyphs, a Chinese joss house, drawings and paintings by Tasmanian colonial artists, and a small collection of English and continental ceramics. In 1930 the museum purchased the Beattie collection of colonial relics and paintings. Research is mainly of a scientific character, but some work has been done on the colonial artists, W.B. Gould, and Thomas and Alfred Bock. *Records* are issued annually in separate parts. The Mond Bequest provides £5000 for the purchase of ceramics and glassware, and the Mary Nicholls Bequest a small income for pictures by Australian artists.

University, College and Library Collection

Museums and galleries of varying quality are to be found in the universities, colleges and libraries throughout Australia. Only a few of the most important will be mentioned here.

The Nicholson Museum of the University of Sydney, an archaeological museum specializing in Near-Eastern, Greek and Roman antiquities is the best museum of its kind in the southern hemisphere. The original collection was bequeathed by Sir Charles Nicholson, Chancellor of the university from 1854 to 1862. There is a small but representative collection of Greek vases of good quality, a collection of classical coins, of *ostraca*, and of Roman sepulchral inscriptions. The Cyprus collection is superior in its representative range to anything outside Cyprus, except for the Swedish Cyprus Collection, Stockholm. Items have been added with the needs of university teaching very much in mind. A *Handbook* (first ed. 1945, second ed. 1948), and a *Guide to the Casts of Greek and Roman Sculpture* (1941) have been published. The university also contains a collection of paintings which includes some fine works from the original collection of Sir Charles Nicholson.

The Museum of Modern Art of Australia (1958), Tavistock Place, Melbourne, is devoted to the visual presentation of modern art and design in all its forms. Exhibitions are held regularly and the nucleus of a permanent collection has been created by Mr and Mrs John Reed's gift (September 1958) of their collection of paintings to the museum. The museum is supported by the private subscription of its members and administered by a governing council.

The Melbourne University contains a small but growing collection of drawings and paintings given by the Society of Collectors (1950). A museum that will house both the ethnological collection assembled by Dr Leonhard Adam and the university's small collection of classical antiquities is at present being planned. The Ewing Art Gallery of Australian art was bequeathed to the University Union by Dr S.A. Ewing in 1938. Both the University of Tasmania (Hobart) and University House, Canberra, contain small but interesting collections of Greek pottery. Valuable collections of paintings are held by several public libraries. Two of these collections together comprise the most important repository of drawings and paintings relating to colonial Australia and the Pacific. The Public Library of New South Wales contains both the Mitchell (1910) and the Dixson (1929) galleries. They contain portraits, views, miniatures, medallions, prints and photographic plates relating to the fields mentioned above. The nucleus of the Mitchell collection was bequeathed by David Scott Mitchell. The Dixson galleries were opened in 1929 with items donated by Sir William Dixson, these being added to during his life and since his death in 1952. The material in both galleries has been assembled in close association with the literary material of the Mitchell and Dixson collections. Both galleries are efficiently administered, admirably catalogued for research purposes, and widely used by scholars, but the pictures are not well displayed, the walls being badly overcrowded and poorly lit. Storage conditions are so primitive that much graphic material, valuable both artistically and historically, is in real danger of deterioration. There is a need for a printed catalogue of at least the more important original paintings in both collections. The Public Library of Victoria possesses a collection of drawings and paintings relating mainly to the early history of Victoria.

The Armidale Teachers' College, N.S.W., contains a large and valuable collection of drawings and paintings, mostly Australian, donated by Howard Hinton between 1929 and his death in 1947. Smaller collections of paintings exist in other teachers' colleges throughout Australia.

The University of Sydney Gallery of Fine Arts has been built as a memorial to members of the university who died in World War II, and consists of an exhibition hall (50 feet x 17 feet) which will be used, from the beginning of 1959, for art exhibitions and related functions. It will be conducted under the direction of a committee of management and a part-time director.

Private Collections

Of the private museums the most important, so far as research is concerned, is that at Mount Pleasant, Bathurst. It is not open to the public, being a research centre for excavations undertaken in Cyprus. When items excavated have been catalogued and their details published, they are distributed to museums acceptable to the Department of Antiquities of the Cyprus Government under conditions required by the Antiquities Law. The museum is equipped with mending rooms, a drawing office, and a photographic studio. A professional draughtsman is available, and most archaeological technical work is carried out. A private collection of medieval coins from the eastern Mediterranean is used for research, and there is a small collection of Near Eastern pottery used for comparative purposes. Publication (in series) of the Cyprus Expedition sponsored by the University of Melbourne is at present being prepared, the first volume being published in 1957.

The Art Gallery and Nautical Museum of the Port Adelaide Institute (1872) is privately maintained with the help of the Port Adelaide Corporation. Its present policy is to collect only nautical items. The Kyancutta Museum, South Australia (1929), is based on the original collection of Robert Bedford. Apart from its geological and natural history collections it contains some examples of Egyptian and Chinese art together with Australian and American ethnological material, and it publishes *Memoirs*. The Melbourne Ward Gallery of Natural History and Native Art, Medlow Bath, N.S.W. (1943), contains among other things a collection of ethnological material relating to Tasmania and Australia, and some Pacific Island material. A small collection of Tasmanian and Pacific ethnology is also to be found at the Pett Falls Museum, Ridgley, north-west Tasmania.

Museums, Galleries and Research

Since the end of the second world war most Australian museums and galleries have extended their educational activities and improved their methods of presentation and display. The art galleries have wisely adopted a more tolerant approach to the purchase of contemporary art (including abstract and non-objective work), and have made some attempt to guide public taste in commercial and industrial design. However, apart from the purely scientific work of the museums—outside the scope of this Survey—research of a scholarly nature has been confined largely to archaeology and anthropology, fields wherein scientific methods are well established. While it is, of course, desirable that museums and galleries should be made as pleasant as possible for the general public, it is most important that the trustees and executives of these institutions do not lose sight of the special requirements of scholars and the exacting demands of scholarship, for the standard of Australia's collections will never be better than the scholarship and critical judgment of those involved in their acquisition, classification and criticism.

Most museums and galleries display only a small proportion of their collections to the general public. The remainder should be housed systematically so that it is readily available to students, scholars and interested persons at all times at short notice. A room should be available where drawings, prints, paintings and other works of art may be studied by accredited persons as comfortably as they can read a book in a public library.

Few Australian art galleries engage upon serious research relating to material in their possession or make much attempt to attract the interests of scholars. The catalogues of most collections are out of print and hopelessly out of date. True, in the larger galleries general catalogues are now, because of the amount and diversity of the material involved, quite unsuitable. In these cases sectional catalogues are most desirable. Excellent work is being done in some galleries by means of quarterly bulletins, which enable recent accessions to be described in some detail. The educational value of many collections would be increased tenfold by the production of suitable handbooks, such as the admirable *Handbook to the Nicholson Museum*. But very little work of this nature, requiring as it does expert knowledge of the field surveyed, has been undertaken. The maintenance of well-catalogued and efficiently administered print collections is an essential aspect of a collection which is to be of use to scholars. In this respect the print collection of the National Gallery of Victoria might well serve as a model for other institutions. Scientific equipment, such as microscopes, ultra-violet, infra-red and X-rays, is also essential for detailed physical examinations of works of art. All the larger collections should possess a well-equipped laboratory and photographer's dark room. In this regard the work of conservation carried out at the National Gallery of New South Wales and the University of Sydney in recent years might be examined with profit by other institutions.

The cataloguing and examination of paintings involve questions of attribution. Many paintings in our galleries have been ascribed to artists on doubtful grounds. Trustees and directors should encourage qualified scholars—whether employed by them or not—to take an interest in such attributions. Certainly, such questions are often complex and difficult, consequently all opinions, however qualified, must be examined critically and often treated with reserve. Nevertheless it is most desirable that no attempt be made to cover up old mistakes or to erect barriers to investigation by those qualified to make them. In this regard the trustees of the Public Library of New South Wales, more experienced (through their control of the Mitchell and Dixson collections) than most trusts of similar Australian institutions in meeting the requirements of scholars, might be followed with advantage. This trust has made available to accredited scholars documents relating to the acquisition of valuable works in their possession, permitted detailed examination with appropriate equipment, and allowed photographs, relevant to ascription, to be taken. Such enlightened procedure is unfortunately still not general in Australia.

Australian art collections tend to be narrow in their range of interests: in the majority of collections British and Australian art since about 1880 occupy a place out of all proportion to their significance in the whole history of art. This imbalance has arisen partly from the desire to be "modern" at all costs; it is only the idea of what is modern that has changed —with frequently embarrassing results. The growing tendency to spend increasing amounts of money upon the purchase of contemporary work is not wholly to be commended, though clearly some purchases in the contemporary field should always be made. Whilst it is admittedly more difficult to collect in some fields than in others it is felt that many museums and galleries might do more to develop specialized collections, with consequent benefit to the diversity and richness of Australia's cultural facilities. Australia possesses no comprehensive collection of African or Indian art, or of the arts of North and South America.

Reliable catalogues, handbooks and bulletins, efficiently administered print rooms, better and more balanced collections all require professionally trained staffs. In museum and gallery administration the day of the well-intentioned amateur has passed. Those who rise to positions of responsibility in our museums and galleries must be trained. A large part of this training must take place within the institutions themselves, though the universities, too, can play their part. The question of the recruitment, training and subsequent professional advancement of the members of the curatorial profession is fundamental to the status and quality of Australia's museums and galleries. It is a question to which far more attention might be profitably given.

DRAMA AND THEATRE IN TERTIARY EDUCATION

BY DONOVAN CLARKE

Theatre Facilities

In keeping with the accepted policy in Australian universities that practical theatre shall be extra-curricular, the university senates have not felt called upon to provide adequate theatre facilities for their students. This has been left to the student bodies themselves. Pending such provision the senates have, however, made available makeshift accommodation by adapting lecture theatres of the auditorium type to dramatic performances.

At the University of Queensland and at the Newcastle University College, this makeshift accommodation remains the only one available. At the University of Sydney there is in addition a general purposes hall provided by the Students' Union. The University of New England has a general purposes hall provided by the Senate. At the University of New South Wales there is a better equipped general purposes theatre. The University of Western Australia has a small open-air theatre, a large open-air auditorium, and a general purposes enclosed hall. The universities of Melbourne and Adelaide alone possess properly designed and equipped theatres. These have been provided in Melbourne by the student bodies and in Adelaide by public subscription assisted by the University Council. The University of Tasmania has no theatre facilities of any kind; use is made of either the Theatre Royal or the Hobart Repertory Theatre for university productions. At the University of Sydney the Students' Union has plans for replacing the present Union Hall by a thoroughly up-to-date theatre. In Queensland there are plans for a general purposes hall.

Dramatic Societies

All the universities have active dramatic societies. For instance, Adelaide has three: the Adelaide Theatre Guild (graduate body); the A.U. Dramatic Society and the Footlights Club (undergraduate bodies). The University of Melbourne sponsors a fully professional repertory company, which has been in existence for over four years, and in addition there are several student societies: the College Dramatic Clubs, the Marlowe Society, the Secondary Teachers' Society, and the Melbourne University Dramatic Club. All the other universities have similar societies.

Interstate Drama Festivals

The National Union of Australian University Students sponsors an annual Drama Festival, held usually in the second term vacation in each of the capital cities in turn. One of the university dramatic societies acts as host and the festival is held in the major theatre available to the host university. The conduct of the festival is vested in the Festival Organizing Committee. Travel allowances are paid by the National Union from the Drama Festival Travelling Expenses Fund, for not more than seven persons from each participating university.

The host organization is responsible for the entertainment, accommodation and expenses of the visiting casts, but it is provided that the individual students unions may subsidize the host to the extent of £60 for general revenue. Profits of the festival are paid into a profit and loss account. All university students who are members of their respective unions are entitled to participate in the festival. The producers are not required to be such members. For an indication of the parlous state of this festival see the report of the drama critic in the *Sydney Morning Herald* on 26th August 1957. The festival is financially precarious, and the standards of production and acting are in many instances poor.

The teachers' colleges of Adelaide and Perth sponsor an interstate committee which organizes an interstate drama competition, held alternately in Perth and Adelaide. This competition is financed by the college administrations and students combined. Each of the four colleges (two in Adelaide and two in Perth) acts in turn as host, and each college presents a one-act play.

In the other states the students' bodies and the colleges, together with bodies such as the British Drama League and the Arts Council, organize or participate in various local festivals. For example, Queensland participates in the annual Ipswich festival of one-act plays; Sydney participates in an annual festival of music and drama; Western Australia, in the festival of Perth.

Productions

The direction of students' plays is by staff members, or outsiders who are usually paid out-of-pocket expenses, but no fees. The support for undergraduate plays comes from a relatively small number of students interested in drama. With a few exceptions all plays produced are by professional authors. Lent and Trinity terms are the most favoured periods, and performances are always in the evening. Except by occasional mismanagement plays are not run at a loss, usually playing for two or three evenings, though in Western Australia the average length of season is six or seven evenings.

As an example of a typical year's theatre programme, we may take the following from Melbourne University (1956):

The Mad Woman of Chaillot: Giraudoux (Melbourne University Dramatic Club)

Time Remembered: Anouilh (Marlowe Society)
This Happy Breed: Coward (Secondary Teachers)
A Winter's Tale: Shakespeare (Trinity College)
Revue: *Up an Atom*, written by students and sponsored by the Students'
Representative Council
The Crucible: Miller (Ormond College)
Gaslight: Hamilton (M.U.D.C.)
Lady 213: Guitton (Newman College)
The Eagle Has Two Heads: Cocteau (Marlowe Society)
Golden Boy: Odets (Queen's College)
Chilypolika: (Russian Dept)
Tomb: Goethe (German Dept)

It will be seen that the type of play produced is for the most part "repertory type", with some representation of the period play, and a student-authored revue. This is typical of all universities. Adelaide is outstanding for its encouragement of locally written plays. Occasional Australian plays are presented elsewhere.

Tours of student productions are the exception. None of these tours is officially sponsored, and all are expected to pay their own way, with the exception, as stated above, of the entries for the Drama Festival.

Drama in the Arts Faculties

All the Arts faculties of the several universities admit a study of English drama in the schools of English, from the beginnings to the present day, with a special emphasis upon Shakespeare and the Elizabethans. In the fourth year (honours) a selection of modern American and British plays is usually studied. No theatre practice is given. Plays are read and criticized and sufficient account is taken of the theatrical qualities of the plays studied to develop an interest in, and an understanding of drama generally. The foreign language departments usually produce one or two plays in the foreign language, more or less as a part of the year's work of students. Use is made in most faculties of long-play records where these are available and are of satisfactory quality.

An Australian School of Drama

In 1959 a School of Drama, sponsored by the Elizabethan Theatre Trust in conjunction with the University of New South Wales, opened in Sydney. It will provide a full two-year course in the dramatic arts, and will include, in addition to practical classes, a course of lectures of university type, with written examinations. The lecturers will be members of staff of the university of New South Wales.

Adult Education Facilities

Only four Australian universities have departments of Adult Education: Adelaide, Western Australia, Sydney and New England. These bodies organize adult evening classes in drama, where plays are read and criticized. At Sydney courses are conducted in the writing of plays. All departments conduct occasional weekend and ten-day schools, when the techniques of acting and production are taught by staff tutors, part-time lecturers, or visiting professional actors or authorities in drama study.

Some Conclusions

It must not be assumed that because theatrical crafts are not included in the university curricula, Australian universities are failing to make any contribution to Australian theatre or that a greater contribution would automatically result if they were included. In America, for instance, despite the flourishing of university schools of drama, and a high degree of correlation between the theory, criticism and practice of the art, there is virtually no professional stage outside New York. Most of the graduates of American drama schools become school teachers of drama, or technicians in the various university theatres, rather than actors or technicians in the commercial theatres. University policy alone can effect little in the face of wider cultural and economic factors. Our universities are making an important contribution to professional and amateur theatre in Australia, by educating an audience for good plays, and by providing a few outstanding recruits to the professions of dramatist, producer, actor and critic. It was, for instance, at the Melbourne Union Theatre that the *Summer of the Seventeenth Doll* was first performed, and it was there too, that the author of that play received some of his training in theatre technique. Sydney University has given Australia two of its outstanding producers in May Hollingworth and Peter Osborn (now in London).

The universities provide a proportion of students (those who wish it) with the opportunity to develop as amateurs such acting and producing talents as they possess. The enlightened student may provide his own correlation between theory and practice; and not a few try to do this. But it may well be asked whether some practical assistance towards this end might not be forthcoming from the faculty authorities. At present there is little or none. The founding of the Elizabethan Trust Drama School is, however, a major step in this direction. To date the University of Melbourne is the only Australian university to attempt to establish a Chair of Drama, and after a frustrating experience the occupant of the chair resigned and returned to his traditional faculty work.

LEARNED SOCIETIES

BY A.D. TRENDALL FROM INFORMATION SUPPLIED BY H.L. WHITE

The Australian people maintain in the federal and state capitals, and even in some of the country centres, a considerable number of learned societies, some of which are connected with the universities, while others are supported by governments and the public in efforts to further culture.[1] Some of these organizations exist to promote the humanities in fields such as the languages, philosophy, history and Australian literature; others are primarily concerned with the physical and social sciences such as education, economics and political science, but their discussions and publications cannot be disregarded for they frequently enter such humanist fields as history. Reference should also be made to the Australian and New Zealand Association for the Advancement of Science, which, through the work of Archibald Liversidge and others, evolved from the Philosophical Society of New South Wales and held its first meeting in Sydney in 1888. The association has sections which deal with history and with education, psychology and philosophy, but unfortunately now publishes only the presidential address of each section in the *Australian Journal of Science*. A.N.Z.A.A.S. receives government recognition and financial help, as do other organizations of this nature.

The existence of a number of learned societies throughout Australia is a not unimportant factor in encouraging the study of the humanities and making them known to a wider audience than that of the professional scholar. Most such societies serve the dual purpose of giving scope for the scholar to present for critical discussion a learned paper on some aspect of his own work, and also of endeavouring, by means of popular lectures, to interest the general public in the subject in question and to keep people informed of recent developments and discoveries. Classics, English, modern languages, philosophy, history and fine arts are all supported in various parts of the country, and several of the societies publish scholarly journals in which original contributions and summaries of addresses appear, while others sponsor literary magazines containing poems, essays, short stories and critical articles.

From very early times the Australian pioneers attempted to institute and

---

[1] As far as can be ascertained, no adequate list of the Australian learned societies, their objectives and their publications, has ever been compiled. This section of the Survey makes no claim to meet the need, and is purely selective. It is based on information supplied by H.L. White, the Commonwealth Librarian, and from the following: "Societies, Learned," *Australian Encyclopaedia*, Angus and Robertson, Sydney, 1926; *A Directory of Adult Education in New South Wales*, Australasian Publishing Co., Sydney, 1945; *Australian Encyclopaedia*, vol. x, Index with numerous references, Angus and Robertson, Sydney, 1958; *Press Directory of Australia and New Zealand*, 14th edition, Sydney, 1958.

conduct literary, philosophical, scientific and book societies, together with mechanics' institutes. Some of these bodies imported small quantities of books and made pathetic and frequently brief efforts to promote a culture which often included the arts. Two of the earliest of these bodies were the short-lived Philosophical Society of Australia, founded by Sir Thomas Brisbane in Sydney in 1821, and the Royal Society of Tasmania, founded by Sir John Franklin in 1839. Amongst the first organizations to gain a footing and to give real help to the humanities were geographical societies, which entered the historical field directly they were founded and issued important publications. The year 1885, for example, saw the establishment of the Royal Geographical Society of Australasia with branches in New South Wales, Victoria, South Australia and Queensland. The New South Wales and Victorian branches failed, but the South Australian body purchased in London the magnificent York Gate Library which contains amongst many historical treasures Joseph Banks's original journal of his expedition to Labrador. The state government now provides this society with accommodation and subsidizes its publications, of which a large proportion consists of historical research and of documents, such as Colonel William Light's journal covering the controversy over the choice of the Adelaide site. The Queensland branch also survived and now possesses commodious quarters and receives government aid. Each body publishes regularly a journal or proceedings containing research, and these publications have gained some status overseas.

Later in origin but of considerable importance are the historical societies, both those in metropolitan cities and those which in a number of country centres are conducting some useful local research before the documentary and other evidence disappears. Of the metropolitan bodies the Royal Historical Society of Australia, which was founded in 1901, has a membership of nearly one thousand and possesses excellent premises in Sydney. Its journal has published important research, such as the work of T.D. Mutch on Jansz's discovery of Australia, and that of F.J. Bayldon on the Spanish discovery of Torres Strait. The Royal Historical Society of Victoria, established in 1909, publishes the *Victorian Historical Magazine*. Of special importance to historical scholarship are *Historical Studies*, published twice a year by the University of Melbourne, and the *Journal of History and Politics* of the University of Queensland.

In the language field there are six local branches of the Classical Association, of which the most flourishing are in Sydney and Melbourne, each of which is able to maintain a regular publication—the *Bulletin* and *Iris* respectively—giving summaries of addresses as well as notes and news. Other branches are in Adelaide, Armidale, Brisbane and Canberra, and these carry out programmes of lectures, readings and discussions. The classical languages have recently combined with the modern languages to form the Australasian Universities' Language and Literature Association, which now replaces the former Modern Languages Association. It publishes proceedings of its congresses, a newsletter, and since 1953, *AUMLA*—a journal of literary criticism, philology and linguistics—which is now issued twice yearly from the University of Canterbury (N.Z.). The association fosters exchanges of scholars and is also concerned with such projects as a union catalogue of German language and literature material. Like most other associations of this kind, it is hampered by lack of numbers and of financial support. The Modern Language Teachers' Association of Victoria has been issuing *Babel* in duplicated form at irregular intervals since 1956. Other aspects of European culture are fostered by the Alliance Française, the Goethe Society and the Dante Alighieri Society, most of which have branches in the main centres.

The English Association has active branches in Queensland and Sydney; the latter, founded in 1923, being responsible for *Southerly*, which has achieved international repute as a literary quarterly during the nineteen years of its existence. Many "little magazines" have appeared and disappeared in Australia, as a subsidy of some kind is almost always essential if journals with such a limited circulation are to survive. At present the Commonwealth Literary Fund is giving substantial aid to *Southerly* and to *Meanjin*, a literary journal located in the University of Melbourne and having a history of seventeen years. The existence of *Westerly* in Perth and *Australian Letters* in the University of Adelaide is evidence of a determined effort to keep alive literary publications of a high quality. *Meanjin* claimed in 1957 that it received submissions of about one thousand poems and two hundred and fifty stories a year.

The Commonwealth Council of the Fellowships of Australian Writers, co-ordinating the work of the various branch fellowships, encourages creative writing and is working for the establishment of a Henry Lawson Prize for Literature. In the past few years the Canberra Fellowship has edited two worthwhile anthologies of Australian writing, *Australia Writes* (1953) and *Australian Signpost* (1956) and in 1958 *Span*, an anthology of the work of Australian and Asian writers.

One of the stronger societies has been the Australasian Association of Psychology and Philosophy, which, now that psychology has its own professional association, has been renamed the Australasian Association of Philosophy. Since its inception in 1923 it has published the *Australasian Journal of Philosophy* and has made itself responsible for the holding of regular philosophical conferences.

Scholars from the comparatively young schools of Oriental Studies in Sydney and Canberra joined in founding the Oriental Society of Australia in April 1956, a group whose interest is in the history and culture of East Asian countries and related subjects. With fellows, members and associates now numbering over one hundred, the society contemplates an annual publication, but at present contents itself with a duplicated newsletter.

In conclusion it may be stated that, although some of the learned societies have tended to become rather antiquarian in character and their work varies in its importance and scholarly value, the majority give useful service by assisting scholars and by emphasizing the importance of the Australian humanities both in this country and to people overseas. The various governments should continue their grants to the organizations, and where claims are supported by expert bodies such as the universities, the Advisory Board of the Commonwealth Literary Fund, or this Council, grants in aid might well be increased. The smaller societies, whose budgets are of necessity often very restricted, would particularly appreciate any support that would enable them to avail themselves of the opportunities afforded by the visits of distinguished scholars from overseas or elsewhere in Australia.

VISUAL AIDS

By BERNARD SMITH

It would seem, on the present indications, that the discovery of photography in the early nineteenth century will produce a revolution in our forms of communication barely less far-reaching than that wrought by the discovery of printing in the later fifteenth century. By contrast with our Victorian ancestors we now rely far less upon verbal forms both for conveying information and providing entertainment. Such a shift in emphasis from largely verbal forms to mixed forms of communication, in which the written and spoken word is supplemented by the visual image, constitutes a challenge to university teachers. And it is a challenge directed at the humanities for which the word, both written and spoken, has always meant, and must continue to mean so much. Since there is every indication that the visual image is going to play an even more important role in communication in the future it is most desirable that it should be enlisted wherever possible for the preservation of academic standards. It is obvious enough how easily it can be enlisted for their destruction. As it happens, the Australian university teacher is reasonably well aware of the possibilities of visual aids for his work, but a good deal remains to be done in order to find out how they may best serve the purposes of academic instruction and research.

Obviously, the value of visual aids varies greatly from subject to subject. In the teaching of architecture, fine arts and geography they are essential; in the higher levels of language teaching they provide little more than a pleasant embellishment. It should be remembered, however, that visual aids at present in use in universities range from the provision of photographs of buildings, sculpture and paintings to the provision of maps, models, statistical tables, motion films and television.

Language departments make use of visual aids mainly for background studies. All departments of Classics possess stocks of slides to illustrate classical art and archaeology, the Greek theatre, etc., though these vary in size greatly from university to university. Modern language departments make use of visual material for studying the life and art of the societies with which they are concerned. Such "civilization" courses are usually given during the first and second years and have been found of great value in developing a deeper interest in the wider implications of linguistic studies. As might be expected, departments of English have not found quite the same need for visual aids as other language departments. The Department of English of the University of New South Wales however, has experimented with the showing of films of set texts, e.g. *The Importance of being Earnest*, where it has been found that they assisted considerably in stimulating the student's critical understanding of the texts.

Visual aids, mainly in the form of projection slides, have been used by History departments for many years, largely as supplementary material for the study of ancient history. Most teachers of language and history tend to agree, however, that their use, while being of considerable value in arousing and deepening interest, especially among pass students, is not central to the discipline of such subjects. For other subjects they are absolutely essential. Fine arts and archaeology cannot be taught without a constant supply of visual material, mainly in the form of slides; and for architecture, geography and town planning, visual material is no less important. Such subjects make use of slides constantly, and of motion films occasionally.

It is the departments of Psychology which make by far the greatest use of the motion film for general teaching purposes. The Department of Psychology in the University of Queensland, for example, shows at least two 16-mm. films a week, while that in the University of New South Wales projects films for at least six hours per week. Teaching techniques are being developed to make the best use of the film as an educational medium. The Department of Psychology at Melbourne, for instance, prepares classes by means of questionnaires, etc. prior to viewing a film. Other departments make use of the 16-mm. film rather as an extra-curricular activity, held in the lunch hour or the evening, partly to supplement teaching and partly for entertainment. For most departments the 16-mm. film is by no means as useful for general teaching purposes as the projection slide. A common complaint is that the films are either too elementary or too general to be of much use in university teaching. Thus the Department of Psychology in the University of Adelaide has found "that the majority of 16-mm. films on psychology and related topics . . . are . . . addressed to a different kind of audience than is found in first year psychology classes". The Department of Geography of the University of New England has found many 16-mm. films available through the usual agencies "too elementary and too general to be of much use". University departments borrow films from a variety of sources such as the Commonwealth National Library, Canberra, the New South Wales Film Council, the Canadian High Commissioner's office, and foreign consular agencies. At present, however, the 16-mm. film suited to university teaching is the exception rather than the rule.

In order to be effective in university teaching visual aids must be serviced adequately. An adequate service requires: firstly, a central organization concerned largely with production and research, and secondly, an officer responsible for their maintenance in each department in which they are used regularly. The captioning, storage and classification of slides, the care of maps and models, and the provision of material for photographing, etc. must be the concern of the department which uses them. In some departments this work can be carried out as part of the duties of a member of the academic staff, in other departments the amount of material involved will require the undivided attention of a full-time officer. For, as with libraries, the value of visual aids depends in large measure upon the speed with which new material can be produced when needed, and old material assembled for use with a minimum of time and fuss. Furthermore, the services of one or more officers skilled and experienced in projecting films and slides is an essential feature of this aspect of university teaching. Such officers are usually responsible for the maintenance of screens and projectors.

Some universities make provision for the production of photographs, slides, film strips, etc. for the use of those departments which require them. The University of Tasmania, for example, possesses a photographic section. In other universities each department provides its own visual material as best it can. The faculty of Architecture of Sydney University, for example, has produced a great deal of material for its own use, and has been able to obtain the services of its graduates and friends in photographing buildings overseas for use in the school. Only the University of Melbourne, however, possesses a department of audio-visual aids which undertakes not only to provide for all the visual aid requirements of the university, but also undertakes research in problems associated with the use of audio-visual aid

Q

material. For this reason it seems desirable to include here a brief outline of the history of the department and the scope of its work.[1]

The Melbourne University Department of Audio-Visual Aids was established in 1946 as a result of an agreement between the Royal Australian Air Force and the university. During the war the R.A.A.F. built up a substantial visual training section and carried out research into methods of using audio-visual materials and their efficiency. As the war ended it was felt that the organization and resources available should not be allowed to disappear but should be maintained for the use of the R.A.A.F. in peace time and for educational purposes in general. By an agreement later reached between the R.A.A.F. and the university, the Air Force contributed basic equipment and films, and the university, accommodation and staff. The department began in October 1946, first in a small attic room, and after the middle of 1947 was accommodated in army huts, where it gradually extended its activities until the opening of its present new building in March 1957. The dark rooms, offices and all heavy equipment are on the ground floor with a theatrette and projection room. Coaxial cables for television have been built into the walls and there is a complete closed circuit television system, which includes a "flying-spot" film scanner and an image-orthicon studio television camera. On the first floor there are a large art studio for the preparation of non-projected visual aids, a photographic studio, rooms for the research staff, a film library and a storeroom.

The department is divided into two sections. One is essentially a service department for the university producing all types of visual aids to instruction, from charts and diagrams to sound motion pictures. The other is concerned with communication research, from the relative values of colour and black and white in illustrative materials to the impact of films and television on children and adolescents. The combination of production and research under single control makes it possible to avoid limiting research to "apparatus" which happens to be available. It is an aim of the department to ensure that the nature of the research undertaken should, as far as possible, determine the type of apparatus used, and not, as so often happens, that the apparatus available should decide the nature of the research. The department is administered by a director responsible to the Vice-Chancellor and the Council. Three specialist officers, in charge of three aspects of the department's activities, function under the director. The Art Department is in the charge of an eminent Australian artist whose responsibilities cover all aspects of illustration, particularly those relating to medicine and science, and includes line-work, titling for films and film-strips, modelling and preparation of illustrations for reproduction. The Photography Department

---

[1] For the outline of the department's work which follows I am indebted to Mr Newman Rosenthal.

is concerned with microfilming, photostating, and all aspects of photographic reproduction, together with the manufacture of slides, film-strips and silent and sound motion pictures. It has made several full-length medical films, two recent ones being "Normal Delivery", a teaching film for the Department of Obstetrics and Gynaecology, and "Pyeloplasty with Nephrosis" for Surgery.

In addition to providing for the general needs of other university departments, the photographic section is engaged in technical research. It has become a source of information and advice on all branches of scientific photography to both industry and educational institutions. Its facilities include equipment for high-speed and time-lapse photography, three-dimensional projection both still and motion picture. Its closed circuit television system is used primarily for controlled experiments in audience reaction and in the likely uses of television for specialized instruction and general education. The department receives a grant from the university's general fund, and makes charges for services rendered and for materials supplied to other university departments. Specialized work from industry and educational institutions is undertaken. Much research is financed by government or industry. The present investigations into the effects of television have been sponsored by the Australian Broadcasting Control Board, the controlling authority for Australian commercial television programmes.

The department's facilities are in constant demand by public bodies such as the National Gallery of Victoria, which it assists from time to time in the physical examination of paintings. For the secondary school courses prescribed in Victoria by the university, the department produces film-strips to help instruction in various subjects, such as background information in modern languages, laboratory practice in the physical sciences, masterpieces of painting for fine arts, and teacher training in education. The department also provides a series of lectures for teachers on the use of audio-visual aids, and conducts seminars from time to time, such as the joint Indo-Australian Audio-Visual Aids Seminar, which it was responsible for organizing at Lucknow, India, for South-East Asian educationists. Following this seminar students from the several countries of South-East Asia have come to Melbourne under the Colombo Plan for a six months' course of training. An examination at the end of the course leads to a certificate of proficiency in the theory and practice of audio-visual aids in education. The department also publishes a journal, the *Visual Aids Review* which appears irregularly when suitable material for publication is available.

Apart from its invaluable service to teaching and its own researches in communication the Department of Audio-Visual Aids also contributes significantly by its services to research being conducted throughout the university. And it is to be remembered that in the field of the humanities, visual aids can be of the greatest help to the research worker, providing him with photostats of manuscripts, articles, and sections of books; and with photographs of the visual documents which are the concern of the archaeologist, ethnologist, anthropologist, art historian, architect, geographer and town planner. To quote only one example: the detailed history of Australian architecture depends in no small measure upon the assembling of large photographic collections of Australian and overseas buildings, without which detailed descriptive and comparative work is not possible. Indeed for all studies concerned with the material remains of man's past—a by no means small sector of the humanist inquiry—visual aids have a crucial part to play both in teaching and in research.

RADIO

BY R.J.F. BOYER

Introduction

While both radio systems, National and Commercial, have contributed to the study and appreciation of humanities in Australia, the Australian Broadcasting Commission by its charter and through provision of public funds, has had the obligation and the opportunity of utilizing the medium to a much greater extent than the commercial system. The following survey, therefore, is confined to the activities of the Commission in this field.

By its nature radio is pre-eminently an instrument for the extension of all its material to the general public, reaching out well beyond the bounds of the normal impact of academic and artistic activities. There is no part of the Australian community which today is not exposed to the output of the National Broadcasting Service. It is this extension work which is fundamental to radio rather than the intensive work of artistic and learned societies and the universities. Its contribution, therefore, while necessarily diffused, has been very real. On the other hand, the charter which was granted to promote actively artistic creativeness as well as to radiate existing output in the humanities has meant that considerable positive and creative work has been accomplished. This is particularly true in the field of music which is a natural area of activity for sound broadcasting, but it is also true of drama, literary composition and philosophic discussion. Indeed, if one concedes the term "humanities" as covering the full range of the activities of the human spirit which cannot be described as utilitarian, it is difficult to find any field in which a contribution has not been made. As the record hereunder will show, the entry of radio into the field of fine music has meant not only consistent broadcasts of classical and contemporary works to all ages and to all levels of popular appreciation, but has actually led to the creation of symphony orchestras, musical ensembles of various kinds and the operation of the largest concert activity in this country. Less spectacular, but equally important, has been the creative work initiated in drama, literature (notably poetry), and in philosophical discussion on topics ranging from religion and civics to metaphysics.

In education of a formal character, school broadcasts have been an extension service of the education curriculum of the various states of the Commonwealth, and their importance in that field has been quite invaluable.

Of particular interest in all the fields of humanities has been the ability of radio to take advantage of overseas scholarship and artistic performances by means of recordings, and in this respect I should like particularly to refer to the excellent material which has been made available in this country from the British Broadcasting Corporation's Home and Third programmes. While television is outside the terms of reference of this submission, it should be added that prospects for the more effective use of the electronic medium through television appear even more promising than has been possible in sound radio, with the exception, perhaps, of fine music. It would seem that television in the future will bring in a much wider audience in the intellectual field than radio has been able to muster. The addition of sight to sound provides a factor of greater ease in attention of the listener-viewer to broadcasts requiring serious thought than has been possible with the disembodied broadcast of sound alone. It might be worth adding to these introductory remarks the rather astonishing reaction in the United Kingdom to a proposal by the B.B.C. to discontinue part, at least, of its Third Programme, which may, I think, be taken as evidence of the deep interest and strong influence of broadcasting at the high levels of art and criticism, even though the audience may have been a minority one when compared with popular listening figures. In Australia it can be said that broadcasting in humanities has had a valuable and significant though not a major audience for such sessions. Indeed, strong disapproval is normally expressed from every section of the community when any proposals to limit such broadcasts in favour of lighter entertainment have been made, indicating that efforts in this direction have gone deeply into the community, even though at a minority level. Under the following headings the factual history of the Commission's efforts are briefly summarized.

Music

When the A.B.C. took over in 1932, there were two "orchestras" of fifteen players each in Sydney and Melbourne. Within a year these were built to twenty-four players and four years later the Commission completed plans to establish studio concert orchestras in all states, the Sydney and

Melbourne players numbering thirty-five and forty-five respectively. There is now a permanent symphony orchestra established in each state of the Commonwealth, with the exception of Tasmania, where, however, an important nucleus exists which is augmented for the frequent concerts given.

In 1936 a subscription series of concerts began, and 2522 subscribers were enlisted in support. In 1956 over 50,000 people subscribed to the various concert series arranged by the A.B.C., and as well as this number many thousands of people attended the various individual concerts presented in all states. An important feature of the subscription series has been the building of a youth subscription orchestral concerts series for an audience under the age of twenty-five. No less than 12,031 young Australians subscribed to this series in 1956. In addition to this the A.B.C. has built in every state of the Commonwealth a series of free orchestral concerts for school children, which tens of thousands of children attend. These concerts are given not only in the capital cities but also in country centres. Additionally, the A.B.C. co-operates with municipal authorities in presenting many free concerts, chiefly on Sundays, in town halls and public gardens throughout the Commonwealth. Many thousands of people may attend any one of these concerts.

The A.B.C. has pursued a vigorous policy of bringing to Australia international artists of world status. Prior to the Commission's advent in this field, it was rare for Australia to be visited by more than one or two international artists each year, and sometimes not by that number. The A.B.C. now brings regularly to Australia twelve to fourteen international figures annually, and special attempts are made to include outstanding Australian artists resident overseas.

In all, the Commission has for a number of years regularly arranged and presented over 700 concerts in more than eighty cities and country towns. However, perhaps the most important part of the service is bringing into the home of the people good music programmes for a number of hours each day. Music sessions are broadcast at certain times each morning, afternoon and evening, and this has a most important influence on the building of appreciation and so enlarging the numbers of those who wish to go and hear the outstanding artists and conductors of the world.

Drama and Literature

The A.B.C. has always devoted considerable attention to the classical drama. As an instance, some years ago a Shakespeare to Shaw Festival was programmed; on another occasion all the plays of Shakespeare were broadcast in series, this probably being unique among broadcasting organizations. There have been series of the great Elizabethan and the Restoration dramatists, and the dramatists of the late nineteenth century. Many translations of plays by outstanding dramatists of other lands have been broadcast, these including Sartre, Victor Hugo, Anouilh, Cocteau, Ibsen, Strindberg, Pirandello and Capek. The half-hour serial has always been a popular form of A.B.C. entertainment, and many standard literary works have been treated in this programme fashion.

Special attention has been paid to verse, and there is a weekly session "Quality Street" broadcast on Sunday evenings, devoted to critical comment and assessment of great poetry and prose. Another regular session is Poets' Corner, where examples are given of the major poets of the English tongue, both classical and modern. There is also broadcast a regular quarterly "Poetry Review", devoted to the assessment of recent works by Australian poets.

Book reviews have been a long-standing feature of A.B.C. programmes, and books of all types are brought before the notice of listeners. On Sundays for many years there have been broadcast regular talks series devoted to literary themes. There is also a regular morning book-reading in which all types of books from the *Pride and Prejudice* type to recent works by Australian authors are read by special readers.

School Broadcasts

Broadcasts to schools have been an important feature of A.B.C. programmes since 1932. A very wide audience of school pupils from kindergarten to the leaving certificate has been built up for the weekly output of some thirty broadcast series throughout the school year. To this school audience must be added the large number of teachers who listen to the broadcasts with the children and greatly increase their fund of information, and experience fresh methods of presentation of educational material. Also there are many adult listeners outside the schools, particularly women, who find in many of the broadcasts great interest or ideas which can later be discussed with their children. More than 8000 Australian schools, or 84% of all schools throughout the Commonwealth, possess radio receivers. These figures imply a regular audience of about one million children, for whom well over a million illustrated programme booklets are annually distributed.

The subject-matter of school broadcasts covers a broad range of school studies, but particularly music and the humanities, such as drama, literature, history and languages. Current Affairs broadcasts provide an opportunity to introduce children to the background events of the day, while a large amount of time is devoted to the provision of graduated musical experience which can accompany the child as he moves up in his school career. Broadcasts in literature are closely associated with the stimulation of children's reading and there is convincing evidence from school and municipal libraries of the degree to which reading of books follows from interest aroused by broadcasts. Some sessions are designed to introduce teachers and children to new subjects and broadcasts of folk dancing, singing or dramatizations of history permit children to have experiences which, particularly in the country, would be denied to them.

The country school is particularly catered for. Broadcast sessions permit teachers in small schools to use their time more economically and effectively and break down the isolation of both schools and teachers. To these schools, broadcasts bring the experience of hearing people who could never visit them, such as Sir Bernard Heinze, and they bring participation in national events, such as the Anzac Day ceremonies of the great cities. Broadcasts in French give country children the opportunity to hear French spoken by French people and broadcasts in literature and history bring them into touch with the best university authorities. For the child still further isolated in sparsely populated areas without schools, broadcasts bring the Correspondence Schools closer by making it possible for these children to hear the voices of their teachers and to receive some oral instruction.

Finally, the A.B.C. since 1942 has broadcast a daily session for kindergarten children. The Kindergarten of the Air not only entertains in a most constructive manner a really large child audience, but it has done important work in introducing the kindergarten idea, particularly in country towns. It is significant that the first television educational broadcast for children should be Kindergarten Playtime.

A.M.E.B. Broadcasts

For a very long time the A.B.C. has broadcast a weekly half-hour for the assistance of students taking A.M.E.B. examinations. These students range from small children doing the lower grades, to adults of all ages studying for the higher grades and for Licentiates. The best available teacher is chosen for each subject, such as piano, violin, 'cello or art of speech, and for each grade at which the examinations are conducted. The broadcasts consist of demonstrations and explanations, and give valuable advice to students. Of first-rate importance has always been the opportunity to hear the music required for the examination played by really good artists. The same advantage is enjoyed by students of the art of speech. They have the opportunity to hear good speakers, live or recorded, speaking the passages of prose, poetry or drama upon which they are themselves working.

Adult Education

For some years the A.B.C. has co-operated with the Australian Institute of International Affairs in bringing out to Australia an eminent visitor each year; these have included men of the calibre of Bertrand Russell, de Madariaga and Arnold Toynbee. Co-operation has also been extended to the Committee for Cultural Freedom, and talks series have been broadcast by Malcolm Muggeridge and James T. Farrell.

The principal contribution of the A.B.C. in this field, however, apart from the broadcasts of eminent scholars and humanists mentioned above, has been through the medium of public discussion. Eminent Australians have been brought to the microphone to discuss not only economic, literary and political matters, but such fundamental issues as the meaning of life, the problem of immortality and the existence of God. All such broadcasts have promoted wide public interest and controversy.

TELEVISION

By NEWMAN ROSENTHAL

Television stations have been operating in Australia for less than three years and then only in Sydney and Melbourne. Nevertheless, this recent invention if wisely utilized may afford substantial help to the humanities.

The history of the introduction of television to Australia can best commence with the work of the Paton Royal Commission, which in 1954 faced divided evidence and divided public opinion, one section considering that television should be introduced immediately and without controls, another that the innovation would produce a catastrophic collapse in the standards of culture and morals. The inquiry created more temperate opinions and a sober and balanced report that television should be adopted, but on a gradual scale, in view of the economic and financial problems caused by the isolation and size of the continent and the distribution of its scattered population.

The resulting Broadcasting and Television Act of 1956 made the Australian Broadcasting Commission the national television authority, and national stations opened in Sydney and Melbourne in November 1956, to be quickly followed by licensed commercial stations, largely owned by the great newspapers. During 1957 and 1958 plans were made to extend the system to Brisbane, Perth, Hobart and Adelaide. Although the cost of receiving sets has remained high, by the middle of 1958 over 200,000 sets were in operation in Victoria and New South Wales, costing nearly £40,000,000.

The establishment of television in Australia has already produced several fundamental problems which are very vital to the future of the humanities in this country. For example, can and will the Australian stations produce high quality programmes, and can Australian artists play an adequate part in the production of such programmes? In 1956-7 the national stations in Sydney and Melbourne were transmitting for some thirty hours a week, and the commercials from thirty-nine to forty-seven hours. The major part of the programmes were drama, adventure and crime, which averaged 30%; comedy took 15%, children's programmes 12%, sport 10%, quiz and panel programmes 6%, talks and interviews 2% and religious matters 2%. There was, however, a marked diminution in the time which the commercial stations were devoting to documentary and information films, although the national stations persevered with this better type of material. In September 1957 the Australian Broadcasting Control Board reported to Parliament that the four commercial stations in Melbourne and Sydney were devoting from 45% to 66% of the total hours of service to Australian items.

The Australian Broadcasting Control Board has arranged with the Commonwealth Film Censorship a different classification of films to that which applies to films for theatrical exhibition. This classification runs: (i) unrestricted for television ("G"); (ii) not suitable for children ("A"); (iii) not to be televised before 8.30 p.m. ("A.O."), and (iv) not suitable for television. The Australian Broadcasting Control Board has the powers to enforce film censorship on commercial stations but it has no control over the standards (and censorship) accepted by the Australian Broadcasting Commission. The Board's code is comprehensive and reasonable. The standards which it requires are: (a) ordinary good taste and common sense; (b) respect for the individual opinions of the public; (c) proper regard for the special needs of children, and (d) respect for the law and social institutions. Simple as this code sounds, its application is by no means easy. Opinions may differ in regard to the exact meaning of "ordinary good taste" and educationists may disagree as to the "special needs of children".

It must of course be remembered that even in great overseas countries, such as the United States, television is an infant, albeit an infant which may soon become a giant in the eyes and interest of human society. Hence the nations which are adopting television are facing a plethora of problems which already create a vital challenge to their universities. Thus the Australian Broadcasting Control Board has already established a Special Research Advisory Committee to explore problems of a fundamental nature, for example with the help of the Department of Audio-Visual Aids in Melbourne University. Authorities believe that this type of research may decide once and for all what is harmful and what is not. Even now, after only two or three years of television in Australia, there is obvious need for statistical surveys and research, for it has become clear that the present television station audience rating is lowest in the national stations; in other words, a larger percentage of the Australian public is attracted to the commercial than to the national stations, which allot a greater amount of time to information, education and general culture.

This fact is an imperative challenge to Australian educationists, including those in the Arts faculties of the universities. Television has arrived, and from the experience of countries such as Britain and the United States, it has not only come to stay, but it is likely to become an outstanding feature in the school curricula and in the leisure hours of children, and even an important factor in university education. Those who are operating the system in Australia are impressed by the potentialities of the new medium. They are, however, still groping with the task of finding and setting standards; their chief and pressing concern is to offer programmes which will be of high quality, yet of sufficient attraction for viewers to want to see them.

THE COMMONWEALTH LITERARY FUND

BY A. GRENFELL PRICE

Although the federal and state governments undoubtedly give immense help to national literature by indirect channels such as the universities and the Australian Broadcasting Commission, the Federal Government also grants direct aid by means of an unusual agency—the Commonwealth Literary Fund. This fund is administered by a non-party committee of federal leaders, the Rt Hon. R.G. Menzies the Prime Minister (Liberal); Rt Hon. J. McEwen (Country Party), and the Rt Hon. Dr H.V. Evatt (Labour), assisted by an Advisory Board of five literary people—A. Grenfell Price, C.M.G., Chairman, T. Inglis Moore, O.B.E., A.R. Chisholm, O.Leg.d'H., K. Slessor, O.B.E., and Douglas Stewart. H.L. White (Commonwealth Librarian) is co-opted to the board, and W.R. Cumming, C.V.O., of the Prime Minister's Department is secretary. The members of the Advisory Board are unsalaried like the members of the British Council, but like the British members they receive expenses, and also—a recent innovation—reading fees.

The Government provides the fund with an income of £12,000 a year, of which a maximum of £6000 is used to assist some thirty literary persons or the dependants of literary persons who require help, and the remaining £6000 is used to advance literature in a number of fields. Thus the committee grants an annual sum of £1000 each to two established literary magazines, Meanjin and Southerly. It subsidizes lectures in Australian literature in all Australian universities. It awards annually two or three fellowships to promising writers and it gives grants or guarantees against loss to assist publication. A recent and important innovation was the introduction in 1956-9 of "pilot projects" to bring national literature before the people of Tasmania, Queensland and South and Western Australia. The tours conducted by the late Vance Palmer, T. Inglis Moore, Kylie Tennant and others were popular and successful and increased the sale of Australian books. These pilot projects will be extended to the remaining states.

Although the fund has its critics, both among the members of the Federal Parliament and among literary people and the public, it has won considerable confidence, and a realization that for an expenditure of £12,000 a year it is securing some valuable and, in a few cases, remarkable results, which compare favourably with the assistance given to national literature overseas. Although there is constant pressure on the fund to increase pensions, there is no doubt that by standards abroad Australia has been generous. The United States, Canada and New Zealand give no special help to literary pensioners, while Sir William Williams, the Secretary-General of the British Arts Council, checked the Australian figures against the literary pensions in the British Consolidated Fund, and considered that in comparison the Australian allotment was liberal. In Britain Parliament permitted Queen Victoria to grant pensions "limited to the total amount of £1200 per annum" for distinguished services in literature, arts or science, and to the dependants of those who had given these services. The figure was later raised to a total of £2500 but the individual aid granted seems in general to have been slight.

Alfred Deakin formed the Commonwealth Literary Fund in 1908 solely to distribute a few small pensions to infirm or aged authors, and when the Hon. James Scullin secured the extension of the fund in 1938, pensions still occupied the first place on the list of objectives. By 1953 pensioners numbered about thirty, and with the inflation, the amount per individual had increased from a maximum of 40s. per week to 90s. for authors and 67s. 6d. for dependants, sums which, where relevant, could be supplemented by 70s. a week for married, invalid or old age pensioners, and 50s. for the unmarried. At this time the total income of the fund was £10,000 per annum, and as the pension expenditure had reached nearly £6000, the fund was finding difficulty in fulfilling its other important objectives—the furthering in various ways of literary work.

In these circumstances the Advisory Board recommended, and the Prime Minister agreed, that the total income of the fund should be increased to £12,000.

In 1959 the Board stressed the difficulties of authors and publishers in view of increasing costs, and Mr Menzies undertook to raise the income for 1960 to £20,000.

As regards fellowships, the Australian system was altered in 1956. Increased living costs had made the former fellowship allowance of £600 per annum quite inadequate, and the fund had reason to believe that fellows, particularly married fellows, had been forced for reasons of finance, to continue much of their usual money-earning labours. Under the new system, the committee raised the fellowship stipend to £1000 per annum and expected a fellow to obtain a year's leave from his usual employment and devote the period of his fellowship entirely to literary work, as is usually the case when awards are made by the Rockefeller, Carnegie, and Guggenheim foundations, or by the Rhodes Trust. From the viewpoint of the fund, fellowships are, of course, tricky things, somewhat in the nature of gambles. There is no guarantee that a fellow will produce any work of value, that he will keep to the subject for which the award is given, or indeed that he will produce anything at all, so that assistance towards the publication of manuscripts actually before the committee is undoubtedly a safer proposition. Nevertheless, although the fund has suffered some disappointments from all the above causes, the majority of fellows have made honourable and successful efforts to justify their selection, and there is little doubt that the system will continue.

It is fair to claim that the aid granted by the Commonwealth Literary Fund to the literary journals and universities has been very valuable. The journals are one of the very few mediums through which Australian writers can ventilate their ideas. They have only a small circulation to an expert clientele, and for this reason their unfortunate editors frequently conduct them as a labour of love to the loss of their own capital. With ever-increasing publication costs, the financial position of *Meanjin* and *Southerly* is by no means easy, and they require larger grants from the fund to keep in circulation. Recently several new journals have appeared, and have made approaches to the fund, which now faces some very difficult alternatives in the use of its resources.

The grants to the universities are also highly effective as they have proved enticing bait to induce university English departments, in some cases apathetic, to cast their lines in new and virgin waters which have proved unexpectedly productive. Some universities prefer to use their own staff as lecturers, but in many cases the universities seek experts from other states, with the result that there is wide interchanges of ideas in Australian literature.

The final and not least important activity of the fund has been the subsidization of publication, a very difficult field, particularly in recent times when costs have increased so dangerously. It is a well-known fact too, that whereas necessary, popular or exciting publications—text-books, fiction and so forth—are commercial and paying propositions, the special, the dull and the poor manuscripts, which no publisher dare touch, seek assistance from organizations such as the Commonwealth Literary Fund.

All sorts of remedies have been suggested both in Australia and overseas. The Americans, for example, are reducing costs by publishing books in paper covers. Length is being curtailed—sometimes to advantage. Authors are expected to accept low royalties or even to abstain from remuneration in order to secure publication.

Many of the old hands have published at sacrifices of many kinds. They know only too well that few books other than text-books and popular fiction cover costs. The outlook is becoming increasingly serious. Even the great American foundations are beginning to fear that they must switch some of the money which they are now expending on many fellowships to the publication of the results of a reduced number of awards. This and many other problems the Australian writer shares with authors abroad, but only in countries such as Sweden do authors gain greater or more sympathetic help from the central government and governmental instrumentalities or from the publishers.

In June 1958 John Lehmann, the editor of the *London Magazine*, made very favourable comments on the support given by the Commonwealth Literary Fund to maintain the two leading Australian literary magazines, writing that the far younger, less wealthy and less powerful cousins of the British people made a genuine effort to support that English literature which "would remain one of the great lights of the world". In contrast the British Arts Council spent an annual income of nearly a million pounds on opera and ballet, which were tourist attractions, and only £5000 on poetry and drama, granting to other literary activities and to literary magazines nothing at all.

The Commonwealth Literary Fund will always meet with criticisms of various types, and no doubt some of those criticisms will be justified. Nevertheless, it has been conceived by Australian statesmen who for fifty years have shown most helpful interest in Australian literature.

In addition to the Commonwealth Literary Fund other federal organizations—the Historic Memorials Committee and Art Advisory Board, assist the humanities. In 1911 the then Prime Minister, Andrew Fisher, set up a Parliamentary Committee to give consultation and advice in reference to the expenditure of money voted for historical memorials of representative men. In 1912 the Commonwealth Art Advisory Board, consisting of distinguished Australian artists, was appointed to advise the Historical Memorials Committee.

Both the committee and the board have been and are active. The committee, with the advice of the board, commissions portraits of Governors-General, Prime Ministers, Presidents of the Federal Senate, Speakers of the House of Representatives and other distinguished Australians. Over the years the committee has also commissioned paintings of scenes of historic interest, for example Ivor Hele's picture of the opening of the Commonwealth Parliament by Her Majesty the Queen in 1954. The committee, on the advice of the board, also purchases paintings of historic and aesthetic interest from the Australian point of view, and buys paintings with Australian backgrounds for government establishments, such as the missions in countries overseas.

CHAPTER IX

Conclusions

A T A GENERAL MEETING IN CANBERRA ON 12TH NOVEMBER 1958 THE members of the Humanities Research Council, after detailed consideration of drafts of the main chapters of the Survey, arrived at the following conclusions on matters which, in their opinion, call for immediate action.

THE UNIVERSITIES

1. That since recent difficulties in the Australian universities have in some instances borne with particular severity on the faculties of Arts, the new Universities Commission should take immediate steps, wherever they lie within its power, to remedy the defects revealed by the Murray Committee and by this Survey. The Council wishes to draw particular attention to the views expressed by the Murray Committee that "the Australian universities are sadly lacking in accommodation for all their important activities"; that in Sydney and Melbourne "the worst overcrowding occurs in . . . the Faculties of Arts and of Science"; that "the situation in the University of Tasmania almost beggars description", the faculties of Arts, Economics and Education being "housed under shocking conditions".

2. That whenever there is established an institution officially designated "a university" it should, from the outset, contain a faculty of Arts, in which the humanities, as they are traditionally understood, are taught to an advanced level in a systematic way.

3. That the Universities Commission, bearing in mind the varying and peculiar conditions which exist in Australia, and the comments of the Murray Committee on the overcrowding of the larger universities, should conduct an inquiry into the size above which, or below which, universities cannot function effectively. The Council recommends that the Universities Commission should consult with the Australian Academy of Science, the Australian Humanities Research Council and the Social Science Research Council before coming to any final decision on this, and comparable, questions.

4. That the university authorities should take steps to increase the administrative and secretarial staff within faculties of Arts, and should provide

236

appropriate equipment (for example, tape recorders and projectors) wherever this may be necessary.

5. That the university authorities should consider whether, in order to lighten the load of administrative burdens on heads of departments, administrative duties in the larger departments might be rotated.

6. That although the consolidation of existing departments in universities must have first priority, consideration should be given to the introduction of new disciplines, e.g. new areas of linguistic and literary studies. In order to avoid unnecessary overlapping, however, such innovations should be preceded by inter-university consultation.

7. That in order to increase the number of fully-trained graduates, every effort should be made to encourage good students to enrol in, and complete, honours courses.

8. That post-graduate studies in Arts should be considerably developed. The Council welcomes the increased grants recently made available by the Commonwealth Government for this purpose, but considers that still more must be done to induce good students to undertake post-graduate work.

9. That a committee of the Australian Academy of Science, the Australian Humanities Research Council and the Social Science Research Council, with other representatives, should be set up to examine the relations between universities and teachers' training colleges, particularly under the following heads:
   (a) The position of students and graduates under bond.
   (b) The effect on administration, teaching and other aspects of university life of admitting unmatriculated students into universities.
   (c) The attitude of education departments to honours courses.
   (d) The removal of full-time students from the universities before they have completed their degrees.
   (e) The control of teachers' training colleges.

10. That the Universities Commission should closely consider the problems raised by the granting of university status and degrees to external students who have had no substantial experience of university life.

11. That provision should be made to enable students to move more freely within Australia to those universities within which their special studies can most effectively be advanced.

12. That greater opportunities should be made available for the exchange of university teachers within Australia, for long or short periods.

LIBRARIES

13. That immediate steps should be taken to ensure that in all Australian universities and university colleges library accommodation, facilities and

R

services are raised to accepted international standards, with special provision for honours and post-graduate students.

14. That the universities should considerably increase the number of senior trained library staff.

15. That provision should be made within universities for the training of librarians at the post-graduate stage.

16. That undergraduate book collections should be reviewed in the light of the great increase in student numbers, and that steps should be taken to ensure an adequate provision of basic reference material for university courses, including multiple copies of essential and expensive books.

17. That the universities should pay immediate attention to the building up of library collections to a level at which advanced research in the humanities can be satisfactorily undertaken. At the same time, an investigation should be made into the possibility of rationalizing the holdings of books and periodicals in Australian libraries.

18. That the Federal Government should provide funds for the urgent compilation of a union catalogue of books held in university, public and major private collections.

19. That the university and public librarians should consider methods of improving facilities for inter-library lending.

20. That there is particular need for rapidly building up the libraries of the new universities and university colleges. The Council emphasizes that whenever a new college or university is established, or a new subject is introduced into an existing curriculum, considerable sums must be set aside for the provision of adequate library services.

21. That governments and universities should be urged to pay close attention to the assembly and maintenance of archives.

22. That the Council warmly supports efforts to improve and strengthen the National Library and the various state libraries. (The Council notes with regret that the recommendation by the Paton Committee that work should be begun forthwith on a national library building has not yet been put into effect.)

23. That representation of the humanities on the Australian Advisory Council on Bibliographical Services should be increased.

24. That the state governments should ensure that the universities are given a greater voice in the governing bodies of the public libraries, and that there should be a scholar of distinction in the humanities on the National Library Board if and when that board is formed.

25. That the post of University Librarian should be regarded by universities as a senior academic appointment.

26. That Commonwealth Scholarships awarded to students should include a sum set aside for the purchase of basic text-books, thereby diminishing the need for libraries to purchase multiple copies.

RESEARCH AND PUBLICATIONS

27. That the universities should make more satisfactory provisions for study-leave, allowing the choice either of a full year's leave at regular intervals or of short periods at more frequent intervals, with adequate financial assistance.

28. That financial assistance should be provided to facilitate visits by eminent scholars from overseas, including scholars from Europe and the Asian countries.

29. That since conferences of scholars working in the various disciplines of the humanities in Australia are of the first importance to the encouragement of research, the universities should, by granting financial aid, encourage the holding of conferences and facilitate the participation of university teachers and students in them, particularly teachers and students from the more remote universities.

30. That more funds should be made available to provide overseas scholarships for recent graduates who are desirous of pursuing further studies abroad, whether at the undergraduate or post-graduate level, and that, in particular, greater opportunities be provided for scholars in the humanities to study in America, Europe and Asia.

31. That funds should be made available to bring scholars to Australia from those countries which now provide scholarships for Australians to study there.

32. That as increasing costs are adversely affecting the publication of research work, special provision should be made for the support of worthwhile publications in the field of the humanities. The Council hopes to assist by granting subsidies towards the publication of humane studies, but will need the financial support of the universities, as was forthcoming in Canada, if its work is to be on an adequate scale.

SECONDARY SCHOOLS

33. That the Council should conduct an investigation into the aims and principles of secondary education in Australia, with special reference to its relations with the universities.

34. That the Council reaffirms the value of the study of ancient and modern foreign languages and literatures as part of a general liberal secondary education, and expresses its concern at the decline in opportunities for the study of foreign languages in the secondary schools.

35. That the Council expresses its opposition to premature specialization in the secondary schools.

36. That further financial assistance should be offered by the appropriate government authorities to enable talented children, who so desire, to complete their secondary education or enter a university, without being obliged to enter into any sort of bond.

37. That all committees set up by governments to survey the organization of studies in secondary schools should include scholars actively engaged in humane studies at the highest level.

OUTSIDE THE UNIVERSITIES

38. That although its Survey hardly touches on the state of the humanities outside the universities, the Council has seen enough to recommend that the Commonwealth Government appoint, as did the Canadian Government, a committee of inquiry to consider the public facilities provided in Australia for the encouragement of music, drama, literature and art.

39. That the trustees of the museums and the state art galleries of Australia be requested

    (a) to employ a greater proportion of university-trained scholars upon the staffs of their institutions in order to raise the standards of curatorial work and of cataloguing to acceptable international standards;

    (b) to provide better facilities for research;

    (c) to undertake the publication of scholarly catalogues, handbooks, and to encourage research.

40. That while the Council appreciates the successful work which the Australian Broadcasting Commission has carried out in the field of music, it considers that the Commission could now do more for literature and drama. It regrets that commercial broadcasting stations are so little help to the humanities. It hopes that the television programmes will in the end be of greater assistance to the humanities than they at present are.

Note—It is the intention of the Council to publish shortly a brief supplement to the present survey reviewing the improvement in university conditions resulting from the recommendations of the Murray Committee.

Bibliography

BY H.A.K. HUNT WITH THE CO-OPERATION OF H.L. WHITE
AND ASSISTED BY R.StC. JOHNSON

INTRODUCTION

THE MAIN PURPOSE OF THE BIBLIOGRAPHY IS TO PRESENT A BROAD PICTURE OF the publications of present members of the Australian universities in the various departments of the humanities. But in order to fill out the picture of research in the humanities in Australia as a whole, we have included lists of works by some writers not on university staffs, of whom there are many in history, literature and philosophy.

The Bibliography is intended to be selective rather than comprehensive; many omissions of persons and publications have been imposed by limitations of space. Some of the scholars listed have published in other fields, but we have included only their work in the humanities. Under history we do not include work of a technical kind in social and economic history, since the Social Science Research Council publishes a register of that. Similarly we have omitted scholars whose main work is in education, to which the Australian Council for Educational Research adequately draws attention.

Scholars are listed in the sections in which they hold university appointments or in which their main work is done, and no attempt has been made to devise a system of cross-references for those who have written on more than one subject. For we are content if this list shows who are the people who write about the humanities and the sort of topics that each of them deals with. It will be found, for example, that various scholars of English and modern languages write about history and current affairs, while among the theologians, most of whom are not on university staffs, the interests range over philosophy, history, linguistics and various other subjects.

We have not included the lists of scholars who have died or have left Australia to work elsewhere, except those of three original members of the interim committee which launched the Humanities Research Council, of whom M.D. Goldman died during the writing of the Survey, while R.G. Howarth and A.N. Jeffares have gone to chairs in South Africa and Great Britain. As a mark of affection and respect for a young historian of great promise and courage, we have included also the list of Margaret Kiddle, whose death is very recent. We should also here record with a deep sense of loss the death of Vance Palmer in July 1959. Under the headings "At Press" and "In Progress" we have had space to mention only works whose publication is proceeding or clearly promised. Most of the universities publish research reports which show what projects are proceeding but not yet in process of publication.

In general the bibliography extends to the end of 1958.

Scholars not on university staffs are indicated by private addresses.[1]

Abbreviations: Most titles of journals are given in full with the following exceptions:

A.J.P. and *A.J.P.P.*—see note in Philosophy section.

A.O.—*Australian Outlook*, Sydney.

A.Q.—*Australian Quarterly*, Sydney.

A.U.M.L.A.—Australasian Universities Modern Languages Association.

C.A.B.—The *Current Affairs Bulletin* published by the Department of Tutorial Classes, University of Sydney.

H.S.—*Historical Studies, Australia and New Zealand*, published in Melbourne.

P.A.—*Pacific Affairs*, New York.

R.A.H.S.—*Journal and Proceedings* of the Royal Australian Historical Society, Sydney.

R.G.S.Q. ⎫ *Proceedings* of the Royal Geographical Society of Australasia, Queens-
R.G.S.S.A. ⎭ land Branch, Brisbane, and South Australian Branch, Adelaide.

University Presses:

C.U.P.—Cambridge University Press.

M.U.P.—Melbourne University Press.

O.U.P.—Oxford University Press.

Q.U.P.—Queensland University Press.

U.W.A.P.—University of Western Australia Press.

Note on journals: It will be seen from the lists that for space in journals Australian scholars are indebted to the generosity of their colleagues particularly in the United Kingdom, Northern America and Europe. Nevertheless there is a growing number of journals published in Australia, for which see the section on "Learned Societies" (Chapter VIII).

Classical Studies and Archaeology

BARBOUR, R.R.P., B.A. (Qld), M.A. (Oxon and Melb.), Senior Lecturer, Department of Classical Studies, University of Melbourne.

BOOK

Ethical Theory. Adelaide: Hassell, 1933.

COOPER, C.G., M.A. (St Andrews), Professor of Classics, University of Queensland.

[1] The Editorial Board notes that creative writing such as poetry and drama is included only when it is relevant to the field in which the scholar's work has been done.

BOOKS

The Logic of Latin. London, Ontario: University of Western Ontario, 1929.
An Introduction to the Latin Hexameter. Melbourne: Macmillan, 1952.
Journey to Hesperia (scenes from the first six books of Virgil's "Aeneid", linked by English narrative). London: Macmillan, 1959.

PAMPHLETS

Classics in Modern Education. Brisbane: Q.U.P., 1951.
Numerous articles in periodicals in Britain, Canada, New Zealand and Australia.

DUNSTON, A.J., M.A. (Cantab.), Professor of Latin, University of Sydney.

ARTICLES

Two Manuscripts of Suetonius' "De Vita Caesarum", *Classical Quarterly*, New Series, II, nos 3 and 4.
The Romulus-Pliny from St Benigne's Abbey at Dijon recovered in MSS. Burney 59 and Hamilton 517, *Scriptorium*, VII, 2, 1953.
The Teacher in Ancient Greece and Rome, *Forum of Education*, XVI, 1, July 1957.

ELLIOTT, J.R., B.A. (Syd.), M.A., Dip.Class.Arch. (Cantab.), Professor of Classics, University of Tasmania.

BOOK

Outline of Greek Art. Wellington, N.Z.: Whitcombe and Tombs, 1939.

FRENCH, A., M.A. (Cantab.), Senior Lecturer, Department of Classics, University of Adelaide.

BOOK

A Book of Czech Verse. London: Macmillan, 1958.

ARTICLES

Pidgin English in New Guinea, *A.Q.*, XXV, 4, 1953.
A Linguistic Problem in Trust Territory, *Eastern World*, IX, 1, 1955.
The Spartan Earthquake, *Greece and Rome*, II, 3, 1955.
The Economic Background to Solon's Reforms, *Classical Quarterly*, VI, nos 1 and 2, 1956.
Solon and the Megarian Question, *Journal of Hellenic Studies*, LXXVII, 1957.

HENNESSY, J.B., B.A. (Syd.), Lecturer, Department of Archaeology, University of Sydney.

ARTICLE

Excavations at Sphagion in Cyprus, *Papers of the British School at Rome*, XXII, 1954.

HUNT, H.A.K., B.A. (Syd.), M.A. (Oxon), Litt.D., Dip.Ed. (Melb.), Professor of Classical Studies, University of Melbourne.

BOOKS

Training through Latin. Melbourne: M.U.P., 1948.
The Humanism of Cicero. Melbourne: M.U.P., 1954.

ARTICLES

The Teaching of Japanese in Australia (co-author with A.R. Chisholm), *A.Q.*, XII, 1, 1940.

Population Problems of the Roman Republic, *Historical Studies*, I, 3, Apr. 1941, and 4, Oct. 1941.
A Special Course for Beginners in Greek, *Greece and Rome*, XV, 45, Oct. 1946.
Classical Studies and Adult Education, *Adult Education*, XIX, 4, June 1947.

JOHNSON, R.StC., M.A., Dip.Ed. (Syd.), Lecturer, Department of Classical Studies, University of Melbourne.

ARTICLES

The Number of Isocrates' Pupils, *American Journal of Philology*, LXXVIII, 3, July 1957.
Isocrates' Methods of Teaching, *ibid.*, LXXX, 1, Jan. 1959.

AT PRESS

The Poet and the Orator, for *Classical Philology*.

KELLY, M.N., M.A. (Syd.), Dip.Ed. (N.E.), Lecturer, Department of Classics, University of New England.

ARTICLE

Linguistic Developments in Fourth Century Attic, *AUMLA Proceedings*, 1957.

LETTERS, F.J.H., M.A., LL.B. (Syd.), Hon. D.Litt. (N.U.I.), Associate Professor, Head of the Department of Classics, University of New England.

BOOKS

Joris Karl Huysmans. A Study. Sydney: privately printed, 1945.
An Introduction to Thomas Mann. Sydney: privately printed, 1945.
Virgil. London and New York: Sheed and Ward, 1946.
The Life and Work of Sophocles. London and New York: Sheed and Ward, 1953.

McKAY, K.J., M.A. (Melb.), Lecturer, Department of Classical Studies, University of Melbourne.

ARTICLE

Further Thoughts on Hesiod "Theogony" 35, *Mnemosyne*, S.IV, vol. XI, 1958.

AT PRESS

Hesiod's Rejuvenation for *Classical Quarterly*.
Stentor and Cerberus; and An Unnoticed Dramatic Tension in "Odyssey" Bk. VI, for *American Journal of Philology*.

MASTERMAN, K.C., B.A. (Tas.), M.A. (Oxon), Associate Professor of Classics, Canberra University College.

BOOK

The Power of Speech. Melbourne and London: Longmans Green, 1952.

ARTICLE

Grammatical Terminology, *AUMLA Proceedings*, 1957.

NICHOLLS, J.J., B.A. (Syd.), M.A. (Cantab.), Senior Lecturer, Department of Latin, University of Sydney.

ARTICLE

The Reform of the Comitia Centuriata, *American Journal of Philology*, LXXVII, 3, July 1956.

QUINCEY, J.H., M.A. (Oxon), Senior Lecturer, Department of Greek, University of Sydney.

BOOKLET

The Fire of London (an original Latin poem awarded the Chancellor's Prize). Oxford: Blackwell, 1947.

ARTICLES

The Metaphorical Sense of λήκυθος and Ampulla, *Classical Quarterly*, XLIII, 1949.
Juvenal Satire VIII, ll. 192-6 *Mnemosyne*, 1959.

QUINN, K.F., B.A. (N.Z.), M.A. (Cantab.), Senior Lecturer, Department of Classical Studies, University of Melbourne.

BOOKS

A First Greek Grammar for University Students. 1st edition, Wellington, N.Z.: Victoria University College, 1955; 2nd edition, Melbourne: University of Melbourne, 1957.
The Catullan Revolution M.U.P., 1959.

ARTICLES

Logic, Psychology and Mechanism in Language, *University of New Zealand Journal*, Mar. 1953.
Les études latines en Nouvelle-Zélande, *Revue des études latines*, XXXIII, 1955.
Two Crises in Horace's Poetical Career, *AUMLA*, V, 1956.
The Changing Face of Classical Literature, *ibid.*, VI, 1957.

AT PRESS

"Horace" for *Encyclopaedia Britannica*.

SHIPP, G.P., M.A. (Cantab.), D.Litt. (Syd.), Professor of Greek, University of Sydney.

BOOKS

Livy Book XXII (co-editor with Powe, A.B.). Sydney: Government Printer, 1936.
Andria of Terence (Introduction and Notes). Oxford: O.U.P., 1938. (Revised edition at press.)
Studies in the Language of Homer. Cambridge: C.U.P., 1953.

ARTICLES

"Cock" in Latin, *Classical Review*, L, 1936.
"Chance" in the Latin Vocabulary, *ibid.*, LI, 1937.
Carina and other Latin notes, *Classical Philology*, XXXIX, 1944.
Notes on Comic Fragments, *ibid.*
Two Notes on the Latin Vocabulary, *Glotta*, XXXI, 1951.
Greek in Plautus, *Wiener Studien*, LXVI, 1953.
Plautine Terms for Greek and Roman Things, *Glotta*, XXXIV, 1954.
The Phonology of Modern Greek, *Glotta*, XXXVIII, 1958.

STEWART, J.R.B., M.A. (Cantab.), F.R.N.S., Senior Lecturer in Archaeology, University of Sydney.

BOOKS

Handbook to the Nicholson Museum. (Part I—"The Ancient Near and Middle East"; Part II—"The Greek Mainland and the Aegean, Cyprus"). Sydney: University of Sydney, 2nd edition, 1948.
Tell el-Ajjul. Sydney: Department of Archaeology, University of Sydney, 1949.
Vounous 1937-8: Field Report on the Excavations Sponsored by the British School of Archaeology at Athens. Lund: C.W.K. Gleerup, 1950. (Skrifter utgivna av Svenska Institutet i Rom, XIV.)

ARTICLES

Excavations at Kusura Afyon Karahisar: The Cemetery, *Archaeologia*, LXXXVI, 1936.
A Turkish Water Bottle, *Antiquity*, 1937.
Decorated Tomb Façades, Cyprus, *ibid.*, 1939.
Toggle Pins in Cyprus, *ibid.*, 1940.
An Imported Pot from Cyprus, *Palestine Exploration Quarterly*, 1939.
Ein Gräberfeld der Yortan-Kultur bei Babaköy (with Professor K. Bittel), *Archiv für Orientforschung*, XIII, 1940.
Kazaphani, *Liverpool Annals of Archaeology and Anthropology*, XXVIII, 1948.
A Latin-Byzantine Hybrid Coin, *Studies Presented to David Moore Robinson*, II, 1953.

TRENDALL, A.D., K.C.S.G., M.A. (Cantab.), Litt.D. (N.Z. and Melb.), F.S.A., Master of University House and Deputy Vice-Chancellor, Australian National University, Canberra.

BOOKS

Paestan Pottery. London: British School at Rome, 1936.
Frühitaliotische Vasen. Leipzig: Keller, 1938.
The Shellal Mosaic. Canberra: Australian War Memorial, 1942; 2nd edition, 1957.
Handbook to the Nicholson Museum. Parts III-V: University of Sydney, 1st edition, 1945, 2nd edition, 1948.
Vasi antichi dipinti del Vaticano—Vasi italioti ed etruschi a figure rosse. Citta del Vaticano, vol. I, 1953, vol. II, 1955.
The Felton Greek Vases, A.H.R.C. Canberra, 1958.

ARTICLES

A Volute Krater in Taranto, *Journal of Hellenic Studies*, LIV, 1934.
Early Paestan Pottery, *ibid.*, LV, 1935.
Greek Vases in the Otago Museum, *ibid.*, LVI, 1936.
Attic Vases in Australia and New Zealand, *Journal of Hellenic Studies*, LXXI, 1951.
Two Skyphoid Pyxides in Moscow, *Bulletin . . . Antieke Beschaving*, XXIV-VI, 1949-51.
Paestan Pottery: A Revision and a Supplement, *Papers of the British School at Rome*, XX, 1952.
The Choephoroi Painter, *Studies presented to D.M. Robinson*, II, 1953.
Paestan Post-script, *Papers of the British School at Rome*, XXI, 1953.
The Medicine Man and the Medical Man (Arthur E. Mills Memorial Oration, 1954), *Medical Journal of Australia*, 1954.
A New Polychrome Vase from Centuripe, *Bulletin of the Metropolitan Museum of Art* (New York), XIII, 1955.

Archaeology in Sicily and Magna Graecia, *Journal of Hellenic Studies*, supplement to vol. LXXVI, 1956; and *ibid.*, LXXVIII, 1958.
Three Vases in Sydney, *Charites (Festschrift für E. Langlotz)*, 1957.

AT PRESS

Phlyax Vases, London, Institute of Classical Studies, 1959.

TREVASKIS, J.R., M.A. (Cantab.), Professor of Classics, University of Adelaide.

ARTICLE

The Sophistry of Noble Lineage (Plato, "Sophist", 230a 5-232b 9), *Phronesis*, I, 1955.

TREWEEK, A.P., B.A. (Syd.), Ph.D.(Lond.), Senior Lecturer, Department of Greek, University of Sydney.

ARTICLES

Chain Reaction or House of Cards? (The Ventris Decipherment), *University of London, Institute of Classical Studies Bulletin*, no. 4, 1957.
Pappus of Alexandria: The Manuscript Tradition of the "Collectio Mathematica", *Scriptorium*, XI, 1957.

WEAVER, P.R.C., M.A. (N.Z.), B.A. (Cantab.), Lecturer, Department of Classics and Ancient History, University of Western Australia.

ARTICLE

Hellenica Oxyrhynchia and Some Related Problems, *AUMLA*, VII, Nov. 1957.

English

ALLEN, L.H., M.A. (Syd.), Ph.D. (Leipzig), formerly Lecturer in Classics, Canberra University College.

BOOKS

Gods and Wood-things. Sydney: Angus and Robertson, 1913.
Translation of Hebbel's "Gyges and his Ring" and "Herod and Mariamne". London: Everyman, 1914.
Introduction to Marcus Clarke's *For the Term of his Natural Life*. London: World's Classics, 1951.

ARTICLES

On Horace Odes. I. 20, *Classical Review*, 1911.
The Ignorance of Antilochus, *ibid.*, 1920.
Plagiarism, Sources, and Influence in Shelley's "Alastor", *Modern Language Review*, 1923.
William Blake, *Proceedings, Australian-English Association of Sydney*, 1927.

ANDERSON, H.McD., 18 Nepean Highway, Mordialloc, Victoria.

BOOKS

A Guide to ten Australian poets. Melbourne: Hawdon Davidson, 1953.
Frank Wilmot (Furnley Maurice). Melbourne: M.U.P., 1955.
Colonial Ballads. Ferntree Gully: Rams Skull Press, 1955; revised and enlarged,

Cheshire, Melbourne, 1959.
Shaw Neilson. Cremorne: Stone (*Studies in Australian Bibliography*), 1956.
Botany Bay Broadsides. Ferntree Gully: Rams Skull, 1956.
Australian Song Index, 1828-1956. Ferntree Gully: Rams Skull, 1957.
Goldrush Songster. Ferntree Gully: Rams Skull, 1958.

ARTICLES

Eleanor Dark: A handlist, *Biblionews*, VII, 9, 1954.
The Making of Shaw Neilson's Honeymoon Song, *ibid.*, IX, 8, 1956.
Green Singer, *Southerly*, XVII, 1, 1956.
Robert FitzGerald, humanist, *ibid.*, XIX, 1, 1958.
Steele Rudd—Checklist of stories, *Biblionews*, XI, 5, 1958.

BAKER, S.J., c/o Angus and Robertson, Castlereagh Street, Sydney, N.S.W.

BOOKS

New Zealand Slang. Christchurch: Whitcombe and Tombs, 1940.
Dictionary of Australian Slang. Melbourne: Robertson and Mullens, 1943 (3rd edition).
The Australian Language. Sydney: Angus and Robertson, 1945.
Australian Pronunciation. Sydney: Angus and Robertson, 1947.
Australia Speaks. Sydney: Shakespeare Head, 1953.

ARTICLES

Origins of the Words Pakeha and Maori, *Journal of Polynesian Society*, LIV, 1945.
Speech Disturbances: A Case for a Wider View of Paraphasias, *Psychiatry*, XI, 1948.
The Failure of Philosophy, *Psychiatric Quarterly Supplement*, XXIII, 1949.
Speech and Sexual Taboos, *International Journal of Sexology*, III, Nov. 1949.
Language and Dreams, *International Journal of Psycho-Analysis*, XXXI, 1950.
Autonomic Resistances in Word Association Tests, *Psycho-Analytic Quarterly*, XX, 1951.
The Mathematics of the Unconscious, *Journal of Clinical and Experimental Psychopathology*, XII, 1951.
The Pattern of Language, *Journal of General Psychology*, XLII, 1950.
A Linguistic Law of Constancy, *ibid.*, XLIII, 1950.
A Linguistic Law of Constancy, II, *ibid.*, XLIV, 1951.
Ontogenetic Evidence of a Correlation between the Form and Frequency of Words, *ibid.*
Constancy Factors in Language: Introduction to the Mechanics of Thought, *ibid.*, LII, 1955.
The Theory of Silences, *ibid.*, LIII, 1955.
The Instinctual Origin of Language, *ibid.*

BARNARD, Marjorie Faith, B.A. (Syd.), 2 Stuart Street, Longueville, N.S.W.

BOOKS

Essays in Australian Fiction (with F.S.P. Eldershaw). Melbourne: M.U.P., 1938.
Phillip of Australia (with F.S.P. Eldershaw). Sydney: Harrap, 1938.
My Australia (with F.S.P. Eldershaw). London: Jarrolds, 1939.
The Life and Times of Captain John Piper (with F.S.P. Eldershaw). Sydney: Australian Limited Editions Society, 1939.

Macquarie's World. Sydney: Australian Limited Editions Society, 1941.
Sydney: the story of a city. Melbourne: M.U.P., 1956.

AT PRESS

A History of Australia. Sydney: Angus and Robertson.

BEDFORD, Ruth Marjory, 347 Edgecliff Road, Edgecliff, N.S.W.

BOOK

Think of Stephen: a family chronicle. Sydney: Angus and Robertson, 1954.

BIGGINS, D.B.O'D., M.A. (Southampton), B.A. (Lond.), Lecturer in English, Newcastle University College.

ARTICLE

Source Notes for Dryden, Wycherley and Otway, *Notes and Queries*, III, 7, 1956.

BRADLEY, D., B.A. (Melb. and Cantab.), Lecturer in English, University of Western Australia.

BOOKS

Mediaeval English Verse: A Selection (ed. with J.D. Tweedie).
Charitable Malice: A Choice of Augustan Satirical Poetry (ed. with L. Burrows). Perth: U.W.A.P., 1955.

ARTICLES

Christina Rossetti, *Winthrop Review*, I, 3, 1953.
Arnold's Liberalism, *Westerly*, no. 3, 1956.

BRISSENDEN, R.F., M.A. (Syd.), Ph.D. (Leeds), Lecturer, Department of English, Canberra University College.

PAMPHLET

Samuel Richardson, *Writers and their Work*, British Council and Longmans Green, 1958.

ARTICLE

The Poetry of Judith Wright, *Meanjin*, XII, 1953.

BUCKLEY, V.T., M.A. (Melb.), First Lockie Teaching Fellow in Australian Literature, University of Melbourne.

BOOKS

Essays in Poetry, Mainly Australian. Melbourne: M.U.P., 1957.
Poetry and Morality: Critical Studies in the Views of Matthew Arnold, T.S. Eliot, and F.R. Leavis. London: Chatto and Windus, 1958.

ARTICLES

Selected Poems of Thomas Merton, *Twentieth Century*, V, 4, 1951.
Australian Poetry from 1900, *ibid.*, VI, 2, 1952.
Some Thoughts on Graham Greene, *ibid.*, 3, 1952.
The Spirit of Criticism, *ibid.*, VIII, 4, 1954.
The Poetry of Kenneth Slessor, *Meanjin*, XI, 1, 1952.
The Poetry of Francis Webb, *ibid.*, XII, 1, 1953.
Helicon at Jordan, *ibid.*, XIII, 4, 1954.
The Poet, the Anthologist, and the Critic, *Southerly*, XIV, 3, 1953.
The Bardic Heresy: Notes on Dylan Thomas, *Direction*, I, 3, 1954.
The Poetry of A.D. Hope, *ibid.*, 4, 1955.

Bread rather than Blossoms, *Delta*, no. 10, 1956.
Notes on Religious Poetry, *Encounter*, IX, 3, 1957.
(Some of the above were subsequently re-published, with or without alterations, in *Essays in Poetry: Mainly Australian*, 1957.)

BURGESS, O.N., M.A., Dip.Ed. (Syd.), Senior Lecturer, Department of English, University of New South Wales.

ARTICLES

Hugh McCrae and Robert Frost, *Southerly*, XVII, 3, 1956.
Joseph Conrad: The Old and the New Criticism, *A.Q.*, XXIX, 1, 1957.

BURROWS, L.R., M.A. (Sheffield), Senior Lecturer in English, University of Western Australia.

BOOKS

Browning: An Introductory Essay. Perth: U.W.A.P., 1952.
Charitable Malice (in collaboration with D. Bradley). Perth: U.W.A.P., 1955.

CLARKE, D.C., B.A. (Melb.), Senior Staff Tutor, Department of Tutorial Classes, University of Sydney.

ARTICLES

The Poetry of Peter Hopegood, *Southerly*, VIII, 1947.
Modern Australian Poetry, *C.A.B.*, XV, 7, Jan. 1955.
Henry Kendall—A Study in Imagery, *A.Q.*, XXIX, Dec. 1957, XXX, Mar. 1958.

CROSS, K.G.W., M.A., Ph.D., H.Dip.Ed. (Dublin), Senior Lecturer in English Literature, University of Sydney.

ARTICLES

Notes on the Vocabulary of John Marston, *Notes and Queries*, New Series, I, 1954, II, 1955, III, 1956, IV, 1957, V, 1958, (continuing).
Notes on Webster's "The White Devil", *ibid.*, Mar. 1956.
Blind Gue's Ghost: A Correction for the O.E.D., *ibid.*, Apr. 1956.
Ovid Metamorphosed: Marston, Webster and Nathaniel Lee, *ibid.*, June and Dec. 1956.
Manningham's Libel on Marston, *ibid.*, Sept. 1956.
Sir Thomas More's "Historie of Richard III" and the Plot of "Lust's Dominion", *ibid.*, May 1957.
The Way of All Flesh: Provenance of a Proverb, *ibid.*, June 1958.
"Balm" in Donne and Shakespeare: Ironic Intention in "The Extasie", *Modern Language Notes*, LXXI, Nov. 1956.
The Date of Marston's "Antonio and Mellida", *ibid.*, LXXII, May 1957.
Robert Wild's "Epitaph for a Godly Man's Tomb" (in collaboration with R.P. Draper), *Explicator*, XV, 8, May 1957.
The Art of Comedy, *Verve*, I, 1, July 1957.
The Vocabulary of "Lust's Dominion", *Neuphilologische Mitteilungen*, LIX, 1958.
The Authorship of "Lust's Dominion", *Studies in Philology*, LV, 1958.

DAVIES, M. Bryn., B.A. (Wales), M.A. (Oxon), Reader, Department of English, University of Adelaide.

BOOK

The Scientific Background (with A.N. Jeffares). London: Pitman, 1958.

ARTICLES

Henry Salt, *Bulletin of the Faculty of Arts*, Fuad I University, 1931.
The Celtic Twilight, *ibid.*, 1938.
Jeremy Bentham in Egypt, *ibid.*, 1939.
Suffolk's Expedition to Montdidier 1523 (a contemporary narrative), *ibid.*, 1944.
Some Tendencies in Modern Biography, *ibid.*, 1948.
The Enterprises of Paris and Boulogne, *ibid.*, 1949.
Boulogne and Calais from 1545-50, *ibid.*, 1950.

DAVISON, D., M.A. (Sheffield), Lecturer in English, University of New England.

BOOK

Andrew Marvell: Selected Poetry and Prose. London: Harrap, 1952.

ARTICLES

Mr Uniades, *Times Literary Supplement*, 11 June 1954.
Aubrey's "Mr Uniades", *Notes and Queries*, Sept. 1954.
A Marvell Allusion in Ward's Diary, *ibid.*, Jan. 1955.
Marvell and Politics, *ibid.*, May 1955.
Francis Jessop, *ibid.*, Jan., 1956.
The Wanderer: From the Anglo-Saxon, *Theoria*, 6, Nov. 1954.
Word and Sound in Yeats' "Byzantium", *ibid.*, 7, Nov. 1955 (see C.J.D. Harvey, *ibid.*, 8, Nov. 1956).
Marvell's "The Definition of Love", *Review of English Studies*, VI, 22, Apr. 1955 (see F. Kermode, *ibid.*, VII, 26, Apr. 1958).
Phonetics to the Rescue, *Standpunkte*, IX, 5, 1955.

DOYLE, Rev. J.W., S.J., B.A., Prefect of Studies, St. Ignatius' College, Riverview, N.S.W.

BOOK

Adam, a Play (translated from the Anglo-Norman). Sydney: Shakespeare Head Press, 1948.

ARTICLES

The Teaching of Languages, *Australasian Catholic Record*, XIV, 1937.
Literature in Education, Art or Science?, *ibid.*, XV, 1938.
Two Years at Sea (Jane Roberts's *Two Years at Sea*, London, 1834: journey to V.D.L.), *Catholic Review* (Auckland), Jan. 1948.
Ave, Porta Paradisi (transcript from thirteenth century MS. 096/R66 in Melbourne Public Library), *Australasian Catholic Record*, XVII, 1940.

EDWARDS, W.A., M.A. (Cantab.), Professor of English, University of Western Australia.

BOOKS

Plagiarism (Le Bas Prize Essay for 1932). Cambridge: Heffer, 1933.
The Rainbow Bird: A Selection of Stories by Vance Palmer, ed. with introduction. Sydney: Angus and Robertson, 1957.

ARTICLE

John Webster, *Scrutiny*, II, 1, 1933.

ELDERSHAW, Flora, B.A. (Syd.), "Sackville", Wagga, N.S.W. See Barnard, M.F.

ELKIN, P.K., B.A., Dip.Ed. (Syd.), B.Litt. (Oxon), Senior Lecturer in English, University of New South Wales.

ARTICLES

Basis of the Neoclassical Conception of Poetry, *University of Ceylon Review*, X, 1, 1952.
Neoclassical View of the Language of Poetry, *ibid.*, X, 3, 1952.
The Neoclassical Conception of Instruction in Poetry, *Symposium*, no. 2, 1952.
Stories within Stories, *Southerly*, XV, 2, 1954.
The Translation of Aboriginal Myths, *ibid.*, XVIII, 2, 1957.
In Defence of Hippocentaurs, *AUMLA*, 5, 1956.

ELLIOTT, B.R., M.A. (W.A.), D.Litt. (Adel.), Senior Lecturer, Department of English, University of Adelaide.

BOOKS

James Hardy Vaux, A Literary Rogue in Australia. Adelaide: Wakefield Press, 1944.
Leviathan's Inch. Sydney: Angus and Robertson, 1946.
Singing to the Cattle. Melbourne: Georgian House, 1947.
Marcus Clarke. Oxford: Clarendon Press, 1958.

ARTICLES

Ballads of Australia, *Pacific Spectator*, Winter 1949.
Our Wandering Wild Colonial Boy, *Biblionews*, VII, 11, Oct. 1954.
The Novels of Martin Boyd, *Meanjin*, 1, 1957.
Australia Touches the Tape, *Colorado Quarterly*, Winter 1957.
An American-Australian Novelist of the Nineteenth Century—W.H. Thomas, *A.Q.*, Sept. 1957.
Birds without Song and Flowers without Smell, *Southerly*, 3, 1957.

GEERING, R.G., M.A., Dip.Ed. (Syd.), Senior Lecturer, Department of English, University of New South Wales.

ARTICLES

The Critics' Neglect of Joyce Cary, *A.Q.*, XXVII, 4, 1955.
Swift's Struldbruggs: The Critics Considered, *AUMLA*, 7, Nov. 1957.

GOLDBERG, S.L., B.A. (Melb.), B.Litt. (Oxon), Senior Lecturer, Department of English, University of Melbourne.

ARTICLES

Sir John Hayward, "Politic" Historian, *Review of English Studies*, New Series, VI, 1955.
A Note on John Wolfe, Elizabethan Printer, *Historical Studies*, VII, 1955.
The Development of American Literary Criticism (ed. Floyd Stovall) in *Comparative Literature*, VIII, 1956.
Art and Freedom: The Aesthetic of Ulysses, *ELH*, XIV, 1957.
Sir John Hayward, *Notes and Queries*, New Series, IV, 1957.
The Poet as Hero: A.D. Hope's "The Wandering Islands", *Meanjin*, XVI, 1957.

GREEN, H.M., B.A., LL.B. (Syd.), former Librarian of the Fisher Library. Burrandowan, Warwick, Queensland.

BOOKS

An Outline of Australian Literature. Sydney: Whitcombe and Tombs, 1938.
Fourteen Minutes. A book based on wireless talks. Sydney: Angus and Robertson, 1944.
Australian Literature 1900-1950. Melbourne: M.U.P., 1951.

PAMPHLETS

The Poetry of W.B. Yeats. Sydney: Australian English Association, 1931.
Christopher Brennan. Sydney: Angus and Robertson, 1939.

GRIFFITHS, D.C., M.A., M.Ed. (Melb.), Lecturer, Sydney Teachers' College; Teaching Fellow, University of Sydney.

BOOK

The Psychology of Literary Appreciation. Melbourne: Australian Council for Educational Research, 1932.

MOODIE HEDDLE, Enid, M.A., Dip.Ed. (Melb.), c/o Longmans Green and Co., Lonsdale Street, Melbourne.

BOOKS

Modern English Literature. Melbourne: Cheshire, 1947.
Australian Literature Now. Melbourne: Longmans, 1949.
Boy on a Horse: the story of Adam Lindsay Gordon (in collaboration with H.J. Samuel). Melbourne: Cheshire, 1957.

HODDINOTT, Alison Mary, M.A. (Tas.), Part-time Lecturer in Old English, University of Tasmania.

ARTICLES
(in collaboration with F.W. Harwood)

Inflections of the English Verb, Noun and Pronoun, *Tasmanian Education*, IX, 2, Apr. 1954.
Statistical Study of English Word Formation, *Language*, XXXII, 2, Apr.-June 1956.

HOPE, A.D., B.A. (Syd. and Oxon), Professor of English, Canberra University College.

ARTICLES

The Esthetic Theory of James Joyce, *A.J.P.P.*, XXI, 1943.
Henry Handel Richardson's "Maurice Guest", *Meanjin*, 2, 1955.
Steele Rudd and Henry Lawson, *ibid.*, 1, 1956.
Vance Palmer Reconsidered, *Southerly*, 4, 1955.
The Discursive Mode: Reflections on the Ecology of Poetry, *Quadrant*, 1, 1956.

HORNE, C.J., M.A. (Melb., Oxon, Adel.), B.Litt. (Oxon), Dip.Ed. (Melb.), Jury Professor of English Language and Literature in the University of Adelaide.

BOOK

Swift on his Age. Selected Prose and Verse. Edited with introduction, notes and bibliography. London: Harrap, 1953.

S

ARTICLES

Early Parody of Scientific Jargon, *Notes and Queries*, CLXXXIV, 3, 1943.
Dr William King's Miscellanies in Prose and Verse, *The Library* for June–Sept. 1944 (*Transactions of the Bibliographical Society*, New Series, XXV, nos 1-2).
Steele and the Beef-Steak Club, *Review of English Studies*, XXI, 83, 1945.
The Phalaris Controversy: King versus Bentley, *ibid.*, XXII, 88, 1946.
Palgrave's "Golden Treasury", *English Studies*, 1949 (Essays and Studies by Members of the English Association).
Literature and Science (pp. 188-202) and biographical-bibliographical appendixes (pp. 443-512), in *From Dryden to Johnson. Pelican Guide to English Literature*, vol. 4, 1957.

HOWARTH, R.G., B.A. (Syd.), B.Litt. (Oxon), F.R.S.L., Professor of English Literature, University of Cape Town. (Formerly Reader in English, Sydney University.)

BOOKS

Minor Poets of the Seventeenth Century, edition with introduction. London: Dent and Sons (Everyman's Library), 1931; 2nd edition, revised, 1953.
Letters and the Second Diary of Samuel Pepys, edition with introduction and notes. London: Dent and Sons (Illustrated Classics), 1932.
Letters of Lord Byron, edition with notes (introduction by André Maurois). London: Dent and Sons (Illustrated Classics), 1933; 2nd edition, revised, London: Everyman's Library, 1936.
Forests of Pan, by Hugh McCrae, edition with foreword. Brisbane: Meanjin Press, 1944.
Voice of the Forest, by Hugh McCrae, edition with foreword. Sydney: Angus and Robertson, 1945.
Literary Particles. Sydney: Angus and Robertson, 1946.
Rigby's Romance, by Joseph Furphy, edition of the complete text, with foreword. Sydney: Angus and Robertson, 1946.
Story-Book Only, by Hugh McCrae, collection with foreword, illustrated. Sydney: Angus and Robertson, 1948.
Writings on Elizabethan Drama, by J. Le Gay Brereton, collection with introduction and bibliography, illustrated. Melbourne: M.U.P., 1948.
The Buln-Buln and the Brolga, by Joseph Furphy, edition with foreword. Sydney: Angus and Robertson, 1948.
Notes on Modern Poetic Technique, English and Australian. Sydney: Angus and Robertson, 1949.
Poems, by Wolfe Fairbridge, edition (in collaboration with T. Inglis Moore). Sydney: Angus and Robertson, 1953.
Two Elizabethan Writers of Fiction, Thomas Nashe and Thomas Deloney. Cape Town: University of Cape Town Editorial Board, 1956.
The Penguin Book of Australian Verse, edited in collaboration with Kenneth Slessor and John Thompson, introduction. London: Penguin Books, 1958.

PAMPHLETS

Shakespeare's "Tempest". Sydney: Australian English Association, 1936, reprinted in Sydney University Library Publications. 2nd edition, revised, 1947.
Literature of the Theatre: Marlowe to Shirley. Sydney: 1953.
The Life of Literature: Inaugural Lecture. Cape Town: University of Cape Town, 1956.

JEFFARES, A.N., M.A., Ph.D. (Dublin), M.A., D.Phil. (Oxon), M.A. (Adel.), Jury Professor of English Language and Literature, University of Adelaide, 1951-6; Professor and Head of the Department of English Literature in the University of Leeds since 1957.

BOOKS

Trinity College Dublin: Drawings and Description. Dublin: Alex. Thom, 1944, 1945.
A Poet and a Theatre. Groningen and Batavia: Wolters, 1946.
W.B. Yeats: Man and Poet. London: Routledge and Kegan Paul, 1949; Yale: Yale University Press, 1949.
Maria Edgeworth's Tales (edited with introduction). Edinburgh: Thomas Nelson, 1953.
Disraeli, *Sybil* (edited with introduction). Edinburgh: Thomas Nelson, 1957.
Disraeli, *Lothair* (edited with introduction). Edinburgh: Thomas Nelson, 1957.

JOHNSON, H.V., M.A., Ph.D. (Manchester), Lecturer in English, University of New England.

ARTICLE

Pater and the Victorian Anti-Romantics, *Essays in Criticism*, IV, 1, 1954.

JOHNSTON, G.K.W., M.A. (N.Z.), B.A. (Oxon), Senior Lecturer, Department of English, Canberra University College.

ARTICLES

Two Passages in "Sawles Warde", *Modern Language Review*, LII, 1957.
A Prayer of the Five Joys, *Notes and Queries*, New Series, IV, 1957.
Classical Influences in Old English Poetry, *AUMLA Proceedings*, 1957.

AT PRESS

An article on "Pearl" for *Review of English Studies*.

KING, A., M.A. (Oxon), Senior Lecturer in English, University of Western Australia.

BOOKS

The Control of Language (in collaboration with M. Ketley). London: Longmans Green, 1940.
Everybody's Business. Melbourne: M.U.P., 1946.
Writing. Melbourne: Longmans Green, 1955.

KRAMER, Leonie Judith, B.A. (Melb.), D.Phil. (Oxon), Lecturer in English, University of New South Wales.

BOOKLETS

Henry Handel Richardson and some of her sources. Melbourne: M.U.P., 1954.
Henry Kingsley: Some Novels of Australian Life. Canberra: Canberra University College, 1954.
James McAuley: Tradition in Australian Poetry. Canberra: Canberra University College, 1957.

ARTICLE

Henry Handel Richardson, *Dictionary of National Biography*. Supplement, Clarendon Press, Oxford.

MACARTNEY, F.T.B., 66 Stanley Street, Black Rock, Victoria.

BOOKS

Furnley Maurice (Frank Wilmot). Sydney: Angus and Robertson, 1955.
Australian Literature: A bibliography to 1938 by E. Morris Miller, M.A., Litt.D.; extended to 1950; edited with an historical outline and descriptive commentaries by Frederick T. Macartney. Sydney: Angus and Robertson, 1956.
The Sonnet in Australasia: A Survey and Selection by Louis Lavater, edited with a Foreword by Frederick T. Macartney. Sydney: Angus and Robertson, 1956.
Australian Literary Essays. Sydney: Angus and Robertson, 1957.
An Historical Outline of Australian Literature. Sydney: Angus and Robertson, 1958.

BOOKLETS

The Increased Price of Liberty; An Odious Comparison; A Noticeable Man; Carols of Cant and Wont (Bulldozer Booklets, nos 1-4). Melbourne: published privately, 1955-8.

MACKANESS, G., O.B.E., M.A., Litt.D. (Syd. and Melb.), F.R.A.H.S., formerly Senior Lecturer in English, Sydney Teachers' College.

BOOKS

Notes on Scott's "A Legend of Montrose". Sydney: Angus and Robertson, 1911.
Inspirational Teaching: A Record of Experimental Work in the Teaching of English. London: Dent, 1928; New York: Dutton, 1928.
Tales of the South Seas, by Louis Becke (selected and annotated). London: Nelson, 1929.
The Life of Vice-Admiral William Bligh, R.N., F.R.S., two volumes. Sydney: Angus and Robertson, 1931; New York: Farrar and Rinehart, 1933; new and revised edition in one volume, reset Sydney: Angus and Robertson, 1951.
Sir Joseph Banks: His Relations with Australia. Sydney: Angus and Robertson, 1936.
The Life of Admiral Arthur Phillip, R.N., Founder and First Governor of New South Wales. Sydney: Angus and Robertson, 1937.
A History of the United Grand Lodge of Ancient Free and Accepted Masons in New South Wales, in two volumes (in collaboration with K.R. Cramp). Sydney: Angus and Robertson, 1938.
A Book of the Bounty. London: Dent, 1938.
An Annotated Bibliography of Henry Lawson. Sydney: Angus and Robertson, 1951.
The Books of the Bulletin: An Annotated Bibliography (in collaboration with Walter Stone). Sydney: Angus and Robertson, 1955.
Collins's New Twentieth Century Dictionary, Australian and New Zealand Supplement. London: Collins, 1956.
The Art of Book-collecting in Australia. Sydney: Angus and Robertson, 1956.
The Story of the Queen Victoria Homes 1897-1957. Sydney: Waite and Bull, 1957.

AT PRESS

A History of Van Diemen's Land to 1835, by Henry Melville, in two parts, edited with an introduction and notes.
The Australian Journal of William Strutt, A.R.A., edited with a Memoir of Strutt, introduction and notes, in two parts.

McKenzie, K.A., M.A. (Melb.), D. de l'U. (Paris), Senior Lecturer in English, University of New England.

BOOK

Christopher Smart, sa vie et ses oeuvres. Paris: Les Presses Universitaires de France, 1925.

Mares, F.H., B.A. (Durham), B.Litt. (Oxon), Lecturer in English, University of Adelaide.

ARTICLES

Judith Wright and Australian Poetry, *Durham University Journal*, L, (New Series XIX), 2, Mar. 1958.
The Origin of the Figure called the "Vice" in Tudor Drama; *Huntington Library Quarterly*, 1958.

Maxwell, I.R., B.A., LL.B. (Melb.), B.Litt. (Oxon), Professor of English, University of Melbourne.

BOOK

French Farce and John Heywood. Melbourne: M.U.P., 1946.

ARTICLE

La farce de Thévot le maire, Perruche sa femme, et Colin leur fils (ed.), *Humanisme et renaissance*, VI, 1939.

Milgate, W., M.A. (Syd.), Professor of English Literature, University of Sydney.

ARTICLES

Donne the Lawyer, *Times Literary Supplement*, 1942.
The Date of Donne's Birth, *Notes and Queries*, CXCI, 1946.
Dr Donne's Art Gallery, *ibid.*, CXCIV, 1949.
The Early References to John Donne, *ibid.*, CXCV, 1950.
References to Donne, *ibid.*, CXCVIII, 1953.
Reading Shelley, *Essays in Criticism*, IV, 1954.

Miller, E. Morris, M.A. (Edin.), Litt.D., (Melb.), Professor Emeritus, University of Tasmania.

BOOKS

Libraries and Education. Melbourne: Robertson, 1912.
Kant's Doctrine of Freedom. Melbourne: Robertson, 1913.
The Basis of Freedom: A Study of Kant's Theory. Sydney: A.A.P.P., Monograph no. 3, 1924.
Brain Capacity and Intelligence. Sydney: A.A.P.P., Monograph no. 4, 1926.
Moral Law and the Highest Good: A Study of Kant's Doctrine. Melbourne: M.U.P., 1928.
Australian Literature from its Beginnings to 1935: A Descriptive and Bibliographical Survey. Melbourne: M.U.P., 1940, 2 vols.
Same. Bibliography (excluding Criticism), extended to 1950, with Commentaries by F. T. Macartney. Sydney: Angus and Robertson, 1956.
Pressmen and Governors: Australian Editors and Writers in Early Tasmania. Sydney: Angus and Robertson, 1952.

PAMPHLETS

Some Phases of Preference in Imperial Policy (Address to Imperial Federation League). Melbourne: 1911.

Australia's First Two Novels: Origins and Backgrounds. Hobart: Tasmanian Historical Research Association, 1958 (limited edition of 150 copies).

ARTICLES

The Beginnings of Philosophy in Australia and the Work of Henry Laurie (Presidential Address), *A.J.P.P.*, VII, 4, 1929; VIII, 1, 1930.

"The Early Tasmanian Press and its Writers" in *Across the Years*, ed. C. Barrett. Melbourne: Seward, 1948.

Also, contributions to *Meanjin*, *Southerly*, *A.J.P.P.*, and other periodicals.

MITCHELL, A.G., M.A. (Syd.), Ph.D. (London), Member of the Council of the International Phonetic Association, Professor of Early English Literature and Language, University of Sydney.

BOOKS

The Pronunciation of English in Australia. Sydney: Angus and Robertson, 1946; reprinted 1947, 1951, 1957.

Lady Meed and the Art of Piers Plowman (Third Chambers Memorial Lecture). London: H.K. Lewis, 1956.

Spoken English. London: Macmillan, 1957.

ARTICLES

Notes on the C-Text of "Piers Plowman", *London Mediaeval Studies*, I, 3, 1939.

"Such is Life": The Title and the Structure of the Book, *Southerly*, VI, 3, 1945.

Australian English, *A.Q.*, XXIII, 1951.

The Australian Accent, *C.A.B.*, vol. 10, no. 9, 1952.

An Australian Glossary—Supplement in *Chambers's Twentieth Century Dictionary*, 1952.

The Copernican Step in Education, *Union Book of 1952.*

Speech Education: The Underlying Assumptions, *Forum of Education*, X, 1951-2.

The Three Texts of "Piers Plowman" (in collaboration with G.H. Russell), *Journal of English and Germanic Philology*, LII, 1953.

MOORE, T. Inglis, O.B.E., B.A. (Syd.), M.A. (Oxon), Senior Lecturer in Australian Literature, Canberra University College.

BOOKS

Six Australian Poets. Melbourne: Robertson and Mullens, 1942.

Australia Writes: An Anthology (ed.). Melbourne: Cheshire, 1953.

Selected Poems of Henry Kendall (ed. with biographical and critical introduction and select bibliography). Sydney: Angus and Robertson, 1957.

PAMPHLETS

Modern American Poetry. Sydney: Australian English Association, 1935, offprint of no. 18.

The Misfortunes of Henry Handel Richardson (Commonwealth Literary Fund Lectures). Canberra: Canberra University College, 1957.

PREFACE

My Father and My Father's Friends by Hugh McCrae. Sydney: Angus and Robertson, 1935.

CHAPTERS

"The Arts in Australia" in *Compton's Cyclopedia*. Chicago, 1937.
"Australian Literature" in *This is Australia*. Sydney, 1938.
"Australian Literature" in *Australian Blue Book*. Sydney, 1950.

ARTICLES

Kenneth Slessor, *Southerly*, VIII, 4, 1947.
Mary Gilmore, *ibid.*, X, 3, 1949.
Frank Wilmot as "Furnley Maurice", *ibid.*, XII, 3, 1951.
The Tragi-Comedies of Kylie Tennant, *ibid.*, XVIII, 1957.
Australian Poetry Today, *Poetry Commonwealth* (England), no. 4, 1949.
Australian Poetry, *Fortnightly* (England), no. 1000, New Series, Apr. 1950.
The Rise and Fall of Henry Lawson, *Meanjin*, XVI, 1957.
The Quest of Judith Wright, *ibid.*, XVII, 3, 1958.

MUECKE, D.C., B.A. (Adel.), M.A. (Oxon), Senior Lecturer in English, Newcastle
University College.

ARTICLES

Vacancy exists for Lecturer in Trivium, *Universities Quarterly*, VII, 4, 1953.
New Directions for Literary Research, *Universities Review*, XXVI, 1, 1953.
The Dove's Flight, *Nineteenth Century Fiction*, IX, 1, 1954.
Some Notes on Vinaver's "Malory", *Modern Language Notes*, LXX, May 1955.
Two Errors in Literary Theory, *Quadrant*, no. 7, Winter 1958.

OLIVER, H.J., M.A. (Syd.), Senior Lecturer, Department of English, University of
Sydney.

BOOKS

The Problem of John Ford. Melbourne: M.U.P., 1955.
Timon of Athens, the New Arden Edition. London: Methuen, 1958.

ARTICLES

Charles Morgan, in *Some Modern Writers*, 1940.
Joseph Furphy and "Tom Collins", *Southerly*, V, 3, 1944.
Izaak Walton's Prose Style, *Review of English Studies*, XXI, 1946.
The Composition and Revisions of "The Compleat Angler", *Modern Languages Review*, XLII, 1947.
Another Source of "Gulliver's Travels"?, *Notes and Queries*, June 1947.
A Note on Joseph Conrad, *Times Literary Supplement*, 1947.
Izaak Walton as Author of "Love and Truth" and "Thealma and Clearchus", *Review of English Studies*, XXV, 1949.
John Steinbeck, *A.Q.*, XXIII, 1951.
The Progress of Ernest Hemingway, *ibid.*
Victor Daley and Roderic Quinn, *Meanjin*, X, 1951.
Louis Stone, *ibid.*, XIII, 1954.
The Achievement of R.D. FitzGerald, *ibid.*
The Mysticism of Henry Vaughan: A Reply, *Journal of English and Germanic Philology*, LIII, 1954.
Tom Collins, Lyre-Bird, *Southerly*, XV, 1954.
A More Versatile Neilson: The Manuscript Evidence, *ibid.*, XVII, 1956.
E.M. Forster: The Early Novels, *Critique: Studies in Modern Fiction*, Summer 1957.
Coriolanus as Tragic Hero, *Shakespeare Quarterly*, 1958.

AT PRESS

Monograph on E.M. Forster for A.H.R.C.

PALMER, Janet Gertrude, M.A. (Melb.), Diploma of International Phonetic Association. 7 Ridgeway Avenue, Kew, Victoria.

BOOKS

Modern Australian Literature. Melbourne: Lothian, 1924.
Henry Bournes Higgins (Biography). London: Harrap, 1931.
Talking it over (Essays, mainly literary). Sydney: Angus and Robertson, 1932.
Fourteen Years (Notes from a Journal, mainly literary). Privately printed, 1945.
Henry Handel Richardson: A Study. Sydney: Angus and Robertson, 1956.

PALMER, V. (died 1959), 7 Ridgeway Avenue, Kew, Victoria.

BOOKS

National Portraits. Sydney: Angus and Robertson, 1940; 3rd edition, 1954.
A. G. Stephens: His Life and Work. Melbourne: Robertson and Mullens, 1941.
Legend of the Nineties. Melbourne: M.U.P., 1954.

PIPER, H.W., B.A. (Adel.), M.A. (Oxon), Professor of English, University of New England.

BOOK

Nature and the Supernatural in The Ancient Mariner. Sydney: University of New England, Halstead Press, 1957.

ARTICLES

Keats and W.C. Wells, *Review of English Studies*, Apr. 1949.
Shakespeare's Thirty-first Sonnet, *Times Literary Supplement*, Apr. 1951.
Wordsworth in Revolutionary Paris, *AUMLA*, Aug. 1955.
Mythology in the English Romantic Poets, *ibid.*, Feb. 1957.
Maturin the Innovator (with A.N. Jeffares), *Huntington Library Quarterly*, 1958.

AT PRESS

The pantheistic sources of Coleridge's early poetry (to appear in *Journal of the History of Ideas*).

REES, G.L.C., B.A. (W.A.), Senior Drama Editor, Australian Broadcasting Commission, Hon. Chairman, Playwrights' Advisory Board, Sydney.

BOOKS

Australian Radio Plays (with introduction and notes. Selected and edited). Sydney: Angus and Robertson, 1946.
Towards an Australian Drama. Sydney: Angus and Robertson, 1953.

ARTICLES

Australian Drama in relation to Literature, *Australian Writers Speak*. Sydney: Angus and Robertson, 1942.
Is the Critic Creative?, *Meanjin*, V, 1946.

ROBINSON, F.W., M.A. (Syd.), Ph.D. (Jena), Associate Professor of English, University of Queensland.

BOOKS

Marius, Saturninus und Glaucia, Beiträge zur Geschichte der Jahre 106-100 vor Chr. (in German), published as no. 3 in the "Jena Historical Research Series". Bonn: Marcus und Weber, 1912.

Canberra's First Hundred Years. Canberra: W.C. Penfold and Co. Ltd, 1927.

Shakespeare's Comedy of a Midsummer Night's Dream (ed.). Melbourne: O.U.P., 1940 with later reprints.

ARTICLES

The Grand Style and the Sublime, Leaflet no. 9 of the *Australian English Association* (Sydney), 1929.

The Great Hall of the University of Sydney and Voices of the Past, *Book of University Union*, Sydney University Centenary, 1952.

RODERICK, C., M.A., Ph.D. (Qld), M.Ed. (Melb.), Education Editor, Publishing Department, Angus and Robertson Ltd.

BOOKS

A Companion to "Speaking Personally" (Walter Murdoch), with an Appendix on the Essay in Australia. Sydney: Brooks, 1945.

The Australian Novel. Sydney: Brooks, 1946.

Twenty Australian Novelists. Sydney: Angus and Robertson, 1947.

In Mortal Bondage: The Strange Life of Rosa Praed. Sydney: Angus and Robertson, 1948.

Introduction to Australian Fiction. Sydney: Angus and Robertson, 1950.

Ralph Rashleigh (James Tucker). Sydney: Angus and Robertson, 1952.

Australian Round-up (The Short Story from 1790 to 1950). Sydney: Angus and Robertson, 1953.

Jemmy Green in Australia (James Tucker) (with introduction on the Early Australian Theatre). Sydney: Angus and Robertson, 1955.

ARTICLES

Christina Stead, *Southerly*, no. 2, 1946.

A Woman of Some Importance (Mrs Campbell Praed), *ibid.*, 3, 1947.

Kenneth (Seaforth) Mackenzie: An Appreciation, *ibid.*, 4, 1954.

Australian Novels of 1947, *Education Magazine* (Melbourne), Mar. 1948.

Social Criticism and Nationalism in Australian Fiction, *ibid.*, June 1948.

Australian Novels of 1948, *ibid.*, Mar. 1949.

Australian Writing 1950, *ibid.*, Mar. 1951.

Roderic Quinn, Child of the Muse, *ibid.*, May 1951.

The Mystery of a Hansom Cab, *ibid.*, Nov., 1954.

The Personality of Henry Handel Richardson, *A.Q.*, Dec. 1948.

The Wanderer of the Ways of All the World (Christopher Brennan), *ibid.*, Mar. 1951.

The Authorship of "Ralph Rashleigh", *Sydney Bulletin*, 24 Dec. 1952.

The Tasmanian "Pickwick Papers", *Biblionews* (Sydney), VI, 10, Oct. 1953.

Literary Research in Australian Archives, *Australian Library Journal* (Sydney), IV, 4, Oct. 1955.

T.A. Scott and his Work at Port Macquarie: With an Account of James Williams per Neptune 1820, *R.A.H.S.*, XLIV, 1, 1958.

RUSSELL, G.H., M.A. (N.Z.), Ph.D. (Cantab.), Reader in English Language, University of Sydney.

ARTICLES

Philip Woodward: Elizabethan Pamphleteer and Translator, *Library*, Fifth Series, IV, 1, 1949.
The Three Texts of "Piers Plowman", *Journal of English and Germanic Philology*, LII, 4, 1953.
Scientia Literarum: Some Notes on the Letters of Bernard of Clairvaux, *Manna*, no. 2, 1958.

SCOTT, W.A.G., B.A. (Melb.), B.Litt. (Oxon), Reader in English, University of Melbourne.

ARTICLES

Smollett, Dr John Hill, and the Failure of "Peregrine Pickle", *Notes and Queries*, Sept. 1955.
Mottoes from the English Poets as Chapter Headings in the Novel, *ibid.*, Nov. 1957.
Smollett's "The Tears of Scotland", *Review of English Studies*, XXIX, 1957.

STEPHENSEN, P.R., B.A. (Qld and Oxon), Publishers' Editor and Authors' Agent, 56 Cremorne Road, Cremorne, N.S.W.

BOOKS

The Antichrist of Nietzsche (version in English with an introduction; illustrations by Norman Lindsay). London: Fanfrolico Press, 1928.
The Bushwhackers, sketches of life in the Australian outback. London: The Mandrake Press, 1929.
The Legend of Aleister Crowley. London: Mandrake Press, 1930.
Anna Pavlova (in association with Walford Hyden). London: Constable and Co. Ltd, 1931.
The Foundations of Culture in Australia, an essay towards national self-respect. Sydney: W.J. Miles, 1936.
The Life and Works of A.G. Stephens. Sydney: "The Bookfellow", 1940.
Wild Colonial Boys by Frank Clune (in literary collaboration with P.R. Stephensen). Sydney: Angus and Robertson, 1948.
The Viking of Van Diemen's Land, the stormy life of Jorgen Jorgensen by Frank Clune and P.R. Stephensen. Sydney: Angus and Robertson, 1954.
Kookaburras and Satyrs, some recollections of the Fanfrolico Press. Sydney: Fanfrolico Press, 1954.
The Cape Horn Breed, my experiences as an apprentice in sail, by W.H.S. Jones, Master Mariner, as told to P.R. Stephensen. London: Andrew Melrose, 1956; New York, 1956. Translated into Norwegian, Spanish and German.

STOKES, E., M.A., (Syd.), A.M. (Harvard) Senior Lecturer in English, University of Tasmania.

ARTICLES

Lafcadio Hearn's "Chita", *AUMLA*, no. 5, 1956.
Henry Green, Dispossessed Poet, *A.Q.*, XXVIII, 4, 1956.

STORMON, Rev. Fr E.J., S.J., M.A. (Melb.), Dean of Newman College, University of Melbourne.

ARTICLES

The Catholic Contribution to English Prose, *Australasian Catholic Record*, XVI, 2, 1939, and XVII, 1, 1940.
Scotus Redivivus, *ibid.*, XIX, 1, 1942.
Time and Mr T.S. Eliot, *Meanjin*, III, 2, 1944.
Eliot Through a Medium, *Mirrabooka*, vol. 2, 1946.
Virgil and the Modern Poet, *Meanjin*, VI, 1, 1947.

AT PRESS

Ricardus Heremita, 3 vols. London and New York: Sheed and Ward.

TODD, F.M., M.A. (N.Z.), Ph.D. (Lond.), Professor of English, University of Tasmania.

BOOK

Politics and the Poet: A Story of Wordsworth. London: Methuen, 1957.

ARTICLES

Wordsworth, Helen Maria Williams, and France, *Modern Language Review*, XLIII, 4, 1948.
Wordsworth in Germany, *ibid.*, XLVII, 4, 1952.
Wordsworth's Monody on Lamb: Another Copy, *ibid.*, L, 1, 1955.
Webster and Cervantes, *ibid.*, LI, 3, 1956.
Henry Lawson, *Twentieth Century*, IV, 3, 1950.
R.D. FitzGerald, *ibid.*, IX, 1, 1954.
The Poetry of Bernard O'Dowd, *Meanjin*, XIV, 1, 1955.

WILKES, G.A., M.A. (Syd.), D.Phil. (Oxon), Senior Lecturer, Department of English, University of Sydney.

ARTICLES

The Progress of Eleanor Dark, *Southerly*, XII, 1951.
The Novels of Katharine Susannah Prichard, *ibid.*, XIV, 1953.
Brennan and Blake, *ibid.*, XV, 1954.
Christopher John Brennan 1870-1932, *Union Book of 1952*.
The Writings of C.J. Brennan: A checklist, *Meanjin*, XV, 1956.
The Authorship of "The Passionate Man's Pilgrimages", *Notes and Queries*, IV, 1957.

PAMPHLETS

New Perspective on Brennan's Poetry. Sydney, 1953 (offprint from *Southerly*).
Some Trends in Australian Verse: The Problem of the Long Poem (Commonwealth Literary Fund Lecture). Canberra: Canberra University College, 1956.

AT PRESS

Australian Literature in the Nineties, *Proceedings of the Sydney University Arts Association*.
The Sequence of the Writings of Fulke Greville, Lord Brooke, *Studies in Philology*.

Fine Arts

ADAM, L.S., LL.D. (Greifswald), Dr Phil. (Bonn), F.R.A.I., Honorary Curator of the Ethnographical Museum, University of Melbourne.

BOOKS

Hochasiatische Kunst. Stuttgart, 1923.
Buddha Statuen. Stuttgart, 1925.
Primitive Art. London: Pelican, 3rd edition, 1954; Spanish edition, Buenos Aires, 1947; French edition in preparation, Grenoble: Arthaud.

ARTICLES

Nordwestamerikanische Indianerkunst, *Orbis Pictus* (Berlin), XVII, 1923.
Die Kunst des alten Amerika und die Alte Welt, *Cicerone* (Leipzig), 1927.
Ein indisches Relief und Ein chinesisches Relief, *ibid.*
Parallele entre les masques du Nord-Ouest de l'Amerique et les masques japonais, *Cahiers d'Art,* 1928.
L'animal dans l'Art de l'ancienne Amerique, *ibid.*, 1929.
Le portrait dans l'Art de l'ancienne Amerique, *ibid.*, 1930.
Das Problem der asiatisch-altamerikanischen Kulturbeziehungen mit besonderer Berücksichtigung der Kunst, *Wiener Beiträge zur Kunst- u. Kulturgeschichte Asiens,* 1931.
Is de Oud-Amerikaansche Kunst uit Oost-Azie afkomstig? *Wereldkroniek,* Dec. 1933.
Northwest American Indian Art and Its Early Chinese Parallels, *Man,* 1936.
Die kombinierten ghi-Kannen und Dochtlampen von Nepal, *Ostasiatische Zeitschrift,* N.F., XIII, 1937.
Arts of Primitive Peoples, *Journal of the Royal Soc. of Arts,* 4564, London, 1940.
Comments on some recent contributions to the prehistory of New Guinea, *Mankind,* III, 9, 1946.
Some uncommon perforated stone implements from the Morobe and Mt Hagen areas, New Guinea, *ibid.*, 12, 1947.
Aboriginal Bark paintings from Groote Eylandt, *Meanjin,* 1950.
"The Last Judgment" (a Chinese tempera painting), *ibid,* 1953.
The Bark Paintings from Groote Eylandt in the Melbourne University Collection, *Südsee-Studien* (Basel), 1951.
Observations on the Bark Paintings of Eastern Arnhem Land, especially of Milingimbi, *Tribus* (Stuttgart), N.F., IV-V. 1954-5.
Bildende Kunst, *Lehrbuch der Völkerkunde,* 3rd edition with Trimborn, Stuttgart, 1958.
Anthropomorphe Darstellungen auf australischen Ritualgeräten, *Anthropos,* LIII, 1958.
Note. In addition Dr Adam has published widely on ethnology and primitive law in general, on technology and archaeology in relation to the study of primitive peoples and on other scholarly matters. Bibliographies of his work have appeared in *Zeitschrift für Ethnologie* (Braunschweig), Bd. 81, 1956, pp. 312-14 and *Zeitschrift für vergleichende Rechtswissenschaft* (Stuttgart), Bd. 59, 1957, pp. 3-6.

Burke, J.T., O.B.E., M.A. (Lond., Yale, Melb.), Professor of Fine Arts, University of Melbourne.

BOOKS

Hogarth and Reynolds: A Contrast in English Art Theory (Charlton Memorial Lecture). Oxford: O.U.P., 1943.
William Hogarth's "The Analysis of Beauty", with the rejected passages from the manuscript drafts and autobiographical fragments (ed. with introduction). Oxford: O.U.P., 1955.

ARTICLES

Some English Embroidered Vestments at Danzig, *Burlington Magazine*, LXX, 1508, Mar. 1937.
A Classical Aspect of Hogarth's Theory of Art, *Journal of the Warburg and Courtauld Institutes*, VI, 1943.
Archbishop Abbot's Tomb: A Problem in Carolean Iconography, *ibid.*, XII, 1949.

IN PROGRESS

Vol. IX (1714-1800) of *Oxford History of English Art*.

Herman, M., B.Arch.(Syd.), F.R.A.I.A., 173 Darlinghurst Rd., Sydney, N.S.W.

BOOKS

The Early Australian Architects and their Work (illustrated by author). Sydney: Angus and Robertson, 1954.
The Architecture of Victorian Sydney (with Boyd Wilkinson). Sydney: Angus and Robertson, 1956.

Hoff, Ursula, Dr Phil.(Hamburg), Lecturer, Department of Fine Arts, University of Melbourne; Curator of Prints and Drawings, National Gallery of Victoria.

BOOKS

Rembrandt und England. Hamburg: privately printed, 1935.
Charles I, Patron of the Arts. London: Collins, 1942.
Masterpieces of the National Gallery of Victoria (ed. and main contributor). Melbourne: Cheshire, 1949.

ARTICLES

Some Aspects of Adam Elsheimer's Artistic Development, *Burlington Magazine*, vol. LXXV, 1939.
Reflections on the Heidelberg School, *Meanjin*, X, 2, 1951.
Albrecht Dürer, the Barlow Collection of Prints in the National Gallery of Victoria, *ibid.*, XVI, 2, 1957.
Various articles in the *Bulletin of the National Gallery of Victoria* and *Meanjin*.

Mountford, C.P., O.B.E., 25 First Avenue, St Peters, Adelaide, S.A.

BOOKS

Brown Men and Red Sand. Melbourne: Robertson and Mullens, 1948.
Australia: Aboriginal Paintings—Arnhem Land. Explanation, and bark and cave paintings. U.N.E.S.C.O. World Art Series: Paris, 1954.
Art, Myth and Symbolism, American-Australian Expedition to Arnhem Land, 1948. M.U.P., 1956.
The Tiwi, their Art, Myth and Ceremony. London: Phoenix House, 1958.

PHILIPP, F.A., B.A. (Melb.), Senior Lecturer, Department of Fine Arts, University of Melbourne.

ARTICLES

Two Medieval Stained Glass Medallions, *Bulletin of the National Gallery of Victoria*, VI, 1, 1952.

A Lamentation of Christ attributed to Bartolomeo Bellano, *ibid.*, VIII, 2, 1954.

Jacopo Tintoretto's Portrait of the Doge Pietro Loredano, *ibid.*, XI, 2, 1957.

SMITH, B.W., B.A.(Syd.), Ph.D. (A.N.U.), F.S.A., Senior Lecturer, Department of Fine Arts, University of Melbourne.

BOOKS

Place, Taste and Tradition: A Study of Australian Art since 1788. Sydney: Ure Smith, 1945.

A Catalogue of Australian Oil Paintings in the National Art Gallery of New South Wales, 1875-1952. Sydney: National Art Gallery of New South Wales, 1953.

Art and Education in Australia: A Symposium. Melbourne: M.U.P., 1958.

ARTICLES

European Vision and the South Pacific, *Journal of the Warburg and Courtauld Institutes*, XIII, 1950.

Coleridge's "Ancient Mariner" and Cook's Second Voyage, *ibid.*, XIX, 1956.

AT PRESS

In association with R.A. Skelton, a catalogue of original drawings and paintings made by the artists who travelled with Captain Cook, to be published in vol. IV of *The Journals of Captain James Cook*, C.U.P., for the Hakluyt Society. Articles: "Topographical Art" and "Australian Art" for *Oxford Companion to Art*. Oxford: Clarendon Press.

European Vision and the South Pacific, 1768-1850: A Study in the History of Art and Ideas. Oxford: Clarendon Press.

History

ALEXANDER, F., M.A. (Melb. and Oxon), Professor of Modern History, University of Western Australia.

BOOKS AND CHAPTERS

From Paris to Locarno and After, 1919-1928. London: Dent, 1928.

"Australia Since the War", chapter XX of *Cambridge History of the British Empire*, vol. VII, pt 1, Australia. Cambridge: C.U.P., 1933.

Australia and the United States. Boston: World Peace Foundation, 1941.

"Australia at War"—pt I, Australia's War Effort, W.Y. Elliott (ed.), *The British Commonwealth at War*, chapter VIII, pt I. New York: Knopf, 1943.

Moving Frontiers: An American Theme and its Application to Australian History. Melbourne: M.U.P., 1947.

"The Australian People and the World", chapter 7, G. Caiger (ed.), *The Australian Way of Life*. London: Heinemann, 1953.

The Origins of the Eastern Goldfields Water Scheme in Western Australia (in collaboration with F.K. Crowley and J.D. Legge). Perth: U.W.A.P., 1954.

Four Bishops and their See: Perth, Western Australia, 1857-1957. Perth: U.W.A.P., 1957 (Editor).

"The Australian Community", chapter I of *Australia in World Affairs, 1950-1955*. Melbourne: Cheshire, 1957.
"Australia 1956", *Chambers's Encyclopaedia World Survey 1956*. London, 1957.
"Western Australia", *Encyclopaedia Britannica*. Chicago, London and Toronto, 1957.

ARTICLES

The Governor-General and Dissolution, *A.Q.*, Sept. 1930.
The State Governor and his Powers, *ibid.*, June 1931.
Inter-Imperial Consultation, *ibid.*, X, 3, 1938.
Australia and the United States, *ibid.*, XIII, 2, 1941.
Sydney University and the W.E.A., 1913-1919, *ibid.*, XXVII, 4, 1955.
The Nazi State, *University Studies in History and Economics* (Perth), I, 1, 1934.
America, the British Commonwealth and the Far East, *America and Japan, Annals of the American Academy of Political and Social Science* (Philadelphia), CCXV, 1941.
Direct Relations between Dominions: An Approach to Mutual Exchanges, *Commonwealth and Empire Review* (London), LXXXIV, 534.
South African Race Patterns, etc. (three articles on South Africa), *Foreign Policy Bulletin* (New York), XXIX, nos 44, 45, 46, 1950.
South Africa's Indian Problem, *Far Eastern Survey*, XXIX, 21.
America 1950: An Impression, *A.O.*, V, I, 1951.
The Simon-Stimson Myth—Japanese Aggression in Manchuria and Anglo-American Relations 1931-1954, *ibid.*, IX, I, 1955.
Australia in World Affairs: Post-War Australian Foreign Policy vis-à-vis the United States, with special reference to South-East Asia, *ibid.*, X, 1, 1956.

AT PRESS

"Australien: Ein Vielgestaltiger Kontinent", for *Europa und die Welt*, vol. I. Zurich: Max S. Metz.
"Australia: History", in *Encyclopedia Americana*, New York and Chicago.

AUCHMUTY, J.J., M.A., Ph.D.(Dublin), M.R.I.A., F.R.Hist.S., Professor of History, Newcastle University College.

BOOKS

The United States Government and Latin American Independence, 1810-30. London: P.S. King, 1937.
Irish Education: A Historical Survey. London: Harrap; Dublin: Hodges Figgis, 1937.
Sir Thomas Wyse 1791-1862: The Life and Career of an Educator and Diplomat. London: P.S. King, 1939.
Lecky: A Biographical and Critical Essay. London: Longmans; Dublin: Hodges Figgis, 1946.

ARTICLES

Acton's Election as an Irish Member of Parliament, *English Historical Review*, LXI, 241, 1946.
Ireland and the Celtic Peoples in Toynbee's "Study of History", *Hermathena*, LXX, Nov. 1947.
The Place of Egypt in Toynbee's "Study of History", *Proceedings of the Royal Society of Historical Studies* (Cairo), I, 1951.
History and the Historian, *Bulletin of the Faculty of Arts*, Farouk I University (Alexandria), IV, 1948.

Acton as a Member of the House of Commons, *ibid.*, V, 1949.
Lord Acton's Morality: Theory and Practice, *ibid.*, VI-VII, 1952-3.
Lachlan Macquarie and the Anglo-Indian Expedition to Egypt 1801, *Proceedings of the Royal Society of Historical Studies* (Cairo), II, 1953.
The Background to the Early Australian Governors, *H.S.*, VI, 23, 1954.
The Background of Australian History, *R.A.H.S.*, XLI, 3.
The Lecky-Lea Correspondence in the Henry Charles Lea Library of the University of Pennsylvania, Philadelphia, U.S.A., *Hermathena*, XCII, Nov. 1958.

BARRY, J.V., Q.C., Judge of the Supreme Court of Victoria.

BOOK

Alexander Maconochie. Melbourne: O.U.P., 1958.

BASSETT, Marnie N., 133 Kooyong Road, Armadale, Victoria.

BOOKS

The Governor's Lady. London: O.U.P., 1940; 2nd edition, 1956.
The Hentys: An Australian Colonial Tapestry. London: O.U.P., 1954.

ARTICLES

Thomas Muir (in collaboration with Franklin Jameson), *American Historical Review*, XXIX, 1, Oct. 1923.
Governor Arthur and the Opposite Coast, *Tasmanian Historical Research Association*, II, 1953.

BASTIN, J.S., M.A. (Melb.), Ph.D. (Leyden), D.Phil. (Oxon), former Fellow, Department of Pacific History, Australian National University.

BOOKS

Raffles' Ideas on the Land Rent System in Java and the MacKenzie Land Tenure Commission. The Hague: Smits, 1954; republished as vol. XIV of the *Verhandelingen* series of the Koninklijk Inst. T.L.V., The Hague.
The Native Policies of Sir Stamford Raffles in Java and Sumatra: An Economic Interpretation. Oxford: O.U.P., 1957.
The Journal of Thomas Otho Travers, 1813-20 (ed.). Singapore: Memoirs of the Raffles Museum, 1957.

ARTICLES

Palembang in 1811 and 1812, *BKI* (The Hague), CIX, 1953 and CX, 1954.
Colonel Colin MacKenzie and Javanese Antiquities, *ibid.*, CIX, 1953.
The Rivalry between Dirk van Hogendorp and S.C. Nederburgh, *Indonesië*, VI, 1953.
The Chinese Estates in East Java during the British Administration, *ibid.* (The Hague), VII, 1954.
Raffles and British Policy in the Indian Archipelago, 1811-16, *JMBRAS* (Singapore), XXVII, 1954.
Indonesian and Malayan Studies in Australia, *BKI*, CXIII, 1957.

BLAINEY, G.N., The Boulevard, Ivanhoe, Victoria.

BOOKS

The Peaks of Lyell. Melbourne: M.U.P., 1954.
The University of Melbourne: A Centenary Portrait (in collaboration with N.H. Olver). Melbourne: M.U.P., 1956.

A Centenary History of the University of Melbourne. Melbourne: M.U.P., 1957.
Introducing Victoria (ed. G. Leeper). Melbourne: M.U.P., 1955; chapter I, "A History of Victoria".
Sir Samuel Wadham: Selected Addresses. Melbourne: M.U.P., 1956; chapter I, "A Biographical Study".
Gold and Paper. Melbourne: Georgian House, 1959.

AT PRESS

A History of Mount Isa Mines, Queensland.

BRAMSTED, E., Ph.D. (London), Dr Phil. (Berlin), Senior Lecturer in History, University of Sydney.

BOOKS AND CHAPTERS

Aristocracy and the Middle Classes in Germany: Social Types in German Literature, 1830-1900 (with a foreword by G.P. Gooch). London: King, 1937.
"Society and Political Thought in France", chapter VII of *Political Thought: The European Tradition* (ed. J.P. Mayer, introduction by Professor R.H. Tawney). London: Dent, 1939.
Dictatorship and Political Police: The Technique of Control by Fear. London: Kegan Paul, 1945; Japanese edition: Tokyo, 1952.
Joint Editor of *Documents on German Foreign Policy, 1918-1945: From the Archives of the German Foreign Ministry*, Series D, 1937-45, vols. I-IV. London: H.M. Stationery Office, 1949-53.
Joint Editor of *Akten zur deutschen auswärtigen Politik 1918-1945*, Series D, 1937-45, Band I-V, Baden-Baden, 1950-3 (edition of the originals in German of *Documents on German Foreign Policy*).
Joint editor with Professor H. Gerth of *Freedom, Power and Democratic Planning* by the late Karl Mannheim. New York: O.U.P., 1950; London: Routledge and Kegan Paul, 1951.

ARTICLES

Probleme der Literatursoziologie, *Neue Jahrbücher für Wissenschaft und Jugendbildung* (Leipzig), VII, 8.
Über die Strukturidentität von Weltanschauung und Staatsauffassung bei Spinoza, *Logos* (Tübingen), XVII, 1928.
Condorcet und das Geschichtsbild der späten Aufklärung, *Archiv für Kulturgeschichte* (Leipzig), XX, 1929.
Lord Haldane and Germany, *Contemporary Review*, CLVII, May 1940.
Croce and the Philosophy of Liberty, *ibid.*, CLXVIII, Nov. 1945.
Joseph Goebbels and National Socialist Propaganda 1926-39: Some Aspects, *A.O.*, VIII, 2, 1954.
Opportunist or Patriot? The Case of Franz von Papen, *A.O.*, VI, 4, 1954.
What Goebbels left out: Some significant Omissions in his Wartime Books, *Wiener Library Bulletin* (London), IX, nos 1-2, 1955, and nos 3-4, 1955.
British Attitudes in National Socialist Eyes: Joseph Goebbels, the English and Mr Churchill, 1939-45, *Australian Journal of Politics and History*, I, 2, 1956.
Joseph Goebbels as a Propagandist; The Lure of Historical Parallels, 1939-45, *H.S.*, VII, 26, 1956.

T

CLARK, C.M.H., M.A. (Melb.), Professor of History, Canberra University College.

BOOKS

Select Documents in Australian History, 1788-1850. Sydney: Angus and Robertson, 1950.

Select Documents in Australian History, 1851-1900. Sydney: Angus and Robertson, 1955.

Sources of Australian History. London: World's Classics, 1957.

ARTICLES

Foreword to *Settlers and Convicts.* Melbourne: M.U.P., 1953.

G.A. Wood, *Twentieth Century*, Dec. 1955.

The Origins of Convicts transported to Eastern Australia, *H.S.*, pt I, May 1956; pt II, Nov. 1956.

The Rewriting of Australian History, in *Australian Signpost* (ed. T.A.G. Hungerford). Melbourne: Cheshire, 1956.

COOPER, H.M., South Australian Museum, North Terrace, Adelaide, S.A.

BOOKS

Australian Aboriginal Words and their Meanings. Adelaide: South Australian Museum, 1949, 1952 and 1957.

A Naval History of South Australia. Adelaide: H.M. Cooper, 1950.

French Exploration in South Australia 1802-3. Adelaide: H.M. Cooper, 1952.

The Unknown Coast. Adelaide: H.M. Cooper, 1953.

The Unknown Coast: A Supplement. Adelaide: H.M. Cooper, 1955.

CRANFIELD, G.A., B.A., Ph.D. (Cantab.), Senior Lecturer in History, Newcastle University College.

PAMPHLET

A Handlist of English Provincial Newspapers and Periodicals 1700-1760. Cambridge: Bowes and Bowes, 1952.

ARTICLES

The Early Career of Robert Raikes, I and II, *Notes and Queries*, CXCVI, 6, 1951.

The First Cambridge Newspapers, *Proceedings of the Cambridge Antiquarian Society*, XLV, 1952.

The Conception of the Just War, *A.O.*, IX, 2, 1955.

Handlist of English Provincial Newspapers and Periodicals, 1700-1760, Additions and Corrections, *Transactions of the Cambridge Bibliographical Society*, VI, 3, 1956.

CRAWFORD, R.M., B.A. (Syd.), M.A. (Oxon and Melb.), Professor of History, University of Melbourne.

BOOKS AND CHAPTERS

The Study of History. Melbourne: M.U.P., 1939.

Ourselves and the Pacific. Melbourne: M.U.P., 1st edition, 1941; 3rd edition, 1952; various reprints.

The Renaissance and Other Essays. Melbourne: M.U.P., 1945; revised, 1947.

The Gold Rushes and their Aftermath, 1851-1901 (in collaboration with G.F. James), chapter IV of C. Hartley Grattan (ed.) *Australia.* University of California Press, United Nations Series, 1947.

Australia. London: Hutchinson's University Library, 1952; reprinted, 1955.

"Historical Aspects of the Problem of Recurrent Wars", chapter I in *Paths to Peace* (ed. Victor H. Wallace). M.U.P., 1957.

ARTICLES

The Letters of Dorothy Osborne, *Australian English Association* (Sydney), 1935, offprint no. 19.

History as a Science, *H.S.*, III, 1947.

The Renaissance Mirror, *ibid.*, VI, 1955.

The Australian National Character, Myth and Reality, *Journal of World History*, II, 1955.

CROWLEY, F.K., M.A., Ph.D. (Melb.), D.Phil. (Oxon), F.S.S. (Lond.), Senior Lecturer in History, University of Western Australia.

BOOKS AND CHAPTERS

A Guide to the Principal Documents and Publications relating to the History of Western Australia. Perth: U.W.A.P., 1949.

The Records of Western Australia, vol. I. Perth: U.W.A.P., 1954.

The Origins of the Eastern Goldfields Water Scheme in Western Australia (in collaboration with F. Alexander and J.D. Legge). Perth: U.W.A.P., 1954.

The Foundation Years: 1788-1821, chapter I in *Australia: A Social and Political History* (ed. G. Greenwood). Sydney: Angus and Robertson, 1955.

Historical Development of the Metropolitan Region, chapter I in *Plan for the Metropolitan Region: Perth and Fremantle, Western Australia.* Perth: Government Printer, 1955.

Church and State in Western Australia, chapter in *Four Bishops and their See: Perth, Western Australia 1857-1957* (ed. F. Alexander). Perth: U.W.A.P., 1957.

ARTICLES

The Present State of Research in Western Australian History, *University Studies in History and Economics* (Perth), II, 1, 1953.

The British Contribution to the Australian Population: 1860-1919, *ibid.*, II, 2, 1954.

Master and Servant in Western Australia: 1829-51, and 1851-1901, *Journal of the Historical Society of Western Australia*, 1953 and 1954.

AT PRESS

Australia's Western Third, for Macmillan, London.

A Pocket History of Western Australia, for Macmillan, London.

CURREY, C.H., 19 Llandilo Avenue, Strathfield, N.S.W.

BOOKS

British Colonial Policy, 1783-1915. Oxford: O.U.P., 1916.

British History 1485-1815 by S.H. Roberts and C.H. Currey. Sydney: Angus and Robertson, 1949.

The British Commonwealth since 1815. Sydney: Angus and Robertson, 1950.

A Brief History of the British Commonwealth since Waterloo. Sydney: Angus and Robertson, 1954.

The Irish at Eureka. Sydney: Angus and Robertson, 1954.

DAVIDSON, J.W., M.A. (N.Z.), Ph.D. (Cantab.), Professor of Pacific History, Australian National University.

BOOK

The Northern Rhodesia Legislative Council. London: Faber and Faber, 1948.

ARTICLES

The History of Empire, *Economic History Review*, XVI, 1, 1946.

Political Development in Western Samoa, *P.A.*, XXI, 2, 1948.

Colonial Government in *Chambers' Encyclopaedia* (London), III, 1950.

The Changing Political Role of Pacific Island Peoples, *New Zealand Journal of Public Administration*, XIV, 1, 1951.

The Price of Political Dependency, *A.O.*, VI, 2, 1952.

New Zealand, 1820-1870: An Essay in Re-interpretation, *H.S.*, V, 20, 1953.

The Study of Pacific History (Inaugural Lecture). Canberra: Australian National University, 1955.

Peter Dillon and the Discovery of Sandalwood in the New Hebrides, *Journal de la Société des Océanistes* (Paris), XII, 1956.

Scholarship and the Government of Colonies, *H.S.*, VII, 28, 1957.

DRUS, Ethel, M.A. (Cape Town), F.R.Hist.S., Research Fellow, Department of Pacific History, Australian National University.

ARTICLES

The Colonial Office and the Annexation of Fiji, *Transactions of the Royal Historical Society*, Fourth Series, XXXII, 1950.

A Report on the Papers of Joseph Chamberlain relating to the Jameson Raid and the Inquiry, *Bulletin of the Institute of Historical Research* (London), XXV, 1952.

Select Documents from the Chamberlain Papers concerning Anglo-Transvaal Relations, 1896-1899, *ibid.*, XXVII, 1954.

The Question of Imperial Complicity in the Jameson Raid, *English Historical Review*, Oct. 1953.

Ed. of *A Journal of Events during the Gladstone Ministry, 1868-74* by John, First Earl of Kimberley, published by the Royal Historical Society in the Camden Miscellany, vol. XXI, 1958.

ELLIS, M.H., F.R.Hist.S., 18 Reed Street, Cremorne, N.S.W.

BOOKS

Lachlan Macquarie: Some aspects of his life. Brisbane: University of Queensland, 1942.

Lachlan Macquarie: his life, adventures and times. Sydney: Dymock, editions 1947 and 1952.

Francis Greenway. Sydney: The Shepherd Press, editions 1949 and 1952.

John Macarthur. Sydney: Angus and Robertson, 1955.

EVATT, Rt Hon. H.V., D.Litt., LL.D. (Syd.), D.Sc.(hon.), F.R.A.H.S.

BOOKS

Liberalism in Australia. Sydney, 1918.

The British Dominions as Mandatories. Melbourne: Law Book Co., 1935.

The King and his Dominion Governors: a study of the reserve powers of the Crown in Great Britain and the Dominions. London: O.U.P., 1936.

Injustice within the Law: A study of the case of the Dorsetshire labourers. Sydney: Law Book Co., 1937.

Rum Rebellion: A study of the overthrow of Governor Bligh by John Macarthur and the New South Wales Corps. Sydney: Angus and Robertson, 1938 and 1955.

Australian Labour Leader. The Story of W.A. Holman and the Labour Movement. Sydney: Angus and Robertson, 1940; abridged edition, 1954.
Foreign Policy of Australia: speeches (introduction by W. Macmahon Ball). Sydney: Angus and Robertson, 1945.
Australia in World Affairs. Sydney: Angus and Robertson, 1946.

FERGUSON, J.A., Hon. Mr Justice, O.B.E., B.A., LL.B., D.Litt. (Syd.), F.R.A.H.S.

BOOKS

A Bibliography of the New Hebrides and a History of the Mission Press. Sydney: Angus and Robertson, pt I, 1917; pt II, 1918; pt III, 1945; pt IV in MS.
The Howes and their Press (in collaboration with Mrs A.G. Foster and H.M. Green). Sydney: Sunnybrook Press, 1936.
Bibliography of Australia. Sydney: Angus and Robertson, *vol. I: 1784-1830*, 1941; *vol. II: 1831-1838*, 1945; *vol. III: 1839-1845*, 1951; *vol. IV: 1846-1850*, 1955; *vol. V: 1851-1901*, in preparation.

ARTICLES

The Tasmanian "Pickwick Papers", *R.A.H.S.*, vol. IV.
The Literature of the Darling Controversies, *ibid.*, IX.
The Literature relating to "The Scottish Martyrs", *ibid.*, XIII.
Bibliography and National Library Service, *The Australian Library Journal*, III, 1954.

AT PRESS

Bibliography of the Gilbert and Ellice Islands and Nauru (part author and editor with Dr Kunz). Sydney: Public Library of New South Wales.

FITZGERALD, C.P., Professor of Far Eastern History, Australian National University.

BOOKS

Son of Heaven: A Biography of Li Shih-min, Founder of the T'ang Dynasty. London: C.U.P., 1933.
China: A Short Cultural History. London: Cresset Press, 1935.
The Tower of Five Glories: A Study of the Min Chia at Ta Li, Yunnan. London: Cresset Press, 1941.
Revolution in China. London: Cresset Press, 1952.
The Empress Wu. Melbourne: Cheshire, 1956; London: Cresset Press, 1956.

ARTICLES

The Chinese Revolution and the West. *P.A.*, XXIV, 1, Mar. 1951.
The Revolutionary Tradition in China (Morrison Oration), *H.S.*, 1952.
A Chinese discovery of Australia? in *Australia Writes.* Melbourne: Cheshire, 1953.
China, Korea, and Indo-China, in *Australian Policies toward Asia.* Melbourne: Australian Institute of International Affairs, 1954.
The Character of Far Eastern History (Inaugural Lecture). Canberra: Australian National University, 1955.
Continuity in Chinese History, *H.S.*, 1955.
The Restoration of the Chinese Empire under the Sui and T'ang Dynasties, *A.O.*, Dec. 1956.

FITZHARDINGE, L.F., B.A. (Syd.), M.A., B.Litt. (Oxon), Reader in Australian History, Australian National University.

BOOKS AND CHAPTERS

St John's Church and Canberra. Canberra: Verity Hewitt, 1941; new edition in press.

Political and Public Life, pt II of *Nation Building in Australia: The Life and Work of Sir Littleton Ernest Groom.* Sydney: Angus and Robertson, 1941.

The Commonwealth, 1901-1939, chapter 5 of *Australia* (ed. C. Hartley Grattan). University of California Press, 1947.

In Search of a Capital City and Old Canberra and District, 1820-1910, chapters 1 and 2 of *Canberra: A Nation's Capital* (ed. H.L. White). Sydney: Angus and Robertson, 1954.

ARTICLES

A Roman Governor: Pliny in Bithynia, *Public Administration,* V, 1, New Series, 1944.

Immigration Policy: A Survey. *A.Q.,* XXI, 2, 1949.

W.M. Hughes in New South Wales Politics, 1890-1900, *R.A.H.S.,* XXXVII, 3, 1951.

Naval Epitaphs from Misenum in the Nicholson Museum, Sydney, *Journal of Roman Studies,* XLI, 1951.

W.M. Hughes and the Waterside Workers, *Australian Journal of Politics and History,* II, 2, 1957.

FITZPATRICK, B., M.A. (Melb.), 22A Clendon Road, Toorak, Victoria.

BOOKS AND CHAPTERS

British Imperialism and Australia 1783-1833: An Economic History of Australasia. London: George Allen and Unwin, 1939.

A Short History of the Australian Labour Movement. Melbourne: Rawson's Book Shop, 1940; 2nd edition, 1944.

The British Empire in Australia: An Economic History 1834-1939. Melbourne: M.U.P., 1941; 2nd edition, 1949.

The Australian People 1788-1945. Melbourne: M.U.P., 1946; 2nd edition, 1951.

Secondary Industries in the Economy, chapter in *Australia* (ed. C. Hartley Grattan). University of California Press, 1947.

The Australian Commonwealth: A Picture of the Community 1901-1955. Melbourne: Cheshire, 1956.

The Irish in Australia, in *The Character of Ireland* (ed. Louis MacNeice and W.R. Rogers). Oxford: Clarendon Press, 1958.

ARTICLES

Studies in Political Conflict, *Meanjin,* XIV, 1, 1955.

The Contentious Eureka Legend, *ibid.,* 2, 1955.

The Importance of being Earnest about Liberty, *ibid.,* XV, 1, 1956.

FITZPATRICK, Kathleen Elizabeth, B.A. (Melb.), M.A. (Oxon), Associate Professor of History, University of Melbourne.

BOOKS

Sir John Franklin in Tasmania, 1837-1843. Melbourne: M.U.P., 1949.

Australian Explorers (selection from their journals, with introduction). London: World Classics, 1958.

ARTICLES

Mr Gladstone and the Governor: The Recall of Sir John Eardley-Wilmot from Van Diemen's Land, 1846, *H.S.*, I, 1, 1940.
The Puritans and the Theatre, *ibid.*, III, 12, 1949.

FORSYTH, W.D., O.B.E., M.A. (Melb.), B.Litt. (Oxon), 88 Banks Street, Yarralumla, A.C.T.

BOOKS

Governor Arthur's Convict System. London: Longmans Green, 1935.
The Myth of Open Spaces: Australian, British and World Trends of Population and Migration. M.U.P. and O.U.P., 1942.

GOLLAN, R.A., M.A. (Syd.), Ph.D. (Lond.), Fellow, Department of History, Australian National University.

CHAPTER

Nationalism, the Labour Movement and the Commonwealth, 1880-1900, chapter 4 of *Australia: A Social and Political History* (ed. G. Greenwood). Sydney: Angus and Robertson, 1955.

ARTICLES

The Trade Unions and Labour Parties, 1890-94, *H.S.*, VII, 25, Nov. 1955.
Nationalism and Politics in Australia, *Australian Journal of Politics and History*, I, 1, Nov. 1955.

GREENWOOD, G., M.A. (Syd.), Ph.D. (Lond.), Professor of History and Political Science, University of Queensland.

BOOKS

Early American-Australian Relations. Melbourne: M.U.P., 1944.
The Future of Australian Federalism. Melbourne: M.U.P., 1946.
Australia: A Social and Political History (editor and contributor). Sydney: Angus and Robertson, 1955.
Australia in World Affairs 1950-55 (editor with N. Harper, and contributor). Melbourne: Cheshire, 1957.

CHAPTERS AND PAMPHLETS

Australia's Interest in the South Pacific Islands, in *Australia* (ed. C. Hartley Grattan). University of California Press, 1947.
The Case for Extended Commonwealth Powers, chapter in *Federalism in Australia*. Melbourne: Cheshire, 1949.
The Present State of Teaching and Research in the Australian Universities— An Estimate, *H.S.*, VI, 23, 1954, and *A.N.Z.A.A.S. Report of the Thirtieth Meeting, Canberra 1954*, Sydney, 1955.
Australia's Triangular Foreign Policy, *Foreign Affairs*, XXXV, 4, July 1957.

HANCOCK, W.K., Kt, M.A. (Oxon), D.Litt. (Rhodes), Litt.D. (Cantab.), F.B.A., Director, Research School of Social Sciences and Professor of History, Australian National University.

BOOKS

Ricasoli and the Risorgimento in Tuscany. London: Faber and Gwyer, 1926.
Australia. London: Ernest Benn, 1930.
Survey of British Commonwealth Affairs. London: O.U.P., 1937, 1940, 1942.
Argument of Empire. London: Penguin Books, 1943.

Politics in Pitcairn. London: Macmillan, 1947.
British War Economy (in collaboration with M.M. Gowing). London: H.M. Stationery Office, 1949.
Wealth of Colonies. Cambridge: C.U.P., 1950.
The History of our Times. London: Athlone Press, 1951.
Country and Calling. London: Faber and Faber, 1956.
The Smuts Papers. London: Athlone Press, 1956.
Colonial Self-Government (Cust Foundation Lecture). University of Nottingham, 1956.

ARTICLES

Ferdinando Ranalli, A Lonely Patriot, *Proceedings of the British Academy*, XXVII, 1941.
Agenda for the Study of British Imperial Economy, 1850-1950, *Journal of Economic History*, XIII, 3, Summer 1953.
The Underdeveloped Economies, *Economic History Review*, VI, 3, 1954.
Exploring the Life of Smuts, *Australian Journal of Politics and History*, I, Nov. 1955.
Official History, *Times Literary Supplement*, 6 Jan. 1956.

IN PROGRESS

Biography of Field-Marshal J.C. Smuts.
A four-volume edition of Smuts papers with notes.
(Both to be published by C.U.P.)

HARPER, N.D., M.A., B.Ed. (Melb.), Associate Professor of History, University of Melbourne.

BOOKS

Our Pacific Neighbours (with G.S. Browne). Melbourne: Cheshire, 1953.
Reflections on Australian Foreign Policy (ed. with F.W. Eggleston). Melbourne: Cheshire and A.I.I.A., 1957.
Australia and the United States, and Australia and Suez, in *Australia in World Affairs 1950-5* (ed. G. Greenwood and N. Harper). Melbourne: Cheshire and A.I.I.A., 1957.

ARTICLES

Some Historical Aspects of Race and Culture Contact, *H.S.*, III, 1944.
Australian Policy towards Japan, *A.O.*, I, 1947.
Jawaharlal Nehru, *ibid.*, II, 1948.
Security in the South West Pacific, *P.A.*, XXIV, 1951.
Turner the Historian: Hypothesis or Process?, *University of Kansas City Review*, XVIII, 1951.
Frontier and Section: A Turner Myth?, *H.S.*, V, 1952.
American Foreign Policy, *A.O.*, VI, 1952.
Pacific Security and Australia, *International Organisation* (Boston), VII, 1953.
Race Relations and the Commonwealth of Nations, *A.O.*, VIII, 1954.
Revision of the United Nations Charter, *India Quarterly* (New Delhi), XI, 1955, reprinted in S.L. Poplai (ed.), *Revision of the United Nations Charter*. O.U.P. and Indian Council of World Affairs, 1956.
Australia and South-East Asia, *P.A.*, XXVIII, 1955.
Australian Foreign Policy 1956, *Australian Journal of Politics and History*, II, 1956.

AT PRESS

N.D. Harper and D.C.G. Sissons, *Australia and the United Nations*. New York: Manhattan, 1959.

The Turner Hypothesis and its Relevance to Australia, in *Australia in World Affairs 1956-8* (ed. with G. Greenwood).

HASLUCK, Alexandra, 2 Adams Road, Dalkeith, Western Australia.

BOOK

Portrait with Background: A Life of Georgiana Molloy. London: O.U.P., 1955.

HASLUCK, P. M. C., M.A. (W.A.), Minister for Territories, Canberra, A.C.T.

BOOKS

Black Australians. A survey of Native Policy in Western Australia, 1829-1897. M.U.P. and O.U.P., 1942.

Workshop of Security. Melbourne: Cheshire, 1948.

The Government and People, 1939-41. Australia in the War of 1939-45, Series 4 (Civil), no. 1. Canberra: Australian War Memorial, 1952.

Native Welfare in Australia. Speeches and Addresses. Perth, W.A.: Paterson, Brokensha, 1953.

Australia's Task in Papua and New Guinea. Melbourne: Australian Institute of International Affairs, 1956.

The Progress of the Australian Territories. Canberra, 1957.

ARTICLES

Problem of Research on Contemporary Official Records, *H.S.*, V, 17, 1951.

Norfolk Island, *R.G.S.S.A.*, Dec. 1957.

HIGGINS, E.MacD., M.A. (Melb.), Assistant Director of Tutorial Classes, University of Sydney.

BOOK

David Stewart and the W.E.A. Sydney: Workers' Educational Association of N.S.W., 1957.

HUGHES, C.A., M.A., Ph.D. (Qld), Lecturer in Political Science, Department of External Studies, University of Queensland.

ARTICLES

Race Relations in the Bahamas, *Venture*, VIII, 6, Nov. 1956.

Adult Suffrage in the Party System in Trinidad, 1946-56, *Parliamentary Affairs*, X, 1, 1957.

Party and Parliament in Queensland, *ibid.*, 4, 1957.

INGLIS, K.S., M.A. (Melb.), D.Phil. (Oxon), Senior Lecturer, Department of History, University of Adelaide.

BOOK

Hospital and Community: A History of the Royal Melbourne Hospital. Melbourne: M.U.P., 1958.

ARTICLE

Churches and Working Classes in Nineteenth Century England, *H.S.*, XXIX, Nov. 1957.

JACOBS, Marjorie G., M.A. (Syd.), Senior Lecturer in History, University of Sydney.

ARTICLES

Bismarck and the Annexation of New Guinea, *H.S.*, V, 17, 1951.
The Colonial Office and New Guinea, 1874-84, *ibid.*, 18, 1952.
Oriental Studies in the University of Sydney, *A.Q.*, XXV, 2, 1953.
A New Approach to Departmental Records, *Public Administration*, XIV, 2, New Series, 1955.

JOYCE, R.B., B.A. (Qld), LL.B., M.Litt. (Cantab.), Lecturer in History, University of Queensland.

PAMPHLET AND CHAPTER

Australian Foreign Policy. Sydney: Department of Tutorial Classes, 1956.
The South-West Pacific, chapter VIII in *Australia in World Affairs 1950-5* (ed. G. Greenwood and N. Harper). Melbourne: Cheshire, 1957.

ARTICLE

The British New Guinea Syndicate Affair of 1898, *Historical Society of Queensland*, V, 1, 1953.

JUDGE, E.A., B.A. (Cantab.), M.A. (N.Z.), Lecturer in Ancient History, University of Sydney.

PAMPHLET

Social Obligation in the New Testament (Tyndale New Testament Lecture), Cambridge. London: Tyndale Press, 1957.

KENT, H.S.K., M.A. (N.Z.), Ph.D. (Cantab.), Senior Lecturer, Department of History, University of Adelaide.

ARTICLES

The Background to Anglo-Norwegian Relations, *Norseman*, XI, 3, 1953.
The Scandinavian Community in 17th and 18th Century London, *ibid.*, XII, 6, 1954.
The Historical Origins of the Three-Mile Limit, *American Journal of International Law*, XLVIII, 4, 1954.

KIDDLE, Margaret Loch, M.A., Dip.Ed. (Melb.), formerly Senior Tutor in History, University of Melbourne. Died 1958.

BOOK

Caroline Chisholm. Melbourne: M.U.P., 1950; 2nd edition, 1957.

ARTICLES

Caroline Chisholm in New South Wales, 1838-46, *H.S.*, II, 1943.
Caroline Chisholm and Charles Dickens, *ibid.*, III, 1945.
Vandemonian Colonists in Port Phillip, 1834-1850, *Tasmanian Historical Research Association*, May 1954.

LA NAUZE, J.A., B.A. (W.A.), M.A. (Oxon), Ernest Scott Professor of History, University of Melbourne.

BOOKS

Political Economy in Australia—Historical Studies. Melbourne: M.U.P., 1949.
Alfred Deakin, The Crisis in Victorian Politics, 1879-1881: A Personal Retrospect (ed. with R.M. Crawford). Melbourne: M.U.P., 1957.

The Hopetoun Blunder. Australian Humanities Research Council Monograph. Melbourne: M.U.P., 1957.

ARTICLES

A Manuscript attributed to Adam Smith, *Economic Journal*, LV, 1945.

Australian Tariffs and Imperial Control, *Economic Record*, XXIV, 1948.

Alfred Deakin and the "Morning Post", *H.S.*, VII, 1955.

LEGGE, J.D., M.A. (Melb.), D.Phil. (Oxon), Senior Lecturer in History, University of Western Australia.

BOOKS

The Origins of the Eastern Goldfields Water Scheme (with F. Alexander and F.K. Crowley). Perth: U.W.A.P., 1954.

Australian Colonial Policy (under the auspices of the Australian Institute of International Affairs). Sydney: Angus and Robertson, 1956.

Problems of Regional Autonomy in Contemporary Indonesia. Interim Report Series, Cornell Modern Indonesia Project, Ithaca (N.Y.), 1957.

ARTICLES

Patterns in History, *Report of the Twenty-Sixth Meeting of A.N.Z.A.A.S.*, Perth, 1947.

Australia and New Guinea to the Establishment of the British Protectorate, *H.S.*, IV, 13, 1949.

Central Supervision of Local Government in Indonesia, *Australian Journal of Politics and History*, III, 1, 1957.

AT PRESS

British Policy towards Fiji, 1858-1880, to be published by Macmillan for U.W.A.P.

MACCALLUM, D., B.A. (Syd.), Lecturer in History, University of Sydney.

ARTICLE

Some Aspects of Defence in the 1850's in New South Wales, *R.A.H.S.*, XLIV, 2, 1958.

McMANNERS, J., M.A. (Oxon), Dip.Th. (Durham), F.R.Hist.S., Officer of the Order of King George I of the Hellenes, Professor of History, University of Tasmania.

CHAPTERS

France, in *The European Nobility in the 18th Century* (ed. A. Goodwin). London: Black, 1955.

The Revolution and its Antecedents 1774-94, in *France, Government and Society* (ed. with M. Wallace-Hadrill). London: Methuen, 1957.

ARTICLE

Les Psalteurs de la cathédrale d'Angers, *Anjou historique*, 1956.

AT PRESS

Chapter on the historiography of the French Revolution for the new *Cambridge Modern History*.

MACMILLAN, D.S., M.A. (Glasgow), Archivist, University of Sydney.

BOOK

A Squatter Went to Sea (the story of Sir William Macleay's New Guinea Expedition, 1875). Sydney: Currawong Publishing Co., 1957.

ARTICLES

The Public Records in Scotland, *Australian Archives Bulletin*, vol. I, 1955.
The Future of Australian Archives, *H.S.*, vol. VII, 1955.
An Australian Aristocrat: Sir Charles Nicholson, *A.Q.*, vol. XXVIII, 1956.
The Arrangement and Description of Private Papers, *Archives and Manuscripts*, 1957.
Archives in New South Wales, *American Archivist*, vol. XX, 1957.
The Australians in London, 1857–1880, *R.A.H.S.*, vol. XLIV, 1958.

McRAE, M.D., B.A., Lecturer in History, University of Tasmania.

ARTICLES

Some Aspects of the Origins of the Tasmanian Labour Party, *Tasmanian Historical Research Association*, III, 2, 1954.
The Tasmanian Labour Party and Trade Unions, 1903–23, *ibid.*, V, 1, 1956.

MAIN, J.M., B.A. (Melb.), B.Litt. (Oxon), Senior Lecturer in History, University of Melbourne.

ARTICLES

Working-class Politics in Manchester from Peterloo to the Reform Bill, 1819–32, *H.S.*, VI, 24, 1955.
Making Constitutions in New South Wales and Victoria, 1853–54, *ibid.*, VII, 28, 1957.

MANSFIELD, B.E., M.A. (Syd.), Lecturer in History, University of Sydney.

ARTICLES

The Background of Radical Republicanism in New South Wales in the 1880's, *H.S.*, V, 20, 1953.
The Origins of "White Australia", *A.Q.*, XXVI, 4, 1954.
Party Organization in the N.S.W. Elections of February 1889, *R.A.H.S.*, XLI, pt II, 1955.
The Socialism of William Morris: England and Australia, *H.S.*, VII, 27, 1956.

MARTIN, A.W., M.A., Dip.Ed. (Syd.), Ph.D. (A.N.U.), Lecturer in History, University of Melbourne.

ARTICLES

Economic Influences in the "New Federation Movement", *H.S.*, VI, 21, 1953.
Free Trade and Protectionist Parties in New South Wales, *ibid.*, 23, 1954.
William McMillan—A Merchant in Politics, *R.A.H.S.*, XL, pt 4, 1955.
The Legislative Assembly of New South Wales, 1856–1900, *Australian Journal of Politics and History*, II, 1, 1956.

MENZIES, Rt Hon. R.G., C.H., Q.C., LL.M. (Melb.), LL.D., C.L., D.Sc., Prime Minister of Australia.

BOOKS AND CHAPTERS

Place of a University in the Modern Community. Melbourne: M.U.P., 1939.
Australian Economy during the War. Adelaide: Joseph Fisher Lecture in Commerce, no. 20, 1942.
Forgotten People and other studies in Democracy. Sydney: Angus and Robertson, 1943.

Post War Reconstruction in Australia (ed. D.A.S. Campbell and with other contributors). Sydney: Australasian Publishing Co., 1944.
Speech is of Time. Selected Speeches and Writings. London: Cassell, 1958.

MULVANEY, D.J., M.A. (Melb.), B.A. (Cantab.), Senior Lecturer in History, University of Melbourne.

ARTICLES

Research into the Prehistory of Victoria: A Criticism and a Report on a Field Survey, *H.S.*, VIII, Nov. 1957.
Prehistoric Man: The Material Evidence, *Twentieth Century*, XI, 1957.
The Australian Aboriginal 1606-1929: Opinion and Field Work, *H.S.*, VIII, May 1958 and Nov. 1958.

NAIRN, N.B., M.A. (Syd.), Senior Lecturer, Department of History, University of New South Wales.

ARTICLES

A Survey of the History of the White Australia Policy in the 19th Century, *A.Q.*, XXVIII, 3, 1956.
The Role of the Trades and Labour Council in New South Wales, 1871-1891, *H.S.*, VII, 28, 1957.

NEALE, R.G., M.A., Dip.Ed. (Qld), Chief Lecturer in History, University of Queensland.

CHAPTERS

India, chapter in *Australia in World Affairs 1950-5* (ed. G. Greenwood and N. Harper). Melbourne: Cheshire, 1957.
History of Queensland, in *Australian Encyclopaedia.* Sydney: Angus and Robertson, 1958.

ARTICLES

New States Movements, *A.Q.*, XXII, 1950.
New State Movement in Queensland, *H.S.*, IV, 1950.
British-American Relations during the Spanish-American War: Some Problems, *ibid.*, VI, 1953.
The New England New State, *A.Q.*, XXVII, 1955.

O'BRIEN, The Most Rev. E.M., C.M.G., M.A. (Syd. and N.U.I.), Ph.D. (Louvain), F.R. Hist.S., F.R.A.H.S., Archbishop of Canberra and Goulburn.

BOOKS

Foundation of Catholicism in Australia, 2 vols. Sydney: Angus and Robertson, 1922.
The Dawn of Catholicism in Australia, 2 vols. Sydney: Angus and Robertson, 1928.
The Foundation of Australia. 1st edition, London: Sheed and Ward, 1937; 2nd edition, Sydney: Angus and Robertson, 1950.

OLDHAM, W., M.A. (Adel.), Ph.D. (Lond.), formerly Senior Lecturer, Department of History, University of Adelaide. Died 1959.

BOOK AND CHAPTER

The Land Policy of South Australia 1830-42. Adelaide: Public Library, 1917.
The Character of the Population, chapter in *Centenary History of South Australia.* Adelaide: R.G.S.S.A., 1936.

ARTICLES

How Adelaide was Bought and Sold, *R.G.S.S.A.*, vol. 45, 1943-4.
The Discovery of Port Adelaide, *ibid.*, vol. 48, 1947.

PIKE, D.H., M.A., D.Litt. (Adel.), Reader, Department of History, University of Adelaide.

BOOK AND CHAPTERS

Paradise of Dissent: South Australia 1829-57. London: Longmans, 1957.
Legal Pluralities and Corporate Personality, in *Church and State* (ed. Leicester Webb). Melbourne: M.U.P., 1958.
Three chapters in *Melbourne Studies in Education* (ed. Edgar French). Melbourne: M.U.P., 1958.

ARTICLE

Wilmot Horton and the National Colonisation Society, *H.S.*, VII, 26, May 1956.

PRICE, A. Grenfell, C.M.G., M.A., Dip.Ed. (Oxon), D.Litt. (Adel.), Chairman of the Advisory Board of the Commonwealth Literary Fund, University of Adelaide.

BOOKS, CHAPTERS AND PAMPHLETS

Foundation and Settlement of South Australia. Adelaide: Preece, 1924.
Founders and Pioneers of South Australia. Adelaide: Preece, 1929.
History and Problems of the Northern Territory (Macrossan Lectures, University of Queensland). Adelaide: Hassell Press, 1930.
Experiments in Colonisation, chapter 8 in *Cambridge History of the British Empire*, vol. VII, pt 1, Australia. Cambridge: C.U.P., 1933.
Centenary History of South Australia, chapters 3, 4, 5 and part of 7. Adelaide: R.G.S.S.A., 1936.
White Settlers in the Tropics. Special Research Publication No. 23. New York: American Geographical Society, 1939.
Australia Comes of Age. Melbourne: Georgian House, 1945.
The Collegiate School of St Peter 1847-1947. Adelaide: St. Peter's College, 1947.
White Settlers and Native Peoples. Melbourne: Georgian House, 1949 and C.U.P., 1950.
The Social Challenge, in *Northern Australia: A Task for a Nation*, pt IV, 2. Sydney: Angus and Robertson, 1954.
Lake Eyre, South Australia, The Great Flooding of 1949-50. Introduction and Historical Geography. Adelaide: R.G.S.S.A., 1955.
The Explorations of Captain James Cook in the Pacific as told by his own Journals. New York: Limited Editions Club, 1957 and Heritage Press, 1958; Melbourne: Georgian House, 1958.

ARTICLES

The Work of Captain Collett Barker in South Australia, R.G.S.S.A., XXVI, 1926.
South Australian Efforts to Control the Murray, *A.N.Z.A.A.S.*, XVIII, 1926.
Captain Cook (Bicentennial Address), *R.G.S.S.A.*, XXIX, 1929.
The Founders of South Australia, *ibid.*
White Settlement in Saba Island, Dutch West Indies, *Geographical Review* (New York), Jan. 1934.
White Settlement in the Panama Canal Zone, *ibid.*, Jan. 1935.

The Mystery of Leichhardt: The South Australian Government Expedition of 1938 (Presidential Address), *R.G.S.S.A.*, vol. XXXIX, 1939.
Moving Frontiers and Changing Landscapes in the Pacific and its Continents (Presidential Address, A.N.Z.A.A.S., Section P., Dunedin), Sydney, *Australian Journal of Science*, May 1957. Western influences in the Pacific and its Continents, A.H.R.C., Adelaide, 1959.

PRICE, C.A., B.A. (Adel.), M.A., D.Phil. (Oxon), Research Fellow, Department of Demography, Australian National University.

BOOKS

German Settlers in South Australia. Melbourne: M.U.P., 1945.
Malta and the Maltese: A Study of Nineteenth Century Migration. Melbourne: Georgian House, 1954.

ARTICLE

The Effects of Post-War Immigration on the growth of Population, Ethnic Composition and Religious Structure of Australia, *A.Q.*, Dec. 1957.

REESE, T.R., B.A. (Sheffield), Ph.D. (Lond.), Lecturer in History, Newcastle University College.

ARTICLES

Benjamin Martyn, Secretary to the Georgia Trustees, *Georgia Historical Quarterly*, XXXVIII, June 1954.
Harman Verelst, Accountant to the Georgia Trustees, *ibid.*, Dec. 1955.
Understanding American Foreign Policy, *A.O.*, II, Dec. 1957.
Georgia in Anglo-Spanish Diplomacy, 1736-1739. *William and Mary Quarterly*, XV, 2, Apr. 1958.

ROBERTS, S.H., C.M.G., M.A., Litt.D. (Melb.), LL.D. (Bristol and British Columbia), D.Sc.Econ. (Lond.), D.C.L. (Durham), D.Litt.(N.E.), Vice-Chancellor, University of Sydney.

BOOKS

History of Australian Land Settlement (1788-1820). Melbourne: Macmillan and M.U.P., 1924.
Population Problems of the Pacific. London: Routledge, 1927.
History of French Colonial Policy, 2 vols. London: London School of Economics Studies in Economics and Political Science, no. 95, 1929.
The House that Hitler Built. London: Methuen, 1937.
British History 1488-1815 (with C. H. Currey). Sydney: Angus and Robertson, 1949.

CHAPTERS

Racial and Labour Problems, in *The Australian Mandate for New Guinea*. Melbourne: Macmillan and M.U.P., 1928.
The Wool Trade and the Squatters, chapter VII in *Cambridge History of the British Empire*, vol. VII, pt 1, Australia. Cambridge: C.U.P., 1933.

ROWLEY, C.D., M.A. (Syd.), Principal, Australian School of Pacific Administration, Canberra.

BOOK

The Australians in German New Guinea 1914-1921. Melbourne: M.U.P., 1958.

ARTICLES

Clarence River Separatism in 1860: A Problem of Communications, *H.S.*, I, 1941.
Native Officials and Magistrates of German New Guinea 1897-1921, *South Pacific*, VII, 1954.

SERLE, A.G., B.A. (Melb.), D.Phil. (Oxon), Senior Lecturer in History, University of Melbourne.

BOOK

The Melbourne Scene, 1803-1956. Melbourne: M.U.P., 1957.

ARTICLES

The Victorian Legislative Council, 1856-1950, *H.S.*, VI, 1954.
The Causes of Eureka, *ibid.*, Eureka Supplement, Dec. 1954.

SHAW, A.G.L., B.A. (Melb.), M.A. (Oxon), Senior Lecturer in History, University of Sydney.

BOOKS

The Australian Coal Industry (with G.R. Bruns). Melbourne: M.U.P., 1947.
The Economic Development of Australia. Melbourne: Longmans Green, 1944; new edition, 1955.
The Story of Australia. London: Faber, 1954; New York, 1956.

ARTICLES

The Australian Coal Industry 1929-1939, *Economic Record*, XIX, 36, 1943.
Economics and History, *H.S.*, III, 12, 1949.
Missing Land Grants in N.S.W., 1792-1800, *ibid.*, V, 17, 1951 and V, 19, 1952.
Some Principles of International Relations, *A.O.*, VI, 3, 1952.
The British Criminal and Transportation, *Tasmanian Historical Research Association*, II, 2, 1953.
The British Criminal and Transportation—A Rejoinder, *ibid.*, 6, 1953.
Origins of the Probation System in Van Diemen's Land, *H.S.*, VI, 21, 1953.
Articles in *Australian Encyclopaedia* on Convicts and Transportation, Coal, Economic Development, Finance—Public, New South Wales, Secondary Industry, Working Conditions and Hours, *et al.*

TAPP, E.J., M.A. (N.Z.), Associate Professor, Department of History, University of New England.

BOOK

Early New Zealand: A Dependency of New South Wales, 1788-1841. Melbourne: M.U.P., 1958.

PAMPHLET

From the League to United Nations. Armidale: Armidale Express, 1950.

ARTICLES

Australian and New Zealand Relations, 1900-1950, *A.O.*, V, 3 and 4, 1951.
Some Aspects of Causation in History, *Journal of Philosophy*, XLIX, 3, 1952.
New Zealand and Australian Federation, *H.S.*, V, 19, 1952.
The Role of the Individual in History, *A.Q.*, XXX, 1, 1958.
Knowing the Past, *Journal of Philosophy*, LV, II, 1958.

TURNER, L.C.F., M.A. (Rand), Lecturer in History, University of New England.

BOOKS

Crisis in the Desert, May-July 1942 (in collaboration with J.A.I. Agar-Hamilton). Oxford: O.U.P., 1952.

Translator and editor of *Panzer Battles 1939-45* by General F.W. von Mellenthin. London: Cassell, 1955; 2nd edition, 1956; and University of Oklahoma Press, 1956; 2nd edition, 1956; 3rd edition, 1958.

The Sidi Rezeg Battles 1941 (in collaboration with J.A.I. Agar-Hamilton). Oxford: O.U.P., 1957.

IN PROGRESS

The War in the Southern Oceans 1939-45, to be published by O.U.P. 1959.

WARD, J.M., M.A., LL.B. (Syd.), Professor of History, University of Sydney.

BOOKS AND CHAPTERS

The Triumph of the Pastoral Economy, 1821-1851, chapter III of *Australia* (ed. C. Hartley Grattan). University of California Press, 1947.

British Policy in the South Pacific, 1786-1893. Sydney: Australasian Publishing Company, 1948 and 1950.

From Mandates to Trusteeship, chapter I; Western Samoa, chapter III; Strategic Areas under Trusteeship, chapter IV, of *Trusteeship in the Pacific* (ed. A.H. McDonald). Sydney: Angus and Robertson, 1949.

Australia's First Governor-General: Sir Charles Fitzroy, 1851-55. Sydney: University of Sydney, Wood Memorial Lecture Fund, 1953.

Earl Grey and the Australian Colonies, 1846-57. Melbourne: M.U.P., 1958.

ARTICLES

Collaboration for Welfare in the South West Pacific: The Historical Background, *A.O.*, I, 1, 1947.

The New Japanese Constitution, *ibid.*, 3, 1947.

The "Germ of Federation" in Australia, *H.S.*, IV, 15, 1950.

Foundation of the University of Sydney, *R.A.H.S.*, XXXVII, 5, 1952.

The British Federal Policy for Australia, 1847-48, *Tasmanian Historical Research Association*, II, 3, 1953.

Some Overseas Historians, *R.A.H.S.*, XL, 1, 1954.

The Third Earl Grey and Federalism, 1846-52, *Australian Journal of Politics and History*, III, 1, 1957.

WARD, R., M.A. (Adel.), Ph.D. (A.N.U.), Dip.Ed., Lecturer in History, University of New England.

BOOK

The Australian Legend. Melbourne: O.U.P., 1958.

ARTICLES

Australian Folk Ballads and Singers, *Meanjin*, XIII, 3, 1954.

Felons and Folksongs, *ibid.*, XV, 3, 1956.

Collectivist Notions of a Nomad Tribe, *H.S.*, VI, 24, 1955.

"Waltzing Matilda" in *Australian Signpost* (ed. Tom Hungerford). Melbourne: Cheshire, 1955.

Social Roots of Australian Nationalism, *Australian Journal of Politics and History*, I, 2, 1956.

U

YULE, G.S.S., M.A. (Melb.), Professor of Church History, Ormond College, formerly Lecturer in History, University of Melbourne.

BOOK

The Independents and the English Civil War. Melbourne: M.U.P., 1958.

ARTICLE

The Independents—Decentralized Calvinism in the 17th Century, *Reformed Theological Review*, June 1956.

Linguistics

CAPELL, A., M.A. (Syd.), Ph.D. (Lond.), Reader in Oceanic Languages, University of Sydney.

BOOKS AND MAJOR WORKS

Netaiyi ugi Ruth (the Book of Ruth, translated into the language of Eromanga, New Hebrides). London: British and Foreign Bible Society, 1932.
Languages of the Northern Kimberley Division, Western Australia (in collaboration with A.P. Elkin), *Oceania*, vol. VIII, no. 2, and *Oceania Monograph* no. 3.
A New Fijian Dictionary. Sydney: Prepared for the Government of Fiji, 1943.
The Linguistic Position of South-Eastern Papua. Sydney, 1943.
A Linguistic Survey of the South Western Pacific. Noumea: South Pacific Commission, Technical Paper no. 72, 1954.
Methods and Materials for recording Papuan and New Guinea Languages. New Guinea Department of Education, 1952.
A New Approach to Australian Linguistics (*Oceania Linguistic Monograph* no. 1). Sydney: University of Sydney, 1956.

ARTICLES

Dr Capell has written some forty articles, mostly on Australian Aboriginal and Oceanic languages and cultures, in various learned journals.

CHURCHWARD, Rev. C.M., M.A., Litt.D. (Melb.), Hay, N.S.W.

BOOKS

Tales of a Lonely Island (Rotuman legends with translation and notes) (*Oceania Monograph* no. 4). Sydney: Australasian Medical Publishing Co. for National Research Council, 1939.
Rotuman Grammar and Dictionary. Sydney: Aust. Med. Publ. Co. for Methodist Church, 1940.
A New Fijian Grammar. Sydney: Aust. Med. Publ. Co. for Government of Fiji, 1941.
Tongan Grammar. Oxford: O.U.P., 1953.

ARTICLES

Relative Pronouns in Samoan, *Journal of Polynesian Society*, XLII, 1934.
The History of Rotuma as Reflected in its Language, *Oceania*, IX, 1, 1938.
Personal Pronouns ending in -self or -selves, *English Language Teaching* (British Council), IX, 4.
The Unstressed "There", *ibid.*, XI, 1.

AT PRESS
Tongan Dictionary, to be published by O.U.P.

DOUGLAS, W.H., missionary linguist, 222 Boulder Road, Kalgoorlie W.A.
BOOKS
Wangka, Books 1-5 (primers in the Aboriginal Language of Warburton Ranges, W.A.). Melbourne: United Aborigines Mission, 1954.
An Introduction to the Western Desert Languages (*Oceania Linguistic Monograph* no. 4). Sydney: University of Sydney, 1958.
ARTICLE
Phonology of the Australian Aboriginal Language spoken at Ooldea, South Australia, 1951-2, *Oceania*, XXV, 3, 1955.

HARWOOD, F.W., M.A. (Melb.), Senior Lecturer in English, University of Tasmania.
BOOK
An Introduction to English Syntax (in collaboration with B.G. Mitchell). Hobart: Oldham, Beddome and Meredith, 1957.
ARTICLES
Axiomatic Syntax, *Language*, XXXI, 3, 1955.
Statistical Study of English Word Formation (in collaboration with A.M. Wright), *ibid.*, XXXII, 2, 1956.
Language and Automation, *Australian Quarterly*, XXVIII, 2, 1956.

STREHLOW, T.G.H., M.A. (Adel.), Reader in Australian Linguistics, University of Adelaide.
BOOKS AND PAMPHLETS
Aranda Phonetics and Grammar (*Oceania Monograph*), 1944.
Aranda Traditions. Melbourne: M.U.P., 1947.
Anthropology and the Study of Languages. Adelaide: Hassell Press, 1948.
An Australian Viewpoint. Melbourne: Hawthorn Press, 1950.
The Sustaining Ideals of Australian Aboriginal Societies. Melbourne: Hawthorn Press, 1956.
Friendship with South-East Asia: A Cultural Approach. Reprint from *Forum* (Melbourne), IX, 1-2, 1956.
Dark and White Australians. Melbourne: Riall, 1958.
ARTICLES
Ankotarinja, an Aranda Myth, *Oceania*, IV, 2, 1933.
Notes on Native Evidence and its Value, *ibid.*, VI, 3, 1936.
The Future of Aboriginal Education in Australia, *New Horizons* (Sydney), no. 3, 1949.
Foreword to Rex Battarbee's *Modern Australian Aboriginal Artists*. Sydney: Angus and Robertson, 1951.
Trends in Australian Native Policy, *Anti-Slavery Reporter* (London), Jan. 1952.
Australian Aboriginal Songs, *Journal of the International Folk Music Council* (London), VII, 1955.
"Australian Languages" in latest edition of *Encyclopaedia Britannica*.
"Australian Primitive Religion" (Australien: Religionsgeschichtlich) in *Die Religion in Geschichte und Gegenwart*, Tübingen, 1957.
Articles on Central Australian Myths and Central Australian Songs in *Australian Encyclopaedia*, vol. 1.

WORMS, Rev. Fr E.A., S.A.C., Rector of the Pallottine College, Manly, N.S.W.

BOOKS

Australian Languages (in collaboration with H. Nekes). Five parts, grammar, comparative dictionaries, texts (*Micro-Bibliotheca Anthropos*, vol. X). Posieux-Fribourg, Switzerland: Anthropos Institute, 1953.

ARTICLES

Initiationsfeiern in Nord-Westaustralien, *Annali Lateranensi* (Rome), II, 1938.
Die religiösen Anschauungen einiger Stämme in Nord-Westaustralien in fünfzig Legenden, *ibid.*, IV, 1940.
Gorangara-Feier im australischen Kimberley, *ibid.*, VI, 1942.
Onomatopeia in some Tribes of North-Western Australia, *Oceania*, VIII, 1937-8.
Foreign Words in some Kimberley Tribes in North-Western Australia, *ibid.* (*Note*. Last two also published in *Studies in Australian Linguistics* (*Oceania Monograph* no. 3), 1938.)
Sense of Smell of the Australian Aborigines, *Oceania*, XIII, 1943.
Aboriginal Place Names in Kimberley, Western Australia, *ibid.*, XIV, 1944.
An Australian Migratory Myth, *Primitive Man* (Washington, D.C.), XXII, 1949.
Djamar, the Creator, *Anthropos* (Posieux-Fribourg), XLV, 1950.
Djamar and his relation to other Culture Heroes, *ibid.*, XLVIII, 1952.
Australian Ghost Drums, Trumpets and Poles, *ibid.*, 1953.
Prehistoric Petroglyphs of the Upper Yule River, North-Western Australia, *ibid.*, XLIX, 1954.
Contemporary and Prehistoric Rock Paintings in Central and Northern North Kimberley, *ibid.*, L, 1955.
Australian Mythological Terms: Their Etymology and Dispersion, *ibid.*, LII, 1957.
Mythologische Selbstbiographie eines australischen Ureinwohners, *Wiener Völkerkundliche Mitteilungen* (Institut für Völkerkunde, Universität Wien), V, I, 1957.

IN PROGRESS

The Poetry of the Yaoro and Bād, North-Western Australia, to appear in *Anthropos*, 1958 or 1959.

WURM, S.A., Dr Phil. (Vienna), Senior Fellow in Linguistics, Australian National University.

BOOKS AND MAJOR PUBLICATIONS

Der Özbekische Dialekt von Andidschan: phonetische und morphologische Studien, part I. Vienna: Akademie der Wissenschaften, Philosophisch-historische Klasse, Sitzungsberichte 224, Bd 3, Abhandlung.
The Karakalpak Language, *Anthropos*, XLVI, 1951.
"Studies in the Kiwai Language, Fly Delta, Papua, New Guinea" in *Acta ethnologica et linguistica*, no. 2, 1951.
The Turkic Languages of Central Asia: Problems of Planned Culture Contact (translation of article entitled "The Turkic Peoples of the U.S.S.R.: The Development of their Languages and Writings", by N.A. Baskakov, with comments by S.A. Wurm), 1952.
Turkic Peoples of the U.S.S.R.: Their Historical Background, their Languages and the Development of the Soviet Linguistic Policy. London: Central Asian Research Centre, 1954.

ARTICLES

The Uzbeck Dialect of Qizil Qujas, *Bulletin of the School of Oriental and African Studies* (London), XII, pt 1, 1947.

The (Kara-) Kirghiz Language, *ibid.*, XIII, pt 1, 1949.

Sind Türksprachen Tonsprachen? Ein Beitrag zur Klassifikation der Tonsprachen, *Wiener Beitrag zur Kulturgeschichte und Linguistik*, IX, 1952.

Über Akzent—und Tonverhältnisse im Özbekischen, *Ural-Altaische Jahrbücher*, Bd 25, Heft 3-4.

Tonal Languages in New Guinea and the Adjacent Islands, *Anthropos*, XLIX, 1954.

Die dringendsten linguistischen Aufgaben in Neuguinea, *Actes du IVeme Congrès international des sciences anthropologiques et ethnologiques*, Vienna, 1956.

Notes on Structural Affinities of Non-Melanesian (Papuan) Languages, *Die Wiener Schule der Völkerkunde, Festschrift zum 25-jährigen Bestand 1929-54*, 1956.

The Indonesian Element in Melanesian: A Reply, *Journal of the Polynesian Society*, LXIII.

AT PRESS

The Present State of Linguistic Research in the New Guinea Area, for *Anthropos*.

The Nivo (Nifilole) Language, Reef Islands, Santa Cruz, an *Oceania Linguistic Monograph*.

Modern European Languages

BATT, Jean C., B.A. (Tas.), Senior Lecturer, Department of Modern Languages, University of Tasmania.

BOOKS

The French Exploration of Australia (in collaboration with L.A. Triebel). Sydney: Editions du Courier Australien, 1943.

The French Exploration of Australia, with Special Reference to Tasmania (in collaboration with L.A. Triebel). Hobart: Government Printer, 1957.

French Pronunciation and Diction. London: Macmillan, 1958.

ARTICLES

The Themes of the Novels and Plays of Albert Camus, *AUMLA*, 6, May 1957.

Albert Camus—From "The Myth" to "The Fall", *Meanjin*, IV, 1957.

BENN, M.B., B.A. (W.A.), M.A. (Lond.), Reader and Head of Department of German, University of Western Australia.

ARTICLES

An Interpretation of the Work of Herman Hesse, *German Life and Letters*, 1950.

Goethe and T.S. Eliot (I), *ibid.*, 1952.

BONNIN, G.M., M.A., Ph.D., Lecturer in German, University of Queensland.

BOOKS

Moral and Intellectual Incentives of the Munich Student Revolt. Stanford (U.S.A.), 1948.

Literary Aspects of the German Underground. Stanford, 1949.

DE BRAY, R.G.A., B.A., Ph.D. (Lond.), Lecturer, Department of Russian, University of Melbourne.

BOOK

Guide to the Slavonic Languages. London: Dent, 1951.

BURGER, Claire Hildegard, M.A. (Melb.), Lecturer, Department of French, University of Melbourne.

BOOK

La France d'hier et d'aujourd'hui (in collaboration with R.L. James). Melbourne: M.U.P., 1955.

ARTICLE

Marguerite d'Autriche, 1480-1530, *AUMLA*, 4, May 1956.

AT PRESS

Monsieur de Pourceaugnac and Baron Ochs von Lerchenau, for *Modern Languages*, 1958.

CANART, P.L.J.G., B.A. (Melb.), Senior Lecturer, Department of French, University of Melbourne.

ARTICLE

Homonymics: French Walloon and Chinese, *AUMLA*, 2, 1954.

CHICOTEAU, M., M.A., L.ès L., Officier de l'Instruction Publique, Vice-Consul for France in Sydney.

BOOK

Studies in Symbolist Psychology. Sydney: Hoertel, 1958.

CHISHOLM, A.R., B.A. (Syd. and Melb.), Officier de l'Instruction Publique, Officier de la Légion d'Honneur, Professor of French, University of Melbourne, 1938-57.

BOOKS

The Art of Arthur Rimbaud. Melbourne: M.U.P., 1930.
Towards Hérodiade, a Literary Genealogy. Melbourne: M.U.P., 1934.
An Approach to M. Valéry's Jeune Parque. Melbourne: M.U.P., 1938.
Christopher Brennan, the Man and his Poetry. Sydney: Angus and Robertson, 1946.
Mallarmé's "Après-midi d'un faune". Melbourne: Australian Humanities Research Council and M.U.P., 1958.
Men were my Milestones. Melbourne: M.U.P., 1958.

ARTICLES

An Appreciation of Three Sonnets by Hérédia, *French Quarterly* (Oxford), III, 1921.
Rimbaud's Fusion of Sea and Sky, *ibid.*, XI, 1929.
Sources and Structure of Rimbaud's *"Bateau Ivre"*, *ibid.*, XII, 1930.
Hérédia: Genealogy of "Floridum Mare", *ibid.*
C'est aussi simple qu'une phrase musicale (Note on Rimbaud), *ibid.*, XIII, 1931.
The Tragedy of the Cosmic Will: A Study of Leconte de Lisle, *ibid.*
Baudelaire: The Duality of "Les Fleurs du Mal", *ibid.*, XIV, 1932.
The Prototype of Dante's Gerione, *Modern Languages Review* (Cambridge), XXIV, 1929.

A Working Exegesis of Mallarmé's "Coup de Dés", *AUMLA*, 1, 1953.
Articles on Rimbaud, Hugo and Valéry in the *New Chambers Encyclopaedia*.
London, Newnes.

AT PRESS

Collected Works of Christopher Brennan. Sydney: Angus and Robertson.

CHRISTESEN, Nina, B.A. (Qld), Senior Lecturer in Charge Russian Language and
Literature, University of Melbourne.

ARTICLES

Some aspects of Mediaeval Russian Literature, *AUMLA Proceedings*, 1953.
Chekhov in English Translation, *ibid.*, 1955.
Notes on Three Soviet Novels, *Meanjin*, 1958.

CLARKE, Margaret Archibald, M.A. (Syd.), D. de l'U. (Paris), Bayswater Road,
Rushcutter's Bay, Sydney.

BOOKS

Heine et la monarchie de juillet. Paris: Rieder, 1927.
Rimbaud and Quinet. Sydney: privately printed, 1945.

ARTICLES

Rimbaud-Michelet-Vico, *Modern Language Review* (London), XXXVII, 1942.
Chesterton the Classicist, *Dublin Review*, CCXXIX, 1955.

COGHLAN, B.L.D., B.A., Ph.D. (Birmingham), Professor of German, University of
New England.

ARTICLES

Hofmannsthal's Christianity, *AUMLA Proceedings*, 1953.
The Development of Hugo von Hofmannsthal during the First World War,
Proceedings of the English Goethe Society, London, 1958.
Traditionelle Form und eigener Stil im Spätwerk Hofmannsthals for *Pro-
ceedings of the VIIth Congress (Heidelberg 1957)* of the Fédération Internationale
des Langues et Littératures Modernes.

CORNELL, J.G., M.A. (Melb.), L.ès L. (Paris), Chevalier de la Légion d'Honneur,
Professor of French, University of Adelaide.

ARTICLES

A propos des notes sur les sources de la préface de Cromwell, *Revue d'Histoire
littéraire de la France*, XLIII, 1, 1936.
The Rhythmical Basis of French Verse, *Australian Educational Review*, IX, 3,
1938.

COVERLID, Dorothea Rebecca, M.A., Dip.Ed. (Melb.), Senior Lecturer in German,
University of Melbourne.
ARTICLE
Seventy Years in the History of Goethe's "Urfaust", *AUMLA*, 1957.

CROSSLEY, R.G., B.A. (W.A.), Dr Phil. (Freiburg i.B.), Senior Lecturer in German,
University of Sydney.
BOOK
Die Kaiserchronik, ein literarhistorisches Problem der altdeutschen Literaturgeschichte.
München: R. Oldenbourg, 1939.

DENAT, A.H.M., L.ès L., Dipl.Et.Sup. (Paris), Lecturer in French, University of Sydney.

ARTICLE

Towards an Ontology of the Poem (from Valéry to Francis Ponge), *AUMLA*, 6, 1957.

FARRELL, R.B., M.A. (Syd.), Dr Phil. (Berlin), Professor of German, University of Sydney.

BOOKS

Stefan Georges Beziehungen zur englischen Dichtung. Berlin: Ebering, 1937.
A Dictionary of German Synonyms. Cambridge: C.U.P., 1953.

ARTICLES

Theme, Motif and Idea as Terms of Literary Criticism, *AUMLA Proceedings*, 1950.
Some German Attitudes, *A.Q.*, XXVI, 1, 1954.
Mörike's Classical Verse, *Publications of the English Goethe Society*, New Series, XXV, 1956.

GAPANOVICH, J.J., B.A., C.Hist. (St Petersburg), Lecturer, Department of Modern Languages, Canberra University College.

BOOKS

The Koriaks: A Siberian Tribe. Peking, 1932 (in Russian).
Russia in Manchuria. Peking, 1933.
Russia in North-Eastern Asia (vol. I, "Russian Colonization: Its Past and Present"; vol. II, "Economic Resources: Their Development"). Peking, 1933-4 (in Russian).
Russian Historiography Outside Russia. China, 1935. French translation, Paris, 1946.
Methods of Historical Synthesis. Hongkong, 1941.
Basic Russian Conversation. Peking, 1953.
Also articles on historical topics in journals in China and Australia.

GOESCH, K.J., B.A., Dip.Ed. (Syd.), D.de l'U. (Paris), Senior Lecturer in French, University of Sydney.

BOOK

Raymond Radiguet: Etude biographique, bibliographie, textes inédits; avant-propos de Jean Cocteau de l'Académie Française, Paris: Editions de la Palatine, 1955.

ARTICLE

Raymond Radiguet and the "roman d'analyse", *AUMLA*, 4, 1956.

GRISHIN, D., Ph.D. (Melb.), Lecturer in Russian, University of Melbourne.

ARTICLES

Gogol in Russia, *Bogatyri*, 4, 1955.
Dissenting Writers in Contemporary Russian Literature, *AUMLA Proceedings*, 1957.

HENNING, I.A., B.A. (Syd.), D.de l'U. (Paris), Professor of French, University of Sydney.

BOOK

L'Allemagne de Mme de Staël et la polémique romantique. Paris: Champion, 1929.

JACKSON, R.F., B.A. (Syd.), M.A. (Melb.), Officier de l'Instruction Publique, Professor of French, University of Melbourne.

ARTICLES

Some Observations on the "Stances" and "Sonnets de la mort" of Jean de Sponde, *AUMLA*, 3, 1955.
French Politics Today, *Current Affairs Bulletin*, XIII, 7, 1954.

KOCH-EMMERY, E.T., M.A. (Adel.), Ph.D. (Vienna and Rome), Senior Lecturer, Department of Modern Languages, Canberra University College.

ARTICLES

When "La Peste" becomes "The Plague", *Meanjin*, IX, 2, 1950.
Thomas Mann in English Translation, *German Life and Letters*, VI, 4, 1953.

AT PRESS

English as a Translator's Language, for *Festschrift* in honour of Professor F. Wild, Vienna, 1958.

LAWLER, J.R., M.A. (Melb.), D.de l'U. (Paris), Senior Lecturer, Department of French, University of Melbourne.

ARTICLES

Apollinaire inédit: le séjour à Stavelot, *Mercure de France*, Feb. 1955.
The Technique of Valéry's *Orphée*, *AUMLA*, 5, 1956.
Guillaume Apollinaire, *Meanjin*, Summer 1956.
Poetry and Music in Apollinaire, *French Studies*, Oct. 1956.

MONOGRAPH

Form and Meaning in Valéry's *Le Cimetière Marin*. M.U.P. for A.H.R.C. 1959.

LODEWYCKX, A., Doctor of Philosophy and Letters (Ghent), M.A. (Good Hope and Melb.), Associate Professor of Germanic Languages (retired), Lecturer in Old Norse, University of Melbourne.

BOOK

Die Deutschen in Australien. Stuttgart, 1932.
A Handbook of Dutch. Melbourne: M.U.P. and C.U.P., 1944.
Overzicht der Nederlandsche Letterkunde. Melbourne: M.U.P., 1946.
Australia Waarheen? Holland: De Terra-Bibliotheek, 1950; 3rd edition, 1954.
Nieuw-Zeeland, een Eden in de Zuidzee. Holland: De Terra-Bibliotheek, 1952; 2nd edition, 1954.
People for Australia. A Study in Population Problems. Melbourne: Cheshire, 1956.
Ultima Thule. Melbourne: M.U.P. for Australian Goethe Society, 1956.

ARTICLES

Een Nieuw Mandeville-Handschrift, *Tijdschrift van de Maatschappij der Nederlandse Letterkunde*, Sept. 1910.
The Name of Australia: Its Origin and Early Use, *Victorian Historical Magazine*, June 1929.
What the Netherlands mean to Australia (Inaugural Lecture), *A.Q.*, Sept. 1943.
Australian Universities Adrift, *ibid.*, June 1947.

De Benamingen van het Vijfde Werelddeel, Historisch en Taalkundig Toegel-
icht, *Tijdschrift van het Koninklijk Nederlandsch Aardrykskundig Genootschap*,
LXVI, 6, Nov. 1949.
Freydis Eiriksdottir Rouda and the Germania of Tacitus, *Arkiv för nordisk
filologi*, LXX, 3-4, Lund (Sweden), 1955.
A full list of works and articles by Dr Lodewyckx appears in an offprint of
AUMLA, 5, 1956.

McCORMICK, C.A., B.A. (Cantab.), Senior Lecturer in Italian, University of Melbourne.

ARTICLE

Ugo Foscolo: A Critical Theory of Translation, *AUMLA*, 5, 1956.

MACLEAN, H., M.A., Ph.D., Dip.Ed. (Melb.), Senior Lecturer in German, University
of Melbourne.

ARTICLES

The Counsel of Despair: A Study of Wolfgang Borchert's "Draussen vor der
Tür", *Studies in Language and Literature presented to Augustin Lodewyckx*, 1951.
The "Job" Drama in Modern Germany, *AUMLA*, 2, 1954.
The Moral Conflict in Georg Büchner's "Dantons Tod", *AUMLA*, 6, 1957.

MEIJER, R.P., M.A. (Amsterdam), Ph.D. (Melb.), Lecturer in Dutch, University of
Melbourne.

ARTICLES

Het Dialectonderzoek in Nederland, *Studies in Language and Literature presented
to Augustin Lodewyckx*, 1951.
Slauerhoffs Chinese bewerkingen en hun Engelse voorbeelden, *De Gids*, CXVIII,
1955.
Expressionist Influences in Marsman's Early Poetry, *AUMLA*, 3, 1955.

MORROW, Christine, B.A. (W.A.), D. de l'U. (Toulouse), Officier de l'Académie,
Lecturer in French, University of Western Australia.

BOOK

Le roman irréaliste dans les littératures de langue française et anglaise. Toulouse:
Didier, 1941.

SAMUEL, R.H., Dr Phil. (Berlin), Ph.D. (Cantab.), M.A. (Melb.), Professor of Germanic Languages, University of Melbourne.

BOOKS

Die poetische Staatas und Geschichtsauffassung Friedrich von Hardenbergs (Novalis)—
Studien zur romantischen Geschichtsphilosophie. Frankfurt, 1926.
Novalis Schriften (in collaboration with P. Kluckhohn), 4 vols. Leipzig: Biblio-
graphisches Institut, 1929. New and enlarged edition at press.
Heinrich von Kleist's Participation in the Political Movements of the Years 1805-1809.
Cambridge, 1938.
Expressionism in German Life, Literature and the Theatre (in collaboration with
R.H. Thomas). Cambridge: Heffers, 1939.
Education and Society in Modern Germany (in collaboration with R.H. Thomas).
London: Routledge, 1949.

H. v. Kleist's "Der zerbrochene Krug", Lustspiel. Critical Edition. London: Macmillan, 1950.

Goethe's "Urfaust". Critical Edition. Melbourne: Cheshire, and London: Allen and Unwin, 1950; 2nd revised edition, London: Macmillan, 1958.

H. v. Kleist's "Prinz Friedrich von Homburg". Critical Edition. London: Harrap, 1957.

ARTICLES

Die Ahnentafel des Dichters und Philosophen Friedrich von Hardenberg (Novalis), *Ahnentafeln berühmter Deutscher* (Leipzig), I, 1929.

Der berufliche Werdegang Friedrich von Hardenbergs, *Romantikforschungen* (Niemeyer, Halle), 1929.

Heinrich Lersch and the German Workers' Poetry, *Modern Languages*, 1937.

The "New Nationalism" in German Literature after the War, *Durham University Journal*, 1937.

Thomas Mann and Hans Grimm, *German Life and Letters*, 1938.

Der Kulturelle Hintergrund von Goethes und Schillers Xenienkampf, *Publications of the English Goethe Society*, XII, 1937.

Goethe-Napoleon-Kleist, ein Beitrag zu dem Thema: Napoleon und die deutsche Geistesgeschichte, *ibid.*, XIV, 1939.

The Constitution of the German Federal Republic, *Australian Outlook*, 1949.

The origin and constitution of the East German Republic, *ibid.*, 1950.

The Liberal Tradition in Germany—Its Failure and its Promise (Inaugural Lecture), *Melbourne Graduate*, III, 2, 1952.

Theodor Fontane (1819-1898), *AUMLA*, 1, 1954.

Heinrich von Kleist und Karl Baron von Altenstein, *Euphorion* (Hamburg), 1955, XLIX.

Goethe and "Die Zauberflöte", *German Life and Letters*, 1956. Eine unbekannte Fassung von H. v. Kleists "Hermannschlacht", *Jahrbuch der deutschen Schillergesellschaft*, I, 1957.

Zur Geschichte des Nachlasses Fr von Hardenbergs (Novalis), *ibid.*, II, 1958.

Articles contributed to *Cassell's Encyclopedia of Literature*, London, 1953, on Literary Groups, Schools and Movements, Classicism, Romanticism, Realism, Naturalism, Impressionism, Imagism, Futurism, Expressionism, Surrealism.

SCALES, D.P., B.A. (Syd.), D. de l'U. (Paris), Professor of French, Canberra University College.

ARTICLES

A Picture of French Manners under the July Monarchy: Louis Reybaud's Humorous Novel "Jérôme Paturot à la recherche d'une position sociale", *AUMLA*, 2, 1954.

Balzac's "Monographie de la presse parisienne", *AUMLA*, 4, 1956.

SINCLAIR, K.V., M.A. (N.Z.), Dip.Phon., L.ès L., D. de l'U. (Paris), Lecturer in French, Canberra University College.

AT PRESS

Monograph on the Melbourne Livy Manuscript for A.H.R.C.

Article on the miniaturists of the Livy Manuscript in the National Gallery Collection for the *Bulletin of the National Gallery of Victoria*, XIII, 1959.

Contributions to *Anglo-Norman Dictionary* for the Anglo-Norman Text Society.

SMIT, J., Litt.D. (Utrecht), M.A. (Melb.), Senior Lecturer in Dutch and Germanic Philology, Department of Germanic Languages, University of Melbourne.

BOOKS

Bijdrage tot de kennis van Potgieters Stijl. Groningen: Wolters, 1937.
E.J. Potgieter, 1808-1875. 's-Gravenhage: Daamen, 1950.
Den Bloemhof van de Nederlantsche Leught (in collaboration with L.M. van Dis). Amsterdam-Antwerp: Wereldbibliotheek, 1955.
Nieuwe Nederlandse Spraakkunst. Groningen: Wolters, vol. I, 1946; vol. II, 1947; vol. III, 1950 (vols. I and III in collaboration with B.H. Erné).
Onder weg in den Regen door E.J. Potgieter. Zwolle: Tjeenk Willink, 1957.
De kosmische vergroting van de dichter bij Bilderdijk, Perk en Marsman (Mededelingen van de Koninklijke Nederlandse Akademie). Amsterdam: Noordhollandse Uitgeversmaatschappij, 1957.

ARTICLE

A Case of Subjectivity in Literary History, *AUMLA*, 1, 1953.
Various articles on literature and philology in journals in Holland.

SMITH, I.H., B.A. (Melb.), D. de l'U. (Paris), Professor of Modern Languages, University of Tasmania.

ARTICLE

Gide's Narcissism, *AUMLA*, 3, 1955.

STUTTERHEIM, K. von, Dr Phil. (Tübingen), Temporary Lecturer in German, University of Sydney.

BOOKS

Die Englische Presse. Berlin: Duncker, 1933. English translation, London: Allen and Unwin, 1933.
England Heute und Morgen. Berlin: Herbig, 1937. English translation, London: Sidgwick and Jackson, 1937.
Zwischen den Zeiten. Berlin: Herbig, 1938. English translation, London: Sidgwick and Jackson, 1939.
Australien. Berlin: Herbig, 1949.

TAUMAN, L., L.èsL., D. de l'U. (Aix), D.èsL. (Paris), Head of Department and Reader in French in the University of Western Australia.

BOOK

Marcel Proust, une vie et une synthèse. Paris: Armand Colin, 1949.

TRIEBEL, L.A., M.A., Dip.Ed. (Lond.), D.Litt. (Tas.), Emeritus Professor of Modern Languages, University of Tasmania.

BOOKS

The Glotta Dictionaries, 2 vols (English-French, French-English, English-German, German-English). London: David Nutt, 1923-6.
The Comedy of the Crocodile. Oxford: O.U.P., 1925.
Storm's *"Hinzelmeier"*, edited. London: Hachette, 1925.
A Phonetic Chart of English, French and German. Cambridge: Heffer, 2nd edition, 1927.
A Handbook to Public Examinations in French. Sydney: Sydney and Melbourne Publishing Company, 2nd edition, 1930.

Gareth and Lynette, edited. Sydney: Sydney and Melbourne Publishing Company, 1932.

French Travellers in Tasmania and in Southern Seas. Sydney: Australasian Publishing Company, 1937.

The French Exploration of Australia (in collaboration with J.C. Batt). Sydney: Editions du Courier Australien, 1943.

Fisher's Ghost and other Essays. Melbourne: Cheshire, 1950.

Facets of France and of French Literature. Sydney: Australasian Publishing Company and London: Harrap, 1952.

Rasser of Alsace. Melbourne: Melbourne and Cambridge University Presses, 1954.

The Literature of Flying and Fliers. Sydney: Editions du Courier Australien, 1955.

The French Exploration of Australia, with Special Reference to Tasmania (in collaboration with J.C. Batt). Hobart: Government Printer, 1957.

"Some French Influences on English Literature" and "The Theatre" in *Light out of France*. Sydney: Angus and Robertson, 1951.

ARTICLES

Notes on Grillparzer, *Modern Language Review* (London), IV, 1910.

Le drame religieux en Allemagne au moyen âge, *ibid.*, I, 1915.

The Scientific Study and Teaching of Languages, *ibid.*, III, 1919.

Victor Hugo's Equipment in Character for his Literary Work, *Australian Teacher*, I, 1937.

The Spirit of Travel in Literature, *A.Q.*, 1937.

French National Ideals, *ibid.*, 1945.

The Humanism of Saint-Exupéry, *ibid.*, 1951.

Un Youm, *Modern Language Review*, XLII, 2, 1947.

The Linguistic Field, *Quarterly Review*, II, 1948.

Some Scientific Factors of Linguistic Change, *ibid.*

A Survey of Western European Stage-craft in the Sixteenth Century, *Modern Language Quarterly* (Seattle), I, 1950.

The "Delectare" Motif and the Sixteenth-century German Stage, *German Life and Letters* (Oxford), 1953.

Neolinguistica from Great Britain, *AUMLA*, 1954.

An Albigensian Trilogy, *ibid.*, 1956.

UGLITZKY, Zinaida, Lecturer in Russian, University of Melbourne.

ARTICLE

Accusative and Genitive with Transitive Verbs preceded by a Negative in Contemporary Russian, *Slavonic and East European Review*, XXXIV, 83, June 1956.

VAN ABBÉ, D., M.A. (Cantab.), Ph.D. (Melb.), Reader in Charge, Department of German, University of Adelaide.

ARTICLES

Some Notes on Cultural Relations between France and Germany in the Nineteenth Century, *Modern Language Quarterly* (Seattle), VIII, 2, 1947.

The MHG Written Language—Fact or Fancy?, *ibid.*, XI, 2, 1950.

Development of Dramatic Form in P. Gengenbach, *Modern Language Review* (Cambridge), XLV, 1, 1950.

Change and Tradition in the Work of N. Manuel, *ibid.*, XLVIII, 2, 1952.

N. Manuel and his Interest in the Reformation, *Journal of Modern History* (Chicago), XXIV, 3, 1952.
Germany—Bismarck or Beethoven?, *A.Q.*, XXV, 3, 1953.
Alternative to Philology?, *AUMLA*, 1, 1953.
Germany's 20th-Century Twin Souls: E. v. Salomon's "Der Fragebogen", *German Life and Letters*, VII, 2, 1954.
The Swings and Roundabouts of Socialist Realism, *Meanjin*, XIII, 2, 1954.
On Correcting Eckermann's Perspectives, *Proceedings of the English Goethe Society*, XXIII, 1954.
Three German Impressions, 1954, *Australian Outlook*, IX, 2, 1955.
Der heutige Stand der deutschen Literatur, *Deutschunterricht für Aüslander*, IV, nos 4-5, 1955.
The Swiss in German Literary History, *German Life and Letters* (Oxford), IX, 2, 1956.
The Germans in South Australia, *A.Q.*, XXVIII, 3, 1956.
E.M. Butler's "Heine", *AUMLA*, 7, 1957.

Oriental Studies

BARNARD, N., B.A. (N.Z.), Ph.D. (A.N.U.), Research Fellow in Far Eastern History, Australian National University.

ARTICLES

A preliminary study of the Ch'u Silk Manuscript, *Monumenta Serica*, XVII, 1958.
A recently excavated inscribed Bronze of western Chou date, *ibid*.

AT PRESS

Some Remarks on the authenticity of a Western Chou style inscribed bronze, for *Monumenta Serica*, XVIII, 1959.
New approaches and research methods in Chin Shih Hsüeh, for *Memoirs of the Toyobunka Kenkyujo*, Tokyo University, XIX, 1959.

BIELENSTEIN, H., fil.dr. (Stockholm), Professor of Oriental Languages, Canberra University College.

BOOK

The Restoration of the Han Dynasty: With Prolegomena on the Historiography of the Hou Han Shu. Göteborg 1953; included in *Bulletin of the Museum of Far Eastern Antiquities* (Stockholm), no. 26, 1954.

ARTICLES

Kinas näringsliv—en aktuell frága, *Ymer*, 1945.
The Census of China during the Period 2-742 A.D., *Bulletin of the Museum of Far Eastern Antiquities* (Stockholm), no. 19, 1947.
An Interpretation of the Portents in the Ts'ien Han Shu, *ibid.*, no. 22, 1950.

VAN DER SPRENKEL, O., B.Sc. (Lond.), Senior Lecturer, School of Oriental Studies, Canberra University College.

CHAPTERS

New China: Three Views (editor and contributor with Michael Lindsay and Robert Guillain). London: Turnstile Press; New York: John Day, 1950.
"China", section IV in *Handbook of Oriental History* (ed. C.H. Philips). London: Royal Historical Society, 1951.

"Law and Government in China", chapter XIV (in collaboration with S. van der Sprenkel) in *Law and Government* (ed. K.C. Wheare). London: Odhams, 1956.

ARTICLES

High Officials of the Ming: A Note on the Ch'i Ch'ing Nien Piao of the Ming History, *Bulletin of the School of Oriental and African Studies*, XIV, pt 1, 1952.
The Chronological Tables of Lei Li: An Important Source for the Study of the Ming Bureaucracy, *ibid.*, pt 2, 1952.
Population Statistics of Ming China, *ibid.*, XV, pt 2, 1953.
Franke's "Geschichte des chinesischen Reiches", *ibid.*, XVIII, pt 2, 1956.

AT PRESS

"Légitimité dynastique et chronologie chinoise" for *Mélanges de l'Institut des Hautes Études Chinoises*, Sorbonne, Paris.
"Changes in the Numbers and Status of Administrative Areas during the Ming Period" for *Oriens Extremus*, Hamburg.
"Geschichte Chinas von der Einführung des Buddhismus bis zur T'ai-p'ing T'ien-Kuo" for *Historia Mundi*, VIII, Bern, Francke, Verlag 1958.

Philosophy

A journal was started in 1923 with the title *Australasian Journal of Psychology and Philosophy* (herein referred to as *A.J.P.P.*). Its name was changed with vol. XXV (1947) to the *Australasian Journal of Philosophy (A.J.P.)*.
Although the psychologists subsequently secured a journal of their own, the name of the society which published the journal remained the *Australasian Association of Psychology and Philosophy* until mid-1958, when it became the *Australasian Association of Philosophy*.
The editors have been: H. Tasman Lovell (1923-34), John Anderson (1935-46), J.A. Passmore (1947-9) and A.K. Stout since 1950.

ANDERSON, J., M.A. (Glasgow), Challis Professor of Philosophy, University of Sydney.

PAMPHLETS

"*Ulysses*". Sydney: Australian English Association, 1930.
Some Questions in Aesthetics. Sydney: Sydney University Literary Society, 1931.
Education and Politics. Sydney: Angus and Robertson, 1932.

ARTICLES

Propositions and Judgments, *Mind*, 1925.
The Truth of Propositions, *ibid.*
The Knower and the Known, *Proceedings of the Aristotelian Society*, XXVII, 1926-7.
Empiricism, *A.J.P.P.*, V, 1927.
Another Outbreak of Virtue, *ibid.*, VI, 1928.
Determinism and Ethics, *ibid.*
Theory and Practice in Morals, *ibid.*, VII, 1929.
"Universals" and Occurrences, *ibid.*
Realism and some of its Critics, *ibid.*, VIII, 1930.

Socrates as an Educator, *ibid.*, IX, 1931.
The Place of Hegel in the History of Philosophy, *ibid.*, X, 1932.
Utilitarianism, *ibid.*
Realism versus Relativism in Ethics, *ibid.*, XI, 1933.
Virtue, *A.J.P.P.*, XII, 1934.
Mind as Feeling, *ibid.*
Some Remarks on Academic Freedom, *ibid.*
Romanticism and Classicism, *Hermes*, 1934.
Marxist Philosophy, *A.J.P.P.*, XIII, 1935.
Production, Distribution and Exchange, *ibid.*
University Reform, *ibid.*
Design, *ibid.*
The Perfect Wagnerite, *Manuscripts* (Melbourne), 1935.
Causality and Logic, *A.J.P.P.*, XIV, 1936.
The "Cogito" of Descartes, *ibid.*
Psycho-Analysis and Romanticism, *ibid.*
The Comic, *Hermes*, 1936.
Marxist Ethics, *A.J.P.P.*, XV, 1937.
The Problem of Causality, *ibid.*, XVI, 1938.
Logic and Ethics, *ibid.*, XVII, 1939.
Logic and Experience, *ibid.*
The Status of Logic, *ibid.*
Freudianism and Society, *ibid.*, XVIII, 1940.
Art and Morality, *ibid.*, XIX, 1941.
The Meaning of Good, *ibid.*, XX, 1942.
The Nature of Ethics, *ibid.*, XXI, 1943.
The Servile State, *ibid.*
Education and Practicality, *ibid.*, XXII, 1944.
Ethics and Advocacy, *ibid.*
The One Good, *ibid.*, XXIII, 1945.
The Freudian Revolution, *A.J.P.*, XXXI, 1953.

REVIEW ARTICLES

S. Alexander, "The Non-Existence of Consciousness: Space, Time and Deity",
ibid., VII, 1929.
F.P. Ramsey, "The Science of Logic: The Foundations of Mathematics";
Richard Robinson, "The Province of Logic"; W. Rivier, "L'empirisme dans
les sciences exactes", *ibid.*, XI, 1933.
Chas A. Campbell, "Scepticism and Construction", *ibid.*, XIII, 1935.
Leonora Cohen Rosenfield, "From Beast-Machine to Man-Machine", *ibid.*
Croce, "Politics and Morals", *A.J.P.*, XXXII, 1954.

ARMSTRONG, D.M., B.A. (Syd.), B.Phil. (Oxon), Lecturer, Department of Philosophy,
University of Melbourne.
ARTICLE
Illusions of Sense, *A.J.P.*, XXXIII, 2, 1955.

BAIER, K.E.M., M.A. (Melb.), D.Phil. (Oxon), Professor of Philosophy, Canberra
University College.
BOOK
The Moral Point of View. Cornell: University Press, 1958, in series *Contemporary
Philosophy*, ed. by Max Black.

ARTICLES

Objectivity in Ethics, *A.J.P.*, XXVI, Dec. 1948.

S. Hampshire, "Fallacies in Moral Philosophy", *Mind*, LIX, 1950.

Doing My Duty, *Philosophy*, XXVI, 1951.

On Describing (together with S.E. Toulmin), *Mind*, LXI, 1952.

The Ordinary Use of Words, *Proceedings of the Aristotelian Society*, LII, 1952.

Good Reasons, *Philosophical Studies*, IV, 1, 1953.

Proving a Moral Judgment, *ibid.*, 3, 1953.

Good Reasons: A Reply to Mr Terrell and Mr Sachs, *ibid.*, V, 4, 1954.

The Point of View of Morality, *A.J.P.*, XXXII, 2, 1954.

Contradiction and Absurdity, *Analysis*, XV, 2, 1954.

Is Punishment Retributive?, *ibid.*, XVI, 2, 1955.

The Meaning of Life (Inaugural Lecture). Canberra: Commonwealth Printer, 1957.

BAKER, A.J., B.A. (Syd.), B.Phil. (Oxon), Lecturer, Department of Philosophy, University of Sydney.

ARTICLES

Logic and Singular Propositions, *A.J.P.*, XXXI, 3, 1953.

Category Mistakes, *ibid.*, XXXIV, 1, 1956.

Incompatible Hypotheticals and the Barber Shop Paradox, *Mind*, no. 255, 1955.

Presupposition and Types of Clause, *ibid.*, no. 259, 1956.

BENJAMIN, B.S., B.A. (Melb.), B.Phil. (Oxon), Senior Lecturer, Department of Philosophy, Canberra University College.

ARTICLE

Remembering, *Mind*, LXV, New Series, 1956.

FOX, A.C., M.A. (Syd.), Professor of Philosophy, University of Western Australia.

ARTICLES

An Examination of Realism, *A.J.P.P.*, VII, 4, 1929.

The Nature of Revelation, *ibid.*, IX, 3, 1931.

The Psychology of Ethical Empiricism, *Philosophy*, IX, 35, 1934.

Professor Alexander's Ethical Views, *International Journal of Ethics*, XLIV, 4, 1934.

Some Reflections on "Sociology of Knowledge", *A.J.P.P.*, XVI, 3, 1938.

The Right and the Good Once More, *ibid.*, XXVIII, I, 1950.

The "Ethic" of Jesus and His "Theology", *Hibbert Journal*, LI, 4, 1953.

Fraternity: Democracy's Neglected Ideal, *Fortnightly Review*, no. 1032, New Series, 1953.

Academic Freedom, *Meanjin*, XIV, 3, 1955.

Skill without Wisdom: A Review of Bertrand Russell's "Human Society in Ethics and Politics", *ibid.*, XVI, 2, 1957.

GASKING, D.A.T., B.A. (Liverpool), M.A. (Cantab.), Associate Professor of Philosophy, University of Melbourne.

PAMPHLET

Examinations and the Aim of Education. Melbourne: M.U.P., 1945.

ARTICLES

Mr Williams on the "a priori", *Analysis*, V-VII, 1939.

Mathematics and the World, *A.J.P.P.*, XVIII, 1940. Reprinted (a) in *Logic and Language*, 2nd Series (ed. A.G.N. Flew). Oxford: Blackwell's, 1953; (b) in *The World of Mathematics* (ed. J.R. Newman) New York: Simon and Schuster, 1956.

Types of Question, *Melbourne University Magazine*, 1946.

History as Science, *Present Opinion* (Melbourne), 1948. Reprinted (in slightly expanded version) under title: The Craft of History and Scientific History, in *H.S.* 1950.

Anderson and the Tractatus Logico-Philosophicus, *A.J.P.*, 1949.

The Philosophy of John Wisdom (in two parts), *ibid.*, 1954.

Causation and Recipes, *Mind*, 1955.

GIBSON, A.B., B.A. (Melb.), M.A. (Oxon), D.Litt. (Cantab.), Professor of Philosophy, University of Melbourne.

BOOKS

The Philosophy of Descartes. London: Methuen, 1932.

Should Philosophers be Kings? Melbourne: M.U.P., 1939.

Thinkers at Work (in collaboration with A.A. Phillips). London: Longmans Green, 1946.

ARTICLES

The Will of God and the Eternal Verities in the Philosophy of Descartes, *Proceedings of the Aristotelian Society*, XXX, 1929-30.

Fact and Ideal in Political Theory, *A.J.P.P.*, XXI, 2, 1934.

Descartes, *Philosophy*, X, 40, 1935.

Freedom (Inaugural Lecture), *A.J.P.P.*, XIV, 4, 1936.

Social Psychology: A Philosophical Analysis, *ibid.*, XIV, 2, 1936.

Can Reason Influence Conduct?, *ibid.*, XVI, 3, 1938.

The Conjugation of Personality, *ibid.*, 2.

Samuel Alexander: An Appreciation, *ibid.*, 3.

The Goodness of producing and the Good produced, *ibid.*, XVIII, 1940.

Preface to a Future Metaphysic, *A.J.P.*, XXV, 3, 1947.

Dogmatism and Scepticism in Aesthetics, *Proceedings of Xth International Congress of Philosophy*, I, 1949.

Philosophers in Council, *A.J.P.*, XXVII, 2, 1949.

Nature and Convention in the Democratic State, *ibid.*, XXIX, 1, 1951.

Natural Theology and Philosophy of Religion, *Proceedings of XIth International Congress of Philosophy*, 1953.

Change and Continuity in Plato's Thought, *Review of Metaphysics*, XI, 2, 1957.

Modern Philosophers Consider Religion, *A.J.P.*, XXXV, 3, 1957.

REVIEW ARTICLES

Henri Bergson, "The Two Sources of Morality and Religion", *A.J.P.P.*, XV, 1, 1937.

Henri Bergson, "The Creative Mind", *A.J.P.*, XXV, 1-2, 1947.

Martin Buber, "Between Man and Man", *ibid.*, XXVI, 1, 1948.

Frederic H. Young, "The Philosophy of Henry James, Sr", *ibid.*, XXXI, 2, 1953.

GIBSON, Q., B.A. (Melb.), M.A. (Oxon), Senior Lecturer, Department of Philosophy, Canberra University College.

BOOK

Facing Philosophical Problems. Melbourne: Cheshire, 1948.

ARTICLES

The Immediate Past in Perception, *A.J.P.P.*, XV, 4, 1937.
The Meaning of "Evolution", *ibid.*, XIX, 1, 1941.
Causation in Social Change, *ibid.*, XXIII, 1945.
Argument from Chances, *A.J.P.*, XXXI, 3, 1953.
Social Forces, *Journal of Philosophy* (New York), LV, 11, 1958.

GODDARD, L., M.A., B.Phil. (St Andrews), Lecturer, Department of Philosophy, University of Melbourne.

ARTICLE

"True" and "Provable", *Mind*, 1958.

AT PRESS

Provability and Necessity to appear in the *Foundations of Logic and Mathematics* series, North-Holland Publishing Company.

GRAVE, S.A., M.A. (N.Z.), Senior Lecturer, Department of Philosophy, University of Western Australia.

ARTICLES

The Shakespearian Pattern, *Theology*, L, 1947.
Aristotelian Philosophy and Functional Design, *A.J.P.*, XXVIII, 1950.
Huxley's Perennial Philosophy, *Landfall*, IV, 1950.
The Ontological Argument of St Anselm, *Philosophy*, XXVII, 1952.
The Foundation of Butler's Ethics, *A.J.P.*, XXX, 1952.
Butler's Analogy, *Cambridge Journal*, VI, 1952.
The Marxist Theory of Mind and Matter, *A.Q.*, XXV, 1953.
On the Perfect Good (Discussion), *A.J.P.*, XXXIII, 1955.
On Evil and Omnipotence (Discussion), *Mind*, LXV, 1956.
Are the Analyses of Moral Concepts Morally Neutral?, *Journal of Philosophy*, LV, 11, May 1958.

GREY, D.R., M.A. (Oxon), Professor of Philosophy, University of New England.

ARTICLES

Art in Plato's "Republic", *Philosophy*, XXVII, 103, 1951.
Subjectivity and the Aesthetic Use of Symbols, *A.J.P.*, XXIX, 2 and 3, 1951.
The Ethical Copula Again, *ibid.*, XXXI, 3, 1953.
The Solipsism of Bishop Berkeley, *Philosophical Quarterly*, II, 9, 1952.
Berkeley on Other Selves, *ibid.*, IV, 14, 1954.

HAMBLIN, C.L., B.Sc., M.A. (Melb.), Ph.D. (Lond.), Lecturer, Department of Philosophy, University of New South Wales.

ARTICLE

Computer Languages, *Australian Journal of Science*, Dec. 1957.

HUTCHINGS, P.A., M.A. (N.Z.), Lecturer, Department of Philosophy, University of Western Australia.

ARTICLES

Some Basic Assumptions of Professor Butts, *Educand*, II, 2, 1955.

What is a Proper Usage of "Illusion"?, *A.J.P.*, XXXIV, 1, 1956.

Necessary Being, *ibid.*, XXXV, 3, 1957.

A Note on Savery's Emotive Theory of Truth, *Mind*, LXVI, New Series, 264, 1957.

JAMES, G., M.A., B.D. (Qld), Lecturer, Department of Philosophy, University of Queensland.

PAMPHLET

Philosophy: A Synopsis. Brisbane: Q.U.P., 1957.

KYLE, W.M., M.A. (Qld), Professor of Philosophy, University of Queensland.

PAMPHLETS

The Elements of Deductive Logic. Brisbane: Q.U.P., 4th edition, 1957.

Lectures on Psychology. Brisbane: Q.U.P., 1944.

Three Sermons on Human Nature by Joseph Butler, edited. Brisbane: Q.U.P., 1947.

Mind and Experience. Brisbane: Q.U.P., 1956.

ARTICLES

British Ethical Theories: The Intuitionist Reaction against Hobbes, *A.J.P.P.*, V, 2, 1927.

British Ethical Theories: The Importance of Bishop Butler, *ibid.*, VII, 4, 1929.

The Measures of Man's Mind (Inaugural Lecture to Theological Hall, Emmanuel College, Brisbane), *Reformed Theological Review* (Melbourne), XIII, 2, 1954.

MARTIN, C.B., Ph.D. (Cantab.), Senior Lecturer, Department of Philosophy, University of Adelaide.

ARTICLES

Mr Hanson on Statements of Fact, *Analysis*, XIII, 3, 1952.

Achilles and the Tortoise (in collaboration with J.M. Hinton), *ibid.*, XIV, 3, 1954.

Identity and Exact Similarity, *ibid.*, XVIII, 4, 1958.

A Religious Way of Knowing, *Mind*, LXI, no. 244, 1952. Reprinted in Flew and MacIntyre, *New Essays in Philosophical Theology*, 1955.

Mr Basson on Immortality, *ibid.*, LXIV, no. 254, 1955.

The Perfect Good, *A.J.P.*, XXXIII, 1, 1955. Reprinted in Flew and MacIntyre, op. cit.

The Perfect Good: Replies, *ibid.*, XXXIV, 1, 1956.

AT PRESS

Religious Belief, for *Contemporary Philosophy* series, Cornell University Press, U.S.A.

McCLOSKEY, H.J., M.A., Ph.D. (Melb.), Senior Lecturer, Department of Philosophy, University of Melbourne.

ARTICLE

An Examination of Restricted Utilitarianism, *Philosophical Review*, LXVI, 4, Oct. 1957.

AT PRESS

The State and Evil, *Ethics* (Chicago).
God and Evil, *Philosophical Quarterly* (St Andrews).

MEDLIN, B.H., B.A. (Adel.), Senior Research Scholar, Department of Philosophy, University of Adelaide.

ARTICLES

Moore's Paradox: Synonymous Expressions and Defining (in collaboration with J.J.C. Smart), *Analysis*, XVII, 1957.
Ultimate Principles and Ethical Egoism, *A.J.P.*, XXXV, 1957.

MILANOV, K., Ph.D. (Berlin), Senior Lecturer, Department of Philosophy, University of Tasmania.

BOOKS

Die Gesetzesbildung, das Verstehen und die anschauliche Abstraktion in geschichtlichem Erkennen. Berlin: 1932.
Basic Problems of Theory of Knowledge. Beograd: Geza Kohn, 1937.
Titoism in Jugoslavia (with introduction by Professor S. Jovanovic). Sloga, 1953.

ARTICLES

Historical Knowledge in the Light of the Theory of Values, *Novi Sad*, vol. 350, 1938.
The Philosophy of the Vienna School, *ibid.*, 352, 1939.
Knowledge in History, *Tasmanian Historical Research Association*, V, 1, 1956.

MITCHELL, Sir W., K.C.M.G., M.A. (Edinburgh), D.Sc., formerly Chancellor and Professor of Philosophy and English, University of Adelaide.

BOOKS

Structure and Growth of the Mind. London: Macmillan, 1907.
Nature and Feeling (Macrossan Lectures, University of Queensland). Adelaide: Hassell Press, 1929.
The Place of Minds in the World (Gifford Lectures 1924 and 1926). London: Macmillan, 1933.

ARTICLE

The Quality of Life (Hertz Annual Lecture in Philosophy at the British Academy in 1935), *Transactions of the British Academy*, 1935.

MONRO, D.H., M.A. (N.Z.), Senior Lecturer, Department of Moral and Political Philosophy, University of Sydney.

BOOKS

Argument of Laughter. Melbourne: M.U.P., 1951.
Godwin's Moral Philosophy. Oxford: O.U.P., 1953.

ARTICLES

The Concept of Myth, *Sociological Review*, XLII, 6, 1950.
In Defence of Hedonism, *Ethics*, LX, 4, 1950.
Subjectivism versus Relativism in Ethics, *Analysis*, XI, 1, 1950.
Archbishop Fénelon versus my Mother, *A.J.P.*, XXVIII, 3, 1950.
Green, Rousseau and the Culture Pattern, *Philosophy*, XXVI, 4, 1951.
Anthropology and Ethics, *A.J.P.*, XXXIII, 3, 1955.
Are Moral Problems Genuine?, *Mind*, LXV, 258, 1956.

PASSMORE, J.A., M.A. (Syd.), Professor of Philosophy, Australian National University.

BOOKS

Ralph Cudworth. Cambridge: C.U.P., 1951.
Hume's Intentions. Cambridge: C.U.P., 1952.
A Hundred Years of Philosophy. London: Duckworth; New York: Macmillan, 1957.

PAMPHLET

T.S. Eliot. Sydney: Sydney University Literary Society, 1935.

ARTICLES

The Nature of Intelligence, *A.J.P.P.*, XIII, 4, 1935.
Psychoanalysis and Aesthetics, *ibid.*, XIV, 2, 1936.
Reason and Inclination, *ibid.*, XV, 1, 1937.
Philosophy and Science, *ibid.*, XVII, 3, 1939.
The Moral Philosophy of Hobbes, *ibid.*, XIX, 1, 1941.
Logical Positivism, I, *ibid.*, XXI, 2-3, 1943.
Logical Positivism, II, *ibid.*, XXII, 3, 1944.
Prediction and Natural Law, *ibid.*, XXIV, 1-2, 1946.
Logical Positivism, III, *A.J.P.*, XXVI, 1, 1948.
T.D. Weldon's "States and Morals" (Critical Notice), *Mind*, LVII, no. 228, 1948.
Philosophy and Scientific Method, *Proceedings of the Aristotelian Society*, 1948-9.
Can the Social Sciences be value-free?, *Proceedings of Xth International Congress of Philosophy*, II, 1948. Reprinted in *Readings in the Philosophy of Science* (ed. H. Feigl and M. Brodbeck). New York: Appleton-Century-Crofts, 1953.
The Dreariness of Aesthetics, *Mind*, LX, no. 239, 1951. Reprinted in *Aesthetics and Language* (ed. W. Elton). Oxford: Blackwell; New York: Philosophical Library, 1954.
G.F. Stout: A Memoir, in G.F. Stout: *God and Nature*. Cambridge: C.U.P., 1952.
Reflections on Logic and Language, *A.J.P.*, XXX, 3, 1952.
Sigmund Freud, *C.A.B.*, 1952.
Descartes, the British Empiricists and Formal Logic, *Philosophical Review*, LXII, 4, 1953.
Professor Ryle's Use of "Use" and "Usage", *ibid.*, LXIII, 1, 1954.
Intentions, *Proceedings of the Aristotelian Society*, Suppl. vol., 1955.
Les Sciences humaines en Australie et en Nouvelle-Zélande, *Revue de Synthèse*, LXXVII, 1, 1956.
Cambridge Platonists: Ralph Cudworth, Arthur Collier, Nathanael Culverwel, *Encyclopaedia Britannica*, revised impression.
Christianity and Positivism, *A.J.P.*, XXXV, 2, 1957.
David Hume, *Encyclopedia Americana*, revised impression.
The Objectivity of History, *Philosophy*, XXXIII, 1958.

PRESLEY, C.F., B.A. (Wales), B.Litt. (Oxon), Lecturer, Department of Philosophy, University of Adelaide.

ARTICLES

Laws and Theories in the Physical Sciences, *A.J.P.*, XXXII, 2, 1954.
Francis Bacon: His Method and His Influence, *Australian Journal of Science*, XIX, 4, 1957.

SMART, J.J.C., M.A. (Glasgow), B.Phil. (Oxon), Professor of Philosophy, University of Adelaide.

ARTICLES

The River of Time, *Mind*, LVIII, 1949. Reprinted with minor alterations in *Essays in Conceptual Analysis*. London: Macmillan, 1956.

Descartes and the Wax, *Philosophical Quarterly*, I, 1950.

Reason and Conduct, *Philosophy*, XXV, 1950.

Excogitation and Induction, *A.J.P.*, XXVIII, 1950.

Heinrich Hertz and the Concept of Force, *ibid.*, XXIX, 1951.

Theory Construction, *Philosophy and Phenomenological Research*, XI, 1951. Reprinted with very minor alterations in *Logic and Language*, Second Series. Oxford: Blackwell, 1953.

The Concept of Force, *A.J.P.*, XXX, 1952.

A Note on Categories, *British Journal for the Philosophy of Science*, IV, 1953.

A Variant of the "Heterological" Paradox (in collaboration with J.L. Mackie), *Analysis*, XIII, 1953.

The Relevance of Modern Analytic Philosophy for Science, *Australian Journal of Science*, XVI, 5, 1954, and *ibid.*, 6.

The Humanitarian Theory of Punishment, *Res Judicatae*, VI, 1954.

The Temporal Asymmetry of the World, *Analysis*, XIV, 1954.

A Variant of the "Heterological" Paradox—A Further Note (in collaboration with J.L. Mackie), *ibid.*

Contradictories and Entailment (in collaboration with U.T. Place), *Philosophy and Phenomenological Research*, XV, 1955.

Critical Notice of Quine's "From a Logical Point of View", *A.J.P.*, XXXIII, 1955.

The Existence of God, *Church Quarterly Review*, CLVI, 1955. Reprinted in *New Essays in Philosophical Theology*. London: S.C.M. Press, 1955.

Metaphysics, Logic and Theology, op. cit.

Mr Mayo on Temporal Asymmetry, *A.J.P.*, XXXIII, 1955.

Spatialising Time, *Mind*, LXIV, 1955.

The Reality of Theoretical Entities, *A.J.P.*, XXXIV, 1956.

Critical Notice of A.N. Prior's "Formal Logic", *ibid.*

Extreme and Restricted Utilitarianism, *Philosophical Quarterly*, VI, 1956.

Plausible Reasoning in Philosophy, *Mind*, LXVI, 1957.

Critical Notice of Hans Reichenbach's "The Direction of Time", *Philosophical Quarterly*, VIII, 1957.

Moore's Paradox: Synonymous Expressions and Defining (in collaboration with B.H. Medlin), *Analysis*, XVII, 1956-7.

Philosophy and Religion, *A.J.P.*, XXXVI, 1958.

STOUT, A.K., M.A. (Oxon), Professor of Philosophy, University of Sydney, Editor of *Australasian Journal of Philosophy* since 1950.

BOOK

God and Nature, G.F. Stout (edited by A.K. Stout). Cambridge: C.U.P., 1952.

ARTICLES

The Basis of Knowledge in Descartes, I, *Mind*, XXXVIII, no. 151, July 1929.

The Basis of Knowledge in Descartes, II, *ibid.*, no. 152, July 1929.

Descartes' Proof of the Existence of Matter, *ibid.*, XLI, no. 162, Apr. 1932.

The Morality of Punishment, *Welsh Outlook*, Nov. 1932.
Can Philosophy determine what is ethically or socially valuable?, *Proceedings of the Aristotelian Society*, Suppl. vol. XV, 1936.
Free Will and Responsibility, *ibid.*, XXXVII, June 1937. Republished in *Readings in Ethical Theory*, Appleton-Century-Crofts, 1952.
The Alleged "Petitio Principii" in Descartes' Appeal to God's Veracity, *Travaux du IXᵉ Congrès International de Philosophie—Congrès Descartes*, Paris, 1937.
Punishment (Inaugural Lecture), *Sydney University Union Recorder*, Oct. 1939.
Motive and the Rightness of an Act, *A.J.P.P.*, XVIII, 1940.
Freewill, *ibid.*
Duty and Inclination, *ibid.*, XX, 1942.
Self Interest versus the Common Good, I and II, *A.Q.*, XV, 1943 and XVI, 1944.
The Functions of a University, *ibid.*, XVIII, 1946.
But Suppose Everyone did the Same, *A.J.P.*, XXXII, 1954.

REVIEW ARTICLES

J.E. Boodin, "Cosmic Evolution", in *Mind*, XXXVI, no. 144, 1927.
E. Hussel, "Méditations Cartésiennes", *ibid.*, XLI, no. 164, 1932.
A. Boyce Gibson, "The Philosophy of Descartes", *ibid.*, XLII, no. 167, 1933.
W.A. Merrylees, "Descartes", *ibid.*, XLIV, no. 175, 1935.

STOVE, D.C., B.A. (Syd.), Lecturer in Philosophy, University of New South Wales.

ARTICLES

A Note on "Relativism", *A.J.P.*, XXX, 3, 1952.
Two Problems about Individuality, *ibid.*, XXXIII, 3, 1955.

REVIEW ARTICLES

W.A. Sinclair, "The Conditions of Knowing", *A.J.P.*, XXX, 1, 1952.
N. Goodman, "Fact, Fiction and Forecast", *ibid.*, XXXIII, 2, 1955.
A.J. Ayer, "Philosophical Essays", *ibid.*, XXXIV, 1, 1956.

THORNTON, J.B., B.A., B.Sc. (Syd.), Associate Professor of Philosophy, University of New South Wales.

ARTICLES

Scientific Entities, I and II, *A.J.P.*, XXXI, 1953.
Materialism and its Critics, *Australian Journal of Science*, XVI, 1953.
Georg Simon Ohm, *ibid.*, XVII, 1954.

Semitic Studies

GOLDMAN, M.D., Ph.D. (Berlin), M.A. (Melb.), Professor of Semitic Studies, University of Melbourne, 1945-57. (Died 1957.)

BOOKS

Hebräisch—A Grammar and Reading Book of the Hebrew Language. Berlin, Charlottenburg: Sefathenu, 1934.
The Story of Meir and Berurie in Arabic Form. Breslau: Z.G.W.F., 1936.

The Book of the Jubilees—Retranslation from the Ethiopic into Hebrew with Critical Commentaries. Tel-Aviv: Meqoroth, Massada, 1947.
"Semitic Studies" in *Light out of France.* Sydney: Angus and Robertson, 1951.

ARTICLES

Problems of Hebrew Adult Education, *Australian Jewish News,* XVIII, 1, 1951.
The Meaning in Yiddish of the Root HZQ as Jesting, based on the same Connotation in Jeremiah XX:7, *ibid.,* 2.
The Origin of a Curious Belief connected with the Feast of Tabernacles, *ibid.,* 6.
The Name of an Angel caused by Misinterpretation of a Verse in Biblical Poetry, *ibid.,* 8.
The Historical Evolution of the Conception of Rozh Hashana, *ibid.,* XIX, 1-2, 1952.
The Isaiah MSS. of the Dead Sea Scrolls, *Australian Biblical Review,* I, 1, 1951.
Lexicographical Notes on the Hebrew Text of the Bible, *ibid.*
Lexicographical Notes on Exegesis, *ibid.,* 3-4.
Humour in the Hebrew Bible, *ibid.,* II, 1-2, 1952.
Was Jeremiah Married?, *ibid.*
Lexicographical Notes on Exegesis, *ibid.*
Authorship of Jeremiah, chapter XXXI, *ibid.,* II, 3-4, 1953.
The Root PLL and its Connotation with Prayer, *ibid.,* III, 1-4, 1953.

GUREWICZ, S.B., B.A., LL.B. (Melb.), F.R.A.S., Tutor in Hebrew, Queen's College, University of Melbourne, Senior Hebrew Master, Mount Scopus College, Melbourne.

ARTICLES

Chapter I of *The Jewish People,* R.A.A.F. Educational Services, 1945-6.
The Mediaeval Jewish Exegetes of the Old Testament, *Australian Biblical Review,* I, 1951.
Prophecy in Israel, *ibid.,* II, 1952.
When did the Cult associated with the "Golden Calves" fully develop in the Northern Kingdom?, *ibid.,* III, 1953.
Some Reflections on the Book of Ruth, *ibid.,* V, 1956.
The Deuteronomic Provisions for Exemption from Military Service, *ibid.,* VI, 1958.
Divorce in Jewish Law, *Res Judicatae,* VII, 1957.

AT PRESS

The Authorship of the Book of Judges, for *Australian Biblical Review,* VII, 1959.

MACLAURIN, E.C.B., B.A., B.D. (Syd.), M.A. (Cantab.), Lecturer in Semitic Studies, University of Sydney.

BOOK

Origin of the Hebrew Sacrificial System. Sydney and Melbourne Publishing Company, 1948.

ARTICLES

The Ancient Family of Rouse, *R.A.H.S.,* XLIII, pt 6, 1957.
Oman and the Trucial Coast, *Australian Quarterly,* XXX, I, Mar. 1958.

Theology

BABBAGE, Very Rev. S.B., M.A. (N.Z.), Ph.D. (London), Th.D. (Aust. Coll of Theol.), Dean of St Paul's Cathedral and Principal of Ridley College, Melbourne, Victoria.

BOOKS
Hauhauism. Wellington, N.Z.: Reed, 1937.
Man in Nature and Grace. Grand Rapids: Eerdmans, 1957.

BENNIE, Rev. G.P.B., M.A. (Melb.), Th.L. (Aust. Coll. of Theol.), Rector of All Saints' Church, Brisbane, Editor of the *Australian Church Quarterly*.

ARTICLES
Lawful Authority in Relation to the Liturgy, *Australian Church Quarterly*, Jan. 1954.
Towards a Doctrine of the Church, *ibid.*, Apr. 1954.
The Poetry of W.H. Auden, *ibid.*, Jan. 1955.
The Authority of the Church in Relation to the Authority of the Bible, *ibid.*, Apr. 1956.

BOOKLET
The Book of Common Prayer. Melbourne: Centenary Press, 1949.

IN PROGRESS
The Church Marriage and the Twentieth Century, book for Anglican Truth Society, early 1959.

COLLOCOTT, Rev. E.E.V., M.A., Litt.D. (Melb.), B.D. (Lond.), Methodist Minister (retired 1958), Donald Street, Epping, N.S.W.

BOOKS
Tales and Poems of Tonga. Honolulu: Bishop Museum, 1928.
Proverbial Sayings of the Tongans (in collaboration with J. Havea). Honolulu: Bishop Museum, 1924.
Koe Ta'u'e Teau (a history of the nineteenth century, in Tongan). London: Clowes.

PAMPHLET
Tongan Astronomy and Calendar. Honolulu: Bishop Museum, 1922.

ARTICLES
Speech of Niua Fo'ou, *Journal of Polynesian Studies*, Dec. 1922.
Sickness, Ghosts and Medicine in Tonga, *ibid.*, Sept. 1923.
Kava Ceremonial in Tonga, *ibid.*, Mar. 1927.
Supplementary Tongan Vocabulary, notes on Measuring and Counting.
Proverbial Expressions and Phases of the Moon, *ibid.*, XXIV, 2 and 3.
Experiment in Tongan History, *ibid.*, XXXIII, 3.
Is there an Absolute Moral Standard?, *A.Q.*, Mar. 1938.
Man and his Religions, *ibid.*
Poetry of the Pacific Islands, *ibid.*, Dec. 1946.
Tongan Myths and Legends, *Folklore*, XXX, XXXII, XXXV.
Notes on Tongan Religion, *Journal of Polynesian Society*, XXX.
Marriage in Tonga, *ibid.*, XXXII, 4.
Supernatural in Tonga, *American Anthropologist*, XXIII.

CULLEN, Right Rev. Monsignor J.H., B.A. (N.U.I. and Tas.), Vicar General Hobart, Tasmania.

BOOKS

Young Ireland in Exile. Eire: Talbot Press, 1928.
Australian Daughters of Mary Aikenhead. Sydney: Pellegrini, 1938.
Catholic Church in Tasmania. Hobart: Examiner Press, 1949.

DALTON, Rev. Fr W.J., S.J., M.A. (Melb.), L.S.S. (Pontifical Biblical Institute, Rome), Professor of Sacred Scripture and Biblical Languages, Canisius College, Pymble, N.S.W.

ARTICLES

Propitiation in the Sacrifice of the Old Testament, *Australian Catholic Record,* XXXIII, Jan. 1956.
The Background and Meaning of the Biblical Flood Narrative, *ibid.,* XXXIV, Oct. 1957; *ibid.,* XXXV, Jan. 1958.
The Fourth Song of the Servant of Yaweh. Is. 52:13—53:12, *Scripture* (English Catholic Biblical Association), X, Jan. 1958.

DUNNE, Rev. E., C.Ss.R., Doctor of Canon Law, Redemptorist College, Ballarat, Victoria.

BOOK

Religious and Priestly Formation. Dublin: Clonmore and Reynolds, 1957.

FLEMING, Rev. T.V., S.J., B.Sc., Professor of Theology, Canisius College, Pymble, N.S.W.

BOOK

Foundations of Philosophy. Sydney, Shakespeare Head Press, 1949.

HAMBLY, Rev. W.F., M.A., B.D. (Melb.), Master, Lincoln College, Adelaide, South Australia.

BOOKS

God in our Times. Melbourne: Australian Student Christian Movement, 1938.
What Christians Stand For. Melbourne: A.S.C.M., 1944.
Bedtime Philosophy. Melbourne: Melbourne Book Depot, 1952.

HEBERT, Rev. Fr A.G., M.A. (Oxon), Hon. D.D. (Aberdeen), Member of the College of the Society of the Sacred Mission, St Michael's House, Crafers, South Australia.

BOOKS

Liturgy and Society. London: Faber and Faber, 1935.
The Parish Communion, a Book of Essays (edited). London: S.P.C.K., 1937.
The Throne of David. London: Faber, 1944.
The Form of the Church. London: Faber, 1944; revised edition, 1954.
The Authority of the Old Testament. London: Faber, 1947.
The Bible from Within. Oxford: O.U.P., 1950.
Fundamentalism and the Church of God. London: S.C.M. Press, 1957.

KENNY, Rev. Fr J.P., S.J., M.A. (Melb.), S.T.D. (Pontifical Gregorian University, Rome), Professor of Dogmatic Theology, Patrology and Liturgy at Canisius College, Pymble, N.S.W.

ARTICLES

(a) Theological—

The Problem of Concupiscence: a recent theory of Professor Karl Rahner, *Australian Catholic Record*, XXIX, 1952, and XXX, 1953.

Beatific Vision, *ibid.*, XXXI, 1954.

Human Nature under the influence of the Supernatural, *ibid.*, XXXIII, 1955.

Reflections on Human Nature and the Supernatural, *Theological Studies* (U.S.A.), XIV, 1953.

Death in the light of Dogmatic Theology, *Transactions of the Catholic Medical Guild of St Luke* (Australia), Series IV, 6, Feb. 1955.

The Mass-Sacrifice of the Whole Christ, *Australian Liturgical Week*, 1955.

(b) Literature, Art, Philosophy—

Poetry—The Soul of Verse and Prose, *A.Q.*, XVI, 1944.

Art and Morality, *Australian Catholic Record*, XXI, 1944.

An Approach to Gerard Manley Hopkins, *Catholic Review* (N.Z.), II, 1946 and III, 1947.

What is a work of art?, *Twentieth Century*, X, 1956.

Is Modern Art Dehumanized?, *Meanjin*, 1957.

PAMPHLET

Reflections on the theory of Maurice de la Taille "Actuation créée par acte incréé", excerpta ex dissertatione ad lauream, in facultate Theologiae Dogmaticae, Pontificae Universitatis Gregorianae, 1950.

PARTLY PUBLISHED

The Deification of Man, a study of the theology of grace. Partly published in *Sursum Corda*, II, 1956, and III, 1957.

Work on the Sacrament of Confirmation, published in part in *Sursum Corda*, 1955.

KIEK, Rev. E.S., M.A. (Oxon and Adel.), B.D. (Lond.), D.D. (Melbourne College of Divinity), Congregational Manse, Katoomba, New South Wales. Died 1959.

BOOKS

The Modern Religious Situation. Edinburgh: T. and T. Clark, 1926.

An Apostle in Australia. London: Independent Press, 1927.

The Battle of Faith. London: James Clarke, 1938.

History of the S.A. Congregational Union. Adelaide.

PAMPHLETS

Group Psychology (Livingstone Lecture). Sydney: Camden College, 1943.

The New Psychology and the Old Faith (Bevan Memorial Lectures, Adelaide). Adelaide: Parkin Trust, 1945.

LOANE, Right Rev. M.L., M.A., Th.D. (Aust. Coll. of Theol.), D.D. (Toronto), Bishop-Coadjutor, Diocese of Sydney, Principal of Moore Theological College.

BOOKS

A Brief Survey of the Synoptic Problem. Sydney: S. John Bacon, 1945.

Oxford and the Evangelical Succession. England: Lutterworth Press, 1950.

Cambridge and the Evangelical Succession. England: Lutterworth Press, 1952.
Masters of the English Reformation. England: Church Book Room Press, 1954.
Centenary History of Moore Theological College. Sydney: Angus and Robertson, 1955.

AT PRESS

Makers of Puritan History, for Eerdmans, U.S.A., 1959.

McCAUGHEY, Rev. J.D., M.A. (Cantab.), Professor of Biblical Studies, Master of Ormond College, Melbourne.

BOOK

Christian Obedience in the University. London: S.C.M. Press, 1958.

ARTICLES

Language about the Church, *Reformed Theological Review,* XV, 1, 1956.
The Gnostic Gospel of Truth and the New Testament, *Australian Biblical Review,* VI, 1, 1958.

PAMPHLET

The Christian Hope. Melbourne: Presbyterian Bookroom, 1954.

MORRIS, Rev. L., B.Sc. (Syd.), M.Th. (Lond.), Ph.D. (Cantab.), Vice-Principal, Ridley College, Melbourne.

BOOKS

The Wages of Sin. London: Tyndale Press, 1955.
The Apostolic Preaching of the Cross. London: Tyndale Press, 1955.
Commentary on I, II Thessalonians. London: Tyndale Press, 1956.
The Story of the Cross. London: Marshall, Morgan and Scott, 1957.
The Lord from Heaven. London: London Intervarsity Fellowship, 1958.
Commentary on I Corinthians. London: Tyndale Press, 1958.

ARTICLES

The Use of Hilaskesthai etc. in Biblical Greek, *Expository Times.* LXII, 1951.
The Wrath of God, *ibid.,* LXIII, 1953.
The Idea of Redemption in the Old Testament, *Reformed Theological Review,* XI, 1952.
The Biblical Idea of Atonement, *Australian Biblical Review,* II, 1952–3.
The Passover in Rabbinic Literature, *ibid.,* IV, 1954–5.
The Biblical Use of the term "Blood", *Journal of Theological Studies,* New Series, III, 1952, and VI, 1955.
Justification by Faith: The Old Testament and Rabbinic Anticipation, *Evangelical Quarterly,* XXIV, 1953.
The Meaning of "Hilasterion" in Romans 3.25, *New Testament Studies,* II, 1955.

AT PRESS

New International Commentary on I, II Thessalonians, with Eerdmans, U.S.A.

NICHOL, Rev. F.W.R., M.A., B.D. (N.Z.), Ph.D. (St Andrews), Director of Theological Studies, Theological Hall of the Presbyterian Church in Western Australia.

ARTICLE

John Oman's Theology, *Reformed Theological Review,* XVI, 2, June 1957.

O'NEILL, J.C., B.A. (Melb.), B.D. (Melbourne College of Divinity), Research Student.

ARTICLES

The Use of ΚΥΡΙΟΣ in the Book of Acts, *Scottish Journal of Theology*, VIII, 1955.
Commentaries on the Acts of the Apostles, *Theology*, LXI, 1958.
The six Amen Sayings in Luke, *Journal of Theological Studies*, N.S. X, 1959.

OSBORN, Rev. E.F., M.A., B.D. (Melb.), Ph.D. (Cantab.), Professor of Biblical Studies, Queen's College, Melbourne.

BOOK

The Philosophy of Clement of Alexandria. Cambridge: C.U.P., 1957.

PAMPHLET

The Faith of the Gospel. Methodist Publishing House, Aldersgate Press, 1957.

O'SHEA, Rev. K., C.Ss.R., Th.D., Ballarat, Victoria.

ARTICLE

The Human Activity of the Word, *Thomist* (U.S.A.), 1958.

PETER, Rev. J.F., B.A., B.D., Dip.Ed. (Syd.), Professor of Theology, Emmanuel College, University of Queensland.

ARTICLES

The Place of Theology in the Church, *Reformed Theological Review*, XI, 2, July 1952.
Warfield on the Scriptures, *ibid.*, XVI, 3, Oct. 1957.
The Redemptive Mission of the Church, *Scottish Journal of Theology*, X, 2, June 1957.

POLLARD, Rev. T.E., B.A., B.D. (Sydney), Ph.D. (St Andrews), Minister, St Columba Presbyterian Church, Woollahra, N.S.W.

ARTICLES

The Impassibility of God, *Scottish Journal of Theology*, VIII, 1955.
Logos and Son in Origen, Arius and Athanasius, *Studia Patristica*, Band 64, 1957.
The Exegesis of John X. 30 in the Early Trinitarian Controversies, *New Testament Studies*, III, 1957.
The Origins of Arianism, *Journal of Theological Studies*, New Series, IX, 1958.

IN PROGRESS

Cosmology and the Prologue of the Fourth Gospel, for *Vigiliae Christianae*.
The Exegesis of Scripture and the Arian Controversy, for the *Bulletin of the John Rylands Library*.
Translation, with introduction and notes, of Eusebius of Caesarea, "Contra Marcellum" and "De Ecclesiastica Theologia", for the series *Ancient Christian Writers*, Catholic University Press of America.

RYAN, Rev. Fr N.J., S.J., M.A., B.Ed. (Melb.), Campion Hall, Kew, Victoria.

ARTICLE

The Assumption in the Early English Pulpit, *Theological Studies* (U.S.A.), XI, 4, Dec. 1950.

SASSE, Rev. H., D.D. (Erlangen), Professor of Immanuel Theological Seminary, South Australia.

BOOKS
(Publications prior to 1946 not listed)
Here We Stand: Nature and Character of the Lutheran Faith. New York, 1938; translations in German and Norwegian; 2nd edition, Minneapolis, 1946.

ARTICLES
Luther's Theologia Crucis, *Lutheran Quarterly*, 1951.
Sacra Scriptura, "Bemerkungen zur Inspirationslehre Augustins", *Festschrift Franz Dornseiff*, Leipzig, 1953, and in *Reformed Theological Review* (Melbourne), 1955.
Concerning the Origin of the Improperia, *Reformed Theological Review*, 1957.
"Die christlichen Kirchen Australiens", in vol. 1 of the encyclopaedia *Die Religion in Geschichte und Gegenwart*, Tübingen, 1957.

AT PRESS
This is my Body. Luther's Contention for the Real Presence in the Sacrament of the Altar. Augsburg Publishing House, Minneapolis, Minn., 1959.

SNELL, Rev. A.A., M.A. (Oxon), Senior Tutor at St Michael's House, Society of the Sacred Mission, Crafers, South Australia.

BOOKS
Understand Your Faith. London and Oxford: Mowbrays, 1942.
In All the Scriptures. London: Church Lit. Association, 1954.

ARTICLE
Lucan, *Greece and Rome*, Feb. 1939.

VOCKLER, Rev. J.C., B.A. (Qld), S.T.B., S.T.M. (Gen. Theol. Seminary, N.Y.), Th.L. (Aust. Coll. of Theol.), Sometime Fellow of the General Theological Seminary, New York, Senior Assistant Priest, Singleton, and Lecturer at St John's College, Morpeth, New South Wales.

ARTICLES
Church Life in England in the 18th century, *Australian Church Quarterly*, Oct. 1957.
Theology and Learning, *Magazine of St John's College*, Morpeth, 1957.
Sound Learning and the Christian Faith, *Anglican*, 1958.
The Purposes of a Theological College, *St Mark's Review*, 12, May 1958.

IN PROGRESS
"Sir Samuel Walker Griffith". A chapter in the symposium *Queensland Political Portraits*, to be published, 1959, by Queensland University Press.
The Elizabethan Vestiarian Controversy, to be published by S.P.C.K., London.

AUSTRALIAN HUMANITIES RESEARCH COUNCIL

LIST OF MEMBERS, 1959

ANDERSON, J., M.A. (Glasgow), Professor Emeritus of Philosophy, University of Sydney.

AUCHMUTY, J.J., M.A., Ph.D. (Dublin), M.R.I.A., F.R.Hist.S., Professor of History, Head of the Department of Arts, Newcastle University College.

BIELENSTEIN, H., fil.dr. (Stockholm), Professor of Oriental Languages, Head of the School of Oriental Studies, Canberra University College.

BRAMSTED, Ernest, Dr.phil. (Berlin), Ph.D. (Lond.), Senior Lecturer in History, University of Sydney.

BURKE, J.T., O.B.E., M.A. (London, Yale and Melbourne), Professor of Fine Arts, University of Melbourne.

CHISHOLM, A.R., O.Lég.d'H., B.A. (Sydney and Melbourne), Professor Emeritus, University of Melbourne.

CRAWFORD, R.M., B.A. (Sydney), M.A. (Oxon and Melbourne), Professor of History, University of Melbourne.

EDWARDS, W.A., M.A. (Cantab.), Professor of English, University of Western Australia.

FARRELL, R.B., M.A. (Sydney), Dr.phil. (Berlin), Professor of German, University of Sydney.

FITZGERALD, C.P., Professor of Far Eastern History, Australian National University.

FITZPATRICK, Kathleen E., B.A. (Melbourne), M.A. (Oxon), Associate Professor of History, University of Melbourne.

GIBSON, A. Boyce, B.A. (Melb.), M.A. (Oxon), Litt.D. (Cantab.), Professor of Philosophy, University of Melbourne.

GREENWOOD, Gordon, M.A. (Sydney), Ph.D. (Lond.), Professor of History and Political Science, University of Queensland.

GREY, D.R., M.A. (Oxon), Professor of Philosophy, University of New England.

HANCOCK, Professor Sir (W.) Keith, M.A. (Oxon.), D.Litt. (Rhodes), Litt.D. (Cantab.), F.B.A., Director of the Research School of Social Sciences, Australian National University.

HOPE, A.D., B.A. (Sydney), B.A. (Oxon), Professor of English, Canberra University College.

HUNT, H.A.K., B.A., (Sydney), M.A. (Oxon), Litt.D., Dip.Ed. (Melbourne), Professor of Classical Studies, University of Melbourne.

LA NAUZE, J.A., B.A. (W.A.), M.A. (Oxon), Ernest Scott Professor of History, University of Melbourne.

MAXWELL, I.R., B.A., LL.B. (Melb.), B.Litt. (Oxon), Professor of English, University of Melbourne.

MITCHELL, A.G., M.A. (Sydney), Ph.D., Dip.Phonetics (Lond.), Professor of Early English Literature and Language, University of Sydney.

PASSMORE, J.A., M.A. (Sydney), Professor of Philosophy, Australian National University.

PRICE, A. Grenfell, C.M.G., M.A., Dip.Ed. (Oxon), D.Litt. (Adel.), Chairman of the Advisory Board, Commonwealth Literary Fund, University of Adelaide.

SAMUEL, R.H., Dr.phil. (Berlin), Ph.D. (Cantab.), Professor of Germanic Languages, University of Melbourne.

SHIPP, G.P., M.A. (Cantab.), D.Litt. (Syd.) Professor of Greek, University of Sydney.

SMITH, Bernard, B.A. (Sydney), Ph.D. (A.N.U.), F.S.A., Senior Lecturer in Fine Arts, University of Melbourne.

STOUT, A.K., M.A. (Oxon), Professor of Philosophy, University of Sydney.

STREHLOW, T.G.H., M.A. (Adel.), Reader in Australian Linguistics, University of Adelaide.

TAUMAN, L., L.-ès-L., D.U. (Aix), D.-ès-L. (Paris), Reader in French and Head of the Department, University of Western Australia.

TRENDALL, A.D., K.C.S.G., M.A. (Cantab.), Litt.D. (N.Z. and Melbourne), F.S.A., Professor Emeritus, University of Sydney; Master of University House, Deputy Vice-Chancellor, Australian National University.

TRIEBEL, L.A., M.A. (Lond.), D.Litt., Dip.Ed. (Tas.), Professor Emeritus, University of Tasmania.

HONORARY MEMBERS

MILLER, E. Morris, M.A., Litt.D. (Melb.), F.B.Ps.S., F.I.A.L., Professor Emeritus, University of Tasmania.

FERGUSON, The Hon. Mr Justice J.A., O.B.E., B.A., LL.B., Litt.D. (Sydney), 81 Clanville Road, Roseville, New South Wales.

SPECIAL MEMBERS

COOMBS, H.C., M.A., Ph.D. (Lond.), LL.D. (Melb.); Governor, Commonwealth Bank of Australia.

WHITE, H.L., M.A. (Melb.), Commonwealth Librarian, Commonwealth National Library, Canberra.

HONORARY CORRESPONDING MEMBERS

BISSELL, C.T., M.A. (Toronto), Ph.D. (Corn.), F.R.S.Can., President of the University of Toronto, Canada.

JEFFARES, A.N., M.A., Ph.D. (Dub.), M.A., D.Phil. (Oxon), Professor of English, University of Leeds, England.

SMITH, D. Nichol, M.A., Litt.D., LL.D., F.B.A. Formerly Merton Professor of English Literature, Oxford.

PUBLICATIONS OF THE
AUSTRALIAN HUMANITIES RESEARCH COUNCIL

Monographs

No. 1. "The Hopetoun Blunder", J.A. La Nauze, M.U.P. 1958.
No. 2. "Mallarmé's *L'Après-midi d'un Faune*", A.R. Chisholm, M.U.P. 1958.
No. 3. "Form and Meaning in Valéry's *Le Cimetière Marin*", J.R. Lawler.

IN THE PRESS

No. 4. "The Art of E.M. Forster", H.J. Oliver.
No. 5. "Bersuire's Translation of Livy", K.V. Sinclair.

Occasional Papers

No. 1. "The Birth of Modern Comedy", T.B.L. Webster, Adelaide, 1959.

No. 2. "Notes on the *Dyskolos* of Menander", J.H. Quincey, W. Ritchie, G.P. Shipp, and A.P. Treweek.

Annual Addresses

1957.   "The Felton Greek Vases", A.D. Trendall.
1958.   "Western Influences in the Pacific and its Continents", A. Grenfell Price.

ILLUSTRATIONS

Sir Charles Nicholson, Sydney.   The Rev. Charles Badham, Sydney.

Sir Ernest Scott, Melbourne.   Sir William Mitchell, Adelaide.

FOUR LEADING AUSTRALIAN HUMANISTS

The Great Hall, University of Sydney.

Wilson Hall, University of Melbourne, from the south-east.

Photos: Visual Aids Department, University of Melbourne

Interior of Wilson Hall.

Photo: Advertiser Newspapers Ltd

The Union Hall (the theatre), University of Adelaide.

The University of Queensland viewed from across the Brisbane River.

Photos: Photographic Department, University of Queensland

The Chemistry Building, University of Queensland, seen through the cloisters
outside the Geology Building.

The Terrace, University House, Australian National University.

The crowded Fisher Library, University of Sydney.

Above: The schoolroom at Trinity Church, Adelaide, the starting place (1847) of St Peter's College. St Peter's is the oldest school on the Australian mainland to remain continuously open.

Right: The Old School House (1852), St Peter's College.

Below: Adelaide Boys' High School (1951).

Photo: Ron Woolmore, Adelaide

N.

W.   A.

PERTH ①

DISTRIBUTION OF
UNIVERSITIES IN AUSTRALIA
1959

SCALE OF MILES
0   100   200   300   400   500